Lecture Notes in Computer Science 3507

Commenced Publication in 1973
Founding and Former Series Editors:
Gerhard Goos, Juris Hartmanis, and Jan van Leeuwen

Fabio Crestani   Ian Ruthven (Eds.)

Context:
Nature, Impact,
and Role

5th International Conference on Conceptions
of Library and Information Sciences, CoLIS 2005
Glasgow, UK, June 4-8, 2005
Proceedings

Volume Editors

Fabio Crestani
Ian Ruthven
University of Strathclyde
Department of Computer and Information Sciences
Livingstone Tower, 26 Richmond Street, Glasgow G1 1XH, UK
E-mail: {f.crestani, ian.ruthven}@cis.strath.ac.uk

Library of Congress Control Number: 2005926658

CR Subject Classification (1998): H.3, H.2, F.2.2, H.4, H.5.4, I.6, I.2

ISSN   0302-9743
ISBN-10   3-540-26178-8 Springer Berlin Heidelberg New York
ISBN-13   978-3-540-26178-0 Springer Berlin Heidelberg New York

Springer is a part of Springer Science+Business Media

springeronline.com

© Springer-Verlag Berlin Heidelberg 2005
Printed in Germany

Typesetting: Camera-ready by author, data conversion by Scientific Publishing Services, Chennai, India
Printed on acid-free paper   SPIN: 11495222   06/3142   5 4 3 2 1 0

Preface

CoLIS 5 was the fifth in the series of international conferences whose general aim is to provide a broad forum for critically exploring and analyzing research in areas such as computer science, information science and library science. CoLIS examines the historical, theoretical, empirical and technical issues relating to our understanding and use of information, promoting an interdisciplinary approach to research. CoLIS seeks to provide a broad platform for the examination of context as it relates to our theoretical, empirical and technical development of information-centered disciplines.

The theme for CoLIS 5 was the nature, impact and role of context within information-centered research. Context is a complex, dynamic and multi- dimensional concept that influences both humans and machines: how they behave individually and how they interact with each other. In CoLIS 5 we took an interdisciplinary approach to the issue of context to help us understand and the theoretical approaches to modelling and understanding context, incorporate contextual reasoning within technology, and develop a shared framework for promoting the exploration of context.

The Organizing Committee would like to thank all the authors who submitted their work for consideration and the participants of CoLIS 5 for making the event a great success. Special thanks are due to the members of the Program Committee who worked very hard to ensure the timely review of all the submitted manuscripts, and to the invited speakers: Prof. David Blair, University of Michigan, Business School, USA and Prof. Elisabeth Davenport, Napier University, School of Computing, UK. We also thank the sponsoring institutions, EPSRC, the Kelvin Institute, the BCS-IRSG and the University of Strathclyde, for their generous financial support of the colloquium, and Glasgow City Council for its civic hospitality.

Thanks are also due to the editorial staff at Springer for their agreement to publish the conference proceedings as part of the Lecture Notes in Computer Science series.

Finally thanks are due to the local team of student volunteers (Mark Baillie, Heather Du, David Elsweiler, Emma Nicol, Fabio Simeoni, Simon Sweeney and Murat Yakici), secretaries (Linda Hunter and Carol-Ann Seath), and the information officer (Paul Smith) whose efforts ensured the smooth organization and running of the colloquium.

June 2005

Fabio Crestani
Ian Ruthven

Organization

Organizing Institutions

CoLIS 5 was organized by the Department of Computer and Information Sciences of the University of Strathclyde, Glasgow, UK.

Organization

Conference Chair: Fabio Crestani, University of Strathclyde, UK

Program Chair: Ian Ruthven, University of Strathclyde, UK

Workshops Chair: Jonathan Furner, University of California, Los Angeles, USA

Tutorials Chair: Monica Landoni, University of Strathclyde, UK

Doctoral Forum Chair: Pia Borlund, Royal School of Library and Information Science, Denmark

Advisory Committee: Peter Ingwersen, Royal School of Library and Information Science, Denmark, and Pertti Vakkari, University of Tampere, Finland

Sponsoring Institutions

Engineering and Physical Sciences Research Council (EPSRC), UK

University of Strathclyde, Glasgow, UK

Kelvin Institute, Glasgow, UK

British Computer Society, Information Retrieval Specialist Group

Glasgow City Council, Glasgow, UK

Program Committee

Alan Smeaton, Dublin City University, Ireland
Andreas Rauber, Vienna University of Technology, Austria
Andrew MacFarlane, City University of London, UK
Anastosios Tombros, Queen Mary University of London, UK
Bernard Jansen, Pennsylvania State University, USA
Birger Hjørland, Royal School of Library and Information Science, Denmark
Birger Larsen, Royal School of Library and Information Science, Denmark
C. J. van Rijsbergen, University of Glasgow, UK
Christine Borgman, University of California, Los Angeles, USA

Dagobert Soergel, University of Maryland, College Park, USA
David Bawden, City University, London, UK
David Hendry, University of Washington, USA
Diane Kelly, University of North Carolina, USA
Dietmar Wolfram, University of Wisconsin, Milwaukee, USA
Douglas Tudhope, University of Glamorgan, UK
Edie Rasmussen, University of British Columbia, Canada
Efthimis Efthimiadis, University of Washington, USA
Erica Cosijn, University of Pretoria, South Africa
Forbes Gibb, University of Strathclyde, UK
Gabriella Pasi, National Council of Research, Italy
Gareth Jones, Dublin City University, Ireland
Gobinda Chowdhury, University of Strathclyde, UK
Harry Bruce, University of Washington, Seattle, USA
Ian Cornelius, University College Dublin, Ireland
Irene Wormell, Swedish School of Library and Information Studies, Sweden
Janna Kekäläinen, University of Tampere, Finland
Jesper Schneider, Royal School of Library and Information Science, Denmark
Joemon Jose, University of Glasgow, UK
Josiane Mothe, Paul Sabatier University, France
Marcia J. Bates, University of California, Los Angeles, USA
Maristella Agosti, University of Padova, Italy
Mark Sanderson, University of Sheffield, UK
Michael Buckland, University of California, Berkeley, USA
Michael Thelwall, University of Wolverhampton, UK
Morten Hertzum, Roskilde University, Denmark
Nils Pharo, Oslo University College, Norway
Paul Solomon, University of North Carolina, USA
Pertti Vakkari, University of Tampere, Finland
Peter Bruza, Distributed Systems Technology Centre, Australia
Peter Ingwersen, Royal School of Library and Information Science, Denmark
Preben Hansen, Swedish Institute of Computer Science, Sweden
Ragnar Nordlie, Oslo University College, Norway
Raya Fidel, University of Washington, USA
Ryen White, University of Maryland, College Park, USA
Sanna Talja, University of Tampere, Finland
Sharon McDonald, University of Sunderland, UK
Stefan Rüger, Imperial College, London, UK
Stefano Mizzaro, University of Udine, Italy
Theo Bothma, University of Pretoria, South Africa

Additional Reviewers

João Magalhães, Imperial College London, UK
Peter Howarth, Imperial College London, UK

Previous Venues of CoLIS

CoLIS 1 was held in 1991 at the University of Tampere, Tampere, Finland.

CoLIS 2 was held in 1996 at the Royal School of Librarianship, Copenhagen, Denmark.

CoLIS 3 was held in 1999 at the Inter-university Centre, Dubrovnik, Croatia.

CoLIS 4 was held in 2002 at the University of Washington, Seattle, USA.

Table of Contents

Contextualised Information Seeking

Agendas for Context

Context and Documents

Workshops

Wittgenstein, Language and Information: "Back to the Rough Ground!"

David C. Blair

University of Michigan Business School

1   Why Language? Why Philosophy? Why Wittgentsein?

First of all, why are the issues of language and meaning important to the study of information systems? Information systems are, of course, tools that are used to search for information of various kinds: data, text, images, etc. Information searches themselves inevitably require the searcher to ask for or describe the information he or she wants and to match those descriptions with the descriptions of the information that is available: in short, when we ask for or describe information we must *mean* something by these statements. This places the requests for information as properly within the study of language and meaning. Surely, requests for information, or descriptions of available information, can be clear or ambiguous, precise or imprecise, just as statements in natural language can. In short, understanding how requests for, and descriptions of, information work, and, more importantly, how they can go wrong, is an issue of language, meaning and understanding.

Why, then, is the focus of this discussion on philosophy? I'm turning to philosophy of language for the principal reason that its *main* concern is with how we *mean* what we say—how language actually works? Another reason why the philosophy of language is particularly pertinent for the present discussion is that for philosophy in general, and Wittgenstein in particular, there is no sharp boundary between understanding language and cognition—how we understand language is closely coupled with how we understand things in general. Not only language, but understanding is important for information systems, too, since information systems are often used to help us understand things better. Since the approach of philosophy of language is the fundamental examination of the issues of meaning, if there are any clear insights into our understanding of meaning, they will likely be found here first. This is why the philosophy of language is so important to the investigation of information retrieval systems.

Why is the philosophy of Wittgenstein particularly important for the study of information retrieval systems? That is, why not just survey the pertinent sections of the Philosophy of Language in general? There are many philosophers of language, and many philosophical theories which have contributed to our understanding of meaning in language. Why should we concentrate our efforts on Wittgenstein's, admittedly difficult, philosophy of language? Surely there are other, easier, routes to furthering our understanding of language and meaning.

But Wittgenstein is unique among philosophers in the following respect: early in his career he was the consummate logician, the intellectual heir apparent to the pioneering logical work of Gottlob Frege and Bertrand Russell. Frege and Russell believed that

F. Crestani and I. Ruthven (Eds.): CoLIS 2005, LNCS 3507, pp. 1–4, 2005.
© Springer-Verlag Berlin Heidelberg 2005

ordinary language was not precise enough to represent the complexity and subtleties of meaning that were becoming increasingly important for analytic philosophy. Russell believed that the goal of analytic philosophy was to clarify what we say about the world. Analytic philosophy should take its inspiration from what Russell believed was the rigor of the scientific method. Since different branches of science often needed their own representational systems to express factual scientific relationships clearly, philosophy would need a similar rigorous representational system to make what it could assert perfectly clear, or so Russell & Frege thought.

What we needed, they believed, was a logical language that could faithfully model these complexities and subtleties of expression, and could be used to clarify whether statements of fact were true or false—a language that could be used to bring out and make explicit the underlying logic of language. Early in his career, Wittgenstein was sympathetic with this view of language, believing, like Russell and Frege, that language could be made more precise through the use of formal logic. In his introduction to Wittgenstein's first published work, **Tractaus Logico-Philosophicus**, Russell describes Wittgenstein as being "concerned with the conditions which would have to be fulfilled by a logically perfect language". Russell goes on to describe a logically perfect language as one which "has rules of syntax which prevent nonsense, and has single symbols which always have a definite and unique meaning".

But as Wittgenstein's thought matured, he began to have serious misgivings about the ability of logic to model or represent the complex and subtle statements of language. Not only was logic inadequate to this task, he thought, ordinary language itself was, if used properly, the best possible medium for linguistic expression, philosophical or otherwise. In short, Wittgenstein's thought evolved from a belief that problems of meaning in language could be clarified by logically analytical methods to a realization that many of the unclarities of language were a result of removing statements from the context, practices and circumstances in which they were commonly used—what Wittgenstein called our "Forms of Life."

What determined the truth or meaning of a statement was not some underlying logic, but how the statement was used and what circumstances it was used in. Ambiguities in language are clarified, not by logical analysis, but by looking at how the words or phrases in question are used in our daily activities and practices. Wittgenstein's transition in his view of language is important for the study of information systems for the following reason: our current most widespread model of information systems is the computer model, in particular, the "data model" of information. This has been a very successful and robust model that has had a remarkably long history of implementation. Computers are, in a fundamental sense, logical machines, so we might say that the current most popular model for information systems is the *logical model*. This logical model, as we will show, has worked well for providing access to the precise, highly determinate content of our data bases—things like names, addresses, phone numbers, account balances, etc. But as more and more of our information is becoming managed by computerized systems we find that we must provide access to less determinate information, like the "intellectual content" of written text, images, and audio recordings—for example, searching for information that analyzes the economic prospects of Central European countries, or information that evaluates the impact of government regulation on small businesses. These kinds of access are not as well served by the logical data model of information, as one can easily see when trying to find some specific subject matter (intellectual content) on the World Wide Web using an Internet search engine.

Current information systems are in some way, the victims of the success of the more determinate data model of information. The logical/data model of information has become the Procrustean Bed to which many information systems are forced to fit. The effort to fit language and information to the logical model was justified because it was assumed that, as Russell and the early Wittgenstein believed, there is an underlying logic of language that governed its correct usage—an underlying logic which must be uncovered if we wanted to insure the clarity of expression. On this view, information systems used to provide access to "intellectual content" are just sloppy or imprecise versions of data retrieval systems. But it was one of Wittgenstein's clearest reassessments of his early philosophy when he said that "...the crystalline purity of logic was, of course, not a result of investigation; it was a requirement"—that is, the logic that Russell and Frege sought to uncover in their analysis of language, did *not* exist latently in language waiting to be uncovered.

The logic of language was something that was a requirement for the analysis *to begin with*—it was something that was imposed on language. Just as Wittgenstein began to have misgivings about the applicability of the logical model, with its requirement for the strict determinacy of sense, to all aspects of language and meaning, some are now having misgivings about how applicable the logical/data model of information is to the more complex and subtle problems of access to less determinate information such as the "intellectual content" of written text, images and audio recordings, a kind of access becoming increasingly widespread as more and more of our information starts out in machine readable form. For the data/logical model to be applicable to all information systems, it is _required_ that the information on the system be represented in extremely precise or determinate ways. But this process will have the effect, not of making better, "more precise" information systems, but, in the case of the search for "intellectual content," of making dysfunctional information systems—systems which are insensitive to the subtleties of language that are required for highly specific access to intellectual content, especially on large systems. As long as we believe that the precision of representation for data retrieval is possible *for all information systems*, we will run the risk of building such dysfunctional systems.

2   Surveying Wittgenstein's Landscape

"....we don't start from certain words, but from certain occasions or activities."[LC p.3]

"Let the use of words teach youtheir meaning." [PI p.220]

"If a lion could talk, we could not understand him." [PI p. 223]

"The best example of an expression with a very specific meaning is a passage in a play."

"When I think in language, there aren't "meanings" going through my mind in addition to the verbal expressions: the language is itself the vehicle of thought." [PI § 329]

"Our language can be seen as an ancient city: a maze of little streets and squares, of old and new houses, and of houses with additions from various periods; and this surrounded by a multitude of new boroughs with straight, regular streets and uniform houses." [PI § 18]

"Many words...then don't have a strict meaning. But this is not a defect. To think it is would be like saying that the light of my reading lamp is no real light at all because it has no sharp boundary." [BB p. 27]

"Frege compares a concept to an area and says that an area with vague boundaries cannot be called an area at all. This presumably means that we cannot do anything with it.–But is it senseless to say: "Stand roughly there"? [PI § 71]

"If a pattern of life is the basis for the use of a word then the word must contain some amount of indefiniteness. The pattern of life, after all, is not one of exact regularity."[LWPP I § 211]

"We want to establish an order in our knowledge of the use of language: an order with a particular end in view; one of many possible orders; not the order." [PI §132]

"My method is not to sunder the hard from the soft, but to see the hardness of the soft." [NB p.44]

"The more narrowly we examine language, the sharper becomes the conflict between it and our requirement. (For the crystalline purity of logic was, of course, not a result of investigation; it was a requirement.) The conflict becomes intolerable; the requirement is now in danger of becoming empty.—We have got onto slippery ice where there is no friction and so in a certain sense the conditions are ideal, but also, just because of that, we are unable to walk. We want to walk; so we need friction. Back to the rough ground!" [PI § 107]

3   Wittgenstein's Main Views of Language

"Meanings" are not linked to words.

"Meanings" are not concepts or any other single thing."

To understand the meaning of a word is not to have some definition in your head, but to be able to use the word correctly in the activities and practices in which it is normally used.

The context of usage is essential for understanding language.

Indeterminacy in language is inevitable, but is not the result of sloppy or irrational usage.

4   Types of Indeterminacy in Information / Content Retrieval:

- Semantic Ambiguity
- Category Overload
- Language Productivity

Text, Co-text, Context and the Documentary Continuum

Elisabeth Davenport

School of Computing Napier University,
Edinburgh EH10 5DT
e.davenport@napier.ac.uk

Abstract. The paper is concerned with ways in which we understand context. In mainstream LIS, context is construed as environment or situation, a place where work gets done, supported more or less by information objects that are retrieved from a different space. The resulting separation of object and agent underlies two significant lines of work in the LIS domain: the search for optimal access to objects and the description of human information behaviour. Performance measurement dominates the former; the latter has led to elaborate and universalist models that have little discriminatory power and whose validity is difficult to establish. Both groups are pre-occupied, in their own way, with matching agent and object, or with relevance, though the question of 'relevant to what?' has many different answers - tasks, life mastery, leisure interests and so on. A recent 'call to order' here suggests that 'tasks and technology' should be the focus of LIS efforts, as these can at least support the validation of empirical work.

Context, however, may be understood differently, in terms of the texts that surround or are linked to a specific text that demands attention at a given moment. (For the purposes of this argument, context is not commensurate with hypertext; hypertext is a technology that supports the recording of context). A text (in terms of functional linguistics) is a meaningful unit of language, and texts vary in size - a clause, an article, a recipe, and (stretching the concept for the purposes of the argument presented here) a collaboratory. To focus thus on texts is not to take the side of 'objects' versus 'agents' - the agent is present in the text and achieves certain ends through texts. These are accomplished within a system of encoding (choices about what is appropriate) that makes meaning possible among those who share the code. For those in the know (members of a group, a discipline, a community) encoding is implicit. Outsiders, in contrast, need to work hard to grasp why choices have been made - what is linked with what, what refers to what, in what ways cohesion is achieved, and this work is often described in terms of literacy. Sociolinguists use a number of terms in discussing these issues - co-text (coding drives textual links to text) and social context (coding drives actions that are non-textual). These are dimensions (along with content) of a continuum - text and function, text and use are tightly coupled.

Within LIS, there are a number of approaches to clustering documents that are based on inter- and intra-textual analysis; this 'co-textual' work, however, has not been perceived as dealing with 'context'. Citation analysis is the most salient of these, with the journal article as the standard unit. It makes visible patterns of social choice and aggregation, and reveals the social encodings that characterise different domains. Citation analysis is concerned with use: sequences of 'uses' establish the texture of a domain and these threads can be traced at a very fine level of detail - a clause (the smallest unit of text) for example, may be tracked across a sequence of documents. Citation analysis may be seen as a prototype

F. Crestani and I. Ruthven (Eds.): CoLIS 2005, LNCS 3507, pp. 5–6, 2005.

for recent systems for social filtering and personalisation (recommender systems, reputational systems). These systems change the texture of work, by providing shifting sets of possibilities for action.

So why foreground an existing technique? The last part of the paper suggests that co-textual analysis is particularly timely in a world of large scale digital collections (or archives) - the aggregates associated with cyber-infrastructures and grid technologies, with e-science, e-learning, e-government, e-commerce. These collaborative spaces for project or service work are constructed on a scale that complicates understanding. They are also complex texts, whose emergent effects contribute to problem framing and problem solving. Existing tools for 'knowledge discovery' in such environments focus on the management of content, or objects that are described and classified (meta-data and meta-languages). But large collaborative texts also require tools for explication (based on co-textual analysis), that address transitivity and trace threads over time, mapping, for example, shifts in the argument of a complex text or shifts in the structure of a complicated document over versions. Visualisations of this kind can be used to track specific couplings of text, co-text and context at different levels of aggregation (what has recently been described as 'textography'); they are also important drivers of literacy - at the level of the domain, or the project.

The Sense of Information: Understanding the Cognitive Conditional Information Concept in Relation to Information Acquisition

Peter Ingwersen[1] and Kalervo Järvelin[2]

[1] Department of Information Studies, Royal School of Library and Information Science,
Birketinget 6 – DK 2300 Copenhagen S – Denmark
pi@db.dk
[2] Department of Information Studies, Tampere University,
FIN-33014 Tampere, Finland
Kalervo.Jarvelin@uta.fi

Abstract. The cognitive information concept is outlined and discussed in relation to selected central conceptions associated to Library and Information Science (LIS). The paper discusses the implication of the conception to information acquisition, both in a narrow information seeking and retrieval sense as well as in more general terms concerned with daily-life situations and scientific discovery from sensory data.

1 Introduction

Information is one of the most central phenomena of interest to information seeking and retrieval (IS&R) and Information Science in general. Understanding information is an imperative for enhancing our conception of other central phenomena, such as, information need formation and development, relevance, knowledge representation, information acquisition, communication and use. Information is the glue that binds these concepts together. We regard IS&R processes to be an important activity of human information acquisition and cognition. IS&R may occur when an actor recognizes a knowledge gap [1] or a state of incompleteness, uncertainty or ASK [2] of itself and acquires information from external knowledge sources in connection to daily-life and work situations. In broad sense information acquisition engages both knowledge sources consisting of human-made signs – *and* involves sensory data as well.

Obviously, the outcome of human daily-life as well as scientific information acquisition is paramount to the further physical and intellectual activities of the actor in question. The understanding of what is nature-bound signals, data intentional signs, meaning, information, and knowledge, leading to cognition, is consequently of outmost importance to Information Science, since it deals with the latter activities.

We outline and discuss the conditional cognitive information concept, originally put forward by Ingwersen [3] and merely concerned with interactive information retrieval (IIR) as an Information Science discipline. We attempt to demonstrate that the same conception can be generalized to cover IS&R as well as human information acquisition

F. Crestani and I. Ruthven (Eds.): CoLIS 2005, LNCS 3507, pp. 7 – 19, 2005.
© Springer-Verlag Berlin Heidelberg 2005

and cognition from sensory data, as performed during scientific discovery. Notwithstanding, the cognitive information conception does not intend to cover also pure biochemical phenomena and physical processes, which do not involve human actors.

The paper is organized as follows. First, the cognitive conditional information concept is briefly outlined and analyzed. This is followed by a discussion of its associations to other central information conceptions from LIS and related information-dependent disciplines, prior to an analysis of the conception in relation to meaning and information acquisition – with scientific discovery from sensory data as the study case.

2   The Cognitive Information Concept

Prerequisites for an information concept for Information Science and information acquisition in general are that it is must be related to knowledge, be definable and operational, i.e., non-situation specific, and it must offer a means for the prediction of effects of information. The latter implies that we are able to compare information, whether it is generated or received – and whether the processing device is man or machine. Hence, we are not looking for a definition of information but for an *understanding* and use of such a concept that may serve Information Science and does not contradict other information-related disciplines. However, at the same time it needs to be specific enough to contribute to the analysis of IS&R phenomena.

2.1   Information Acquisition in Context

Human acquisition of information from any kind of source demonstrates that communication processes play a fundamental role, involving sender, message, channel, recipient, and a degree of *shared context*. The special case for information science, and in particular IS&R lies in the notion of *desired information* and that messages take the form of *intentional signs*. Acquisition from sensory data is a special case of intentionality. A relevant information concept should consequently be associated with all components in the communication process and involve intentionality [4].

Essentially, both the generation *and* reception of information are acts of information processing made in *context* – Fig. 1 – but often at different linguistic levels, commonly known as: morpho-lexical; syntactic; semantic (or contextual); and cognitive (or epistemic) [3, p. 22-23]. All levels are nested. The former three levels belong to the 'linguistic surface levels of communication', Fig. 1. One should not be seduced by the (false) impression that recipients always are human actors. They may be generators as well as recipients and, quite importantly, computers or information systems may likewise play both roles, owing to their embedded (fixed) cognitive models representing a variety of actors.

Fig. 1 is an extension from Ingwersen [3, p. 33] by a) including different situation-specific contexts of generator and recipient, influencing their state of knowledge and cognitive-emotional model[1], and b) by viewing the act of communication at a given point in time, that is, at the instance of reception of signs. The contexts are open-ended,

---

[1] The notion 'cognitive' covers also emotions throughout the paper.

implying that factors from more remote contexts of the environment may influence the current ones (A and B) and the given situations.

At generation time, the situation in context A influences the generator's state of knowledge when producing a message of signs – the left-hand side, Fig. 1. Regardless whether the signs are stored for later communication, for instance in an information system, or immediately communicated, its meaning (sense) and context is lost – named the *cognitive free fall*. The generator has thus lost control of the message.

This is because the signs in the message fall back to a morpho-lexical state. They become data. The original (linguistic) conventions binding them together like grammar, cases and meaning (sense) are also present as signs themselves or have disappeared completely. A text or oral message simply becomes a string of signs, which have to be decoded by means of interpretation of a recipient, e.g., a reader.

That message is communicated at the linguistic surface level of the communication system. At the right-hand side the recipient perceives the signs at a linguistic surface level, in his/her/its context B. Only through the stages of information processing, and supported by the cognitive model of the recipient, may the message (signs) affect the current cognitive state of that recipient. In order to turn into information the signs must transform the cognitive state by means of interpretation. Indeed, the information perceived may be different from that intended by the generator.

The transformation is influenced by the open-ended situation in context B. Signs may indeed have effect on the recipient, but information may not be conceived. The cognitive-emotional state in context B may contain doubt, perceive a problem about the processing and/or interpretation of the signs, and reach a state of uncertainty. In itself this state could be said to hold information (on uncertainty or doubt), but then this information is of generic nature, e.g. "to me the signs seem to be of Asian origin – but I do not understand them".

In *human information processing* and acquisition the cognitive model is the individual cognitive space which controls the perception and further processing of external input, for instance, during communication and IS&R. The space consists of highly dynamic and interchangeable cognitive and emotional structures, including tacit knowledge. This individual cognitive space is determined by the individual perceptions and experiences gained over time in a social and historical context. In the actual situation the acquired information turns into IS&R knowledge and/or domain knowledge – the two knowledge types fundamental to all IS&R activities [3].[2]

In *automatic* (symbolic) *information processing* the cognitive model of the recipient may be dynamic but *not* self-contained. It consists of the human cognitive structures represented in the system prior to processing. Its individual cognitive structures, e.g., in the form of algorithms or textual strings of signs, may interact with one another and with structures generated by humans external to the system – when ordered and capable of doing so. However, the processing will only take place at a *linguistic surface level* of communication – at sign level – never at a cognitive level, see Fig.1.

---

[2] In [3] domain knowledge was frequently also named 'conceptual knowledge', which includes emotions.

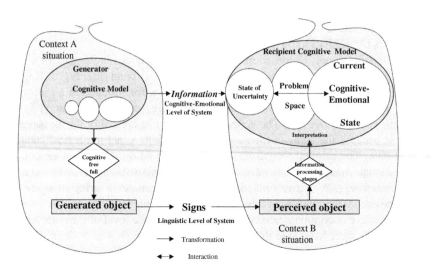

Fig. 1. The cognitive communication system for Information Science, IS&R and information acquisition in general. From [2] and revision of [3]

2.2 The Conditional Information Concept

With the above analysis in mind the concept of information, from the perspective of information science, must satisfy *two conditions* simultaneously [3, p 33]:

On the one hand information being something which is the
  result of a transformation of a generator's knowledge structures
  (by intentionality, model of recipients' states of knowledge, and in the form of signs),
and on the other hand being something which,
  when perceived, affects and transforms the recipient's state of knowledge.

Evidently, any transformation of state of knowledge involves an effect on that state. It is important to stress, however, that an effect on state of knowledge, and an ensuing reaction, does not necessarily require any transformation of a knowledge state. When a computer starts printing due to a perceived and understood print command, it is simply an effect, not a change of state of knowledge. The command remains a sign – not information.

The information concept covers both human and symbolic information processing at both the generator and recipient side of the communication channel. It does not imply that the information acquired should be novel to the recipient or true. It may simply verify the already known. Verification adds to the state of certainty concerning some phenomenon – whereas falsification commonly signifies a radical change of state [5].

From this follows that in the four man-machine relations situations, only when the recipient is a human actor, communication of information *may* take place:

1. Human actor – machine communication, the conveyed data (message or potential information) remains signs at linguistic surface level;

2. Human actor – Human actor communication, the data (message or potential information) *may* turn into information in a cognitive sense, depending on state of knowledge of recipient actor;
3. Machine – human actor communication, the conveyed data (message or potential information) *may* turn into information in a cognitive sense, depending on state of knowledge of recipient actor;
4. Machine – machine communication, the conveyed data (message or potential information) remains signs at linguistic surface level.

2.3 Associated Central Information Conceptions

Between the conditions outlined above by the cognitive information conception a substantial range of concepts can be found [6]. The conditional information concept is strongly influenced by Wersig's analyses [7] by including the notions of problem space and state of uncertainty. It is originally an extension of Brookes' [8] equation and Belkin's [2] information concept. It reflects Belkin's two-level communication model and modifies slightly the idea of information as structure proposed in [2, p. 81]. Further, we explicitly include the contextual/semantic information processing level as part of the linguistic surface level. In particular Brookes equation [8] may offer a workable solution to understanding information acquisition from sensory data.

The majority of alternative conceptions pertinent to Information Science and IS&R associate to specific elements of the conditional cognitive conception and to portions of Fig. 1.

Shannon's information concept, which, to be more accurate, originally was a measure of probability for transfer of signals forming part of his mathematical theory of communication, is very limited in scope [9]. The measure is concerned with the *probability of the reception* of messages or signals in the form of bits through a channel, explicitly not with the semantic aspects of messages. Shannon's conception thus makes information equal to communicated signs (or electronic signals) at the linguistic surface level between generators and recipient. The measure cannot be applied to information seeking and retrieval where meaning in general is related to information. Neither intentionality nor any context exists according to the conception. Hence, neither condition one and two are necessarily satisfied and it cannot deal with acquisition of sensory data, only with data transfer.

Salton [10] identifies information with text *contents*, that is, information objects as represented by the inherent features, such as, words, image colors or (automatically extracted) index keys. Context is limited to such features within objects. This is what Buckland named Information-as-Thing [11]. Searchers may provide relevance feedback, but this fact does not indicate any notion of effect on the searcher, only on the system. Salton's interest is to isolate generated messages (texts) conveyed by signs (words and other attributes) in organized channels (information systems). Hence, implicitly Salton recognizes that contents of information objects contain, carry or have *meaning* (are meaningful or have sense); otherwise the calculation of discriminating word frequencies in texts for indexing purposes would not be meaningful. In the framework of the conditional information conception Salton's notion of information equals the first condition: it is *intentional signs* placed at the linguistic surface level after the cognitive free fall on the generator side, Fig. 1. To Salton information systems are real information systems, not in any metaphorical sense. In practice most experimental researchers in IR base their feature-based search engine algorithms on independent features of objects, that is, at a morpho-lexical level. As a matter of fact, the so-called independence assumptions of document features and relevance assessments are here regarded absolutely necessary for the validity and understanding of common probabilistic IR models.

Ideas of information that regard value-added data as information, e.g. provided by human indexers by means of keyword structures, are close to Salton's conception. Pure documents are thus data, whilst organized information systems are value-added and real information systems. When perceived such entities become knowledge. The value-adding idea does not take into account the 'cognitive free fall' – also of the index terms and other added structures.

With Salton, Shannon and similar understandings the focus of the concept of information has moved from the areas of generated messages (contents of information objects) to the message in a channel (not its meaning). This drift in focus corresponds to a move from the left towards the center in Fig. 1, but at the linguistic surface level. Since none of these information concepts actually are concerned with human recipients, they cannot offer realistic solutions to understanding information acquisition from sensory data.

With Wersig [7] we reach the recipient side of the figure. He devotes attention to a concept associated with the reduction of uncertainty or doubt and the effect of a message on a recipient. Uncertainty (or doubt) is the end product of a *problematic situation*, in which knowledge and experience may not be sufficient in order to solve the doubt. It is important to note that Wersig's information concept operates in a situational and social context. His concept of information only vaguely deals with the senders' states of knowledge. But he extends his information concept and communication model to include the *meaning* of the communicated message, i.e., that it is intentional and makes sense, in order to explain the effect on the recipient: reducing uncertainty. In this concept a message 'has meaning', and may eventually 'give meaning' to the recipient. Only in the latter perspective does it offer explanations associated with acquisition of sensory data.

It is clear that the reduction of uncertainty is a relevant concept in the study of human actors (searchers) and their reasons for desire of information. Uncertainty reduction is but one of several ways a state of knowledge may change. However, it becomes unclear how this understanding of information may be related to generation processes and to non-human recipients, for instance, computers.

Recently Losee has discussed a quite generalized concept of information, suitable for all the disciplines or sciences treating 'information' in some way or another [12]. In order to accommodate the natural sciences and the issues of entropy his concept has the general form: 'information is the result of a process'. This is not the same as Bateson's 'a difference that makes a difference' [13] because the latter difference is assumed created by man as an intellectual circumstance. To Losee any process, whether taking place in nature or instigated by a human actor, will thus result in information, regardless the kind of recipient. The recipient may be a natural artifact, i.e., a World 1 object in Popper's ontology [5]. For instance, it might be a DNA molecule. It may be a World 3 knowledge product, like computers or other signs structures, made by World 2 minds. Losee's concept implies that *all* signals, intentional as well as un-intentional, *are* information in a real sense. This conception corresponds to a heavily condensed cognitive information concept. Condition one is thus reduced to ad hoc signals and natural effectors that incorporate intentional signs as a special case. Condition two becomes reduced to perception and effect – by any kind of recipient.

Fundamentally, Losee takes Shannon's [9] signal theory and alters the meaning of information, signals and data merely to signify a substitution for a 'universal *effector concept*'. The notion of information is hence not needed at all. This is not fruitful to Information Science, although Losee may argue that in special cases or situations, effectors ('information') may indeed conform to the totality of the conditional concept of information. In that case one returns to the starting point: a concept of information for Information Science that may explain when 'something' is or is not information. Losee's concept can be workable with respect to sensory data acquisition at a very general level (has effect on a recipient of any kind).

In the case of entropy, information is commonly regarded as bits of signals that can be formalized. For instance, the more open a sentence is semantically and the more surprising, i.e., the less predictable it is, the larger the amount (bits) of information that is available in the sentence. In the inverse case, that the conveyed set of signals is highly predictable, the approach considers informativeness as very low (= close to zero number of bits). In this perspective, which derives from Shannon [9], information is an objective and quantifiable entity, and completely removed from any cognitive structure, i.e., not associated to interpretation, meaning, context and information in our common sense.[3] Owing to the lack of subjective perception and interpretation entropy offers understanding of (sensory) data acquisition at linguistic surface levels – not at cognitive levels.

Finally, Dretske maintains, like Salton, that the content of information systems *is* information [14]. When accessed, following Dretske's semantic information theory, information may provide meaning, that is, *make sense* to the recipient. Information is consequently reduced to intentional signs only – i.e., identical to the first condition alone of the cognitive information conception. Dretske's information concept equals Ingwersen's understanding of 'potential information', i.e., the signs, signals, data, etc. *prior* to any act of interpretation [3]. In terms of sensory data acquisition Dretske's conception does offer an understanding: when such data (un-intentional signals) are perceived and make sense they are information entities that provide meaning, understood in a semantic sense.

2.4 Information and Meaning

One might argue that becoming informed is a purely social phenomenon, that is, that information similarly is socially dependent. This would imply that context (B), Fig. 1, or the socio-cultural and organizational context, Fig. 2, *determines* the act of becoming informed. From that perspective cognitive models reflect the social environment

---

[3] In a search for 'dog', 'eats' and 'man' it is only known to the information seeker whether a text like 'dog eats man' is meaningful and more informative (due to the unpredictability or 'surprise' value following the entropy line of thought) than 'man eat dog'. Evidently, in a cognitive sense some socio-cultural context is required to determine which understanding of the two sentences that possesses the highest surprise value in an entropy sense. Then, the entropy is not as directly quantifiable and objective as assumed.

and its domain-dependent paradigmatic structures. In a cognitive sense, however, the processes of becoming informed are *not* beyond the control of the individual actor(s). In our view the actor(s) possess relative autonomy and therefore may – *influenced* by the environment – contribute to the change of a scientific domain, of professional work strategies and management, or indeed a paradigm. This combined bottom-up and top-down view of cognition is named the principle of complementary social and cognitive influence [15].

Without that principle scientific disciplines and schools, professional and social domains as well as ideas would and could not change over time. They would stagnate, remain introvert and promote the collective (semantic) understanding of the world as the only valid and true understanding. In the case of several 'schools' in a discipline they ignore or compete with one another. This behavior can be observed by citation studies. Such aspects of information transfer are central – in particular – when discussing information acquisition, whether from documents or sensory data.

The questions then are: how much context that necessarily must be shared between sender and recipient in order to make information acquisition work? – And how does social context and elements of cognitive models reflect on acquisition from (unintentional) sensory data?

To the first question at least so much context must be shared between the actors that the message makes sense to the recipient, i.e. gives meaning. Whether or not the intended information actually becomes conveyed depends on the perception and cognitive state of the receiving mind, influenced by the current situation in context. The more common context between actors, the higher the probability that intended information becomes transferred. This is the idea behind human indexing of documents, and refers back to the first condition of the cognitive information concept: the existence of a model of the future recipients in the mind of the generator. Most often, there is not the necessary context present at any given point in time.

The second question is discussed in the ensuing sections.

Meaning commonly signifies that a message makes sense to or is understood by an actor. At the cognitive stage of information processing information is seen as *supplementary* to the existing cognitive-emotional model of the individual actor. Thus, the information from a message deriving from a human knowledge source is basically the construct by association and *interpretation* of the perceived and understood message.

In this connotation of meaning there is no doubt that information goes *beyond meaning*. Old archives, history studies as well as archaeology or IS&R are full of problems of interpretation of ambiguous sources, due to the lack of adequate context surrounding such sources. This is the reason why modern archival practice attempts to improve future sense-making and informativeness of the archive, and to avoid too much guess work, by adding sufficient context to the sources. The issue here on the thin line between meaning and information is: what is sufficient context to be shared? In some cases [16], owing to insufficient context in knowledge sources, we may observe an endless regression of meaning and interpretation; and new and creative use of expressions is inevitable.

However, jokes told within one culture are *only* fun due to the shared semantic memory, and a recognizable and understood situation. The slight twist of the shared context then creates the surprise and the significance – i.e., the unexpected sense (meaning) becomes the information and the gist of the joke. Here, we regard information as equal to meaning. Jokes can only with difficulty be transferred and provide the laugh (expression of information) in other communities or cultures, not sharing collectively the same context, although indeed linguistically understood. Similarly, deliberate misinformation builds often on known shared semantics from which the expected sense ought to lead to the desired interpretation by the recipients, i.e., to the desired (mis)construct in their minds. Misunderstanding of messages may lead to constructs different from the intended ones. In all these cases of false, wrong, or misinformation, we still talk about information as such.

But how does this bears on information acquisition from un-intentional sensory data? How is it possible to become informed from signals or signs created by nature?

3   Information Acquisition from Sensory Data

With respect to human acquisition of information from sensory data in daily-life situations none of the above Information Science conceptions focusing on the sender of meaningful messages, or on the communication channel alone, are applicable, the left hand side and center, Fig. 1. All conceptions dealing merely with the state of knowledge of recipients of signs are applicable, but only if the signs are allowed to be unintentional signals. If signs presuppose meaning in messages that will exclude sensory data. Left are thus the general information concepts that are not useful to Information Science.

The conditional cognitive information conception is quite workable in IS&R and the Information Science domain, but presupposes intentionality on the sides of the sender *and* recipient. A way to understand information acquisition from sensory data is to propose that the human recipient *simultaneously* act as a kind of go-between sender. Only in that way contexts can be shared between 'actors'. What is required is an *idea* or belief (a perspective) and some rule or logic concerning the original (unintentional) source, the matter and effect of the sensory data. The idea signifies some kind of statement that may lead to derived ideas and some methods for testing them: "The sun is warm, yellow and is seen circling around Earth close by. The stars are also yellow, but smaller and seem to stand still on the sky during the night, when the sun has gone away: The sun is on fire – more during summer than winter – and the stars are smaller fires fixed in the sky far form Earth. The moon is a less warm kind of sun, perhaps burned out, a ghost, even when it is full. Why this is so we do not know." If somebody then observes that the stars actually move around a fix point during a year there might be new ideas about the nature of the celestial bodies. Somebody may even begin to work out some rules about their movements, i.e., making predictions.

What is important is that the idea (or belief) constitutes the shared context between incoming signals (regarded surface-level signs by the recipient) and the recipient. By putting a certain perspective to the perceived sensory data the recipient actor *superimposes* a specific way of making sense and interpretation of the data *as if* he/she had participated in creating them intentionally. The interpretation made by means of rules (conventions), experiences and logic signifies the information acquired. The idea and rules or test methods may be inadequate or completely wrong, or rather; they may start contradicting (what is perceived as) reality or other actors' perspectives of the same phenomena. They may indeed also prevail collectively, leading to similar interpretations for a long span of time.

Exactly this double-sided artificial way of manipulating the sensory data makes developments and changes in cognitive models of individuals possible in relation to context. The gained experiences can then be communicated as intentional messages via social interaction and/or other kinds of knowledge sources to other individuals.

3.1 Scientific Discovery

Scientific discovery follows the same route as in daily-life situations. The difference is that conventions exist for scientific inquiry for the variety of disciplines nowadays is more pointed than for common situations. The conventions assure a minimum of context to be shared scientists in between and between scientists and their objects of inquiry.

The scientist has commonly intentionality (goals), ideas and perhaps an already established theory. From that theory he/she may generate a hypothesis about objects and phenomena. For instance, Tycho Brahe was one of the last astronomers to make observations only by eyesight. He created a vast data collection of positions of the stars and known planets. At that time (late 16th Century) the commonly (semantic) recognized theory about the universe adhered to the so-called Ptolemaic cosmology with the Earth as center and the sun and stars turning around in spheres. The problem was that the planets did not behave as they were supposed to in their orbits, according to this prevailing cosmology shared by the scientific, philosophical and religious communities, see Fig. 2, right hand side. Their courses were erratic. The common hypothesis was that the observations available were not exact enough. Hence the cumbersome work by Tycho Brahe.

In a way we may say that his data collection activity was made in order to *verify* the prevailing theory or perspective (the Ptolemaic cosmology). The hope was the data would make sense, i.e., give improved understanding of reality as perceived during the period. Information would equal meaning. He did not himself manage to carry out the proper calculations of the new orbits. Copernicus did that later on and made a discovery of consequence! The observations did not suit the prevailing cosmology. In fact they suited much better an inverted cosmology, a completely different idea: that of the helio-centric system. The original observations – made for verifying and improving the original cosmology – succeeded in *falsifying* that theory and to suggest a more suitable one. The same observations were later also used by Keppler to produce his Laws.

To Tycho Brahe starlight and his observations of star positions were built on a *hypothesis* (albeit wrong) that guided his way of making the observations. He consequently concentrated his attention on specific patterns of that light and superimposed *his* intentionality on the flow of data. He thus became a generator, substituting the originator from nature, *and* recipient at the same time of the incoming signals. They turned into signs intentionally structured according to the hypothesis (the cognitive model of the recipient actor). Condition one of the cognitive information conception is hence fulfilled although the data originates un-intentionally from natural phenomena and objects.

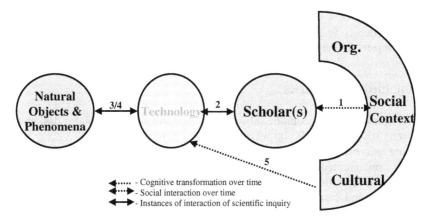

Fig. 2. Cognitive framework for instances of scientific information acquisition from sensory data [15]

The same data set may provide very different information constructs, cognition and knowledge, later to be put into theoretical patterns that may produce novel hypotheses. It all depends on the nature of the *pre-suppositions* and context that are applied as well as creativity and courage to allow a falsification to lead to unexpected conclusions. The danger of this construct is that it may lead to social constructivism or scientific relativism where the prevailing pre-suppositions are stronger than the sense of truth, logic and fairness towards reality. This is also the basic reason behind making available the data sets used in empirical research, as required, e.g., by the journals Nature and Science. In that way, by scientific convention, comparisons can be made between hypotheses, the data collection, the methods used for obtaining that collection and the ensuing results, conclusions and perspectives *and* competing approaches to the same issues. In more analytic disciplines and research traditions, the interpretative elements and speculation are more in front. But comparisons can still be made via logic, communication and academic discussion. In disciplines not dealing directly with sensory data originating form nature, but concerned with the interpretations of such phenomena in the form of knowledge sources (documents), like in History, Literature History, etc., there exists a human originator. However, most often the scientists in those domains also play the 'go-between' the original data and him or herself, in order to manipulate the interpretation. That is why so many interpretations do occur for the same event.

In a general sense Fig. 2 illustrates instances of scientific information acquisition [15]. The scientist interacts with and is influenced by his/her own domain context, including colleagues, recorded knowledge, prevailing research beliefs and traditions of that domain over time, arrow (1). To the left the scientist interacts with the natural phenomena under investigation – arrows (2) and (3/4) – carrying out information acquisition. This situation of scientific inquiry increasingly involves complex technological tools produced by other actors – arrow (5). If the technology component does not exist, however, the model becomes even more simplistic with direct interaction between man and nature – arrows (2=3/4). This was indeed the case in Astronomy during the period of Tycho Brahe prior to the invention of the binocular. If Fig. 2 is intended to depict information acquisition from man-made signs, the component 'Natural Objects & Phenomena' becomes replaced by the notion Information Objects.

4 Concluding Remarks

We have shown that the conditional information conception, originally designed by Ingwersen [3] with a specific Information Science purpose in mind, also is capable of explaining information acquisition from un-intentional signs created by nature. We have also demonstrated that there are alternative information conceptions within and associated to Information Science that do not display similar characteristics. They are either very general concepts of information, and thus not useful to Information Science and IS&R, or they commonly are not concerned with the reception of sensory data. The reason why such data are important is that they constitute the primary source for knowledge generation and thus for the generation of information objects. Consequently, it is of interest when an information concept in Information Science also may cover this central aspect of the information flow and transfer.

Acknowledgement

The authors wish to thank the Nordic Research School for Library and Information Science (NORSLIS) for travel support.

References

1. Dervin, B. From the mind's eye of the user: The sense-making qualitative-quantitative methodology. In: Glazier, R.R., (Ed.): Qualitative Research in Information Management. Libraries Unlimited, Englewood, CO (1992) 61-84.
2. Belkin, N.J. Information Concepts for Information Science. J. of Doc. **34** (1978) 55-85.
3. Ingwersen, P. Information retrieval Interaction. Taylor Graham, London (1992).
4. Searle, J.R. Intentionality and its Place in Nature. Synthese **61** (1984) 3-16.
5. Popper, K. Objective Knowledge: An Evolutionary Approach. Clarendon Press. Oxford, UK (1973).
6. Capurro, R & Hjørland, B.. The Concept of Information. Ann. Rev. Inf. Sc. & Tech. **37**, Chapter 8 (2003) 343-411.
7. Wersig, G. Informationssoziologie: Hinweise zu einem Informationswissenschaftlichen Teilbereich. Athenäum Fischer, Frankfurt, BRD (1973).
8. Brookes, B.C. The Foundation of Information Science: Part 1: Philosophical Aspects. J. Inf. Sc.: Princip. & Prac. **2** (1980) 125-133.
9. Shannon, C.E. & Weaver, W. The Mathematical Theory of Communication. University of Illinois Press, Urbana, IL. (1949).
10. Salton, G. & McGill, J.M. Introduction to Modern Information Retrieval. McGraw-Hill, New York, N.Y. (1983).
11. Buckland, M. Information as Thing. J. Am. Soc. Inf. Sc., **42**(5) (1991) 351-360.
12. Losee, R.M. A discipline independent definition of information. J. Am. Soc. Inf. Sc. **48** (1997) 254-269.

13. Bateson, G. Steps to an Ecology of Mind. Paladin, Frogmore, St. Albans, USA (1973).
14. Dretske, F.I. Knowledge and the Flow of Information. Basil Blackwell, Oxford, UK (1981).
15. Ingwersen, P. & Järvelin, K. The Turning Point: Integration of Information seeking and Retrieval in Context. Springer, London (2005) (in preparation).
16. Blair, D.C. & Maron, M.E. Full-text Information Retrieval: Further Analysis and Clarification. Inf. Proc. & Man, **26**(3) (1990) 437-447.

Practical Implications of Handling Multiple Contexts in the Principle of Polyrepresentation[*]

Birger Larsen

Department of Information Studies,
Royal School of Library and Information Science,
Birketinget 6, DK-2300 Copenhagen S,
Denmark
blar@db.dk

Abstract. The principle of polyrepresentation, proposed more than 10 years ago, offers a holistic theoretical framework for handling multiple contexts in Information Retrieval (IR), and allows integration of representation and matching of both documents as well as the information seeker's information need in context. Relatively few empirically based studies have, however, applied the principle explicitly for IR purposes. This paper examines the principle of polyrepresentation, and analyses the practical implications of applying it to multiple contexts in best match IR research. It is concluded that the principle is inherently Boolean in its foundation in spite of its intentions to be applicable to both exact and best match IR. This may constitute a major obstacle for the application of the principle in main stream IR and information seeking research. A polyrepresentation continuum is proposed as an illustration of this problem, and as a model for developing the principle towards greater practical applicability.

1 Introduction

The principle of polyrepresentation proposed by Ingwersen [8; 9] offers a holistic theoretical framework for handling multiple contexts in Information Retrieval (IR), and allows integration of representation and matching of both documents and the information seeker's information need. In brief, the principle hypothesises that overlaps between different cognitive representations of both the information seeker's situation and documents can be exploited in order to reduce the uncertainties inherent in IR, thereby improving the performance of IR systems. Good results are expected when cognitively unlike representations are used. The document title (made by the author) vs. intellectually assigned descriptors (from indexers) vs. citations (made by other authors over time) are examples of such different cognitive origins. Similarly, the information need is not seen as a static entity, but rather as part of a causal structure in which the work task to be solved plays an essential role, and from which a number of representations can potentially be extracted (See Section 2 below).

---

[*] The work presented is based in part on the author's dissertation work [13].

F. Crestani and I. Ruthven (Eds.): CoLIS 2005, LNCS 3507, pp. 20–31, 2005.

Essentially, the principle is about making use of a variety of *contexts*, and to do so in an intentional manner by focussing on the overlaps between cognitively different representations during interactive IR. Based on Ingwersen's cognitive theory of Information Retrieval [7] the principle of polyrepresentation places the documents, their authors and indexers, the IT solutions that give access to them (e.g., search engines), and the seekers in a comprehensive and coherent theoretical framework. In comparison with the mainstream IR research tradition and the research carried out in the information seeking community, the principle offers a much broader approach than either two. The mainstream system-oriented IR research tradition focuses on document representation and matching algorithms, but not on the actual users of the system, and the user-oriented information seeking community focuses on the user's situation and seeking behaviour, but rarely on the IR systems involved. The principle of polyrepresentation stresses the importance of all agents and the interplay between them as a condition for achieving successful and optimal IR. The potential of the principle is therefore to serve as a common theoretical framework for research that integrates the information seeking perspective on the users with the mainstream IR focus on designing and testing better IR systems. This is much needed and has been called for repeatedly in the literature, but has not been realised to a great extent.

In spite of being highly cited and of its potentials for a more comprehensive approach to IR and seeking research, relatively few empirically based studies have, however, applied the principle of polyrepresentation explicitly for IR purposes. A few studies have reported promising results when applying it on operational databases using exact match approaches [e.g., 4; 12]. The aim of this paper is to analyse the practical implications of applying the principle to multiple contexts, especially the challenges faced when applying the principle in best match IR. Much of Ingwersen's thinking behind the principle seems inherently Boolean, e.g., the emphasis on cognitive overlaps, which might not transfer easily to a best match context.

The paper is structured as follows: Section 2 outlines the principle of polyrepresentation as a basis for the analysis of the practical implications of implementing it in Section 3. Section 4 discusses these and points to future possibilities, and conclusion are given in Section 5.

2   The Principle of Polyrepresentation

The principle of polyrepresentation originates in work on establishing a cognitive theory for interactive information retrieval [see 7], and can be regarded as a result of his efforts to demonstrate the *applicability* of this theory [3]. The cognitive view serves as a unifying perspective by viewing all processes in interactive IR as the result of cognition processes in the involved agents. The principle of polyrepresentation presumes that each agent contributes with their own interpretation of the documents as seen from their context: For instance, a document reflects the knowledge structures and intentions of its author(s), the controlled descriptors and uncontrolled index terms assigned to it are indicative of the indexer's interpretation, and the individual interpretations by subsequent citing authors. In addition, the choices made by designers of IR algorithms and databases have consequences for the representation of the documents, and the resulting systems are seen as reflective of their ideas and intentions. This line of thought and its parallels with Internet meta-search engines are not considered in the present paper. The cognitive view is also applied to the seeker's situation. Ingwersen only regards information retrieval to have taken place when the recipient has perceived the document and interpreted it into her own context. Because the author can only express her intentions and ideas through *signs* (speech, writing, etc.) the information sent by a generator is subjected to a cognitive "free fall", and has to be re-interpreted by the recipient in order to transfer information in a cognitive sense [9]. This inescapable act of interpretation has as a consequence that uncertainties and unpredictabilities are inherent features of *any* of the representations in IR.

In the principle of polyrepresentation the tangible entities in IR, e.g., documents, are regarded as *representations* of the responsible agent's interpretation of the documents from their context. Representations of the same entity can be viewed from two perspectives: If the representations stem from two different agents the representations are regarded as *cognitively different*. Representations from the same agent are regarded as *functionally different*. Polyrepresentation of the seeker's cognitive space is to be achieved by extracting a number of different representations from the seeker. In an ideal situation, at least three potentially different functional representations may be extracted at any one point in time [9, p. 16]:

1. "a 'what', i.e., a request version which includes what is currently known about the unknown (the wish or desire for information);
2. the 'why', i.e. a problem statement as well as;
3. a work task and domain description."

Because the underlying cognitive structures are variable over a session, different versions of each representation may occur over time. Some of the extracted representations may often appear to be similar, e.g., the problem statement and the work task description. This is a consequence of the fact that information needs may be well or ill-defined, as well as more or less stable. These different types of information needs and their development are clearly demonstrated by the empirical studies [See, e.g., 1; 6], as is the role of the librarian in helping the seeker to define and refine her need. Such a set of representations extracted from the information seeker's cognitive space provides a more fertile context of causally structured contexts. The intention in the principle of polyrepresentation is that this enriched set of representations should be used as search terms during interactive IR, and combined with each other to achieve polyrepresentation of the seeker's cognitive space.

A range of both cognitively and functionally different representations can potentially be associated with the documents. This is illustrated in Fig. 1 below in relation to academic documents. Each ellipsis in the figure can be thought of as a different cognitive agent with the agent's role in capitals and examples of the agent's representation in lower case. Within each ellipsis the representations are functionally different, and when compared across ellipses they are cognitively different. The *author* of the documents is important as the originator of a variety of functional representations as shown on the right hand side of the figure. As academic documents have a rich rhetorical structure many functional representations can be extracted from the structure of the documents apart from the full text itself. Other agents include *human indexers*, *thesaurus constructers*, other authors responsible for *citations* to particular documents (and passages in them), and so-called *selectors*. These selectors are agents that are responsible for the availability and accessibility of documents, e.g., journal boards, reviewers, employers etc. who bestow cognitive authority by, e.g., allowing a paper to appear in a given journal or at a conference. Ingwersen added these in the 2002 paper [10], which may be seen as an attempt to broaden the scope of the principle of polyrepresentation into wider contexts.

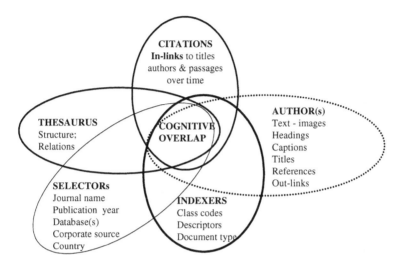

Fig. 1. Polyrepresentative cognitive overlaps of cognitively and functionally different representtations of documents. [Reproduced from 10, p. 294]

The principle of polyrepresentation represents Ingwersen's attempt to exploit the multitude of contexts to achieve successful and optimal IR. The core of the principle of based on the following of hypothesis [9, p. 26]:

1. "all the inconsistencies are self-evident, inescapable, formally unpredictable, and of similar cognitive nature;
2. the more remote in cognitive origin and in time, the less the consistency;
3. the inconsistencies can be applied favourably to improve retrieval because:
4. if different cognitive structures, in defiance of the inconsistency, do, in fact, retrieve overlapping information objects, this cognitive overlap presents more 'relevant/useful/...' information objects than each independent structure;
5. the more different the cognitive structures producing an overlap are in time and by cognitive or functional type, the higher the probability of its 'relevance/usefulness...'."

The principle thus represents an attempt to view the uncertainties and unpredictability as favourable to IR, and to exploit these actively. Inspired by, e.g., Sparck Jones [15], Ingwersen proposes to work through *intentional redundancy*, that is, to represent documents (or information needs) in multiple, complementary ways. Ingwersen calls this redundancy "intentional", since general and non-estimated redundancy in relation to representations of documents may not always be productive in IR [8]. The means to achieve the intentional redundancy is through the identification of the so-called 'cognitive overlaps', which are sets of documents that, in response to a given query, are retrieved when the query matches *several* cognitive or functional representations of the documents. The idea is illustrated in Fig. 1 where a cognitive overlap is created by the cognitive and functional representations discussed above.

3 Practical Implications

The practical implications of implementing the principle of polyrepresentation for IR purposes are analysed below based on Ingwersen's texts and the experiences of those who have implemented the principle in empirical studies.

While there are general hints for what types of representations to use in the hypothesis quoted above (i.e., the ones that are most different in time and in cognitive or functional type), the actual selection of representations and how to combine them is not dealt with in any great detail by Ingwersen. This is mainly left as an issue to be dealt with by the IR system's intermediary mechanism [8, p. 105]:

> "The degree, mode and function of redundancy should be determined by knowledge of the current user's information behaviour, e.g. as inferred or believed by the intermediary mechanism, based on a elaborate model of searcher behaviour.
>
> In other words, from a cognitive perspective as many and as different cognitive structures as possible should be made available and applied during IR interaction, however, in accordance with an estimation which allows for a controlled or calculated selection of exactly such structures that are regarded most appropriate to the current retrieval situation. This issue of estimation is not necessarily seen as a mathematical one but rather a behavioral and psychological issue."

The reliance on the intermediary mechanism clearly shows that Ingwersen's conception of polyrepresentation is highly influenced by his own and other's early studies of the interaction between librarians and patrons [see, e.g., 6]. The idea of an automated intermediary mechanism is clearly inspired by the expert systems envisioned in the late 1980s (see Chapter 7 in [7]) with elaborate user modelling and extended dialogs. This line of research has been abandoned, mainly due to the cost involved in establishing and maintaining the knowledge bases of the systems, and Ingwersen's recent proposals focus on request modelling rather than actual user modelling [10]. Rather than modelling the whole situation of the user, including the user's general competencies, the request modelling is concerned with the three types of questions outlined above (extracting descriptions of the 'what', the 'why', and the work task). Nevertheless, the matter of how to treat these representations of the seeker's context (once these are obtained) largely remains an issue for future research on the principle of polyrepresentation.

The identification and manipulation of the cognitive overlaps are obviously crucial for any practical implementation of the principle. With the focus on *overlaps* Ingwersen's thoughts about the implementation of the principle are inherently *Boolean*. This is apparent in some of the figures used by Ingwersen to illustrate the principle, where the representations are displayed as sets in Venn diagrams with cognitive overlaps between these sets such as in Fig. 1 above. The main practical example of the application of the principle of polyrepresentation given by Ingwersen deals with online searching in an exact match system which further accentuates the Boolean line of thought [9, p. 44-45]. In establishing the cognitive frame around the principle of polyrepresentation it is, however, clear that Ingwersen's *intention* is for the principle also to be applicable in best match systems. An inference network inspired by Turtle and Croft [16] is for instance used to illustrate the matching of document representations with representations of the seeker's context [9, p. 37]. Much of the inspiration for the principle also comes from mainstream IR research into best match systems, e.g., that different best match principles tend to identify slightly different sets of relevant documents in relation to the same query. This intention is also explicit in later papers on the principle [10]. The practical implications of this tension between the Boolean exact match perspective and the best match elements of the principle of polyrepresentation are examined below by analysing implementations of the principle.

A difficulty also noted in Ingwersen is the problem of identifying suitable test environments in which to experiment with the principle of polyrepresentation [9]. The large scale Text REtrieval Conferences (TREC) has two problems in relation to polyrepresentation: the test corpora mainly consist of short news articles in relation to which very few functional and no cognitive representations can be extracted, and the main ad hoc track uses static requests so there can be no polyrepresentation of the seeker's context. Ingwersen analyses the many possibilities offered by academic full text documents in the 1996 article, but at that time no corpora was available for test purposes. This situation has begun to change recently, however, as publishers increasingly produce academic journals and book electronically, e.g., in SGML or XML. Begun in 2002, the INitiative for the Evaluation of XML Retrieval (INEX) is the first IR initiative to use a corpus of highly structured academic full text articles to build a test collection for IR experiments[1] [5]. INEX is still far from the size of TREC, but offers a wide range of possible functional representations of the documents.

Although the principle of polyrepresentation has not resulted in a large body of empirical research that deal with all elements of the principle a few studies work with elements of it. Four of these are examined below in order to identify issues related to the implementation of the principle. Two of the studies were carried out in operational online databases [4; 12], while the other two used test collections [13; 14].

Larsen proposes a new strategy for searching via citations, the so-called 'boomerang effect' [12]. The strategy was tested in a small experiment carried out in the online version of the Science Citation Index (SCI) using one test person's real information needs and subsequent relevance assessments. As the SCI does not contain the full text the number of representations used was limited: titles and abstracts by the author, and Keywords Plus (automatically assigned identifiers) and the network of references and citations by other cognitive agents. The experiment was Boolean because of the online setting, and only static versions of the information needs were

---

[1] INEX uses a corpus of 12,107 full text articles from the IEEE Computer Society's 20 journals corresponding to ½ GB of text. For more information see the INEX web site http://inex.is.informatik.uni-duisburg.de:2004/.

used. Larsen used the principle of polyrepresentation as inspiration for selecting representations, for the automatic identification of seed documents for the citation search, and for refining the results of the strategy. The latter consisted of a number of retrieved document sets ordered in a polyrepresentative overlap structure, and showed that the overlaps generated by many representations consistently contained greater proportions of relevant documents. Although it was possible to implement the strategy, Larsen notes that with more than three or four representations the number of overlaps and the effort required to handle them increase dramatically. He also experienced problems with the initial query formulations, which had to be expanded in order to fit the individual representations. The expansion was also necessary in order ensure that the sets were sufficiently large to produce an overlap. Finally, the output was a semi-ranked list of document sets (similar to the example given in [9]) with no internal ranking within each set. This can present problems to users if a set is large, and this kind of output makes it very hard to compare the strategy to other approaches, including best match systems.

Christoffersen used the online versions of Medline, Embase and SCI to test the proportions of relevant documents in the overlaps between the three databases [4]. Again the study was Boolean because of the online setting. The representations had strong cognitive differences: Title/abstract words (from authors extracted from Embase) vs. MeSH terms (from indexers extracted from Medline) vs. searching by citations (from citing authors in SCI). The relevance assessments were by subject experts, and the results showed that the degree of overlap (i.e., the number of sets a document appeared in) correlated strongly with the percentage of relevant items in a set. As only three representations were used no serious problems were experienced with handling the overlaps. The intersections involved did, however, reduce the number of documents in the overlaps to less than 14 % of the total number of documents retrieved.

Both studies were on small scale and used only a few representations, and the promising results of both are therefore noteworthy. This may be interpreted as a consequence of the strong cognitive differences between the representations used. An equally important factor is the size of the database involved: in both cases the systems were operational and contained several million records each. The principle of polyrepresentation could therefore reduce the uncertainty associated with each individual representation, and still create overlaps that were not empty.

Skov et al. set out to test elements of the principle of polyrepresentation in a best match setting [14]. The small test collection contained 1239 Medline records augmented with references and citations. Despite its small size the collection offered several cognitive and functional representations: words from titles and abstracts (from the author), Minor and Major MeSH headings (by indexers) as well as references and in-going citations (by citing authors). Two types of queries were tested in a best match system: natural language queries and highly structured queries. Both types used Boolean operators to identify overlaps. The highly structured queries also contained indications of query facets and phrases, and had synonyms added intellectually from MeSH. These additions were the results of Skov et al.'s efforts to on one hand improve the quality of the document sets, and on the other ensure that the overlaps were non-empty. Results showed that overlaps generated by several representations had higher precision than those generated from few representations for both query types. Marked differences were also found between representations; in particular the results indicate an increase in precision when documents identified by a citation search strategy formed part of an overlap, stressing the importance of using representations that have strong differences. In all cases the highly structured queries achieved higher precision than the natural language queries, which is explained as a consequence of generating overlaps in a best match system: because the natural language queries only require one search term from the query to be present, the retrieved sets of documents and thus the overlaps may contain documents with very little relation to the information need. Skov et al.'s results indicate that the quality of the initial sets from which overlaps are created can be improved and better results achieved with the principle of polyrepresentation, but only after extensive work on refining the queries.

Larsen tested a best match version of the boomerang effect using the INEX test collection [13]. Because of the complex full text XML structure a number of functional representations could be extracted from the documents: title, abstract, author keywords, cited titles (from the reference list) as well as figure and table captions and the introduction and conclusion sections. In addition, the documents were represented by descriptors from the INSPEC thesaurus and uncontrolled identifiers assigned by INSPEC indexers. The boomerang effect was tested against two baselines: a bag-of-words index where all the representations were mixed into one, and a polyrepresentation baseline, which gave higher weights to documents retrieved from several representations and required that documents were retrieved in at least two representations. The same unstructured queries were used in all three runs. Results showed that the bag-of-words baseline out-performed the other two, and that the polyrepresentation baseline performed slightly better than the citation search strategy in the boomerang effect. Strict Boolean overlaps were not enforced in any of the strategies; Larsen had instead chosen to rely on thresholds to limit the size of the sets. It should be noted that the best performance of the latter two were obtained at relatively low thresholds, i.e., when the sets from each representation contained few documents. This may be explained similarly to Skov et al.'s results: as the best match system only requires at least one of the query terms to be present in the retrieved documents, only the documents at the top of the rank have a sufficiently strong relation to the information need.

The approaches in both studies produced ranked output, which could be compared to standard IR methods. The results show that unstructured applications of the principle of polyrepresentation are not likely to result in performance improvements – rather a decrease in performance can be expected, at least when simplistic fusion strategies such as those in Larsen are used [13]. Thus the implementation of the principle of polyrepresentation in best match systems is not straightforward, as it seems that some structure is needed to ensure the quality of the cognitive overlaps as seen in Skov et al. [14].

4   Discussion and Future Directions

In summary, three possible obstacles for the practical implementation of the principle were identified above from Ingwersen's texts:

1. The need for effective tools to build models of the seeker's request,
2. The inherent Boolean approach to identifying the cognitive overlaps despite the intentions of integrate the principle into a best match setting, and
3. The lack of suitable test environments.

We regard the tension between the Boolean exact match perspective and the best match elements of the principle of polyrepresentation to be the most immediate concern. For any implementations of the principle of polyrepresentation based on exact match the consequence is that a large and complex, but consistent set of overlaps have to be identified. This may be difficult to handle manually, but it can be automated without problems, and the quality of the set that the cognitive retrieval overlaps are based on can be maintained. If the implementation involves best match principles the situation is different. Best match systems will most often place the documents that contain all the query keys at the top of the ranked retrieval output, but will also include any document that contains just one of the query keys at lower positions of the rank. The combination of partial match and ranked output is one of the main advantages of best match systems over exact match systems [2]. However, in relation to the creation of overlaps in the principle of polyrepresentation there is a risk that the quality of the sets that the cognitive retrieval overlaps are based on, as a whole, are too low. For instance, with two search concepts there is the risk that only the first of them is retrieved by some of the lower ranking documents in one representation, and the second in the lower ranks in another representation. Thereby proper polyrepresentation in the true sense of the concept cannot be achieved, and reduced rather than increased performance can be expected.

On a theoretical level, the principle of polyrepresentation seems to be a strong and comprehensive framework for integrating research on IR systems with detailed knowledge of the context of the information seeker. If this is to be achieved within the principle of polyrepresentation, more research needs to be directed towards methods of achieving a flexible match of representations while still retaining the power of the Boolean logics. The studies analysed above show that this is not straightforward, and that much more work needs to be done on the matching of representations before the potentials of the principle can be fully realised. Rather than using either exact match or best match approaches it is our belief that a combination of methods is needed. Therefore we propose the idea of a *polyrepresentation continuum* as illustrated in Fig. 2 below. The continuum is useful as a model for discussing how structured a given implementation of the principle of polyrepresentation is, and may guide the direction of further work on the principle.

At the *structured* pole of the continuum the implementations are based on exact match principles, leading to sets of retrieved documents for each representation from which overlaps can be formed and a pseudo-ranking be constructed. At the *unstructured* pole of the continuum the implementations are based on best match principles leading to a rank of the documents that are retrieved as input for polyrepresentation. Rather than generating overlaps between sets, the implementations at the unstructured pole of the polyrepresentation continuum will fuse the ranks to produce a final ranked output, perhaps aided by thresholds to provide the necessary quality. Between the two poles there is a continuum going from highly structured implementations to highly unstructured implementations. The implementtations in Larsen [12], Christoffersen [4] and the example given in [9] are all placed at the structured pole of the continuum. The polyrepresentation baseline in Larsen [13] is placed at the unstructured pole. The cloud in the middle of the continuum illustrates the current status where we have little knowledge of how to match the cognitive representations in a flexible and effective manner, and identifies the challenges for future research on the principle of polyrepresentation. Skov et al. [14] represents a constructive attempt to move from an exact match approach towards the unstructured pole of the continuum, with their highly structured queries that are run in a best match system. Further moves toward the unstructured pole could include structured queries as investigated in best match systems by Kekäläinen and Järvelin [11], query expansion and query adaptation to individual representations. The latter appears to be important and might lead to more formal IR models which incorporate differentiated normalisation and weighting for different representations.

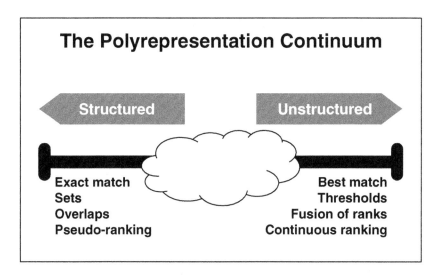

Fig. 2. The polyrepresentation continuum. Inspired by Skov et al. [14] and Larsen [13]

None of the four empirical studies involved polyrepresentation of the information seekers' cognitive space. This is probably a consequence of the lack of tools to extract the representations from the seekers (the request model builder). We regard this as an issue to be dealt with the interface level. Although very complex solutions can be imagined simple versions could be tested initially, e.g., by asking the seeker for different descriptions of the 'what', the 'why', and the work task. Suitable test environments for testing such approaches are beginning to emerge, e.g., within the INEX initiative where an interactive track has been organised for the first time in 2004[2]. In addition to an interactive setting, INEX offers a document collection from which a large range of representations can be extracted.

---

[2] See http://inex.is.informatik.uni-duisburg.de:2004/tracks/int/.

5 Conclusions

The most immediate obstacle identified for the practical implementation of the principle of polyrepresentation in best match IR is its inherent Boolean nature. The major challenge for future research involving the principle is to develop methods that can on one side ensure the quality of the cognitive overlaps and on the other hand add greater flexibility than that provided by means of exact match. The proposed polyrepresentation continuum illustrates this and may guide the direction of further work on the principle. Such work would be facilitated by recent projects such as the INEX initiative.

Acknowledgments

The author is grateful for financial support for the presented work from the Nordic Research School in Library and Information Science (NORSLIS) and the Danish Ministry of Culture (grant no. A2004-06-028). In addition, the author wishes to thank the anonymous referees for constructive comments.

References

1. Belkin, N. J. (1984): Cognitive models and information transfer. *Social Science Information Studies*, 4, 111-129.
2. Belkin, N. J. and Croft, W. B. (1987): Retrieval techniques. In: Williams, M. E. ed. *Annual review of information science and technology (ARIST), volume 22, 1987*. Amsterdam: Elsevier Science, p. 107-145.
3. Borlund, P. (2000): Experimental components for the evaluation of interactive information retrieval systems. *Journal of Documentation*, 56(1), 71-90.
4. Christoffersen, M. (2004): Identifying core documents with a multiple evidence relevance filter. *Scientometrics* , 61(3), 385-394.
5. Gövert, N. and Kazai, G. (2003): Overview of the initiative for the evaluation of XML retrieval (INEX) 2002. In: Fuhr, N., Gövert, N., Kazai, G. and Lalmas, M. eds. *Proceedings of the first workshop of the initiative for the evaluation of XML retrieval (INEX) : December 9-11, 2002, Schloss Dagsthul, International Conference and Research Centre for Computer Science,* p. 1-17. [http://qmir.dcs.qmul.ac.uk/inex/Papers/final_overview_Goevert_etal.pdf]
6. Ingwersen, P. (1982): Search procedures in the library analysed from the cognitive point of view. *Journal of Documentation*, 38(3), 165-191.
7. Ingwersen, P. (1992): *Information retrieval interaction*. London: Taylor Graham. x, 246 p. ISBN: 0-947568-54-9. [http://www.db.dk/pi/iri/, visited 1-11-2003]
8. Ingwersen, P. (1994): Polyrepresentation of information needs and semantic entities : elements of a cognitive theory for information retrieval interaction. In: Croft, W. B. and van Rijsbergen, C. J. eds. *SIGIR '94 : Proceedings of the seventeenth annual international ACM-SIGIR conference on research and development in information retrieval, organised by Dublin City University, 3-6 July 1994, Dublin, Ireland.* London: Springer-Verlag, p. 101-110.
9. Ingwersen, P. (1996): Cognitive perspectives of information retrieval interaction : elements of a cognitive IR theory. *Journal of Documentation*, 52(1), 3-50.

10. Ingwersen, P. (2002): Cognitive perspectives of document representation. In: Bruce, H., Fidel, R., Ingwersen, P. and Vakkari, P. eds. *Emerging frameworks and methods : CoLIS4 : proceedings of the fourth international conference on conceptions of library and information science, Seattle, WA, USA, July 21-25, 2002.* Greenwood Village, Colo.: Libraries Unlimited, p. 285-300.
11. Kekäläinen, J. and Järvelin, K. (1998): The impact of query structure and query expansion on retrieval performance. In: Croft, W. B., Moffat, A., van Rijsbergen, C. J. and Zobel, J. eds. *Proceedings of the 21st Annual International ACM SIGIR Conference on Research and Development in Information Retrieval (ACM SIGIR '98), Melbourne, Australia, August 24-28, 1998.* New York: ACM Press, p. 130-137.
12. Larsen, B. (2002): Exploiting citation overlaps for information retrieval: generating a boomerang effect from the network of scientific papers. *Scientometrics*, 54(2), 155-178.
13. Larsen, B. (2004): *References and citations in automatic indexing and retrieval systems : experiments with the boomerang effect.* Copenhagen: Royal School of Library and Information Science. 297 p. (PhD dissertation) [http://www.db.dk/blar/dissertation]
14. Skov, M., Pedersen, H., Larsen, B. and Ingwersen, P. (2004): Testing the Principle of Polyrepresentation. In: Ingwersen, P., van Rijsbergen, K. and Belkin, N. eds. *ACM SIGIR 2004 Workshop on "Information Retrieval in Context".* Sheffield: [University of Sheffield], p. 47-49. (Workshop proceedings) [http://ir.dcs.gla.ac.uk/context/]
15. Sparck Jones, K. (1990): *Retrieving information or answering questions.* London: The British Library Board. (British Library Annual Research Lecture ; 8)
16. Turtle, H. and Croft, W. B. (1990): Inference networks for document retrieval. In: Vidick, J.-L. ed. *Proceedings of the 13th annual international ACM SIGIR conference on research and development in information retrieval : Brussels, Belgium, 5-7 September, 1990.* New York: The Association for Computing Machinery, p. 1-24.

Information Sharing and Timing:
Findings from Two Finnish Organizations

Gunilla Widén-Wulff and Elisabeth Davenport

Åbo Akademi University, Information Studies,
Tavastgatan 13, 20500 Åbo, Finland
gunilla.widen-wulff@abo.fi
Napier University, School of Computing,
10 Colinton Road, Edinburgh, EH10 5DT, Scotland
e.davenport@napier.ac.uk

Abstract. Timing of organizational information sharing is an under-explored area of research in information science. Timing has been addressed on the individual level in the context of sense-making, or in terms of moves in information seeking. In related areas, time has been treated, largely, in terms of life cycle theories, which then again does not feature information sharing. In this paper we have drawn on a broader range of source materials to investigate timing and information sharing in two very different social environments: an insurance claims department and a biotechnology firm. The key question is "how does timing work in the contexts where information sharing happens?" The study shows that sharing cannot be considered without taking timing into account. The cases reveal that organisational timing depends on the demands of social process as well as on individual disposition.

Topic Areas: Contextual factors, Information seeking and behaviour.

1 Introduction

The timing of information sharing in organizations is a topic that has been under-explored in information science. Where it has been addressed in the domain of human information behaviour (HIB), treatment has been variable: Solomon [1-3], for example, discusses 'time and timing' in the context of sense-making. Other treatments of timing have been in terms of specific moves in information seeking [4], which involve identifiable sequences that may be linear [5] or non-linear [6]. It is not always clear in such studies to what extent the observed sequences (and thus the presentation of time and timing) are artefacts of the research process – many information seeking studies employ the critical incident technique [7, 8], which requires participants to describe their behaviour in terms of a linear narrative.[1] Spink [10], with her colleagues has provided more elaborate versions of episodic models in

---

[1] It may be noted that this problem is not unique to LIS – Czarniaiawska [9.] raises similar issues in a discussion of research in the domain of organizational studies.

F. Crestani and I. Ruthven (Eds.): CoLIS 2005, LNCS 3507, pp. 32–46, 2005.

studies of multiple search strategies. In many of these studies, timing is part of goal directed behaviour; few researchers have considered the timing in searching as arbitrary, or opportunistic; Hert [11] and Cool [12] are among those who cover opportunistic searching in their studies of situated searching, and 'situation'. The majority of these studies consider timing in terms of *individual* behaviour, and link identifiable moves to changes in cognitive state. This somewhat limited appreciation of time and timing is characteristic of much HIB research, which, in general, has not addressed the *organizational* dimensions of information work.

In organizations information sharing happens in a constant mix of purpose, timing, and availability. Information sharing is a motivated process [13, 14] where purpose and availability can be described as roles, status, and social networks influencing the utilization of sources and sharing in organizations [15-19]. In addition to purpose and availability the time aspect is crucial for organisational information sharing [9].

In this paper the objective is to address timing as an important part of structuring internal information sharing in organizations. For the purposes of this paper, information sharing is a reciprocal behaviour that derives sequences of action in sets of changing circumstances. Two cases with different work structures, work pace, and operating in different turbulent environments are investigated in order to compare how time aspects affect information sharing. The studied organizations are an insurance claims department and a start-up company of biotechnology. The data for the paper were gathered in two Finnish companies during 2003-2004. Measures for investigating information sharing were derived from several sources and addressed work related information sharing, conditions, consequences, group behaviour, information interactions, culture and social climate. A more detailed description of the methods is found in [13]. The data consist of responses to questionnaires and interview transcripts. Our account in this paper of timing and information sharing is based largely on the qualitative data in the transcripts. Timing and time issues were not explicitly addressed in either the interviews or the questionnaires, and we have thus avoided instrumental bias.

2   Context and Timing

Information seeking in context has been thoroughly explored (see the ISIC conferences e.g. [20, 21]) and on a broad level context is defined as work life and everyday life, in different organisational and professional settings, e.g. [6, 22-24]. Recent analysis have emphasised a narrower scope; practitioners in specific domains, e.g. [25-29]. Others propose that different sub-fields within the LIS area, studies on information seeking and information retrieval, should be combined with the aim of creating a more coherent picture of the real life work settings where social and cultural issues are addressed [30, 31]. In a review of the concept of situation in information science Cool [12] suggests that "contexts are frameworks of meaning and situations are the dynamic environments within which interpretive processes unfold, become ratified, change and solidify".

In this paper we try to find a focused description of context in relation to information sharing in groups, by asking "how does timing work in the contexts where information sharing happens?" Blurring somewhat the distinction made by Cool [12] between context and situation, we suggest that context can be understood in terms of process, and that information sharing is tightly coupled with the work patterns that characterise this process The context of sharing is built up from several levels of interactions [32] that follow different tempos.

Two pertinent CSCW studies address the mundane work of insurance claims handlers [33, 34], and throw light on the often opportunistic and sometimes ritualistic nature of timing in this environment. A further set of studies on interactions in meetings has provided a basis for exploring the micro-level interactions in bounded time and space; and studies of collaborative work in the natural sciences [35, 36] have thrown light on the ongoing ebb and flow of sharing as instruments and people come together and disperse. Work in systems science and communication science on cooperation in temporary organizations [37] has sensitized us to temporal elements of situation that extend existing treatments in IS; and recent work on 'spacing and timing' in organizational studies [9, 38] has provided us with examples of typology and vocabulary that grapple more fully with organizational timing than standard LIS models. This extended repertoire of sources has supported our attempt to assess how well traditional approaches (episodic, life cycle, chronological) adequately capture time issues in organizational information sharing, and whether an extended approach that takes account of social process is required.

At this point it may be helpful to define additional terms. By timing, we refer to a judgment to make a move, which may be triggered by private motives (the standard model), by the demands of the work process, or a mixture of these. We define information sharing, primarily, in terms of interpersonal interactions that happen in different question/answer modes. Though material that is deposited in commonly accessible databases may be described as "shared information" (and indeed was perceived as such by several participants in the study), the input and accessing of such material is not strictly 'information sharing'.

3   Timing and Sharing in the Claims Handling Process

The first case, Company A, is a claims handling department in a Finnish insurance company. The company offers insurance and financial service to small and medium sized companies, and private persons. There are about 440 employees in the whole organisation. The claims applications unit has about 30 employees. This group is an example of close-knit organization in a stable environment. Information in the claims handling company is held in formal structures (database, Internet) but may also be gained by asking questions of one's colleagues. Both formal and informal dimensions were invoked in answers to questions about information sharing which seems to mean at least two things – making information available where it is publicly accessible, and being responsive when asked about something (the focus of our study). The information activities of the group involved in the fieldwork are presented in Table 1.

Table 1. Information activities in claims handling

Source	Purpose	Access	Timing
Internal database	Rules, clauses, principles, best practise	Easy to access. Equal to everyone.	Updated once a week. Used when on telephone duty. New members use it more regularly.
Internet	Formal information Medical information Customer information	Suitable sources filtered through claims procedure. Commonly assessed in meetings	In claims procedure as an important research tool.
Meetings	Cases and best practise General information	Everybody attends	Regular meetings.
Personal network	Validation of information Access to information for special work tasks Best practise Access to knowledge about other sources	Depends on roles and status in the group Easy to access because the unit is physically located in the same corridor	Colleagues are consulted on daily basis. Informal occasions as coffee breaks, lunch, and corridor discussions.
Intranet	General information about the company, other departments	Easy to access, part of everyone's user interface	Accessed when someone points out that there are important information.

Table 2. Work tasks in the claims handling unit

Persons	Tasks	Years in the unit
A	*Claims handler*	0-1
B	Claims administration (payments)	30
C	Committee procedure	11-15
D	Head user – system administration	11-15
E	Committee procedure	11-15
F	*Claims handler*	2-5
G	*Claims handler*	0-1
H	*Claims handler*	6-10
I	Committee procedure	11-15
J	*Claims handler*	11-15

In many instances, information sharing could not be attributed to a disposition or cognitive style, but is how work gets done in this particular context[2]. Ten persons were interviewed in the unit representing the different roles within the department.

3.1 Routine Timing

We have identified three main types of timing in the work of the claims department. The first is routine timing or judgments that are tightly coupled to work process. Claims handling is a form of distributed cognition [39] and activities around an artefact (the claims documentation) take place in series of moves across the group with each member contributing to the completion of the task. Moves (where judgment is made visible) fall into two categories: reciprocal (question/response) and teleological (a required part of the process is fulfilled). The timing of both of these varies across different sequences of tasks and roles. Routine timing can thus be described in terms of bounded predictability – a quota of claims must be handled each day, though within the day timing and moves are flexible and time can be found in coffee breaks and lunch breaks to complete cases that make heavy demands on time, or non-core activity (like browsing the web) may be given up to accommodate them. To some extent, routine timing is amenable to description in terms of the episodic moves that are typical of the standard timing model in LIS, though in the claims department moves are made by many hands.

3.2 Ad Hoc Timing

The second category of timing that we have identified is what we call 'ad hoc' timing. This may be observed in the handling of what the respondents refer to as "difficult cases". Ad hoc timing works at different levels. For any novices in the group, the first port of call for handling claims is the database of good practice, and any case that cannot be handled with this is considered difficult. In the interests of getting work done quickly they will ask whoever is next to them for help. More experienced staff accept this role as part of their ordinary work. These more experienced employees also take ad hoc action when faced with difficult cases, though they do not rely on physical proximity but use their knowledge of others' expertise to target respondents. These others may be internal colleagues, or outside specialists like medical doctors or actuaries. Although meetings are the main platform for handling difficult cases (we discuss these in more detail below), they are held once a week, every Thursday, and some cases cannot wait for several days. Then it is up to the handler to use all the other sources available (database, Internet, and colleagues), and in the end consult the manager of the unit. *"Sometimes you can't wait with all decisions to Thursday morning. Then you have to ask the manager how to proceed, and of course check with your colleagues." (Head User - D)*

Ad hoc timing is unpredictable – it is not possible to know when a novice, even with training, or when an experienced handler will ask for help; and the availability of expert colleagues cannot be guaranteed. Being an experienced claims handler means

---

[2] This echoes Solomon's observation that : `the participants in the work-planning process did not think of information or actions to collect, process, or use information as something separate from the task or problem to hand`. (p. 1109) [3].

knowing how to accommodate ad hoc information sharing into your work pattern – whether helping those who are less experienced, or seizing the opportunity to tap the expertise of those with more specialised knowledge. This aspect of timing and sharing is less amenable to description in terms of the standard model, as it is embedded in the structural and emotional patterns of the group. The Internet has had an impact on this type of interaction: *"Earlier we had e.g. to find the Financial Newspaper somewhere in the organisation to check out currency rates. Then we occasionally copied the table and distributed it within the department. Now you just go to a currency converter on the net and you have the information within seconds." (Claims handler - H).* With the Internet much of the ad hoc information sharing is now a matter of informing each other of usable sites, and the use of external personal networks is less extensive.

3.3 Ritual or Normative Timing

The third type of timing that we have identified is ritual or normative timing. Meetings are where this timing may be observed. The most difficult claims involve sharing among handlers and specialists, with an added dimension of public debate and communal decision taking. Though such cases are initially opportunistic, as they are concerned with anomalies, the outcome of information sharing and public debate is often reutilisation: the cases are framed in terms of what has happened previously, and an appropriate handling procedure is logged in the database.

The meetings that are the occasion of this process of collective judgment also serve a ritualistic function –judgments depend heavily on the wisdom of tribal elders like "Janet" who has been in the department for thirty years, and who is the source of narratives that legitimate the categorising of a claim as requiring this or that treatment. Collective judgments result in recommendations that are stored in collective memory, a database that is the resource of first resort for novices.

Meetings are well organised in this department and new members of the group emphasised the importance of meetings for learning about practice. There are claims handling meetings every week for general information, news, with most of the time allocated to difficult cases. In addition, there are open departmental meetings every second week where general information and news are disseminated and discussed. Meetings make individual knowledge visible for everyone in the group. *"There is so much to know and remember. In the meetings our different knowledge is brought together. Someone remembers something and another something else. From these different parts a more coherent picture of how to deal with a difficult case is built." (Claims procedure - I)*

Two hours are allocated for most meetings, but sometimes they over-run: *"Sometimes it feels quite tough to sit on these meetings for several hours, but in the end they are so important that everybody attends" (Claims handler - F).* We suggest that the normative timing that is characteristic of the meetings may be compared with Cool's definition of context as "shared frameworks of meaning". Because of their systematic nature an individual claims handler can make sure she knows the most important things about the department activities by attending the meetings.

3.4 Discussion of Company A

Information sharing in Company A is part of a repertoire of interlinked behaviours that are brought into play as the process (more or less protracted) of handling a claim unfolds. Though individual behaviours can be identified (seeking, responding, checking) none on its own can capture the way in which the group's most important asset, collective expertise, is acquired and sustained. Following Wenger [34] who provides an account of insurance work in his monograph on communities of practice, we suggest that this organisational form appropriately describes the work of the claims handling department. Members of the group are engaged in distributed cognition (the claims handling process that we describe above), claims handling procedures are produced and reproduced in a process of situated learning (the normative or ritualistic information sharing that happens in meetings and in routine information sharing) and situated action (ad hoc information sharing) supported by an appropriate social infrastructure[3].

In what ways, then, does the pattern of timing in the claims handling workplace differ from that described in standard accounts involving episodic sequences and life cycles? Though we acknowledge that these may provide some understanding of routine work, we suggest that the added dimensions of social and lived time that must be taken into account, and that a broader conceptual framework is required that addresses the full range of activities (questions, responses, referrals, meetings) and accounts for the ritualistic elements of sharing that are characteristic of community maintenance in the claims department.

4 Timing and Sharing in the Biotechnology Firm

We now turn to the very different world of the technical specialists and intermediary and administrative staff who make up Company B. The company is a small association of experts, who occupy a specialised market niche that is based on a unique product. The company was formed as a university spin-off; it has 14 employees overall divided into six functions of the company (senior management, board, financial, training, marketing, sales department, R & D, communications). Every person has their own area of expertise, which means that the work of the experts in this company is very varied, as is the use of different information sources. Though there are fewer actors than in Company A, each of them operates in a number of intersecting situations. We have found, however, that patterns of timing can be observed that apply across the manifold situations. These, as might be expected, differ from those in Company A, as they are tightly coupled to a specific environment. The operating efficiency of Company B, a loosely bound group of experts, is due to the co-ordination work of key intermediaries, and three of these (corporate communication, administration, training) along with one researcher with responsibility for R & D. All members of Company B rely heavily on each other's judgment. The work tasks of the interviewed persons are presented in table 3.

---

[3] These dimensions of communities of practice are developed in a framework proposed by Davenport and Hall [25].

Table 3. Work tasks in the biotechnology firm

Expert area	Years with the Company
Researcher, R & D	4 years
Communications	2 years
Administration	6 years
Training	2 years

Table 4. Information activities in the biotechnology firm – Personal networks

Source	Purpose	Used by	Access	Timing
Personal network (External)	Suppliers, distributors, customers	All	Based on the personal contacts every expert has	Project based (opportunity)
	Experts in the area (e.g. dentists, professors)	Researcher	Personal contacts	Project based
	Other experts (lawyers, insurance, tax)	Administration	Personal contacts	Cyclic, planning
Personal network (Internal)	Personal network	All	Easy to access, open office landscape, email	Projects
	Meetings (working groups, units, projects)	All	Put together for different purposes	Project based
	Board meetings	Top management, all functions	6/14 employees (persons responsible for different functions)	Regular
	Coffee – lunch breaks	All	In the same building	Daily basis

Work in Company B is hectic and information sharing is closely bound up with project-based work. The researcher, for example, observed *"We have an expert on every key area of the company's activities. This means that the organisation is very flat. We have no units, only a person responsible for his or her area. But then we gather teams for specific purposes, which are responsible for a part of the communication or the continuing communication of a matter. This means it is a challenge to remember and be aware of the right people that are involved in that particular work process."* Top management has overall responsibility for framing company activities and board meetings are the channels for this. Special project meetings facilitate information sharing across the company, but it is up to each expert to decide what is relevant to put forward and not. Decisions on what to share are project based, and there is no common assessment on what should be in a common knowledge base. It may be noted that informal gatherings are important facilitators of information sharing (coffee breaks, open office landscape). It is evident that the work of the interviewed persons varies according to role, though roles are interdependent. Structuring the information sources used is more difficult that in company A. Personal networks are very important for all activities which is shown in table 4.

The trainer's internal duties promote greater awareness about the company's activities. Internal colleagues are the main sources of information, accessed by means of a personal network, and often by e-mail. The coordination between product development and distributors' learning process is the basis for planning training activities. The responsibility to forward information to the right people is paramount: *"A challenge in this kind of organization is to combine information from different sources all the time; be organised and think of who should know about this... You are able to destroy and slow down processes by the fact that you don't share" (Trainer).* The trainer who was interviewed believes that effective information sharing depends on a combination of structured sharing and personal openness. *"Some persons share information spontaneously and some persons you must 'interview'" (Trainer).*

The primary task of the corporate communications expert is to sustain internal and external awareness of developments. For this role to be effective, information sharing is a duty, not an option: *"There is a responsibility to give information. If you don't know you have the responsibility to find out" (Communication).* Communication has an important role of gathering information from all units, processing it and communicating it to an external audience. Again, timing is important. Ability to prioritize is underlined because of the time limits.

Formal information sources are mainly used by the researcher and in the administrative work where the planning processes are central. An overview of formal sources is given in table 5.

The researcher's work, for example, supports innovation, development of products, and production. This entails preparing documentation to support the firm's own innovations, producing, for example, internal studies that compare traditional dental care with new approaches. The researcher also cooperates with internal and external experts (by means of personal networking) and much of the work involves judgments about reliability and trustworthiness. In addition, the researcher evaluates colleagues in terms of their sharing behaviour. Research must also report to the supporting areas so that they can plan their activities in the right timeline.

The work of the administrator involves background information for decisions at board level and managing information for such functions as office organisation, logistics, and service functions. Acting as both a hub and a generator of internal information, the administrator operates across a broad network with active internal collaboration with all units and employees. At times, the role is that of an enforcer, demanding information from colleagues to allow a given process to proceed.

Table 5. Information activities in the biotechnology firm – Formal sources

Source	Purpose	Used by	Access	Timing
Formal sources (External)	Market reports	Research, administration	Databases, accessed personally and through information experts	Project based Planning
	Research articles	Research	Databases	Project based, continually
Formal sources (Internal)	Own research / reports	All	Research department	Project
	Company handbook / to learn about the company	All, mostly new members	Available to all	
	Internal database (IS)	Administration	Poorly updated	Planning, regular
	Customer management program / marketing program (software)	Training, Communication, Administration	Easy to access, intranet	Planning
	Web pages	Administration		"To read about what is happening in the company"

4.1 Compliance Timing

We have identified at least three type of timing in Company B. The first is compliance timing. This involves moves to share information that are triggered by the demands of projects and that may be linked to critical path analysis, as these moves are made so that other moves may follow. One of the interviewees compared the work of those involved in projects to 'baton passing'. Though the work of Company B is in some respects similar to that of Company A (the outcome of group or team effort is collective and achieved on the basis of the partial input of each participating member), the timing patterns are different – compliance timing is not routine, and is shaped by a spreadsheet that records instances when information is sent, and the fact that it has been received and understood.

4.2 Pragmatic Timing

The second type of timing is pragmatic timing, or judgments about when and what to share that are base on calculations about time resources in the broader sense, and the tradeoffs between stimulating extended debate, and ensuring that the company's interests are not put at risk by under-reporting. This type of judgment is often brought into play at meetings: *"There is constant interacting and it is important that everyone participates enough in information sharing. But not too much, there is point in sitting in meetings where you cannot contribute". (Researcher)*

The work tasks are individual and the experts work quite independently, but there is the challenge of sharing information at a specific stage in a process to specific functions and persons. *Time is crucial when we are a small organisation aiming at global markets. You must be very concentrated, but at the same time you need to have the whole process internalised so that you are able to stop and think who might need this information. Even if I'm in a hurry I must respect the duty to share information to others. (Training)*

4.3 Formative Timing

The third type of timing that we observe in the transcripts from Company B is formative timing, or judgments about sharing that contribute to overall awareness across the company of new developments. (The overall responsibility for this, as we note above, belongs to the trainer). Like pragmatic timing, this depends often on a calculus of costs and benefits – often on a 'tit for tat' basis: *"We depend on each others knowledge – do not upset the other or you remain without information!" (Communication)*

The board meetings and the planning cycle are almost the only visible time structures in this organisation. Timing is visible in the administration process where they have 4 months planning cycle involving financial and market planning. It is important to get predictions from different functions in the organisation, as a basis for analysis (market, sales etc.). However, this is not working systematically although forms exist. The top management is responsible for gathering the projects into a coherent workflow. The board meetings function as the "knowledge base" where all functions of the company are reported on a monthly basis. *Half of our staff is members of the board. Even so there is a problem that those who then have subordinates don't always remember to inform them. (Administration).* The open office landscape helps the organisation to shape some level of common knowledge base where everyone can see and hear what the other functions are working with. *The open office landscape means that everything is public information. (Communication).*

4.4 Discussion of Company B

As we note above, information sharing behaviour in Company B different from that of Company A. The experts and their co-ordinator are bound together by an immediate objective – the creation of innovative products to sustain the company, and they work within tight time constraints. The timing typology reflects this. What is shared, or brought to the common attention of the group, is highly selective, and depends on judgments about the consequences of sharing at any given juncture. There is more at stake – each specialist must trust the judgments of the others, as he or she is not competent to assess the quality of another specialist input. And specialist external sources must be filtered by the judgment of resident experts – few information sources can thus be used in common. The habits of the experts in Company B are similar to those that have been reported in accounts of interdisciplinary scientific collaboration among specialist experts in other contexts – water planning [40] public administration [41]. They have a contractual obligation to share, but do not always believe that 'outsider' recipients will fully understand the specialist data that has been sent to them, and will thus be highly selective in what they divulge.

5   Conclusions

In this paper we have explored the question "how does timing work in the context where information sharing happens" with the objective to address timing as an important part of information sharing in organizations. Timing of organizational information sharing has been a neglected area of research in information science and therefore we have brought a broader range of studies to investigate the phenomenon in two different cases. Several types of timing were revealed and it is clear that sharing cannot be considered without taking timing into account. Studying two cases with very different work structures it was possible to focus how time aspects are present in these structures. Our typology of timing shows that sharing requires two parties, timing and availability, and that two parties work in a stimulus response mode that is characterised by different time regimes. The typologies of timing that we have produced for the two cases indicate that these regimes characterise different types of organizational work. Where Company A is labelled by routine, ad hoc, and ritual timing, Company B was more unstructured but was driven by compliance, pragmatic, and formative timing in their information sharing. The examples from the routine or regulated environment are mostly of sharing in response mode. In the non-routine environment, sharing is initiated in response to a perceived opportunity; it might also be described as 'strategic' sharing. This can be seen as of two types: personal, when an expert initiates an exchange that is in their own advantage (as their intervention process is in their own interest), and collective, when an expert releases information that will benefit the group or company.

Our findings, though preliminary and incomplete, demonstrate that accounts of timing in organizations need to take account of the social dimension. Solomon [1], in the first part of his trilogy on time and timing, observes that in information science 'the passage of time is so obvious that we tend to ignore it…time as expressed in the information dynamics of social systems is difficult to capture and comprehend'. He suggests that time has thus been 'simply glossed over in research, theory development and practice'. (p. 1107). We do not agree with all of these statements: though under-explored, a number of important studies in information science (as we note above) have addressed time, notably studies of moves and sequences in information seeking. Moves are a critical concept in any study of time and timing; what is missing in our domain is serious exploration of moves that have consequences in terms of others. As authors interested in the reciprocal phenomenon of information sharing, we agree with Elchardus' [42] definition (quoted with approval by Solomon: 'time is, in a very real sense, a gift of the others, a socially constructed predictability that allows us to live'.

Time as a social construction has been explored in depth by researchers in the domain of organizational studies. Czarniawska [9], for example, speaking of time as a "collective construction" and discusses the interplay of kairotic time (the 'right time' to do something) and chronological time (the sequence of events captured in planning templates, schedules and so on). We can see both of these at work in the case studies. This interplay is highly localised, and it is thus not surprising that there are differences in patterns of timing in the two organizations, though aspects of timing in each are similar to those reported in comparable sectoral studies.

We underline that this study is still at an early stage, and much work is still to be done on context in general and timing in particular. Information sharing is achieved by means of a constant mix of motives, duties, expectations, availability; all of these, in different combinations, contribute to timing, or judgments about when to make moves that will trigger the actions of others. Some of the moves that constitute information sharing, as we note above are embedded in existing social processes of getting work done; others are intentional individual acts that initiate new processes and sequences. Individual and social actions are intertwined in a process that can be explicated in terms of timing.

References

1. Solomon, P.: Discovering information behavior in sense making: I. Time and timing. Journal of the American Society for Information Science 48 (1997) 12 1097-1108.
2. Solomon, P.: Discovering information behavior in sense making: II. The social. Journal of the American Society for Information Science 48 (1997) 12 1109-1126.
3. Solomon, P.: Discovering information behavior in sense making: III. The person. Journal of the American Society for Information Science 48 (1997) 12 1127-1138.
4. Fidel, R.: Moves in online searching. Online Review 9 (1985) 1 61-74.
5. Kuhlthau, C. C.: Seeking meaning: a process approach to library and information services. 2nd ed. Libraries Unlimited, (2004).
6. Ellis, D. and M. Haugan: Modelling the information seeking patterns of engineers and research scientists in an industrial environment. Journal of Documentation 53 (1997) 284-403.
7. Flanagan, J.: The critical incident technique. Psychology Bulletin 51 (1954) 4 327-358.
8. Urquhart, C., et al.: Critical incident technique and explicitation interviewing in studies of information behavior. Library & Information Science Research 25 (2003) 1 63-88.
9. Czarniawska, B.: On space, time and action nets. Organization 11 (2004) 6 773-791.
10. Spink, A., et al.: Modelling users, successive searches in digital environments. D-Lib Magazine (1998) April. Retrieved 01.03.2005 at http://www.dlib.org/dlib/april98/04spink.html
11. Hert, C.: User goals in an online public access catalogue. Journal of the American Society for Information Science 47 (1996) 7 504-518.
12. Cool, C.: Concept of situation in information science. Annual Review of Information Science and Technology 35 (2001) 5-42.
13. Widén-Wulff, G. and M. Ginman: Explaining knowledge sharing in organizations through the dimensions of social capital. Journal of Information Science 30 (2004) 5 448-458.
14. Wittenbaum, G. M., A. B. Hollingshead, and I. C. Botero: From cooperative to motivated information sharing in groups: moving beyond the hidden profile paradigm. Communication Monograph 7 (2004) 3.

15. Thomas-Hunt, M. C., T. Y. Ogden, and M. A. Neale: Who's really sharing? Effects of social and expert status on knowledge exchange within groups. Management Science 49 (2003) 4 464-477.
16. Hertzum, M.: The importance of trust in software engineers' assessment and choice of information sources. Information and Organization 12 (2002) 1-18.
17. O'Reilly, C. A. I.: Variations in decision makers' use of information sources: the impact of quality and accessibility of information. Academy of Management Journal 25 (1982) 4 756-771.
18. Wilson, T. D.: Human information behaviour. Informing Science 3 (2000) 2 49-55.
19. Haythornthwaite, C. and B. Wellman: Work, friendship, and media use for information exchange in a networked organization. Journal of the American Society for Information Science 49 (1998) 12 1101-1114.
20. Vakkari, P., R. Savolainen, and B. Dervin (eds.): Information Seeking in Context. Proceedings of an International Conference on Research in Information Needs, Seeking and Use in Different Contexts. Taylor Graham, London (1996).
21. Wilson, T. D. and D. K. Allen (eds.): Exploring the Contexts of Information Behaviour. Proceedings of the Second International Conference on Research in Information Needs, Seeking and Use in Different Contexts, Sheffield. Taylor Graham, London (1998).
22. Ginman, M.: De intellektuella resurstransformationerna : informationens roll i företagsvärlden. Åbo Akademis förlag, Åbo (1987).
23. Savolainen, R.: Everyday life information seeking: approaching information seeking in the context of "Way of Life". Library & Information Science Research 17 (1995) 259-294.
24. Widén-Wulff, G.: Information as a resource in the insurance business: the impact of structures and processes on organisation information behaviour. New Review of Information Behaviour Research 4 (2003) 79-94.
25. Davenport, E. and H. Hall: Organizational knowledge and communities of practice. Annual Review of Information Science and Technology 36 (2002) 171-227.
26. Hyldegård, J.: Collaborative information behaviour - exploring Kuhlthau's Information Search Process model in a group-based educational setting. Information Processing & Management in press (2004).
27. Mackenzie, M. L.: Information gathering revealed within the social network of line-managers. In: Proceedings of the 66th Annual Meeting of the American Society for Information Science and Technology(2003), 85-94.
28. Solomon, P. (ed.) Information mosaics: patterns of action that structure. Exploring the contexts of information behaviour. Proceedings of the 2nd International Conference on Research in Information Needs, Seeking, and Use in Different Contexts, ed. Wilson, T.D. and D.K. Allen. Taylor Graham, London (1999). 116-135.
29. Talja, S.: Information sharing in academic communities: types and levels of collaboration in information seeking and use. New Review of Information Behaviour Research 3 (2002) 143-159.
30. Byström, K. and P. Hansen: Work tasks as units for analysis in information. In: Bruce, H., et al.: Editors Emerging Frameworks and Methods. Proceedings of the Fourth International Conference on Concepts of Library and Information Science (CoLIS4), Libraries Unlimited, Greenwood Village (2002), 239-251.
31. Järvelin, K. and P. Ingwersen: Information seeking research needs extension towards tasks and technology. Information Research: an International Electronic Journal 10 (2004) 1. Retrieved 01.03.2005 at http://InformationR.net/ir/10-1/paper212.html

32. Reddy, M. and P. Dourish: A finger on the pulse: temporal rhythms and information seeking in medical work. In: Proceedings of the 2002 ACM conference on computer supported cooperative workNew Orleans, Louisiana, USA (2002), 344-353. Retrieved 01.03.2005 at http://doi.acm.org/10.1145/587078.587126

33. Ackerman, M. and C. Halverson: Considering orgnizational memory: processes, boundary objects, and trajectories. In: Proceedings of the 32nd Hawaii international conference on system sciences(1999),

34. Wenger, E.: Communities of practice: learning, meaning, and identity. Cambridge U.P., Cambridge (1998).

35. O'Day, V., et al.: When worlds collide: molecular biology as interdisciplinary collaboration. In: Prinz, W., et al.: Editors Proceedings of the Seventh European Conference on Computer Supported Cooperative Work, 16-20 September 2001, Bonn, Germany, Kluwer Academic, Dordrecht (2001), 399-418.

36. Sonnenwald, D. H., K. Maglaughlin, and M. C. Whitton: Designing to support situation awareness across distances: an example from a scientific collaboratory. Information Processing & Management 40 (2004) 6 989-1011.

37. Weisband, S.: Maintaining awareness in distributed team collaboration: implications for leadership and performance. In: Hinds, P. and S. Kiesler: Editors Distributed work, MIT Press, Cambridge, MA (2002), 311-333.

38. Thrift, N.: Thick time. Organization 11 (2004) 6 873-880.

39. Hutchins, E.: Cognition in the wild. MIT Press, Cambridge, MA (1995).

40. Van House, N.: Digital libraries and collaborative knowledge construction. In: Bishop, A., B. Buttenfield, and N. Van House: Editors Digital library use: social practices in design and evaluation, MIT Press, Cambridge, MA (2003), 271-296.

41. Drake, D., N. Steckler, and M. Koch: Information sharing in and across government agencies. Social Science Computer Review 22 (2004) 1 67-84.

42. Elchardus, M.: In praise of rigidity: on temporal and cultural flexibility. Social Science Information 33 (1994) 459-477.

Contexts of Relevance for Information Retrieval System Design

Erica Cosijn and Theo Bothma

Department of Information Science, School of Information Technology,
University of Pretoria, Pretoria, 2001, South Africa
{erica.cosijn, theo.bothma}@up.ac.za

Abstract. Users judge relevance in various dimensions, but systems traditionally only support matching of queries to documents or document representations on an algorithmic or topical level. We argue that systems should support users in order for them to make relevance judgements on the level of cognitive relevance, situational relevance, and socio-cognitive relevance as well. Current studies in the field of Information Retrieval and Seeking are discussed from a relevance point of view, in order to show how systems might be adapted to assist users in making multi-dimensional relevance judgements.

1 Introduction

Traditionally, the focus of IR research is on topicality as the deciding criterion for relevance. It is essential to understand the manner in which relevance is judged in order to improve the representation of, and access to information. A previous study has confirmed that users also judge relevance on levels other than topicality [1]. The purpose of this paper is to review the larger significance of these results regarding the implementation of the findings in terms of the possible applicability of the framework defined by the model that is briefly described in Section 2. The main question that will be discussed in Section 3 is: *How can systems be improved in order to help users to make relevance judgements on other levels as well?*

The analysis presented here should be seen as a possible contextualisation of the model within current research projects and provides a guideline for future research on relevance. The research in the field has been mapped to the model in order to expose the "bigger picture" of what is being done within relevance research. Although the list of studies reviewed below cannot be regarded as being comprehensive, all the studies mentioned already have as underlying theme the understanding of various types of relevance judgements as made by users of IR systems.

2 Proposed Relevance Model

The different dimensions of relevance have been identified in a theoretical study by Cosijn and Ingwersen [2], and subsequently modeled [1] as a modification of the Ingwersen *Cognitive Model of Information Transfer* [3]. This model is depicted in Figure 1.

F. Crestani and I. Ruthven (Eds.): CoLIS 2005, LNCS 3507, pp. 47–58, 2005.

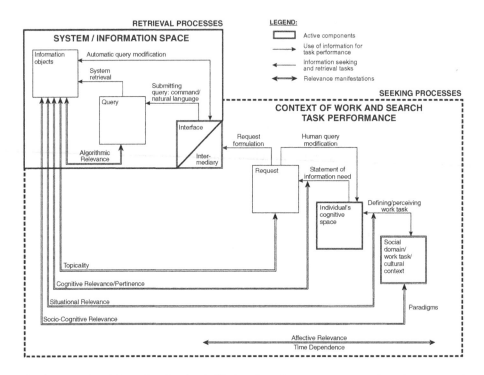

Fig. 1. Interactive Information Retrieval: Work task performance, search task performance and relevance types

In this model, the original elements of the Ingwersen model have been retained, but the dimensions of relevance are defined in terms of the relationships between the information objects (as perceived) and different elements in the information searching process. In this manner, situational relevance can, for example, be defined as the relation between the definition or perception of the work task in the user's mind, on the one hand, and the information objects as perceived by the user, on the other hand. Affective relevance has been shown to operate on a different level and affective relevance judgements can be associated with any of the subjective relevance types.

The model was then empirically tested according to the following issues: usefulness and viability of the model, the influence of the nature of the work task on the application or non-application of documents in work task fulfillment, the influence of work and search task execution on the type of relevance judgements made, whether some relevance dimensions necessarily include others, and the relationships between types of relevance judgements.

Thirty-three users performing three different types of work tasks (undergraduate students writing a guided research essay, masters and doctoral students, and researchers writing articles and conference papers) were asked to judge the relevance of the documents utilized in the execution of the work task. In total, 467 documents were judged, of which 320 were relevant to the works tasks and 147 were retrieved and at least partially read, but were not relevant to the extent that they were cited. The questionnaires and other measuring instruments are described in Cosijn [4]. The empirical testing showed that the model is a valid representation of the types of relevance judgments made by users [1]. Detailed results will be published elsewhere.

3   Dimensions of Relevance for System Design

In Section 3, each of the relevance types is discussed briefly in order to re-establish the parameters of the definitions of the relevance types. These definitions are important, because these are the parameters in which the argument will take place. It is acknowledged that relevance is a fuzzy concept and that definitions vary, but by defining each manifestation clearly and only arguing within those parameters, misunderstandings should be minimized.

For each of these studies, the recent and current research into facilitating these relations in the search process has been analysed, with the focus on the more subjective relevance types of cognitive, situational and socio-cognitive relevance.

3.1   Algorithmic Relevance

In the model as depicted in Figure 1, the relation is defined as that between the query and the information objects. This relation is system-oriented to a very large extent, as it depends on the degree of similarity between the features of the query and the features of the information object. This type of relevance is by nature system-dependent. It is not influenced by the user, nor is it related to any subjective information need the user may have.

System or algorithmic relevance is measured in terms of the comparative effectiveness of logical or statistical similarity of features inferring relevance. There are various models of matching the query (as a representation of the user's need) to the information objects (whether as full-text or as representations). Systems may be Boolean (exact match) or best-match (for example vector space, probabilistic, etc.) in nature, or a combination of both. Although this study limits its scope to the more subjective types of relevance judgements, the concept of algorithmic relevance is, nevertheless, included in the model and therefore a brief review of recent projects aiming to increase the comparative effectiveness of the relation between the query and the information objects has been given.

One of the most enduring debates within the systems approach to IR is the use of natural language versus controlled vocabulary to improve retrieval. A recent study in this field was done by Tomaiuolo and Packer [5]. A subset of this type of research is the work of researchers such as Sanderson [6] on sense disambiguation. Other researchers concentrate on improving relevance feedback methods, for example the research by Voorhees [7] on the role of assessors in measuring relevance feedback, Lee [8] on multiple evidence from relevance feedback methods, Lam-Adesina and Jones [9] on summarization techniques for term selection in relevance feedback, Voorhees [10] on the validity of TREC for using relevance as a measurement of retrieval effectiveness and Voorhees [11] on the role of highly relevant documents in system evaluation. Another recent area of research within the systems relevance is that of partial or graded relevant assessments, for instance the work of Järvelin and

Kekäläinen [12] on discounted cumulative gain which incorporates multiple relevance levels into a single measure and Kekäläinen and Järvelin [13] on graded relevance assessments in IR evaluation.

The focus of the studies mentioned above is algorithmic relevance in the model derived in this study – the relation between the query and the information objects. Traditional Boolean systems facilitate binary relevance judgements, whereas best match systems, or a combination of best match and Boolean systems, are able to rank retrieved information by relevance. It is clear that even in systems relevance research there has been a move away from the traditional binary relevance judgements and a greater appreciation for the fuzziness of relevance judgements made by users and the need for interactive information retrieval (IIR). Therefore, research on retrieval systems improvement should focus more on facilitating fuzzy relevance judgements.

3.2 Topicality

Topical relevance is defined as the relation between the topic of the query and the topic of the assessed information objects. The finding of focus during the formulation of the request by the user, which is then transformed into a query by the system, is the criterion whereby topicality is inferred. The assumption is that both request and the objects may be assessed by a cognitive agent as being about the same or a similar topic, which implies a degree of subjectivity. The assessment is even less reliable if the information objects are represented by human-indexed terms.

Improving the relationship between the request and the information objects in terms of topicality is the focus of IR systems. Interesting new developments in the field of information representation, might prove to be useful in assisting users to judge potentially useful documents on a topical level.

Although not empirically supported, Ford's [14] discussion of the possibilities offered by machine processing of similarities through high order knowledge representation and fuzzy (or parallel) IR is summarised here as a case in point.

3.2.1 High Order Knowledge Representation

Relatively high order knowledge representations may be facilitated by linguistic analysis whereby similarity relationships at a relatively high level of abstraction can be made. A system such as DR-LINK "… can retrieve related articles that would not be found in a Boolean search because they contain the ideas, not the precise words, that were requested" (Feldman as quoted in Ford [14]). This is still not enough, for current research, according to Ford [14], is focused (*within narrow subject domains*) on:

- The computation of argumentation (components and structures of arguments are represented in such a way that patterns of argument and counter-argument may be mapped onto each other and compared for similarities and differences).
- Analogy-based representations and processing to support case-based reasoning (similarities are represented and then matched between stored cases of solved problems so that solution structures of known problems may be applied to new ones).
- The direct modeling of analogical reasoning (attempts to model human analogical reasoning to computers as well as commercial analogical problem-solving systems).

Information abstraction (structured knowledge representation of complex events, situations or relationships are created and then populated with text extracted from unstructured natural language texts).

The common thread in these studies is the specification of relationships between structural components at a level of abstraction higher than mere morphological or syntactical analysis, "and of more complex semantic patterns than relative simple thesaural links" [14].

3.2.2 Fuzzy and Parallel IR

Often neural networks (employing fuzzy, parallel processing though pattern matching), focus on sub-semantic levels (e.g. image processing). Some systems, however, also use nodes to represent keywords and documents on a semantic level. Examples of these representations are taxonomies and ontologies [15] and topic maps [16]. Knowledge of the relationship between query and documents is then stored in the pattern of links between the nodes [14].

By using higher order knowledge representation and fuzzy and parallel IR, systems tend to become more intelligent. Although this type of research is relatively new, it is quite feasible that technologies such as those described above, may aid users in the judging of topically relevant information, by supplying wider information content than simply that which was requested through the query. Typical projects on these matters are for instance those related to sense disambiguation [6], Park's [17] work on inferential representation of documents within subject fields and Choi and Rasmussen's [18] work on image retrieval based on topicality.

3.3 Cognitive Relevance / Pertinence

Pertinence is measured in terms of the relation between the state of knowledge, or cognitive information need of the user, and the information objects as interpreted by that user. The criteria by which pertinence are inferred are cognitive correspondence, informativeness, novelty and information preferences. For instance, a paper may be topically relevant but repeating what the user already knows. Cognitive relevance is clearly a very subjective judgment, as opposed to algorithmic and topical relevance as discussed above. The question on how to induce and facilitate the novelty value of information to users, must therefore by addressed on an entirely different level.

Traditional IR systems allow users to modify queries according to their own understanding of the problem. This, in turn, depends on the user's conceptual knowledge background and his understanding or perception of his information need. Toms [19] uses an interesting set of analogies to describe this aspect of seeking: "Sometimes people seek a target with the precision of a cruise missile. Sometimes they seek a target with the imprecision of a Christmas shopper."

The fact that the success of a query to retrieve cognitively relevant information depends on the user's understanding of both the system and the user's own problem space, tends to limit the possibility of the user finding relevant information. In recent research, however, there has been attempts to induce and facilitate serendipitous information retrieval. To continue with Toms' [19] analogy: "Sometimes a target appears — unexpected and unsought, such as the five dollar bill fluttering in the fall leaves."

According to Toms [19] there are essentially three ways to acquire information:

- Searching for information about well-defined and known objects.
- Searching for information about an object that cannot be described, but which will be recognized on sight.
- Accidental, incidental or serendipitous discovery of an object.

She contends that current information retrieval systems are based on the assumption that users know (or partially know) the object of their search, and that serendipitous information retrieval is largely ignored in information system development and research [20].

According to Figueiredo and Campos [21], classic problem solving first requires a recognition of the problem, then some sort of divergence taking place and ultimately converging into a novel solution for the problem. Serendipity, on the other hand, is a creative process, whereby an attempt to solve a problem leads first to a divergence, and then to a new problem or a solution to a problem that was not known to exist. Serendipity is also defined by Quéau (quoted in Figueiredo & Campos [21]) as "the art of finding what we are not looking for by looking for what we are not finding".

It is generally acknowledged that qualitative research sometimes contains "good fortune", but according to Fine and Deegan [22], serendipity consists in how this fortune is transformed into substantive discovery. Serendipity is therefore not only a "chance encounter" [20], but more than that – it is the "unique and contingent mix of insight coupled with chance" [22]. Furthermore, Spink and Greisdorf [23] found that highly relevant documents do not often change the user's cognitive or information space, but partially relevant documents do.

Serendipity rests on the three principles of insight, chance and discovery [22]. The principles of chance and discovery could be built into systems, for example though improved browsing facilities (see Toms [19] for an example of such a system). However, the first principle, that of insight, rests solely with the user. To quote Louis Pasteur: "Chance favours only the prepared mind" (Oxford Dictionary of Quotations, 1979).

Although the research focus of serendipitous retrieval is not necessarily that of helping users that cannot formulate their own information need satisfactorily, it is plausible that it may be utilised as an aid to users who cannot express their query to a sufficient degree. Research, such as that of Toms [19,20], is very important in terms of the improvement of IR systems in order to assist users to judge relevance on a cognitive (personal) level.

Another important contribution within this focus of cognitive relevance judgements, is the research on profile building for information filtering. Coupled with browsing, personalization of information retrieval can help people to find information with potential value to their information needs. With regard to the Internet, Bowman et al. [24] note "at least 99% of the available data is of no interest to at least 99% of the users". Personalization of information delivery relies on systems that selectively weed out the irrelevant information based on the user's preferences [25]. Although this has been said in a different context, it is clear that *cognitive relevance* is implied.

3.4 Situational Relevance

Situational relevance describes the relationship between the perceived situation, work task or problem at hand and the usefulness of the information objects as perceived by the user. The criteria by which situational relevance is inferred are usefulness in decision-making, appropriateness of information in problem solving and the reduction of uncertainty.

According to Borlund [26] "… the judgement of situational relevance embraces not only the user's evaluation of whether a given information object is capable of satisfying the information need, it offers also the potential of creating new knowledge which may motivate change in the decision maker's cognitive structures. The change may further lead to a modification of the perception of the situation and the succeeding relevance judgement, and in an update of the information need".

Subjective relevance types, including situational relevance, are generally accepted to be both dynamic and multidimensional in nature. In the information seeking process, these relevance types are continually and interactively assessed. This assessment is not binary, but rather judged as degrees of relevance. In order for systems to support the searching behaviour of users in this context, it must allow for interactive information retrieval. See Borlund [26] for the evaluation of such systems, and Savage-Knepshield and Belkin [27] for a historical overview of trends in interactive IR (IIR).

Situational relevance in a previous study [1] was empirically found to be more strongly associated with work task execution than with search task execution. Therefore, interactive IR should also support searching over more than one session, and complex profiling should be able to dynamically include changing situational factors as well.

3.5 Socio-Cognitive Relevance

Socio-cognitive relevance is, together with cognitive, situational and affective relevance, regarded as a subjective relevance type. Socio-cognitive relevance describes the relationship between the situation, the work-task or problem at hand in a given socio-cultural context on the one hand, and the information objects on the other, as perceived by one or more cognitive agents. The social or organizational domain, or cultural context in which the individual finds himself is defined by a paradigm, which dictates what problem explanations may be found to be acceptable.

Retrieval of information limited to particular paradigms or socio-cultural or socio-cognitive domains may not be easily solved by improvement to systems. Facilitating serendipity or IIR may yield somewhat improved results, but in general the nature of socio-cognitive relevance is such that metadata would probably be the best solution to this particular problem.

The purpose of metadata is to describe the structure of the content data, and more importantly, to capture any additional properties that may characterise it. Metadata formats are divided into three categories: simple, rich and structured [28]:

- *Simple formats* are proprietary and based on full text indexing. Search engine crawlers create this type of data. They are easy to use, but are weak for information retrieval purposes, as they do not support field searching.
- *Rich formats* are associated with research and scholarly activity, and require specialist subject knowledge to create and maintain. These formats are usually based on international standards, e.g. MARC (Machine-Readable Cataloguing), FGDC (Federal Geographic Data Committee), ICPSR (Interuniversity Consortium for Political and Social Research – an SGML codebook initiative describing social societies), CIMI (Computer Interchange of Museum Information), EAD (Encoded Archival Description) and CERIF (Common European Research Information Format).
- *Structured formats* are a compromise between simple and rich formats, specially developed for Internet usage. These include data that contain a detailed enough description to allow a user to assess the potential utility or interest of a resource without having to retrieve it. The data are structured and support field searching, but are still domain specific. Some structured formats are the IAFA (Internet Anonymous FTP Archive) templates; RFC (Internet Request for Comments) 1807 (format for bibliographic records); SOIF (Summary Object Interchange Format); and LDAP (Lightweight Directory Access Protocol) Data Interchange Format (LDIF). However, the Dublin Core Metadata Element Set (http://dublincore.org) is one of the first truly universal formats. This metadata element set is intended to facilitate the finding of electronic resources, originally conceived for author-generated descriptions of web resources.

The *de facto* standard for metadata, especially on the Web, is Dublin Core (DC). Dublin Core is a general set of metadata elements and is often enriched by application domain-dependent additions, such as the NDLTD (Networked Digital Library of Theses and Dissertations) and the LOM (Learning Object Metadata). The elements and definitions of DC are based on the official standard for the element set of DC (ANSI/NISO Z39.85-2001). The elements can be seen as describing three different dimensions of metadata, i.e. describing the content or *data*, describing the *source*, and describing the *collection process* to collect the content. This subdivision is very important, since it describes the reality of the aboutness, isness and processing of the information objects [29].

It is especially the data elements that are related to the source that may be of importance for improving access to *socio-cognitively relevant* information objects. Metadata elements such as the following DC elements have great potential to help users to judge the relevance of retrieved information objects with regard to a particular situation, or within a particular socio-organizational domain during the search task:

- Type: Nature or genre of the content of the resource
- Format: Physical or digital manifestation of the resource
- Identifier: Unambiguous reference to the resource within a given context
- Source: Reference to a resource from which the present resource is derived
- Language: Language of the intellectual content of the resource
- Relation: Reference to a related resource, and
- Coverage: Extent or scope of the content of the resource.

Another technique that may be used to facilitate socio-cognitive relevance judgements is that of co-citation analysis. Patterns of co-citation can help a searcher to understand which publications and authors may be grouped together in terms of their approach to a subject. This may then give an indication of acceptability within a particular socio-organizational domain.

An interesting study by Yuan and Meadow [30] showed another possibility of improving access to socio-cognitively relevant documents. Authors in different fields use different words to describe concepts, for example *data* and *information* is used differently in the fields of computer science and information science. Yuan and Meadow [30] found that when two individual papers, or two authors over several works, use the same variables (or terms), it indicates a *similarity in approach* to the subject. According to them, if authors use the same variables, "such usage may be a stronger indication of similarity than co-citation because it represents what the authors did, rather than what they say" [30].

In traditional systems, both topicality and socio-cognitive relevance types were facilitated purely by human input. However, by using technologies such as described above, both these relevance types may be partially facilitated at a systems level.

3.6 Affective Relevance

Affective relevance is described in terms of the relation between the goals, intents and motivations of the user and the information objects. Affective relevance should not be seen as the ultimate subjective relevance in a scale of relevances, but rather as another dimension of relevance judgments that may be associated with the other subjective types of relevance.

At this point it would be prudent to add a note on the time dimension encountered in the judgments of relevance by users. The phenomenon that relevance judgements changes over time has little bearing on algorithmic relevance, but as the relevance judgements become more subjective, changes in cognition over time have an increasingly profound influence on the dynamic process of interpretation, and are especially individualized in affective relevance.

As such, it is probably not possible to improve systems (other than profiling) or information representation to expressly facilitate this manifestation of relevance.

4 Conclusions

This study has aimed to improve our understanding of relevance by providing a model for understanding the concept of relevance in terms of relations between information objects on the one hand and the various aspects of the information seeking and retrieval process on the other.

In the historic development of IR as a field of study, three main research paradigms can be clearly identified – the systems approach, the user approach and the cognitive approach [31]. Recently the emergence of a (tentative) fourth approach has become evident – the socio-cognitive or epistemological approach [32].

Relevance may be regarded as the central and most fundamental concept within the field of information science [33,34,35,36]. We are studying relevant information, not just any information. As such, relevance should not be studied from a limited perspective. Systems may be improved by making their algorithmic relevance scores better correlate with the subject, but users judge relevance from a much broader perspective – not only from a cognitive perspective, but also within an epistemological framework.

The model developed and tested in a previous study [1] and represented here defines the various relevance types and their interconnectivity. From the additional information provided on the various manifestations in this paper it should be clear that these relevance judgements, either individually or jointly, may be and indeed need to be facilitated in some way by improving systems to make intelligent, interactive IR possible.

Through a literature review and meta-analysis, this paper is an effort to show how research in different areas of IR research is already moving towards improving access to information through facilitating users' relevance judgements when searching for information.

Relevance should be the one issue connecting the various approaches within information science. No single research paradigm should claim relevance for its own. In order to understand relevance, it is necessary to view the concept from a holistic perspective, taking into account the systems, the users, the cognitive overlaps of the role players within IR as well as the influence of the epistemological framework in which IR takes place. It is critical that future research in the field of IR should take all these factors into account. The model presented here and subsequent discussion, shows that this model may be viewed as a coherent framework within which this research may take place.

Acknowledgements

We would like to thank the anonymous reviewers for their suggestions.

References

1. Cosijn, E. Relevance Judgements in Information Retrieval. Unpublished DPhil Thesis. University of Pretoria, South Africa (2003)
2. Cosijn, E. & Ingwersen, P. Dimensions of Relevance. Information Processing and Management 6(4) (2000) 533-550
3. Ingwersen, P. Cognitive perspectives of information retrieval interaction: elements of a cognitive IR theory. Journal of Documentation 52(1) (1996) 3-50
4. Cosijn, E. A methodology for testing dimensions of relevance. In: Bothma, T. & Kaniki, A. eds. Progress in Library and Information Science in Southern Africa. Proceedings of the third biennial DISSAnet Conference (ProLISSA3). Pretoria. Infuse. (2004) 279-299 Available http://www.dissanet.com
5. Tomaiuolo, N.G. & Packer, J. Keyword and natural language searching. Online, November/December (1998) 57-60
6. Sanderson, M. Retrieving with good sense. Information Retrieval 2 (2000) 47-67

7. Voorhees, E.M. Variations in relevance judgements and the measurement of retrieval effectiveness. In: Croft, B.C. et al. eds. Proceedings of the 21st Annual International ACM SIGIR Conference on Research and Development in Information Retrieval. Melbourne, Australia. ACM Press (1998) 315-323

8. Lee, J.H. Combining the evidence of different relevance feedback methods for information retrieval. Information Processing and Management 34(6) (1998) 681-691

9. Lam-Adesina, A.M. & Jones, G.J.F. Applying summarization techniques for term selection in relevance feedback. In: Croft, W.B. et al. eds. Proceedings of the 24th Annual International ACM SIGIR conference on Research and Development in Information Retrieval. New Orleans, Louisiana, USA. ACM Press (2001) 1-9

10. Voorhees, E.M. Variations in relevance judgements and the measurement of retrieval effectiveness. Information Processing and Management 36 (2000) 697-716

11. Voorhees, E.M. Evaluation by highly relevant documents. In: Croft, W.B et al. eds. Proceedings of the 24th Annual International ACM SIGIR conference on Research and Development in Information Retrieval. New Orleans, Louisiana, USA. ACM Press (2001) 74-82

12. Järvelin, K. & Kekäläinen, J. IR evaluation methods for retrieving highly relevant documents. In: Belkin, N.J . et al. eds. Proceedings of the 23rd Annual International ACM SIGIR Conference on Research and Development in Information Retrieval. Athens, Greece. New York: ACM Press (2000) 41-48

13. Kekäläinen, J. & Järvelin, K. Using graded relevance assessments in IR evaluation. Journal of the American Society for Information Science and Technology 53(13) (2002) 1120-1129

14. Ford, N. Information retrieval and creativity: towards support for the original thinker. Journal of Documentation 55(5) (1999) 528-542

15. Welty, C. & Guarino, N. Supporting ontological analysis of taxonomic relationships. Institute for systems science and biomedical engineering of the Italian Research Council (CNR). [Online]. Available http://www.labseb.pd.cnr.it/infor/ontology/papers/DKE-2001.pdf (13 March 2003)

16. Pepper, S. The TAO of topic maps: finding the way in the age of infoglut. [Online]. Available http://www.gca.org/papers/xmleurope2000/ papers/s11-01.html. (13 March 2003)

17. Park, H. Inferential representations of science documents. Information Processing and Management 32(4) (1996) 419-429

18. Choi, Y. & Rasmussen, E. User's relevance criteria in image retrieval in American history. Information Processing and Management 38 (2001) 695-726

19. Toms, E. Information exploration of the third kind: the concept of chance encounters. A position paper for the CHI98 Workshop on Information exploration. [Online]. Available: http://www.fxpal.com/ConferencesWorkshops/CHI98IE/submissions/long/toms/Default.htm (21 November 2002)

20. Toms, E. Serendipitous information retrieval. [Online]. Available: http://www.ercim.org/publication/ws-proceedings/DelNoe01/3-Toms.pdf (21 November 2002)

21. Figueiredo, A.D. The serendipity equations. In: Webber, R. and Gresse, C. eds. Proceedings of the Workshop Program at the 4th International Conference on Case-based Reasoning, ICCBR01, Technical Note AIC-01-003. Washington, DC: Naval Research Laboratory, Navy Centre for Applied Research in Artificial Intelligence. [Online]. Available http://www.aic.nrl.navy.mil/papers/2001/AIC-01-003 /ws4/ws4toc2.pdf (21November 2002)

22. Fine, G. & Deegan, J. Three principles of serendip: insight, chance and discovery in qualitative research. [Online]. Available: http://www.ul.ie/~philos/vol2/Deegan.html (21 November 2002)

23. Spink, A. & Greisdorf, H. User's partial relevance judgements during online searching. Online and CDROM Review 21(5) (1997) 271-280

24. Bowman, C.M., Danzig, P.B., Manber, U. & Schwartz, F. (1994). Scalable internet resources discovery: research problems and approaches. Communications of the ACM 37(8) (1994) 98-107

25. Quiroga, L.M. & Mostafa, J. (2001). An experiment in building profiles in information filtering: the role of context of user relevance feedback. Information Processing and Management 38(5) (2001) 671-694

26. Borlund, P. Evaluation of interactive information retrieval systems. Doctoral dissertation. Åbo: Åbo Akademi University Press. (2000)

27. Savage-Knepshield, P.A. & Belkin, N. (1999). Information retrieval interaction: trends over time. Journal of the American Society for Information Science 50(12) (1999) 1067-1082

28. Hakala, J. Internet metadata and library cataloguing. [Online]. Available http://www.lnb.lt/events/ifla/hakala.html (21November 2004)

29. Cosijn, E., Pirkola, A., Bothma, T. & Järvelin, K. Information access in indigenous languages. In: Bruce, H. et al. eds. Emerging frameworks and methods. Proceedings of the Fourth International Conference on Conceptions of Library and Information Science. Greenwood Village, Colorado: Libraries Unlimited (2002) 221-238

30. Yuang, W. & Meadow, C.T. A study of the use of variables in information retrieval user studies. Journal of the American Society for Information Science 50(2) (1999) 140-150

31. Ingwersen, P. (1999). Cognitive information retrieval. In: Williams, M.E. ed. Annual Review of Information Science and Technology (ARIST). Medford, NJ: Learned Information, INC. 34 (1999) 3-52

32. Hjørland, B. Brief communication: Towards a theory of aboutness, topicality, theme, domain, field, content … and relevance. Journal of the American Society for Information Science 52(9) (2001) 774-778

33. Froelich, T.J. Relevance reconsidered – towards an agenda for the 21st century: Introduction to special topic issue on relevance research. Journal of the American Society for Information Science 45 (1994) 124-133

34. Saracevic, T. Relevance reconsidered '96. In: Ingwersen, P. & Pors, N.O. eds. Information Science: Integration in Perspective. Copenhagen, Denmark: Royal School of Library and Information Science (1996) 201-218

35. Saracevic, T. Information science. Journal of the American Society for Information Science 50(12) (1999) 1051-1063

36. Schamber, L., Eisenberg, M.B. & Nilan, M.S. A re-examination of relevance: Toward a dynamic, situational definition. Information Processing and Management 26(6) (1990) 755-776

Searching for Relevance in the Relevance of Search

Elaine G. Toms[1], Heather L. O'Brien[1], Rick Kopak[2],
and Luanne Freund[3]

[1] Faculty of Management, Dalhousie, Halifax,
Nova Scotia B3H 4H8 Canada
{etoms, hlobrien}@dal.ca
[2] SLAIS, University of British Columbia, Vancouver,
British Columbia V6T 1Z3 'Canada
rkopak@interchange.ubc.ca
[3] Faculty of Information Studies, University of Toronto, Toronto,
Ontario M5S 1A1 Canada
freund@fis.utoronto.ca

Abstract. Discussion of relevance has permeated the information science literature for the past 50+ years, and yet we are no closer to resolution of the matter. In this research we developed a set of measures to operationalize the dimensions underpinning Saracevic's manifestations of relevance. We used an existing data set collected from 48 participants who used a web search engine to complete four search tasks that represent four subject domains. From this study which had assessed multiple aspects of the search process – from cognitive to behavioural – we derived a set of measures for cognitive, motivational, situational, topical and system relevances. Using regression analysis, we demonstrate how the measures partially predict search success, and additionally use factor analysis to identify the underlying constructs of relevance. The results show that Saracevic's five manifestations may be merged into three types that represent the user, system and the task.

1 Introduction

Much has been written about the assessment of search output. Many models and frameworks for evaluation have been introduced, many measures suggested, and many solutions proposed. Nevertheless results (for better or worse) seem to be tied to traditional precision and recall measures based on some notion of relevance. While precision and recall are concrete, fully operationalized concepts, the underlying concept of relevance is aloof, by its very definition controversial and difficult to measure.

In common usage, *relevance* describes a relationship in which one thing has a direct bearing on another. There are two sources of ambiguity when this concept is used in information retrieval (IR). First, on what basis can we say that two things are directly related, and second, which two things are we relating? The traditional approach to relevance in IR uses features of the text as indicators of a relationship between queries and documents. In contrast, the information behaviour community

F. Crestani and I. Ruthven (Eds.): CoLIS 2005, LNCS 3507, pp. 59–78, 2005.
© Springer-Verlag Berlin Heidelberg 2005

claims that relevance is in the eye of the user, and is a subjective measure of the applicability of information to a user's need, problem, situation and context.

One of the few frameworks to offer a more precise interpretation of the various meanings of relevance is Saracevic's [18] "manifestations of relevance." However, his conceptual constructs remain largely unmeasured and few metrics have been devised and/or validated. In this research, we propose measures to operationalize each of Saracevic's manifestations, test each with a real life set of data, and examine the underlying dimensions of these manifestations as well as relationships among the measures.

2 Previous Work

Measuring search output begs the question: what is the purpose of the measurement? In the 1950s, initial developers of IR systems established the goal to retrieve relevant output [18]. Relevance has remained the holy grail of success for IR system research and retrieving only relevant information has also been the holy grail of IR system development; yet achieving relevance and knowing when relevance is achieved continues to challenge both researchers and developers to this day.

2.1 Relevance

Relevance has been debated, researched and reviewed, the most significant of these works being Saracevic [17], Schamber [19], and Mizzaro [15], and more recently, a thoughtful examination by Borlund [2]. For the past fifteen years, many proposals have emerged from the debate, from situational relevance [20], to psychological relevance [9] and task-based relevance [5], [16]. Mizzaro [15] proposed a time-driven logical relevance topology, while Saracevic [18] developed five manifestations of relevance.

2.2 Saracevic's Manifestations of Relevance

Saracevic's set of types (manifestations) of relevance was the first holistic approach to delineate the multi-dimensional nature of relevance, and remains the most comprehensive view, although others [2], [5] have suggested revisions. Each type outlined in this conceptual framework expresses a relationship betweens two elements of the triad: query, document, and user.

System/Algorithmic relevance is indicative of the similarity of a query, in essence its features, to a document. This type of relevance asks the question: how close is the fit between the retrieved set of documents and the user's query as determined by the algorithm? This is normally interpreted as an objective relevance – a comparison, but the questions that emerge are what and whose relevance?

Topical relevance indicates the 'aboutness' of a document. How close is the semantic fit between the query and the topics of the documents retrieved? Borlund [2] distinguishes this from algorithmic relevance by referring to it as "intellectual topicality;" a document may be assessed for aboutness independent of the query.

Cognitive relevance or Pertinence relates to how a document suits the "state of knowledge and cognitive information need of a user." What is the user's judgment about the applicability of the retrieved documents to the matter at hand? Saracevic suggests this is related to novelty, informativeness, information quality, and cognitive correspondence. Borlund [2] points out that pertinence is indicative of the dynamic nature of information needs – an item may be pertinent to a person at a point in time, but not necessarily pertinent to another person with the same problem, or indeed pertinent to the same person at a later (or earlier) point in time.

Motivational/Affective relevance relates to how a document corresponds with a user's intentions, goals and motives in seeking the information. It is also related to the user's emotional state and his or her perceived satisfaction and success with the task. Notably, this represents the human drive for information, and is likely inherent in other relevance types [2].

Situational relevance or Utility refers to the fit between the situation, problem space or task of the user and the documents output by the system. Do retrieved items allow the user to complete the task at hand? This form of relevance is driven by the context of users as well as their motivation for the information, and potentially affect other relevance types [5].

Of these types of relevance, System/Algorithmic and Topical relevances are of a lower order, closer to the system, while Cognitive/Pertinence, Situational and Motivational/Affective relevances are of a higher order of relevance, closer to the user. Underpinning all forms of relevance is the notion of interactivity. It is the relationships between the query, the document and/or the user that will determine relevance, rather than an assessment of any one of these in isolation. Rolled up in the concept of relevance then is the expectation that an IR system is capable of effective query processing and is able to deliver documents that are on the topic of the query, are pertinent to the user, leave the user satisfied, and enable task completion.

2.3 Measures of Search Outcome

While consensus may be emerging in defining the multi-dimensional nature of relevance, there is little consensus in how to measure it [2]. Precision and Recall have been used to measure search outcome since the initial experiments of Cleverdon [4]. The limitations of such an approach have been well documented and will not be addressed here (see for example, [10]). Yuan and Meadow [31] analyzed the use of measures in IR research using an approach analogous to co-citation searching. They examined the works of a set of authors from five research groups and found inconsistencies in the selection of measures, and coverage of the problem, demonstrating the confusion of measurement in this field. More recently, an ongoing Delphi study [30] is attempting to reach a consensus on appropriate measures of online searching behaviour. To date, they have found that the search outcome measures ranked most highly by more than 50 researchers including: users' criteria for evaluating retrieved items, satisfaction with the search results, and utility/value of search results. Precision and recall measures have been ranked the lowest, not unlike the finding of Su [23].

One of the most significant and systematic attempts to measure the success of IR systems is that of Su [23] who compared 20 measures that included relevance, efficiency, utility, user satisfaction and overall success. She equated precision with relevance which was the generally accepted view of the day. In her study, participants were more concerned with recall than precision. This observation is not surprising given that the usual expected outcome during this period was to include *all* the documents on a topic. In addition measures such as satisfaction, user confidence, value of the search results, and user knowledge were more tightly correlated with the user's overall assessment of success. In this case success was user response to a scaled variable at the conclusion of the test. This study was conducted in an era when intermediaries conducted the search and the user paid for that service.

More recently, Greisdorf and Spink [8], [21] have attempted to map measures to Saracevic's relevance types, but these measures are subjective and potentially confounding. Users were asked whether or not retrieved items had met an information need based on five self-rated statements corresponding to the five types of relevance. No objective measures were used in the study.

A little know measure devised by Tague-Sutcliffe [25], Informativeness, determines the amount of information resulting from the interaction of a user and a document. Notable about this measure is that it captures the interactivity emphasized by Saracevic [18], the time element suggested by Mizzaro [15], and includes a system penalty when the system fails to deliver relevant documents (rather than the reward for success suggested by Vakkari and Sormunen [29]). Except for the work of Tague-Sutcliffe, this measure has languished (see one of the few applications in Tague-Sutcliffe and Toms [26]).

Many approaches to the measurement of relevance exist [3], [10] and the lack of a standard protocol for measurement impacts the conduct of research and development in this area. Having the ability to do systematic system comparisons has been missing in the interactive retrieval area as is evidenced by the TREC Interactive Track (see http://trec.nist.gov). Although the use of recall-precision measures has been strongly criticized, they have served the IR community for decades as a technique for making system comparisons. The long term objective of our work is to identify a parsimonious set of measures that may be used for research experimentation and by developers to assess system success. We place an emphasis on the notion of parsimony; although Schamber [19] devised a list of more than 80 criteria for assessing relevance, we believe that the essence of the problem is identifying the smallest set that will measure system success. Notably Barry and Schamber [1] in a comparative study found that two different contexts shared relevance criteria suggesting that the same criteria may be used in multiple contexts.

The objective of this study was to identify a set of measures for relevance using Saracevic's types of relevance as a framework for the work. The intent was to identify measures that could be interpreted as either subjective or objective, and could either explicitly or implicitly represent the essence of the relevance type. While some of the types such as Topical relevance are clearly understood with an operational definition that easily prescribes a probable measure, others such as Cognitive relevance have not been illuminated to the same degree. In addition, where warranted for each type of relevance, we wanted to explore the relationships among its measures to determine if a single measure could be used to represent that type. Finally, we were interested in the relationships among the types of relevance. For example, given our selected measures, do some relevance types predict others? Lastly, does each type represent an underlying construct?

Using previously collected data, we derived and tested relevance measures for each of Saracevic's types of relevance. While recognizing that searching is dynamic and interactive and some relevance judgements may change over the course of the search, we assessed search outcomes. System success in the context of IR systems can be determined by how successful users are in completing their tasks.

3   Methods

In 2001, we conducted an exploratory and experimental study of web searching behaviour in the context of the TREC 10 Interactive Track [28]. It was exploratory in that we collected a wide range of data (both qualitative and quantitative, and both objective and subjective) to assess user cognitive and affective behaviours, and to examine how the search was conducted on a process and procedural level. It was experimental because we had several variables with multiple levels including: search tasks from four topical domains and two sources of the search task: researcher-specified or user-personalized. The intent of that work was to examine ways of improving the search process; for the work reported here we focus on our assessment of search outcomes. In this section we elaborate on the design of that study and explain how the data used to explore relevance was collected and analyzed.

3.1   System Used

For the research, we designed a custom search interface to access the Google search engine. The standard Google interface was modified to contain a longer search box of 200 characters with the Google directory categories displayed below. The screen contained the instructions: "please enter your search or select from the directory categories below." Beyond the first page, the standard Google interface screens were retained. The purpose of including the directory was to provide an alternative option – a scan capability – for the user. Choosing Google as the search engine was based on its status as the most widely used search engine.

3.2   Task

Sixteen tasks (which had been devised by the TREC 10 Interactive Track participants) were used in the study. The questions came from four domains: Consumer Health, Research, Travel and Shopping. Of the 16 tasks (four per domain), half were fully specified by the Track (e.g., "Tell me three categories of people who should or should not get a flu shot and why.") and half could be personalized by participants who were instructed to specify an object or a topic based on their interests. Examples of these personalized tasks include "Name three features to consider in buying a(n) [name of product]" and "List two of the generally recommended treatments for [name of disease or condition]." The former are referenced as "researcher-specified" and the latter as "user-personalized" in subsequent discussions.

3.3 Participants

Participants were adult members of the general public who had used the web but who had not taken a professional online search course. Participants represent a sample of convenience; no formal sampling was done and participants self-selected, i.e., were volunteers. They were recruited through advertisement via printed posters posted on bulletin boards on campus, or in libraries and coffee shops in the downtown area, and via e-mail messages posted to listservs or e-notice boards at the research sites. Thirty-two were from Toronto and sixteen were from Vancouver.

The 29 women and 19 men ranged in age from 18 to 20 to over 65, with 71% per cent between 21 and 35 years old. Most had university level education, mainly at the bachelor (18) or masters (14) level, predominantly from the humanities or social sciences. About half were students; the remainder were from a diverse range of occupations. Almost all participants (94%) had been using the web for two or more years, and most were moderate web users. Overall, they were a relatively young, educated group who were experienced in terms of web use.

3.4 Procedure

The participants were recruited in August and September of 2001. Each participant was given four search tasks, one from each of the four subject domains. Of the four assigned tasks, two were research-specified and two could be personalized. We used a modified Latin square method to distribute the questions among the participants. Search tasks were given to participants one at a time. Because we were interested in the full range of searching and browsing behaviour of web searchers, participants were free to use either the search box or the directory categories for all tasks. In anticipation of questions regarding search syntax, we printed a "cheat sheet" of basic search instructions for Google and placed it at the computer. Very few read it.

In each two-hour session, participants, first completed a demographic and web/search experience questionnaire and were assigned four search tasks in sequence. For each search task, they completed four steps as follows:

1) They completed pre-search questionnaire containing a scaled set of questions about their familiarity and expertise with the search topic.
2) They searched for the topic using the web interface. Participants were left uninterrupted for this part of the session. During this time, screen capture video recorded the search activity and a transaction log stored user actions. Participants were requested to print pages they believed useful to the task; these print commands were recorded in the transaction log along with other actions such as the query, categories selected and pages examined.
3) They responded to a post-search questionnaire containing a scaled set of questions about their perception of the search including their satisfaction with the results, the amount of time they had been assigned and their overall assessment of the results.
4) They participated in a semi-structured talk-after interview while reviewing the on-screen video of the search. In this part of the session, the screen capture video was re-played and paused while participants narrated the search process they had undertaken. Participants identified decisions, problems and issues

with task completion. A series of probing questions were used to help the participant articulate the process.

When all search tasks were completed, participants participated in a short structured interview about the problems and challenges of searching the web.

Data were collected in the following ways:

a) on paper for questionnaire type data, namely the demographics and web/search experience, and the pre- and post-search questionnaires;

b) by audio tape recorder for talk-after interviews and the final interview; these were later transcribed;

c) using a transaction log to capture keystroke data; *WinWhatWhere* software captured the titles, URLs of all sites visited, and all keystrokes entered, and time stamped each action. *WinWhatWhere* is a 'spy' software that works at the operating system level (see http://www.winwhatwhere.com for more information).

d) using a screen capture application to capture all events on the screen, and thus to record the user process in a video form. *Lotus ScreenCam* was used for this aspect, and it is no longer being updated.

3.5 Data Analysis

Because of the myriad types of data, we first had to prepare the data for analysis. Some of this preparation was relatively straightforward such as transcribing the paper-based questionnaires into digital form, and some required more substantive actions such as the preparation required for the transaction log files.

First we cleaned the *WinWhatWhere* files, removing duplicate and esoteric data unrelated to our problem, to isolate selected actions including the queries and categories used, and to delimit the four task segments. Some of the data that we deemed important to our further analyses could not easily be identified in the cleaned files. For example, we wanted to determine how many different actions were used in the context of a search and how much time was spent in the results list. This type of process data could not be automatically identified in the logs, and thus we manually coded each participant session. To do this, we reviewed the activity on the ScreenCam video screen capture files to identify and/or verify the nature of recorded action in the *WinWhatWhere* files. We labeled each action from a pre-specified set of codes including: using a query, using a category, examining the results list, reviewing a URL selected from the results list, and viewing a URL selected from a link. In addition, for each website examined we noted its rank on results list, and the verbatim text of the query. This process resulted in a single file per user per task with time and date stamps, queries submitted, and coded actions. These logs were summarized by action within a participant's task to create measures such as Time-in-List (the amount of time spend scanning the results pages), Rank (the average rank of items identified as relevant by the participants), Not-on-List (the proportion of relevant pages examined that did not come from the results pages, and Modified Queries (number of queries used to complete the task).

In addition, we assessed the results – the pages indicated by participants as being useful – for each task using independent judges. Using both the paper printouts from the sessions and the URLs in the transaction log files, we first created a master list of all URLs declared relevant by participants, and saved a copy of that page (to capture the precise text that the user had viewed). Subsequently, each page was examined twice by two external judges. One assessed for aboutness, that is, does the page have anything to do with the search task. A second judge examined the *set* of all pages declared relevant to the task to assess task completeness. No comparison was made between participants to ascertain whether one set was better than another; each was assessed for its own merits. These measures are described in section 4.

Finally data from the pre- and post- search questionnaires and the demographics/ experience survey data were combined with summary data from transaction logs, and the results analysis. This resulted in a set of over 80 variables. Data were analyzed using primarily SPSS univariate General Linear Model to assess differences by the experimental factors. In addition, Regression Analysis and Correlation were used to assess the relationships among the variables within relevance type, and among the relevance types. Factor Analysis was used to explore the underlying constructs of the resulting measures. The 'talk after' interviews (which are outside the scope of this paper) were coded using *Qualrus* qualitative analysis software (see http:// www.qualrus.com for more information about this software).

4   Results

The first challenge in this research was to match appropriate measures from those we had collected, or create new measures from the collected data. This process was partially inductive and partially deductive: it required examining each variable to determine if it was an appropriate measure of a relevance type, and additionally, examining the each relevance type to determine which measures represent its underlying dimensions. We assumed that no single variable was likely to represent a single relevance type, although that proved incorrect given that we could identify only one measure each for Topical relevance and Situational relevance. In addition, none of these measures are binary; Schamber [19] recommended that binary judgments be avoided, and later Tang and Solomon [27] observed the need for more than two levels while Kekäläinen and Järvelin [13] found that graded relevance assessments more reliably identified the distinction among retrieval methods.

After the measures were selected, we assessed them against our data, examining relationships among the measures for each type of relevance. Next we assessed the relationships among the relevance types and finally analyzed the metrics as a set for underlying constructs. These variables were calculated per individual search session (192 in total).

4.1   Measures of Relevance

Table 1 summarizes the measures used to evaluate each type of relevance. For each measure, we provide a definition and identify the source of the data. Some are *objective*, derived from system observations of user search behaviour. Others are based on the *subjective* responses of participants to pre- and post-task questions, or based on the *external assessment* of expert judges. These measures are intended for post task assessment, rather than interval assessment of within-task behaviours/ decisions. Although we agree with Mizarro [15] that relevance may change over time, we assessed the outcome – the success of the user in completing a task.

System/Algorithmic Relevance

Our intention was to identify an objective measure of the fit between the query and the system output, but this proved difficult. Technically, System/Algorithmic relevance reflects the degree to which the system representation of a document and the user initiated query terms match. But how do we assess the system's ability to do its job without confusing this form of relevance with Topical and Situational relevances? Saracevic [18] notes that system relevance is inferred mainly through comparison, which is also supported by Cosijn and Ingwersen [3]. Thus, we can compare one algorithm to another in terms of the efficiency or effectiveness of this matching process, but this is problematic for the evaluation of a single system. Furthermore, observing that one system achieves a different algorithmic relevance than another, that is, produces a different match, says nothing about the merits of the difference. It cannot be objectively decided as there is no absolute benchmark by which to compare the outcome.

In TREC-style assessments based on an identified document collection, a set of tasks, and a set of relevance judgments, the "gold standard" is a set of documents based, a priori, on an external judge's assessment of what is relevant for a given query. In essence, due to the nature of the problem space, a very human problem space, the assessment is always determined by a user, or a surrogate of the user, i.e., an external assessor. Algorithmic relevance as defined by Saracevic [18] may be useful in conceptual discussions, but does not lend itself easily to operationalization. Borlund [2] too had difficulty providing an operational definition of this type, concluding that one could have vector space relevance or probabilistic relevance.

In this study we assume that Algorithmic relevance can be externally assessed. That is, at some point, a human being will decide how well the system does its job; an assumption cannot be made that the system has an appropriate Algorithmic relevance because the algorithm can make a match, irregardless of the quality of the match. Thus, we will do this indirectly using human selection or human workload. In essence, a system that makes a good match will highly rank the documents that are relevant to the query, and will reduce the user's effort. Implicitly, if the system cannot do both, then it cannot be argued that the system has made a good match, and thus has attained a high System/Algorithmic relevance. Much of past work focuses on System/Algorithmic relevance as being related specifically and only to the algorithm; this is an outdated perspective. Despite Saracevic's original definition, and subsequent discussions by many others, the *system* is much more than its algorithm; how results are displayed, how the system is enquired and so on are equally important.

Table 1. Measures for Saracevic's Manifestations of Relevance

Relevance Types [18]	Measure	Operational Definitions	Source of Data
System or Algorithmic Relevance	Rank	Average rank on the Google hitlist of all pages declared relevant by the user	System
	Not-on-List	Portion of relevant pages not on hitlist, but found through some other means	System
	Time-in-List	Time spent examining hitlists (in seconds)	System
Topical or Subject Relevance	Aboutness	Average of all pages examined per task on a scale of 1 to 5, as determined by independent coders	External Judgement
Cognitive Relevance or Pertinence	Certainty	Measured on a scale of 1 to 5; asked users, per task, how certain they were they had found an adequate answer	User
	Modified Queries	Number of queries used in the task	System
Motivational or Affective Relevance	Satisfaction	Measured on a scale of 1 to 5; asked users, per task, how satisfied they were with the search	User
	Ease of Use	Measured on a scale of 1 to 5; asked users, per task, how easy it was to do the search task	User
	Perceived Time	Measured on a scale of 1 to 5; asked users, per task, whether they had sufficient time to do the task	User
	Familiarity	Measured on a scale of 1 to 5; asked users, per task, how familiar they were with the topic of the search	User
Situational Relevance or Utility	Completeness	Measure of how complete the task was based on entire set of relevant webpages selected by participants	External Judgement

For System/Algorithmic relevance, we identified three measures:

1) *Rank*: Highly ranked documents are the ones determined by the system as the best match between the query and the document collection. If a user declares that items highly ranked are the relevant items, then one may conclude that the system is doing its job, and conversely, if the user selects items much lower on the list, then the system is not doing its job. Thus, Rank, the average rank of all items declared relevant, is indicative of this type of relevance.

2) *Not-in-list*: If the relevant hits are not on the results list but are found on secondary pages, then similarly the system has not done its job. Relevant hits should be listed on the results page. Not-on-list is thus the proportion of relevant pages acquired through some other means.

3) *Time-in-list*: This measure is indicative of the amount of effort that it takes a user to scan the results list to select a relevant item. If the user must take a considerable amount of time to select an item, then the system is also not doing its job. This may be due to poor ranking of the relevant documents and/or poor representation of the documents (relevant or not) on the results page. In our view, System/Algorithmic relevance is not just about the ranking algorithm, a traditional view of IR evaluation; it is equally about how that system is represented to the user.

These three measures are implicit measures of relevance. That is, none directly measure System/Algorithmic Relevance, but serve as proxies of this type of relevance. On average, participants found relevant items half-way down the results page (n=192, x=4.4, SD=2.8296) and found a small proportion of the relevant items elsewhere (n=188, x=0.3, SD=0.385) elsewhere on the Web, through hyperlinks from the site that appeared on the results list. In addition, they spent a couple of minutes reviewing the results pages (n=192, x=128.31, SD=193.3) per task.

Topical Relevance

Topical relevance also called subject relevance reflects *aboutness*, a generally agreed upon interpretation [18], [15], [5]. While one could assess aboutness independently of the query [2], in the development of this measure, we considered how well the topics in the document matched the topic represented by the query. In this case, external assessors examined the 395 pages declared relevant by our participants to assign a value as illustrated in table 2. No additional measures emerged from our data collection to either implicitly or explicitly represent this relevance type. Overall, the documents printed by participants were rated highly for *aboutness* (n=181, x=4.54, SD=0.866).

Table 2. Aboutness Measure

Code	Definition
5	pages directly related to the topic and containing clear info on the topic,
4	pages that provide some information that is related, or leads directly to the answer
3	pages that about the topic but may be broader or narrower that the topic
2	tangentially related but not really in the topic area
1	pages that are clearly not about the topic at all

Cognitive Relevance or Pertinence

Cognitive relevance is the most poorly defined of the five relevance types. Cosijn and Ingwersen [5] suggest a wide range of measures for this, noting that it is highly subjective and personal. In our work, we consider this form of relevance as the *opposite* of cognitive dissonance, the psychological conflict within the individual caused by inconsistencies between belief and behaviour.   Therefore, cognitive correspondence is achieved when there are congruities between the searchers' initial queries and the search results.

In this case, we interpreted cognitive relevance as the *certainty* with which participants felt that they had done a good job – a perception of a good match, and a perception of personal success. From a user perspective, a strong measure of certainty may be equated with a perception of overall success. Secondly, we noted the number of times users felt it necessary to modify a query (*modified queries*) as a signal of a probable mismatch.

Participants reported being fairly certain that they had found adequate information to satisfy their queries (n=191, x=3.9, SD=1.069) and modified a small number of queries (n=168, x=0.9, SD=1.428). Pearson's Correlation Coefficient was used to examine the relationships between these two variables. Certainty was negatively correlated with the number of modified queries (R^2=-0.167, p<0.05). The more queries created resulted in a lower degree of certainty.

Motivational or Affective Relevance

As defined by Saracevic [18], motivational relevance deals with intentions and goals and as such is an *a priori* construct that potentially changes over the course of doing a search. This too is subjective and personal [5]. *Familiarity*, the degree to which the topic matter is known to the user (or prior knowledge) can be a powerfully influential force in affecting both motivations and intentions. Affective behaviours, on the other hand, may change over the course of a search, but their state at the end of a search may be related to the cognitive state of the user at the end of the search activity. At the end of each search task, participants indicated the *ease* with which the task was accomplished, the suitability of the amount of time – the *timeframe* – assigned to do the task, and their *satisfaction* with the task. This relevance type contains measures of both pre-search and post-search behaviours.

Participants similarly rated their levels of satisfaction (n=191, x=3.63, SD =1.121), ease of use (n=191, x=3.7, SD =1.139), and perceived time frame (n=191, x=3.47, SD =1.06) for the search tasks. It is, therefore, not surprising that all three variables are significantly correlated: satisfaction and ease of use (R^2=0.76, p<0.001), ease of use and timeframe (R^2=0.527, p<0.001), and satisfaction and timeframe (R^2=0.523, p<0.001).

Situational Relevance or Utility

Situational relevance is a context specific dimension that examines the fit between the documents retrieved and the task. In this study, this perceived fit was artificial in that the tasks were not personal to the participant, and participants did not have to process the information post the search. To assess this aspect, we created a measure called *completeness* which was an expert assessment of the proportion of the task that could be completed with the set of documents declared relevant by the participant. Spink, Greisdorf and Bateman [22] found that partially relevant documents added new knowledge to users' understanding of their problem. Thus all pages identified by a participant as useful to the search task were included in the set, irregardless of the document's aboutness rating, as partially relevant document may contribute some aspect to task completion. The same set of webpages examined for aboutness was reevaluated. In this case, for each participant task, the *set* of documents identified as relevant was assessed. When taken together as a set, how much of the task could be completed? The scale is illustrated in Table 3.

Table 3. Completeness Measure

Code	Definition
5	100% of the problem has been answered.
4	about 75% of the problem has been answered/responded to
3	about 50% of the problem has been answered/responded to
2	about 25% of the problem has been answered/responded to
1	0% of the problem has been answered/responded to

The selected web pages retrieved by users received high ratings ($n=176$, $x=4.39$, SD $=1.2$) according to completeness. In other words, on average, participants selected pages that could be used to satisfy at least 75% of the assigned task.

4.2 Predicting Success in IR Systems

In this section, we examine relationships among the identified measures using multiple regression. While the measures can be defined in terms of the types of relevance and represent underlying dimensions of each type, we wondered how much these measures contributed to search success. Success is an elusive construct in IR evaluation. Among our set of measures, we hypothesized that users in our study would declare success according to certainty – the degree to which they feel they had achieved an appropriate response, a measure of Cognitive relevance. Because of the significant correlations among the various measures used for each relevance type, one measure was selected to represent the types with multiple measures. Thus, rank and satisfaction were selected for System/Algorithmic relevance and Motivational /Affective relevance respectively. Two of the relevances, Topical and Situational had only a single measure: aboutness and completeness, respectively. These four measures were found to significantly predict certainty ($F(4, 146)=25.077$, $p<0.001$), and to explain 39% of the variability in certainty, or as we consider it – success.

Among these five variables, two are responses from the search engine to users' queries: rank and aboutness, and three are based on human judgments: certainty, completeness, and satisfaction. We were interested in the interplay between these two general types of variables. In essence, do user oriented measures predict the system measures, or vice versa? We regressed average page rank and average aboutness score with certainty ($F(2,151)=4.626$, $p<0.05$), completeness ($F(2,149)=67.137$, $p<0.001$), and satisfaction ($F(2,151)=4.081$, $p<0.05$) to triangulate the system and user constructs used to measure relevance. Although significant, they account for only 4.5 to 5% of the variability in certainty. With such a low percentage, we wondered if the relationships among these variables represented a different set of constructs other than the initial five types of relevance.

4.3 Identifying Components of Relevance

Because of the mixed results in looking at the five types of relevance as potential predictors of success, we used factor analysis to ascertain which of the measures might form coherent groupings that are relatively independent of one another (see [24] for an excellent explanation of factor analysis). Were there any potential underlying factors of relevance that were not evident in our previous analyses?

All measures listed in Table 1 were loaded initially, but *familiarity* and *time-in-list* were removed because they were poorly correlated with the other measures. The Kaiser Meyer Olkin measure (.737) and the Bartlett's Test of Sphericity ($\chi2=429.627$, df=28, p< .0001) indicated that the sample was adequate and that the measures were likely to be related. These two tests are conducted to determine if factor analysis is an appropriate technique for this data set.

Factor analysis was conducted using principal components analysis as the method of extraction and varimax as the method of rotation. Principal components analysis looks at linear combinations of variables. The first combination tends to account for the largest amount of variation, the second and subsequent contain successively smaller portions of the total variance, and additionally are independent of one another. Varimax (an orthogonal rotation that results in factors that are uncorrelated) is used to ensure that the resulting factors are interpretable. In essence, do the variables that load together strongly have an identifiable construct? Potentially there can be as many components or factors as there are variables. But that was not the case in this analysis which resulted in three components or factors (see Table 4). In addition, these three factors have internal coherence – they have clearly identifiable meanings. *Ease*, *satisfaction*, *certainty* and *timeframe* are user perception dimensions, indicative of cognitive or user type of relevance. The second factor, *aboutness* and *completeness*, are dimensions of the task relevance, while the third factor contains *not-on-list* and *rank*, dimensions of the system relevance.

Table 4. Factor Loadings

	Factors		
Measure	**User Perception**	**Task**	**System**
Ease	.842		
Satisfaction	.829		
Certainty	.809		
TimeFrame	.731		
Aboutness		.753	
Completeness		.746	
Not-on-List			-.787
Rank			.706

In this analysis, the communality values were high – all greater than .70; all variables loading on the three factors together account for 72% of the variance. All three factors had eigenvalues greater than 1; the factor loadings illustrated in Table 4 indicate the correlations of the variables with the factors. All measures for all factors correlated at greater than .70. These relationships are represented in Figure 1 which has been modified for a two-dimensional presentation.

As illustrated in Figure 1, the first factor (on the extreme right in Figure 1) includes measures of user perceptions and as a set represents variables from both Cognitive and Motivational relevance as defined by Saracevic [18]. The second factor (at the top) includes measures from Topicality and Situational relevance that results in an intersection between the *aboutness* of the document and the task for which it will be used. The third factor (on the lower left) concerns the System/Algorithmic relevance. To summarize, there are three underlying factors represented by the set of measures that were previously identified to fit the five types of relevance. These factors may be interpreted as representing the user (cognition and motivation), the task, and the system.

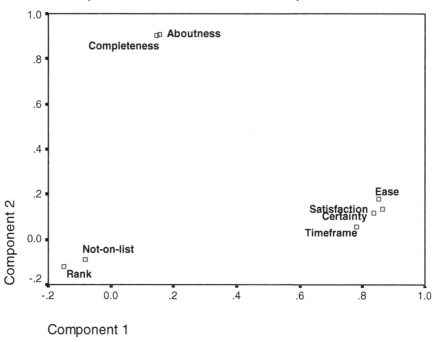

Fig. 1. Relationship between Measure and Factors in a 2-D space

5 Discussion

5.1 Measures for Relevance Types

This research examined the relevance problem, operationalizing the relevance types previously defined by Saracevic [18], and identifying one or more measures for each of the types. Notably, the measures were derived from a holistic study that included 16 web search tasks performed by 48 users; but, the choice of measures was informed primarily by Sarecevic's conceptual framework. Where more than one measure existed for a single type, all of these measures were strongly correlated within that type. While the findings for this particular data set have the usual limitations (e.g., no replication), the relationships among the variables and the underlying factors that emerged from the analysis are noteworthy.

Challenging in the selection of measures was System/Algorithmic relevance. While this type is clearly defined and that definition is widely accepted – the similarity of a query to a document, the definition has to date only been operationalized in TREC style comparative studies that are unable to determine definitively that a system delivers relevant documents; it can only state that system A delivers more relevant documents than system B. Furthermore in web-based studies the notion of precision and recall are incalculable except in an arbitrary way. With the 16 search tasks used in this study, participants often received a 'set' containing thousands if not millions of documents. Balance this point with the fact that people examine on average 1.8 pages of references (as found in the recent PEW studies (http://www.pewinternet.org)); the system designer's notion of a document set is at odds with user perception. Is precision, therefore, to be measured for the set defined by the algorithm or that perceived by the user? TREC studies may calculate precision-recall values for hundreds to thousands of documents, which is useful for comparing systems on a theoretical level, but has no basis in real world activity. An IR system services human activity and, its human users becomes the assessor of its quality and its success. Thus, for this relevance type, we used measures that implicitly evaluate System/Algorithm relevance. As a final footnote to this type, we believe that the definition of System/Algorithm relevance needs expansion. While the system may provide a good match between a query and a document, a user still may not be able to identify the relevant document because of many other characteristics of the system such as how the document set is presented to the user, how the system is queried and so on.

Because Topical relevance has been in use for so long, the choice of a measure, *Aboutness*, was almost self-evident. We wondered what additional sorts of measures might service this type, but like others (e.g., [5], we did not find additional measures.

Cognitive relevance or Pertinence is a multi-dimensional type of relevance, and has been defined as a series of qualities from informativeness to novelty. The one consistent quality that seems to be in general agreement is cognitive correspondence, which we interpret as the opposite of cognitive dissonance. Motivational/Affective relevance, on the other hand, is much more clearly understood although with some dispute as to whether it is a mutually exclusive relevance type (see the argument put forth by Borlund [2]) with regard to the other types. Both of these types of relevance stem from the user, and as seen from our results share the same underlying construct and thus are related.

In the context of our study, a laboratory experiment, Situational relevance was more difficult to assess. The tasks were assigned tasks, although half could be personalized by participants. This form of relevance is generally interpreted as a post system-interaction assessment. Are the results useful in decision-making? Does it reduce uncertainty? Are the results useful? In this case we looked at task completion from an external assessor perspective which was a good surrogate measure for this relevance type. Additional measures are conceivable in non-laboratory studies that see the work task to completion.

5.2 Examining Relationship Among the Measures and Relevance Types

Using the 'standard bearer' measure – rank, aboutness, satisfaction, completeness and certainty – defined for each relevance type, we explored the relationships among the five types. Some of the measures are systems-oriented and some user-oriented; we compared the systems-oriented ones with the user-oriented measures. Interestingly, the System/Algorithmic and Topical relevance measures – aboutness and rank – predict measures for the user specified relevances: Motivational, Situational and Cognitive. This was unexpected, as it is at odds with the current belief concerning system relevance – that relevance is human-driven (see [2], [5], [18], [19]). However, the contribution to variability in those user-specified measures (certainty, satisfaction and completeness) was small, leading us to conclude that success at the systems level is not sufficient to predict success at the user level.

In addition, we proposed that certainty from the user's perspective is the ultimate goal not unlike the success variable used by Su [23]. We may hypothetically have perfect relevance matches in all types, but if the user is uncertain about the results, then appropriate matches either have not been made or have not clearly communicated. Our results demonstrated that the System, Motivational, Topical and Situational relevances predict the Cognitive. Thus a person's level of success with a search – the certainty with which participants believed that had a good response is determined by the satisfaction with which they performed the search, the aboutness of the documents retrieved, the average rank of useful items, and the completeness of the task. Troubling about this finding is that only 39% of the variability in certainty could be explained by these four variables. Notably this is significantly higher than the relationship between systems-oriented and user-oriented measures discussed above. This finding though not ideal brings us a step closer to defining a parsimonious set of measures for relevance, and in particular for measuring system success.

5.3 Re-examining Relevance Types

Initially we examined associations among measures that reflect relationships between any two of query, document and user. These were founded on the five pre-defined relationships described by Saracevic's [18] relevance types. However, once we explored the associations amongst the measures unencumbered by the relevance types, a different pattern became apparent. Rather than five underlying constructs, three emerged from our data: system, task and user. On further inspection, we concluded that Saracevic's original relevance types are heavily oriented toward the user, while Mizzaro's [15] typology is more heavily weighted toward the system; the outcome from our work provides a more balanced blend of the two.

System: it is not surprising that the measures we used – *Rank* and *Not-on-list* – emerged as a single construct, considering our earlier discussion of System/Algorithmic relevance. The definition for this type does not change substantially. It remains a match between query and document according to the system's ability to highly rank useful items.

Task: this was not the case for Topical and Situational relevances; that *Aboutness* and *Completeness* would form a single construct was unexpected. While both were assessed by external judges, the judges for each measure differed. The first measure is used at the level of an individual document while the second is based on a document set. One is a match between query and document while the second is a match between document and the work task. The merging of these two measures suggests a (work) task relevance type. Although task is often separated from situation in discussions of relevance, a situation dictates a task, and a situation may require multiple tasks, each of which in turn may require multiple search tasks. In the case of our study for example, few of the tasks could be handled with a single query. Conceivably, task is unlikely to be mutually exclusive from situation, and thus will inherit many of its characteristics from the situation. Our finding is not unlike the fourth dimension of Mizzaro [15]'s model which contains topic, task and context components, and supports earlier work [16]. Situation, it could be argued, will impact not only the task, but other types of relevance as well [5]. Thus, this type of relevance becomes a match between the documents and the task including both a topical match, and task completion.

User: Cognitive and Motivational relevances form a single construct representing multiple characteristics of the user. Borlund [2] suggests that Motivational relevance is not independent of other types, and in particular of other subjective types; Cosijn and Ingwersen [5] isolate affect as a time-based dimension. Both groups had concerns with these two separate but clearly interrelated types of relevance. Mizzaro [15] has no user-specific component in his model. However, creating a type that combines both Cognitive and Motivational/Affective relevances is not atypical; it corresponds to the 'ABCs' of cognitive psychology: Affect, Behaviour and Cognition. Thus, this type of relevance is a holistic one that includes multiple user dimensions.

Of particular note in this work is the contribution to our understanding of the underlying constructs within the sea of potential measures of relevance. That our probing of relevance would reveal that user, task and system relevances emerge from all of the measures we employed is on one hand unexpected, and on the other, predictable. Our findings are clearly in line with Ingwersen's [11] cognitive model of interactive IR (although interestingly this model diverges from his relevance model [5]); He proposed that interactive IR contained three elements: systems, users and the environment. Similarly Borlund [2] identifies a process that includes a user level, a system level and a surface level. These two frameworks are closely aligned with the one that emerged from our data. Relevance can be defined in terms of three components each with its own dimensions and measures: user, system and task. Although there is much yet to explore concerning these three constructs, together they form a much simpler model than that of Saracevic and Mizzaro.

6 Conclusion

The findings from our study are not unlike that of Delone and McLean [6], [7] who examined many studies of systems evaluation in business to develop a model that predicts systems success. In their model, system, information and data quality affect system use and user satisfaction which, in turn, affect the net benefits of the system.

We have not yet explored our data to examine the multiple effects as presented by Delone and McLean.

Another form of evaluation which is rarely mentioned in the context of IR systems is that of usability, a concept well-known in human-computer interaction and often used in the assessment of interfaces. Usability, as defined by the International Standards Organization, is the "the effectiveness, efficiency and satisfaction with which a specified set of users can achieve a specified set of tasks in particular environments" [12]. Like relevance, it too suffers from an abundance of potential measures with which to assess its underlying dimensions. Usability contains the concepts of efficiency and effectiveness discussed by Borlund [2]. While efficiency and effectiveness are directly related to use as described by Delone and McLean [6] [7], and task as referenced by the relevance community (see for example, [5], [16]), satisfaction represents affective and cognitive behaviours, that tend to be examined by the information behaviour community [1], [19]. Both the Delone and McLean success model and usability would be fruitful directions to explore in our quest for measuring IR system success.

Our research has demonstrated that a combination of system, user and task measures indicate the outcome of the search. These findings fit with the "interactive framework" [18], [2], [5] within which all relevance types operate, and additionally form a more parsimonious set of relevance types. Our work also points to the importance of including subjective measures in investigations of relevance balanced with quantifiable, tangible metrics. While we achieved some success in identifying useful measures of various relevance types, future work will entail testing and validating these measures as well as the relevance types.

Acknowledgements

Work funded by grants to the first author from the Social Sciences and Humanities Council (Canada), the Natural Sciences and Engineering Research Council (Canada), and the Canada Research Chairs Program. Thanks to research assistants Joan Bartlett, Ariel Lebowitz and Louanna Mootoo who worked on the data collection and analysis, and to the three anonymous reviewers whose very helpful suggestions and comments have greatly improved the final manuscript.

References

1. Barry, C.L., Schamber, L.: Users' criteria for relevance evaluation: A cross-situational comparison. INFORM PROCESS MANAG. 34 (1998) 219-236
2. Borlund, P.: The concept of relevance in IR. J AM SOC INFORM SCI. 54(10) (2003) 913-925
3. Borlund, P., Ingwersen, P.: The development of a method for the evaluation of interactive information retrieval systems. J DOC. 53(3) (1997) 225-250
4. Cleverdon, C.W.: Information and its retrieval. ASLIB Proc. 22 (1960) 538-549
5. Cosijn, E., Ingwersen, P: Dimensions of relevance. INFORM PROCESS MANAG. 36 (2000) 533-550
6. DeLone, W.H., McLean, E.R.: Information systems success: the quest for the dependent variable. INFORM SYST RES. 3(1) (1992) 60-95

7. Delone, W.H, McLean, E.R.: Information systems success revisited. 35th HICSS Proc. (2002)
8. Greisdorf, H.: Relevance thresholds: a multi-stage predictive model of how users evaluate information. INFORM PROCESS MANAG. 39(3) (2003) 403-423
9. Harter, S.: Psychological relevance and information science. J AM SOC INFORM SCI. 43 (1992) 602-615
10. Harter, S. P., Hert, C.A.: Evaluation of information retrieval systems: Approaches, issues, and methods. ANNU REV INFORM SCI. 32 (1997) 3-94
11. Ingwersen, P.: Cognitive perspectives of information retrieval interaction: elements of a cognitive IR theory. J DOC 52(1) (1996) 3-50
12. ISO.: Ergonomic requirements for office work with visual display terminals (VDTs): Part 11.Guidance on usability. ISO 9241-11-1998 (1998)
13. Kekäläinen, J. Järvelin, K:. Using graded relevance assessments in IR evaluation. J AM SOC INFORM SCI. 53(13) (2002) 1120-1129
14. Maglaughlin, K.L., Sonnenwald, D.H.: User perspectives on relevance criteria: A comparison among relevant, partially relevant, and not-relevant judgments. J AM SOC INFORM SCI. 53(5) (2002) 327-342
15. Mizzaro, S.: How many relevances in information retrieval? INTERACT COMPUT. 10 (3) (1998) 303-320
16. Reid, J. A new task-oriented paradigm for information retrieval: implications for evaluation of information retrieval systems. CoLIS3 Proc. (1999) 97-108
17. Saracevic, T.: Relevance: a review of and a framework for the thinking on the notionsin information science. J AM SOC INFORM SCI. 26 (1975) 321-343
18. Saracevic, T.: Relevance reconsidered. CoLIS Proc. 2 (1996) 201-218
19. Schamber, L.: Relevance and information behavior. ARIST (1994) 3-48
20. Schamber, L. Eisenberg, M.B. Nilan, M.S.: A re-examination of relevance: toward a dynamic, situational definition. INFORM PROCESS MANAG. 26 (1990) 755-775
21. Spink, A., Greisdorf, H.: Regions and levels: Measuring and mapping users' relevance judgments. J AM SOC INFORM SCI. 52(2) (2001) 161-173
22. Spink, A., Greisdorf, H. Bateman, J.: From highly relevant to not relevant: examining different regions of relevance INFORM PROCESS MANAG. 34 (1998) 599-621
23. Su, L.T.: Evaluation measures for interactive information retrieval. INFORM PROCESS MANAG. 28(4) (1992) 503-516
24. Tabachnick, B.G. Fidell, L.S:. Using multivariate statistics, 4th ed. Allyn & Bacon (2001)
25. Tague-Sutcliffe, J.: Measuring Information. Academic Press, New York (1995)
26. Tague-Sutcliffe, J., Toms, E.G.: Information systems design via the quantitative analysis of user transaction logs. Presented at the 5th ICSI, River Forest, Illinois (1995).
27. Tang, R. Solomon, P.: Towards an understanding of the dynamics of relevance judgments: an analysis of one person's search behavior. INFORM PROCESS MANAG 34 (1998) 237-256.
28. Toms, E.G., Freund, L., Kopak, R., Bartlett, J.C.: The effect of task domain on search. CASCON, IBM, Toronto (2003) 303-312
29. Vakkari, P., Sormunen, E.: The influence of relevance levels on the effectiveness of interactive information retrieval. J AM SOC INFORM SCI. 55 (11) (2004) 963-969
30. Wildemuth, B.M., Barry, C., Luo, L., Oh, S.: Establishing a research agenda for studies of online search behaviors: a Delphi sStudy (2004). (see http://ils.unc.edu/sig_use_delphi/ for details of the study, and preliminary reports).
31. Yuan, W., Meadow, C.T.: A study of the use of variables in information retrieval user studies. J AM SOC INFORM SCI. 50 (1999) 140-150

Information Searching Behavior: Between Two Principles

Nick Buzikashvili

Institute of System Analysis, Russian Academy of Science,
9 prospect 60 Let Oktyabrya, 117312 Moscow, Russia
buzik@cs.isa.ru

Abstract. The paper considers different types of model and real-life information searching behavior. Only two behavioral principles correspond to all the
diversity of information searching: the principle of least effort describing a
model unmediated search and the principle of guarantied results describing a
model mediated search. It is shown that real-life searching follows the same
principles and that the principle of least effort describes not only unmediated
search but also team and pseudo-mediated searches. To explain information
searching behavior the 'coverage space' is considered. This model explains
both choice of the principle and non-monotonicity of this choice. As an application of these results, the universally accepted myth about differences between
searching on the Web and searching in 'traditional' IR systems is reevaluated.

1 Introduction

There are some widely spread but not very compatible opinions about searching behavior. According to the commonly accepted viewpoint, all searchers follow the principle of least effort [3], [5], [22]. However this principle is too general and may be
specified in different ways. Do different specifications lead to different behavior in
one and the same situation? Do searchers indeed follow this principle in any situation? Why searchers hypothetically driven by this universal principle behave too differently on the Web and in traditional IR as another common viewpoint states [14]?
This paper tries to answer these questions.

Section 2 is devoted to the description of information searching behavior (ISB), its
characteristics and observations of ISB. In Section 3 we introduce a service-center
metaphor of search. A notion of logical structure of searching process and a distinction between logical and physical search structures is also introduced. A logical structure includes logical sessions, which may be either distributed between different and
simultaneously conducted physical sessions or be included into the same physical
session. According to a service-center metaphor, IR service is one of the services
supplied by a terminal used for IR and real-life usage of this service is sufficiently
driven by availability of other services (text processing, gaming, news reading, etc.).

In Section 4 we consider two principles of searching, which cover all the diversity
of searching manners. While according to the common point, searchers should follow
the principle of least effort (PLE), all earlier studies of interactions with traditional

F. Crestani and I. Ruthven (Eds.): CoLIS 2005, LNCS 3507, pp. 79–95, 2005.
© Springer-Verlag Berlin Heidelberg 2005

search services showed two quite different manners — PLE-driven unmediated search and classic mediated search driven by the 'principle of the guarantied result' (PGR). Furthermore, considering traditional laboratory studies of searching behavior we observe pseudo-unmediated search conducted for externally assigned tasks and follow PGR rather than PLE. Dealing with the Web we see no traditional mediated search but we discover mass modifications in the form of a cooperative search ([7], [11]) when a pseudo-intermediary (a colleague, friend, etc.) assists a 'patron'. In contrast to a professional intermediary, this assistant is not a search expert and his domain knowledge may be comparable to or greater than the patron's knowledge. Modern searching (e.g. searching on the Web) demonstrates a wide and differently distributed specter of variants of pseudo-mediated search. Most of this diversity is described by PLE.

Then some explicit search criteria are formulated, and 'lazy user' behavior based on PLE and intermediary behavior based on PGR are compared with the optimal strategies. It is shown the PLE-based behavior usually generates suboptimal strategy under uncertainty while the PGR-based searching is not at the average effective.

However, what factors generate PLE- or PGR-based behavior? We suppose that only two coverage means (document coverage, i.e. recall and topic coverage reflecting the subjective uncertainty of the task) determine the principle which a searcher follows. Thus, selection of the principle is determined by the point in the coverage space which corresponds to externally or 'internally' assigned tasks.

Finally, in Section 5 we consider a dramatic example of comparison of unmediated and pseudo-unmediated searching behavior, which have lead to the universally accepted myth about the differences between searching on the Web and searching in 'traditional' search services. We show that the question of differences between the Web and traditional services is confusing and that both a positive answer and its negation are nothing other than artifacts. The myth bases on difference between truly unmediated Web search and pseudo-unmediated laboratory search rather than differences between these search services or their users.

2   Information Searching Behavior: What is Measured?

2.1   Two Classes of Characteristics

The commonly used characteristics of ISB fall into two groups: *quantitative* characteristics and *qualitative* ones. The first group includes session length, the number of terms per query, the fraction of Boolean queries, time characteristics such as intervals between queries, etc.

The qualitative characteristics describe search in terms of search tactics [1], [2], [10]. Bates has enumerated more than 20 tactics of interaction with IR system: the tactics of initial query, tactics of query modification (intersect – *AND*-expansion, reduce – terms elimination, parallel – *OR*-expansion with synonyms) and so on. Considering a logical search session as a sequence of used tactics we can speak about strategies and principles realized by a searcher in this session. Considering quantitative characteristics of a search session we can't speak even about subjective complexity of the task. The qualitative characteristics are the main characteristics of ISB. If two ISB manners are described by the same quantitative but by different qualitative characteristics then these manners are different. On the contrary, any differences in quantitative characteristics with coinciding sequences of tactics don't allow to speak about differences in ISB. For example, let's compare 3 sessions. 1st session consists of 2 queries: one-term initial query and one *OR*-expansion of this query; 2nd session consists of 5 queries: one-term initial query and 4 sequential *OR*-expansions; 3rd session includes 2 queries: 2-term initial query and one-term reduced query. While quantitative characteristics of the 1st and 3rd sessions (2 queries, 1.5 terms per query) differ from the 2nd session (5 queries, 3 terms per query) 1st and 2nd sessions intuitively seem more similar and are realizations of the same strategy of *OR*-expansion.

2.2 Two Sources of Data

The data on ISB fall into two different categories. The first category comes from external observations — transaction log analysis. The former category was formed during the comprehensive studies based on logs, interviews and questionnaire.

Transaction logs observations are objective, representative, potentially unlimited but superficial (for example, we don't known whether the user has found the needed information). Subjects in these studies formulate search goals themselves. In comprehensive studies neither the object of search nor the users are representative. A small group of users consists of colleagues and students of the study's authors. It is more important that earlier studies were frequently based on the externally assigned tasks which differ dramatically from the tasks searchers assign for themselves (if an initial information need seems too complex, people *simplify* it by decomposing it into different tasks or by substituting a more simple task, e.g. one of the decomposed tasks).

3 Search Environment, Search Service, Search Logical Structure

Now we introduce an approach to search as a service and a notion of a logical structure of search as opposed to a physical structure.

3.1 Search Service Instead of Search Environment

We use a notion of search service rather than the notion of search environment. We consider a terminal used for search as a service center (device) or environment (namely, search environment), which supplies one or many services, one of which is a search service realized by one or many search engines (Web search engines, portals, local IR systems, or online public access catalogues — OPACs).

A multi-service center (e.g. a supermarket, a mobil phone, a personal computer) supplies different types of services (e.g., dress, appliance, games). A one-service center (e.g., a mobil phone shop, a phone, old terminal of IR system) supplies the only service. When user comes to specialized one-service IR terminal he comes as a searcher: he has an information need, he realizes this need and he is ready to formulate it. When a user turns to his PC he wants one of the services. Furthermore, he may use it by the force of habit. A search in multi-service environment frequently is not 'planned' but is an 'occasional' one. A search need may appear during his interaction with this service center. While using a one-service center new information needs appear from either outside this environment or as a result of the just completed search, a multi-service center is a self-sufficient environment including the services similar to all services generating information needs outside the one-service center. In other words, all pre-query stages [19] are usually generated before interaction with one-service environment and are the cause for this interaction. On the contrary, these stages are usually generated during interaction with the multi-service environment.

Real-life manners of using of a search service on the one-service center and on a multi-service center are very different regardless of the search engines used. Besides, real-life search manners depend on availability of a center. To search something on an old terminal a user should come to it, wait and perhaps employ imposed additional service of an intermediary. On the contrary, a PC is a really free accessible environment. At the same time, as we show in the next subsection, manners of search are determined by the number (one or more) of windows supported by the center.

Table 1. Environmental factors affecting use of a search service

	Service center (Search environment)	
	[old] IR terminal	PC
Services	one service (search)	many services (text, game,…search)
Windowing search	one-window	multi-window
Search availability	'every-day'	every-second

3.2 Logical Structure of Searching

Contrary to the physical session, we associate a logical session with searching one and the same topic. Let a user search for a certain topic. During this search he may open several 'search windows' and use several engines (IR system, OPAC, or the Web search engine) simultaneously. The logical session may be distributed over different (for example, conducted simultaneously) physical sessions. The user may resume the search of the topic two days and many physical sessions later. Thus, one logical session may be distributed between different physical sessions and one physical session may include (fragments of) more than one logical session. A logical structure of a search is a structure of dependencies between logical sessions: some sessions are mutually independent, whereas some sessions are the results of other sessions or may result in other sessions. Some kind of logical structures known as a multitasking session is studied in [26] and related works.

The most frequent dependency is a tree dependency (Figure 1). The most frequent tree dependency is a branching search: achievement of the current goal generates a set of consequent goals and logical sessions corresponding to these goals. On the contrary, a convergence search is a search with initially recognized hierarchy of subgoals. The simplest one-level hierarchy task: to search all documents containing info about young cats. Because we nill to omit '6-month cat' or 'one-year cat', we decompose the initial task into subtasks. A result may be achieved either by one long query *cat AND (young OR month OR year)* or by several short 'subqueries'.

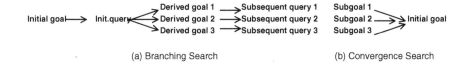

Fig. 1. Two types of tree search structures

The same searcher differently maps the same logical structure onto available physical one. For example, branching search is supported by the multi-window interface of PC environment. Old environments (IR terminals) support only one-window work, and a searcher is forced to 'linearize' branching search trees. As to convergence search, neither new environments nor old environments provide tools to map this logical structure into physical search process.

A logical session is a relative notion. Namely, a new physical session is considered as a continuation of one of the previous logical sessions when both the same topic is searched and the searcher considers new session as a continuation.

Besides logical sessions, users operate in terms of logical terms. A logical term may contain more than one word: "Messbauer effect", "sudden infant death syndrome", or "Ivan the Terrible".

4 Two Search Principles

Considering the diversity of specific ISB forms we can see that any ISB may be described only by one of the two principles: the principle of least effort (PLE) or the principle of the guarantied result (PGR) according to which searchers try to cover all possible interpretations of the information need (essentially, this is the widely known precision–coverage dichotomy). The first is well-known and wide spread. The second has earlier been limited to the classic intermediary behavior and now seems to be dying out. However we are not interested in the matter of popularity but in:

1) whether these two principles are sufficient to describe all ISB variants;
2) both principles being too general, what are their more operational wordings;
3) different operational wordings of the same principle dictate similar or largely different behavior in one and the same situation — in the latter case there are more than two principles;
4) when (depending on what circumstances) the searcher follows this or that principle. The answer to this question may both explain the frequency of using these principles and outline their perspectives. Besides this answer explains the artifact of differences between ISB in traditional IR systems and ISB on the Web which is considered in Section 5 devoted to quantitative characteristics of ISB.

4.1 Model Searching

Up-to-date universal opinion is that searchers' behavior is simple and searchers follow the principle of least effort (PLE). "Countless studies have shown that people use the principle of least effort in their information seeking", "People use least effort because they have always used it, and because, until very recently, it has worked adequately, if not optimally." [5]. On the other hand, already in 1991 Wildemuth et al. [31] showed that the most common ISB is to use simplest tactics. Furthermore, instead of accurate but difficult to formulate (and not necessary effective) query a user is satisfied with a simple rough query.

4.1.1 Classic Unmediated Search: Principle of Least Effort

During unmediated search a searcher performs his own (not externally assigned) task. This task is not a self-valued problem but a supplementary one for a searcher. A mathematician spends years to find the finest proof of the earlier proven theorem, but nobody spends any time to construct the 'finest' query or sequence of query modifications. A searcher follows PLE ([3], [5]). This principle is applied at all levels of information seeking from selecting a source (a talk with a colleague, seeking in a real library or in a base) to specific steps of query modification in successive search.

The unmediated searching style is *interactive* — the current query (including the first query) is not considered as the final one, a search is a multiple-step one and searchers 'say' in queries less than they can say.

4.1.2 Classic Mediated Search: Principle of Guarantied Result

There are a lot of studies of mediated search (e.g. [24]). The main problem they consider is that of a patron–intermediary interaction. We are interested in a simpler and less popular question about an intermediary interaction with IR system, and the principles describing this searching.

ISB of classic intermediaries is quite a different ISB. The task of search is not a supplementary problem for an intermediary. An intermediary *doesn't follow* the principle of least effort. S/he follows the "principle of the maximum query completeness", or *the principle of the guarantied result* (PGR): s/he tries to miss nothing, because s/he doesn't know what is important for the user's information needs. Sometimes this principle results in the same tactics as the principle of the minimum risk.

Interacting with the IR system a searcher faces environmental uncertainty of distribution of desired documents and that of the system behavior as such. Besides these uncertainties, an intermediary faces the uncertainty of the users' information needs (see also [18]). Namely, a classic intermediary usually knows something about 1) the information needs of the users and 2) the subject area. Thus, an intermediary *is forced* to follow PGR. Intermediaries try to make more complete and more general queries [21]. The maximum completeness tactic is the result of the uncertainty of the information needs rather than the intermediaries' professional duty or habit. When she searches for herself or when she clear understands a need and search in the well-known domain, she follows PLE.

The intermediary's searching style is *non-interactive* and corresponds to the situation when, in fact, each query (including the first query) is considered as the final query. An intermediary formulates queries in such a manner, which guarantees the presence of documents corresponding to all possible interpretations of the patron's information need in the search results.

The rule of the mediated search: to search until something is found. I.e., supposedly, one logical session is more rarely broken into several physical sessions. Considering that to get access to the intermediary's one-service center one has to make an extra effort (as a minimum, to got to some place), a user can collect a 'packet of needs' to satisfy. Then a physical session consists of several logical sessions.

Table 2. Model searcher in unmediated and classic mediated search

Searcher	Ability to recognize pertinence	Searcher's aim	Searcher's tactic at each step
Unmediated searcher	Yes	Precision of search results	Least effort tactic
Intermediary	No or Partial	A most complete query	max coverage tactic

4.2 Real-Life Search: Unmentioned Revolution?

We saw dramatically changed environment: from one-service one-search engine one-window to multi-service multi-search engine multi-window environment.

Obviously, changes of the number of services don't affect in any way the laboratory behavior in the case of externally assigned tasks. If the task doesn't dictate an one-search engine one-window search, the laboratory study won't observe the differences in the number of search services and the number of simultaneously used search windows. If the task doesn't demand (e.g. implicitly), their use is restricted by the technical capacity of inter-window [inter-search engine] exchange.

But, are there any real changes in real-life behavior? These changes must be significant. The searcher's behavior must be changed, the needs must be generated differently and differently satisfied (being at the same time subject to technological restrictions by non-supported inter-window inter-search engine exchanges). Today it is a matter of making our guesses. This change is great, obvious but unremarked. However, may the effect of these changes on ISB be no so great and thus be ignored?

A hypothesis is that a physical session in one-window one-service environment contains more logical sessions than a physical session in multi-window multi-service environment. Motivations: (1) a user uses one-service environment only when he has one or more systematized needs, (2) one-window environment supports only linear search, so all logical sessions corresponding the user's needs are included into the same physical session. On the contrary, (1') a user of multi-service environment uses a search service spontaneously, (2') logical sessions tend to be fragmented into different physical sessions.

4.3 Real-Life Search: Diverse Search Manners but Only Two Search Patterns

Two model manners of searcher and intermediary behavior were described. Contrary to the model intermediary, the real one may follow PLE rather than PGR. As well as a real searcher may follow PGR rather than PLE. When? The more confident an intermediary is with the information need, the more s/he diverts from the maximum coverage tactics.

Now the most frequent manner of mediated search is not an iterative user-librarian interaction but a non-iterative procedure: a patron-chief formulates a retrieval task and an intermediary-subordinate performs this task. Unlike the classic mediated search, this intermediary usually knows the subject area. The only uncertainty determining the search principle is the uncertainty of the patron's information need. A non-classic intermediary frequently ignores this uncertainty and follows PLE rather than PGR.

Of course, the same search configuration (chief–subordinate) is not a novel one. More interesting is that this configuration precisely describes pseudo-unmediated laboratory search constructed in earlier studies of information searching. Namely, a participant of such a study performs externally assigned tasks and perfectly plays the same role as an intermediary-subordinate. The exceptions are that 1) a participant frequently follows coverage-oriented PGR, 2) the tasks frequently formulated in re-call-oriented manner (to search as many documents as possible). The tasks in such pseudo-unmediated search are 'twice-coverage oriented'.

Table 3. Non-monotonic intermediary's ISB depending on task uncertainty

Ability to localize (Task uncertainty)	A query of inter-mediary	Search principle	Search situation and its frequency
None	Reproduction of the stated need	min risk [Least effort]	Special inf. need (unreal)
Partial	Broader query	Guaranteed result	Classic mediated search (rare)
Perfect	Narrow query	Least effort	Non-classic me-diated search (frequent)

By virtue of obvious reasons (a lot of searchers, no professional intermediaries) we can't see a classic mediated search on the Web. At the same time a mass manner of the Web search is a cooperative search ([7], [11]). A cooperative ('pseudo-mediated') search differs greatly from the traditional mediated search. An assistant (a colleague, friend, family member, etc.) plays a role of an intermediary. He (1) is a more qualified searcher than a 'patron' but is not a search expert, (2) may know the subject area better than a patron. These situations are mass in modern search, especially the Web search. Such pseudo-mediated cooperative searching on the Web is another variant of a non-classic mediated search. Depending on his domain knowledge and information need uncertainty a pseudo-intermediary may follow PLE or PGR.

4.4   Patterns of Search Interactions

Different search manners differ in patterns (sequences) of interaction (Table 4). Notations used in Table 4: <q> is a multiplier of q, i.e. <q> generates q, qq, etc. E – sEarcher, P – Patron, I – Intermediary, C – Chief, U — sUbordinate, T – Team. In 1996 Bates [4] discovered similar variety of search manners as preferences of the Getty project participants. The majority of the interviewed participants mention different variants of team search as preferable. Thus, we see no changes in the variety of search manners but we see a significant difference between modern (Web or non-Web) search and classic search in fractions of manners put into practice.

Table 4. Model and real patterns of interaction in different search manners

Search manner	Pattern	Examples of interactions
Classic unmediated search	<ES>E	ESE, ESESESE
Classic mediated search	<<PI><SI>P>	PISIP, PIPISIPISISIP
Non-classic mediated search*	C<US>UC	CUSUC, CUSUSUC
Team/pseudo-mediated search	<TS>T	TST, TSTSTST

* Participants of 'traditional' ISB studies were forced to demonstrate the same manner.

As it is seen team/pseudo-mediated search (<TS>T) has the same pattern as classic unmediated search (<ES>E) while non-classic mediated search (C<US>UC) is 'ambivalent' and may be similar to classic unmediated search or to classic mediated search. Thus, all the diversity of search manners falls under two search models.

4.5 Formal Models: A Search Game, Criteria, and Optimal Strategies

There are a lot of conceptual high-level ISB schematizations, which are sometimes over-generalized and are non-operational. At the same time, there is a lack of middle-level models and formalized models in particularly. Classic unmediated search and partly team search follow the principle of least effort (PLE). But what is a measure of the complexity of the searcher behavior and what is a measure of the searcher's effort and in what way these measures are interdependent (if they are)? Surprisingly, but just as in case of 'complexity' ([6], [8], [30]), considering 'effort', we can only speak about subjective effort.

Both matter reveal in any of 'problem solving' stages: 1) to understand the task; 2) to structure the task; 3) to transform this structure into the queries. Each of these things possesses its own complexity, with the formal measures like the Kolmogorov's one applying only to the result of (3). The existing formal complexity measures do not work for task complexity. For examples, a solution of the complex problem may be shorter than a result of the simplest enumeration task.

So far we have been satisfied with intuitively clearance. Zipf's PLE is a universal principle ("the primary principle that governs our entire behavior of all sorts" [33]) but it is known as a conceptual rather than an operational one. To elaborate an operational model we need to specify this principle what may be done in different manners.

Let us consider the following simplified successive search model formulated in terms similar to the Bates-Fidel language of query modifications [1], [2], [10]. Let a searcher use any combination of any terms. Some of the combinations are 'magical', i.e. the combinations for which the viewed part of the retrieved results includes desired documents. The aim of the search is to guess one of the magical combinations. The user may compare the results of successive steps (a query modification possesses worse or improved retrieved results) and add, delete or replace term(s) depending on the changes in the results. This framework allows to consider the following criteria of successive search and to estimate a lazy strategy of least query modifications.

How Optimal are PLE- and PGR-based Searches? Let's briefly consider in brief some explicit search criteria and compare a real PLE- and a PGR-based search with optimal strategies.

The Criterion of Minimum Number of Added Terms (including terms of the initial query). First, the strategy of the least modification (addition, deletion, replacement by exactly one term) at each step is optimal for any degree of uncertainty. In the special case of certainty other optimal strategies also exist — to enter any number of terms at each step.

The Criterion of Minimum Number of Steps. The greater the uncertainty is the less number of terms may be modified at each step. The strategy of minimum (one-term) modifications is the best for high degree of uncertainty.

The Criterion of Minimum Summary Time. The simplest measure of effort is the time used. If we suppose that a system response time and a 'user response time' (to view retrieved results) are intrinsic, we come to the criterion of minimum steps. A more realistic assumption is that the user response time depends on the similarity of results at the current and previous steps (first-order dependency). In this case simple modifications became more preferable, and we come to the 'weak' minimum steps criterion.

Thus, lazy tactics usually form optimal or suboptimal behavior under uncertainty. In distinction from the number of steps of the successive search and the length of the query, the rules of query modification don't depend on any factor as well on a search goal (precision or recall). Contrary to the PLE-based ISB, a search following PGR (a classic intermediary's search) requires more terms, more steps and more time.

4.6 Search Principles in the Coverage Space: Nothing than Two Areas

Let's consider the coverage space, which has two dimensions: a dimension of topic coverage (or task clearance or an ability to recognize document pertinence, see Table 3) and a dimension of documents coverage (recall). Placed in this space (Figure 2a)

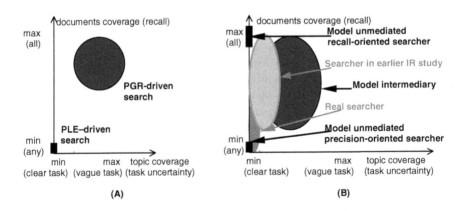

Fig. 2. Model, laboratory and real-life types of search and in the coverage space

searches driven by two model principles are nothing than two areas: a compact area of the certainly understood precision-oriented task and a diffused area of the highly uncertainly understood recall-oriented task. But what principles are induced by the certainly understood recall-oriented task and by the uncertain precision-oriented task?

Due to threshold dependency of the effort (task complexity) ISB is not monotonic over the task uncertainty. While subjective task complexity and efforts are measured on the ordinal scale we can conventionally describe their quantitative behavior. Figure 3 shows dependencies of these measures on the coverage measures.

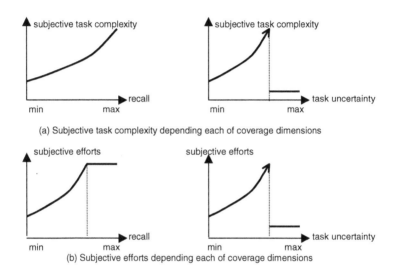

(a) Subjective task complexity depending each of coverage dimensions

(b) Subjective efforts depending each of coverage dimensions

Fig. 3. Dependences of subjective task complexity and subjective effort on coverage measures

5   Do Users of Different Search Services Behave Differently?

Now we consider an example of comparison of pseudo-unmediated and unmediated searching behavior, which have lead to the commonly accepted myth about the differences between searching on the Web and searching in 'traditional' search services. The interesting and provocative analytical work [14] formulates a question and gives a positive answer about the differences between different search services: traditional IR systems (TIRS), OPACs, and the Web. Although [14] says nothing about the reasons causing these differences, it is this very work that together with the previous *Excite* project works [28],[32] forms a basis for the myth about the peculiarities of the search on the Web as a result of the peculiarities of the Web users. "TIR, OPAC, and Web systems differ in terms of interfaces, search models, and document collections. However, do these differences result in different searching characteristics?" [14]

Table 5. Commonly accepted characteristics of the Web, TIRS and OPAC searchers

	Web (1997/99)	TIRS (1993)	OPAC (1993)
Queries per session [14]	1–2	7–16	2–5
Terms per query [14]	2	6–9	1–2
% of Boolean queries [14]	8%	37%	1%
Users (not from [14])	Untrained, poorly educated	Adult, educated, trained	Adult, educated, trained

5.1 Myth

"The comparison indicates that Web searching differs from searching in other environments." [14]. The study [14] together with the works [15],[28],[32] of the *Excite* project has shown the difference between earlier observed searching in TIRS and recently observed searching on the Web (Table 5) At the same time, the myth is considerably different from what these works state. Thus, [14] shows differences but it neither states that the reason for these differences is "the peculiarities of the Web users", nor does it discuss possible reasons for these differences. However, now the commonly suggested cause of the commonly supposed distinction of the Web searching is a certain feature of the Web users, who are too lazy (short sessions, short queries) and ignorant — they use rarely logical operators, which is not surprising since nobody teaches them to do it. As opposed to users of TIRS who are adult, trained and educated, a Web population includes children and uneducated users.[1] Of course, users of the Web are a very different population. But it is by no means an answer to the initial question "Are they a different population of *searchers*?"

5.2 Anti-myth

More recent studies of ISB in non-Web IRSs show no differences from the Web data but great differences from results of the earlier observations of ISB in pre-Web IRSs. Furthermore, [20] shows that there is no difference between searching on the Web and in the online catalogue! It is very surprising taking into account the differences in search capabilities of OPAC and other search engines and probable resulting difference in search tactics.

    ***CTSR* transaction log study** [16] analyses queries to *CSTR* (Computer Science Technical Reports) collection of the New Zealand Digital Library. The *CSTR* base contains thousand of documents neither categorized nor annotated, i.e. is similar to the Web with the exception of its specialization. Users of the *CSTR* are CS specialists, usually considered to be good searchers. They are familiar with the domain of the collection. According to the myth we should expect the exemplary ISB greatly differing from ISB of the Web users. However, as seen from Table 6, except the fraction of Boolean queries, the results of the *CSTR* study are very similar to the results of the *Excite* project.

---

[1] Myth adherents believe that egghead father searches better than his teen son. This is not so. Besides, obviously, a long session and a long query don't mean a quality search.

Table 6. Data of the *Excite* project [15], [25], [28] and *CSTR* study [16]

	Excite				CSTR
	1997 pilot	1997 stage 1	1999 stage 2	2001 stage 3	1996/7
Topics	All the diversity of topics				CS
Queries per session	2.8	2.5	1.9	2.3	2.5
Terms per query	2.3	2.4	2.4	2.6	2.4
Terms per session	6.4	6.0	4.6	6.0	6.0
% of Boolean queries	9%	5%	5%	10%	20%

Comprehensive Studies. Table 7 presents a comparison of earlier and more recent data on session length and query length. 37% as fraction of Boolean queries to TIRS look impressive as long as it remains unknown that the remaining 63% of queries contain just one term. That is the fraction of single-term queries was greater than the fraction in the Web queries, which poorly corresponds to the Web searcher myth.

Table 7. Comparison of earlier and recent data on non-Web search

	Earlier data			Recent data	
	Data [source]	year		Data [source]	Year
Queries/session	7 [14]	1980/90s		1–3 [16],[23] 2–3 [23],[29]	1997 1997/99
Terms/query	7.9 (novice), 14.4 (expert)[10], and contra: 8.8 (novice), 7.2 (expert) [12]	1981 1993		3 (queries without synonyms), 5.5 (queries with synonyms) [29]	1999
% of Boolean	37% [24]	1993		10% [16],[23]	1997

Table 7 presents another example of non-monotonicity: search manners of the beginners are simple, then during learning users complicate their behavior, and than being search experts they simplify their behavior. From this point of view results of [10] and [12] are not contradict.

5.3 Confusing Question and Incomparable Data

Thus, we see two contradicting answers to the question about the differences between quantitative characteristics of ISB. (While [16] claims the first answer is wrong because earlier studies were based on small samples, this is too amusing an explanation for the *systematical* difference of *all* these studies.) What is wrong? The only reason is that the factors really affecting ISB are ignored in the IR categorization used to describe ISB. The 'category name' factor (Web, TIRS) explains nothing. As a result, both answers are no other than artifacts.

As it seen from Figure 4, the values of quantitative characteristics of ISB in IRS are enormously dispersed. Whereas the Web data are compact, the differences between recently observed and 'traditional' ISB in IRS are greater than the difference between ISB in modern IRS and ISB on the Web. Furthermore, the results of recent observations in TIRS differ from the old results in the same TIRS. These are the reasons to speak about a special character of searching in IRS, not on the Web.

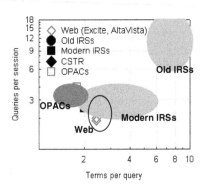

Fig. 4. Quantitative characteristics of searching in TIRSs, in OPACs and on the Web

Surprisingly, although empirical works a priori seem to cover all combinations of factors traditionally considered as ISB determining, it is not so. There is no ground for direct comparison of the Web ISB and non-Web ISB: all the Web studies correspond to those combinations of non-environmental factors, which do not intersect with combinations presented in TIRS studies. The partial exception is the *CSTR* study [16]: specialized users search specialized topics in a manner similar to an average Web user searching an average topic. To compare the Web ISB and non-Web ISB we need additional assumptions or new observations. But these efforts make no sense taking into account the dispersed results of IRS category. On the contrary, to reveal the roles of different factors we need no new data.

5.4   Factors Determining Differences

Let's reconsider the factors presumably affecting ISB. The properties of the search service usually considered as the factors affecting ISB are:

1. *response time* of IR system;
2. *interfaces/search methods* used by IR system;
3. *a number of indexed items* and *a number/fraction of relevant items*.

1. Response time was significant only for IRSs of 1960-70s.

2a. Data of the *CSTR* study in which both Boolean and free-text interfaces were used show no differences between ISBs. Differences between interfaces are revealed in the necessity to train users rather than in the a number of terms used per query.

2b. As it follows from the data compiled in [14], all search methods really used in non-Web or in the Web lead to no differences in quantitative characteristics.

3. Only the number of relevant items plays a little role. It is a threshold factor: this number should be sufficient rather than huge. When it is too small, users need to expand their queries by synonyms regardless of the tasks. However, if this number is small for an average query, then DB is small, which is not an actual case.

The *non-service (non-environmental)* factors are:

1. *user*: specific, specialized (e.g. profession), and average;
2. *topics*: specific, specialized (e.g. medicine, entertainment), and average;
3. *task*: topic and documents coverage orientation.

It should be noted that recent results are elaborated in case of one's own (largely precision-oriented) tasks rather than the externally assigned tasks. If we look at the tasks of studies [12], [17], [24] mentioned in [14] as a base for conclusions about TIR search, we discover a coverage orientation of these externally assigned tasks: a partial coverage of topics and apparent coverage of documents (inquiry to search as many documents as possible). On the contrary, subjects of recent studies of ISB on the Web or in non-Web perform own tasks. A comparison of different non-Web studies shows that only task orientation (common 'precision-oriented' tasks or uncommon 'coverage-oriented' tasks) and topic specialization determine quantitative characteristics.

Thus, besides a task orientation and topic specialization only the DB size may partly lead to different quantitative characteristics of ISB regardless of used search services. A searcher in earlier laboratory studies dealt with external tasks (i.e. it was at least partly 'pseudo-unmediated search' following PGR) and these tasks were more compound (and decomposable) than average real-life tasks. The differences in quantitative characteristics are actually the differences between laboratory and real-life conditions and results [15] rather than between different search services [14].

6   Conclusions and Further Works

We have considered different types of information searching behavior. We have shown that only two behavioral principles correspond to all the diversity of information searching. We have shown that searching based on PLE is more effective according to formal criteria. Finally, as an application of these results, a universally accepted myth about differences between searching on the Web and searching in 'traditional' IR systems was reevaluated. It was shown that suggested differences are the differences between coverage-oriented and precision-oriented searching.

In Section 4 we used simple formal decision models for illustrative purposes. However they deserve a closer examination, in particular in the context of other formal models of ISB. Than it turned out that we don't have available formal complexity concepts to describe task complexity or, in a broader sense, to construct a PLE model. Hopefully this is not so much a disappointing as a stimulating result.

Earlier in this paper we have introduced the notions of search center and search logical structure (LS). However, even these notions worked in the paper they did it only partly. Nevertheless these concepts don't seem to be an for object Occam razor. We saw dramatically changed environment: from one-service one-search engine one-window to multi-service multi-search engine multi-window environment. But, are there any real changes in real-life behavior?

The usefulness of the LS is twofold: to study ISB and to design search interfaces. Although LS depends on the possible search physical structure (as, according to the Sapir Worph thesis, thinking depends on the language), the LS provides a natural and intuitively clear search scheme. LS approach allows to formulate the tasks of interface design proceeding from common positions. Although such tasks as search windows exchange have simplest technical solutions they have not been solved so far —only because they have not been set. LS approach is a source of these tasks.

References

1. Bates, M.: Information Search Tactics. JASIS, 30(4) (1979) 205-214
2. Bates, M.: Where should the person stop and information interface start? Information Processing & Management, 26(5) (1990) 575-591
3. Bates, M.: Task force recommendation 2.3. Research and design review: improving user access to library catalog and portal information. Final Report. (2003)
4. Bates, M.: The Getty end-user online searching project in the humanities: Report #6. College&Research Libraries, 57(6) (1996) 514-523
5. Bates, M.: Toward an integrated model of information seeking and searching, Proc. of 4th Conf. on Information Seeking in Context (2002) 2-14
6. Bell, D., Ruthven, I.: Searchers' assessments of task complexity for Web searching. Proc. of 26th ECIR 2004. LNCS 2997 (2004), 57-71
7. Bruce, H., Fidel, R., Pejtersen, A. M, Dumais, S., Grudin, J., Poltrock, S. A comparison of the collaborative information retrieval behaviour of two design teams. New Review of Information Behaviour Research, 4(1) (2003) 139 -153
8. Buckland, M., Florian, D.: Expertise, task complexity, and artificial intelligence: A conceptual framework. JASIS, 42(9) (1991) 635-643
9. Fenichel, C.: Online searching: Measures that discriminate among users with different types of experience. JASIS, 32 (1981) 23-32
10. Fidel, R.: Moves in Online Searching. Online Review, 9(1) (1985) 61-74
11. Fidel, R. Pejtersen, A.M., Cleal, B., Bruce, H.: A multidimensional approach to the study of human-information interaction. JASIST, 55(11) (2004) 939-953
12. Hsieh-Yee, I.: Effects of search experience and subject knowledge on the search tactics of novice and experienced searchers. JASIST, 44(3) (1993) 161-174
13. Holscher, C., Strube, G.: Web search behavior of internet experts and newbies. Int. J. Comput. Telecommun. Networks. 33 (1–6) 337-346
14. Jansen, B., Pooch, U.: A review of Web searching studies and a framework for future research, JASIST, 52(3) (2001) 235-246
15. Jansen, B., Spink, A., Saracevic, T.: Real life, real users, and real needs: a study and analysis of user queries on the Web. Information Processing&Management, 36(2) (2000) 207-227
16. Jones, S., Cunningham, S., McNab, R., Boddie, S.: A transaction log analysis of a digital library. Int. J. on Digital Libraries, 3(2) (2000) 152-169
17. Koenemann, J., Belkin, N.: A case for interaction: a study of interactive information retrieval behavior and effectiveness. Proc. of CHI-96 (1996) 205-212
18. Kuhlthau, C.: A principle of uncertainty for information seeking. Journal of Documentation, 49(4) (1993), 339-355

19. Kuhlthau, C.: Seeking meaning: a process approach to library and information services. Noewood, NY: Ablex (1993)
20. Niu, X., Bizants, A.: The effects of search environment and task realism on search behavior, *Human Factors and Ergonomics Society 45th Annual Meeting* (2001).
21. Nordlie, R.: Unmediated and Mediated Information Searching in the Public Library. ASIS 1996 Annual Conf. Proc., (1996) http://www.asis.org/annual-96/ElectronicProceedings
22. Sandstrom, P.: Scholars as subsistence foragers. Bulletin of ASIS, 25(3) (1999), 17-20
23. Seiden, P., Szymborski, K., Norelli, B.: Undergraduate students in the Digital Library: Information seeking behavior in an heterogenous environment. ACRL National Conference (1997) http://www.ala.org/acrl/paperhtm/c26.html
24. Siegfried, S., Bates, M., Wilde, D.: A profile of end-user searching by humanities scholars. JASIS, 44(5) (1993) 273-291
25. Spink, A., Jansen, B., Wolfram, D., Saracevic, T.: From e-sex to e-commerce: Web search changes. Computer, March 2002, 107-109
26. Spink, A., Ozmutlu, H.C., Ozmutlu, S.: Multitasking information seeking and searching processes. JASIST, 53(8) 639-652
27. Spink, A., Wilson, T. D., Ford, N., Foster, A., Ellis, D.: Information seeking and mediated searching study. Part 1. JASIST, 53(9) (2002) 695-703
28. Spink, A., Wolfram, D., Jansen, B., Saracevic, T.: Searching the Web: The Public and their queries. JASIST, 52(3) (2001) 226-234
29. Vakkari, P.: eCognition and changes of search terms and tactics during task performance. Proc. of RIAO 2000, 894-907
30. Vakkari, P.: Task complexity, problem structure and information actions. Information Processing & Management, 35(6) (1999) 819-837
31. Wildemuth, B., Jacob, E., Fullington, A., de Blieck, R., Friedman, C.: A detailed analysis of end-user search behaviors. Proc. of 54 ASIS Annual Meeting (1991) 302-312
32. Wolfram, D., Spink, A., Jansen, B., Saracevic, T.: Vox populi: the public searching of the Web. JASIST, 52(12) (2001) 1073–1074
33. Zipf, G.: Human behavior and the principle of least effort. Addison-Wesley, Cambridge, MA (1949)

Bradford's Law of Scattering: Ambiguities in the Concept of "Subject"*

Birger Hjørland and Jeppe Nicolaisen

Royal School of Library and Information Science,
Birketinget 6, DK-2300 Copenhagen S., Denmark
{bh, jni}@db.dk

Abstract. Bradford's law of scattering is said to be about *subject scattering* in information sources. However, in spite of a corpus of writings about the meaning of the word "subject" and equivalent terms such as "aboutness" or "topicality", the meaning of "subject" has never been explicitly addressed in relation to Bradford's law. This paper introduces a distinction between Lexical scattering, Semantic scattering, and Subject scattering. Neither Bradford himself nor any follower has explicitly considered the differences between these three and the implications for the practical applications of Bradford's law. Traditionally, Bradford's law has been seen as a neutral and objective tool for the selection of the most central information sources in a field. However, it is hard to find actual reports that describe how Bradford's law has been applied in practical library and information services. Theoretical as well as historical evidence suggest that the selection of journals based on Bradford-distributions tend to favor dominant theories and views while suppressing views other than the mainstream at a given time.

1 Introduction: Bradford's Law

Bradford's law of scattering (of subjects in information sources), first published in 1934, is often mentioned together with Zipf's law (about word frequencies in natural language texts) and Lotka's law (about distribution of authors' productivity) as one among the three most important bibliometric laws, and is often considered the best model or example of scientific research that is available within Library and Information Science (LIS). Bradford's law states that documents on a given "subject" is distributed (scattered) according to a certain mathematical function so that a growth in papers on a subject requires a growth in the number of journals/information sources. The numbers of the groups of journals to produce nearly equal numbers of articles is roughly in proportion to 1: n: n^2 ..., where n is called *the Bradford multiplier[1]*. Ex-

---

* The authors are currently investigating various issues relating to Bradford's law of scattering. The project is partly sponsored by The Danish Ministry of Culture [A2004 06-026].

[1] Bradford believed n to be constant in the different zones ($n_1 = n_2 = n$); Results reported by Rao [1] indicates, however, that Bradford's assumption was wrong: Bradford multipliers vary from zone to zone.

F. Crestani and I. Ruthven (Eds.): CoLIS 2005, LNCS 3507, pp. 96–106, 2005.
© Springer-Verlag Berlin Heidelberg 2005

plained in words, Bradford's law states that a small core of, for example, journals have as many papers on a given subject as a much larger number of journals, n, which again has as many papers on the subject as n^2 journals.

Bradford himself provided both a graphical and a verbal formulation of his law that have later been found not to be mathematical equivalent. The exact mathematical function has been subject to much subsequent research, and the very question what a Bradford distribution is has been debated. As the distribution is very sensitive to different subjects and conventions, Heine [2] found that it is unclear under which circumstances a distribution should be regarded as a Bradford distribution.

Bradford's law has been used as an argument about how to build collections, how to select journals to be indexed in bibliographies, how to measure the coverage of bibliographies, how to solve practical problems related to information seeking and retrieval, and by Bradford himself as an argument for a new way to organize bibliographical work and scientific documentation.

Bradford's law is explicitly about the scattering of documents on specific subjects. The meaning of the term "subject" (and related terms such as aboutness, topicality, and theme) as applied in subject indexing, classification and knowledge organization, has been investigated in LIS for about a hundred years. Among the important contributions are Cutter [3], Wilson [4], Hutchins [5, 6, 7], Maron [8], Miksa [9], Soergel [10], and Hjørland [11, 12]. Since Bradford published his works, there has also been an impressive literature about Bradford's law. The peculiar thing is, however, that with a few exceptions nobody have thus far tried to outline the consequences of different conceptions of "subject" for Bradford's law of (subject) scattering. The two lines of research have never really met.

2   Applications of Bradford's Law

B.C. Brookes was among the first to address the possible applications of Bradford's law. In a short note in *Nature* he wrote that the law "seems to offer the only means discernible at present to reducing the present quantitative untidiness of scientific documentation, information systems and library services to a more orderly state of affairs capable of being rationally and economically planned and organized" [13, p. 953].

Several commentators have suggested using Bradford's law to solve practical journal collection management problems. The basic idea is to conduct Bradford analyses of journals - i.e., to sort the journals in Bradford zones – and thus identify which belong to the core and which does not. Any Bradford analysis involves three steps [14, pp. 16-17]:

1. Identify many or all items (usually articles) published in this field;
2. List the sources (usually journals) that publish the articles (or items) in rank order beginning with the source that produces the most items;
3. While retaining the order of the sources, divide this list into groups (or zones) so that the number of items produced by each group of sources is about the same.

Nisonger [15, pp. 139-140] argues in his textbook *Management of Serials in Libraries* that the following points are some of the "most obvious potentials" of Bradford analyses:

- Selection/deselection
- Defining the core
- Collection evaluation
- The law of diminishing returns
- Calculation of cost at various coverage
- Setting priorities among journals

Other commentators have suggested using Bradford's law to solve practical problems related to information seeking and retrieval. Howard D. White [16] proposed an automatic option for sorting the output from online searches of journal literature, which he argued would help online users. What he had in mind was a "computerized sorting of hits by the journals in which they appear, and then of journals, high to low, by the number of hits appearing in each" [16, p. 47]. He termed the procedure "Bradfordizing", and argued that "the ability to retrieve items selectively by journal after learning contributing titles and their yields, would seem to be the greatest single advantage of the proposed option" [16, p. 50]. The reason for his optimism is spelled out in the article. According to White it is easy to imagine situations in which the searcher would want to retrieve hits only in the core journals of a literature. He mentions that it is often troublesome to track down the articles in the tail of a Bradford distribution, and concludes that "one may have the prejudice that items published in the core journals of a subject are generally superior to those scattered over journals in the tail, which is tantamount to believing that journals publishing the most items on a topic also publish the items most worth reading, as a rule" [16, p. 50][2]. Perhaps as responses to White's suggestion, the proposed option is today a standard option in the products of most database vendors.

However, it is hard to find actual reports that describe how Bradford's law has been applied in practical library & information services[3]. The near absence of such reports is hard to comprehend in light of the many suggestions for applications. It is furthermore a bit strange as G. Edward Evans in his primer on collection management writes that:

> "Special libraries and information officers make good use of data generated by bibliometric techniques in selecting and maintaining collections of the most needed serials. Bradford's law, Lotka's law, Zipf's law, and citation analysis <u>have</u> contributed to the effective operation of special libraries" [18, p. 104; emphasis added].

Unfortunately, Evans does not provide any details or references on this.

There is no reason to believe that the assumptions about universalism and neutrality underlying the application of Bradford's law can be combined with the demands on pluralism, which may be expected from libraries and information systems. In other words: The application of Bradford's law to the selection of information sources may

---

[2] This prejudice is probably quite common. Sandstrom [17, p. 584], for instance, argues: "Knowing how the core is constructed and integrated with other research concerns makes it easier for scholars to track down necessary information".

[3] One exception is the ISI databases. The ISI journal selection process is partly based on Bradford analyses
[http://scientific.thomson.com/knowtrend/essays/selectionofmaterial/journalselection/].

not be just a neutral tool, but may possibly turn out to function discriminatorily against minority views. Cognitivism has dominated American psychology (and thus also international psychology) since the early 1970's. Before that time behaviorism was the dominant approach in psychology (see [19]). However, historians of psychology have found that cognitive approaches may be tracked long back in the history of psychology. Greenwood [20] identifies sources of cognitive psychology in the hey-days of behaviorism, often in more remote psychological journals. It is reasonable to expect that if Bradford's law had been applied to select (or deselect) journals to libraries and databases around 1930, then the result would have been that journals with an exclusive behavioral orientation would have been too strongly represented and that journals more open towards, for example, the cognitive approach, would have been too weakly represented. The cognitive view later developed to a majority view. If journals open to the cognitive view had been deselected due to the application of Bradford's law, this may well have made it more difficult for the view to develop, why the application of Bradford's law would have counteracted scientific progress. This is the opposite of what library and information services are supposed to do.

3 The Underlying Mechanisms

Bradford [21, p. 110, 22, p. 148] wrote under the heading *The scattering of articles on a given subject:*

> "It is, therefore, necessary to examine the extent to which articles on a given subject actually occur in periodicals devoted to quite other subjects: as, for instance, a paper on the mechanism of the heart, contributed to the *Proceedings of Physical Society*, or one on genetics, occurring in an agricultural magazine. Investigation shows that this distribution follows a certain law, which can be deduced both theoretically from the principle of the unity of science and practically from examination of the references.
>
> According to this principle every scientific subject is related, more or less remotely, to every other scientific subject.
>
> It follows that from time to time, a periodical devoted to a special subject may contain an article of interest from the point of view of another subject. In other words, the articles of interest to a specialist must occur not only in the periodicals specializing on his subject, but also, from time to time, in other periodicals, which grow in number as the relation of their fields to that of his subject lessens and the number of articles on his subject in each periodical diminishes".

Bradford's empirical data are well known and well considered in the literature. The principle of which he felt he could deduce his famous law, is, however, extremely superficially treated in [21] (equal to [22]; and not mentioned at all in Bradford's 1934 paper [23]). To our knowledge this theoretical principle has also been unnoticed by subsequent research. Disregarding the short quotation given above, no discussion of this principle of the unity of the sciences[4] and the consequences for the organization of the scientific literature has to our knowledge been produced. Although it seems very probable and fruitful to us, we do have difficulties in deducing any specific statistical distribution of papers or subjects from it. In fact in the original paper [23], two different distributions were hypothetically mentioned in the beginning. This indicates that at this time, at least, Bradford himself did not deduce or anticipate or had intuitions that the distribution, which was later widely recognized as *Bradford's law,* followed from the principle of the unity of the sciences.

A more productive understanding related to the unity of science would probably be to connect the phenomenon of scattering with the concept of *interdisciplinarity.* It seems rather obvious that the more interdisciplinary a field of research (or a tradition or a "culture" of research) is, the more scattered the subject will be over different disciplines and clusters of journals. The kind of distribution in terms of mathematical functions should be expected to depend on the nature of the borders between fields. If such borders are strictly and formally defined and if the contribution to such fields demand conditions that can only be met by a small group of scientists, then the degree of scattering should be low (high concentration) and the distribution rather discontinuous. Experimental science depending on very special equipment should have a high concentration, while contributions to philosophical problems should have a high scattering because such problems have a high degree of generality and at the same time many different professions have the qualifications and conditions to make a contribution. The social sciences are generally considered very interdisciplinary (see e.g., [26]), with legal science as an exception. The degree of interdisciplinarity probably influences phenomena of scattering. In some journals (e.g. in some psychoanalytic journals) only authors with a specific training are allowed to publish. Such regulations may also influence phenomena of scattering. Unfortunately, Bradford did not consider such more sociologically oriented thoughts. His thoughts were dominated by the metaphysical view to find in reality an a priory pattern or law to which his empirical data would fit.

Bradford himself had very little interest in the underlying mechanisms that produced the observed distributions. His motivation to do the investigations was to show that the existing documentary system was incomplete and "chaotic". His conception of subject matter was in our opinion rather primitive, and what interested him was primarily a better coverage of abstracting and indexing services, which he demonstrated was very low: "Less than half the useful scientific papers published are abstracted in the abstracting periodicals and more than half the useful discoveries and inventions are recorded, only to lie useless and unnoticed on the library shelves" [22, p. 146].

4 Bradford's Conception of "Subject"

As Bradford never explicitly discussed the meaning of "subject", we have to infer his meaning of this concept indirectly by considering how he uses this word. We have

---

[4] That Bradford mentions the concept "unity of science" in 1948 is no surprise. This concept was a hot issue at that time due to the influence of the logical positivists who published the International Encyclopedia of Unified Science. The first issue came in 1938. The last in 1962 (cf. [24] and [25]).

already seen that "a paper on the mechanism of the heart, contributed to the *Proceedings of Physical Society*, or one on genetics, occurring in an agricultural magazine" are considered "quite other [different] subjects". But do these examples really exemplify "quite different subjects"? The heart can be regarded from a physical point of view and a paper on this subject can be regarded as part of the interdisciplinary field of biophysics. The paper can thus be considered a subject on (or rather for) both human biology and physics. The same argument may be applied to the paper on genetics appearing in an agricultural magazine. Bradford's conception of "subject" reflects a view close to *naïve realism* [11].

Bradford's empirical distribution was based on the sources indexed in four years of the current bibliography *Applied Geophysics* and two and a-half years of the current bibliography *Lubrication,* both prepared by *the Science Library* in London, of which Bradford was the keeper. There is no discussion, however, of how papers were assigned subject descriptors (e.g. classification codes) and how this assignment may have influenced the actual distributions. Indirectly however, we may get a little insight of his thinking about this issue and its consequences for his law.

Bradford realized the needs for deep indexing addressed towards specific subject areas (such as lubrication). His library, however, could not provide bibliographies with sufficient coverage of the relevant documents. Because the sources were too scattered, no special library could cover all the needed documents, and no compilatory team of a realistic size could manage to scan all the needed sources. Because of this insight Bradford suggested a two-step procedure. All journals and other information sources should be indexed by source, not by subject. That is: one team should make a crude indexing of journals one by one. Then other teams of information specialists could make specialized indexing to special purposes. "On the average, a general abstract requires two classification numbers to specify the main subjects of the paper [...]. A special abstract, which included every substance mentioned and every piece of apparatus described, might well need as many as twelve classification numbers" [22, p. 145].

Bradford imagined that 12 classification numbers per document would hardly be worthwhile, as many of these numbers might never be consulted. This is in contrast to present-day information retrieval in which every word in documents may be used as subject access point (in full text retrieval), where all references may be used as access points (in citation indexes), and where many kinds of subject access points and retrieval techniques may be applied. Bradford's view reveals a mix of theoretical considerations and practical constraints that probably are typical and harmful in the development of general knowledge in information science.

Concerning indexing and the concept of "subject" the quotation given reveals something about how Bradford looked at things. A comprehensive indexing should list "every substance mentioned and every piece of apparatus described". This is a kind of thinking related to a listing of all "substantive" words. When he suggests that these words should be indexed with the UDC classification, it is not the words, but the concepts (words including synonyms and excluding homonyms) that are indexed. This may therefore be interpreted as indexing of concepts rather than by subjects proper. But what difference does this make?

A proposal for the differentiation between concept indexing and subject indexing is given by Bernier [27]. In his opinion subject indexes are different from, and can be contrasted with, indexes to concepts, topics and words. Subjects are what authors are working and reporting on. A document can have the subject of *Chromatography* if this is what the author wishes to inform about. Papers using Chromatography as a research method or discussing it in a subsection do not have Chromatography as subjects. Indexers can easily drift into indexing concepts and words rather than subjects, but this is not good indexing[5].

5 Kinds of Scattering

The idea about different kinds of scattering came up when the first author served as referee on a paper by Hood & Wilson [28]. This paper examines - in the tradition from Bradford [23] - the distribution of bibliographic records in online bibliographic databases using 14 different search topics, which are searched in DIALOG (see table 1.).

The first author's suggestion to the authors was that these 14 questions represent three different kinds of questions. This is acknowledged in the paper, in which Hood & Wilson [28, pp.1253-1254] write:

> "Hjørland [[29]] suggests that at a deeper and more theoretical level, scattering among databases is related to different kinds of scattering within the journal articles. He proposes three types of scatter: lexical scatter or the scatter of one word as in search #4 (shakespeare); semantic scatter or the scatter of one concept with different synonyms as in search #10 (dark matter); and subject scatter or the scatter of concepts useful to a problem [[11]] as in search #9 (hair loss). The gradation of scatter is from simple to complex, with lexical scatter being the most objective and subject scatter the most problematic, requiring a comprehensive search formulation. Further, the degree of semantic and subject scatter may be important indicators of interdisciplinarity. A logical progression of this research is to investigate further the underlying mechanisms for the types of literature scatter so as to answer suggested questions, such as: "To what degree is the overlap caused by overlap in the indexing of the same journals in different databases?" and "To what degree does overlapping terminology and concepts in different fields cause the overlap?"

---

[5] Bernier does not, however, differentiate author's subjects from those of the information seeker. A user may want a document about a subject, which is different from the one intended by its author. *From the point of view of information systems, the subject of a document is related to the questions that the document can answer for the users.* Such a distinction between a content oriented and a request-oriented approach is emphasized by Soergel [10]. The implication of a request-oriented approach is that subject analysis should predict the questions that the document is going to help answering (See e.g., [8]). Based on such analyses, Hjørland [11, 12] proposes that subjects are the epistemological or informative potentials of documents, and sees the job of the indexer as that of making a prognosis of the most important future applications of the document. This view corresponds to the functional theory about sources in history, which states that what count as an information source is always relative to the question that it is supposed to answer.

Thus, there are at least three different kinds of scattering:

- Lexical scattering is the scattering of <u>words</u> in texts and in collections of texts.
- Semantic scattering is the scattering of <u>concepts</u> in texts and in collections of texts.
- Subject scattering is the scattering of items useful to a given <u>task or problem</u>.

These three kinds of scattering are not independent of each other. There are, of course, internal relations between them.

<u>Concerning lexical scattering:</u> A word may, for example, be defined operationally as a sequence of letters surrounded by blanks. The most known formula for this kind of scattering is Zipf's law that states that the number of occurrences of a given word in a long stretch of text is the reciprocal of the order of frequency of occurrence.

<u>Concerning semantic scattering:</u> A concept may, for example, be defined operationally as nouns and their synonyms. Classes in classification systems and descriptors in thesauri are the most operationally available lists of concepts in domains and in databases. They do not, however, exhaust the number of concepts in a given domain and they may be subject to different interpretations.

Table 1. Queries used in DIALOG by Hood & Wilson [28]

1	fuzzy(w)set? ?
2	(informetric? ? or bibliometric? ? or scientometric? ?)
3	bradford?(5n)((law? or distribut? or dispers? or scatter? or zipf? or lotka or multiplier? or bibliograph? or rank? or bibliometr? or analys? or technique? or yield or method? or constant? or curve? or zone?))
4	Shakespeare
5	disease?(5n)eye?
6	(domestic or family)(5n)(violen? or abus?)
7	supervene or supervenes or supervened or supervening or supervenient or supervenience or supervention
8	librar?(5n)(privati? or outsourc?)
9	(finasteride or minoxidil or proscar or propecia) and (bald???? or alopecia or (hair(4n)(thin???? or loss)))
10	(Dark(w)matter or (weakly(w)interacting(w)massive(w)particles) or (massive(w)compact(w)halo(w)objects))
11	(el(w)nino or la(w)nina) and (climat?(5n)change?)
12	neandert?
13	((euro(w)dollar?) or (euro (5n) currency))
14	Cladism? or cladist? or cladogram? or cladogen?

Concerning subject scattering: This is what Bradford's law is supposed to be about. What is useful to a given task is, however, determined by given theories in the subject field, and different theories imply different views of what is relevant in case (cf. [30]). Subject scatter is difficult to operationalize. Probably the best expression of what different theories or "paradigms" identifies as useful to given tasks can be operationalized by studying patterns in citations because citations are supposed to reflect subject relations as relations of relevance or usefulness (see [19] and [31]).

6   Implications

What are the implications of the three kinds of scattering for the practical use of Bradford's law?

If core journals (or other information sources) are selected from the frequencies of words or concepts, rather that subjects proper, then such cores may contain journals that are not relevant to users. The core may be "polluted" with journals not belonging to "the subject". Such journals may take the place from other journals "on the subject" that use different words or concepts. In other words: an adequate indexing of documents is as relevant for providing Bradford distributions as for providing relevant documents to users.

Besides, while the distribution of documents according to word frequencies is a rather mechanical, neutral, and "objective" process, the distribution of information sources according to subject matter is a much more interpretative and political process. It is much more difficult to make operational implications of "subjects". What is a subject for one person need not be the same subject for another. The best way to generalize views about subjects is probably to consider different theoretical views or epistemologies regarding subjects. A pure mechanical view of selection must consequently be replaced by a reflective view in which the selector must justify the selection on axiological arguments.

7   Conclusion

Urquhart [32, p. 25] notes that the way Bradford's law has been handled by information scientists is "a good illustration of the unfortunate effects of the academic approach to information science". We have done our utmost to break with that tradition. In this paper we have put forward serious arguments against the received view on Bradford's law. The fact that it is difficult to find any examples of its actual use in practice may be an indication that such problems have intuitively been foreseen. Future research comparing and explaining different kinds of scattering in information sources should decide the potentials of Bradford's law.

References

1. Rao, I.K.R. (1998). An analysis of Bradford multipliers and a model to explain law of scattering. *Scientometrics, 41*(1/2): 93-100.
2. Heine, M.H. (1998). Bradford ranking conventions and their application to a growing literature. *Journal of Documentation, 54*(3): 303-331.

3. Cutter, C.A. (1904). *Rules for a Dictionary Catalog*. Washington, DC: Government Printing Office.
4. Wilson, P. (1968). *Two Kinds of Power: An Essay on Bibliographical Control*. Berkeley, CA: University of California Press.
5. Hutchins, W. J. (1975). *Languages of Indexing and Classification: A Linguistic Study of Structures and Functions*. London, UK: Peter Peregrinus.
6. Hutchins, W.J. (1977). On the problem of "aboutness" in document analysis. *Journal of Informatics, 1*: 17-35.
7. Hutchins, W.J. (1978). The concept of "aboutness" in subject indexing. *Aslib Proceedings, 30*: 172-181.
8. Maron, M. E. (1977). On indexing, retrieval and the meaning of about. *Journal of the American Society for Information Science*, 28: 38-43.
9. Miksa, F. (1983). *The Subject in the Dictionary Catalog from Cutter to the Present*. Chicago, IL: American Library Association.
10. Soergel, D. (1985). *Organizing Information: Principles of Data Base and Retrieval Systems*. Orlando, FL: Academic Press.
11. Hjørland, B. (1992). The concept of "subject" in Information Science. *Journal of Documentation, 48*(2): 172-200.
12. Hjørland, B. (1997): *Information Seeking and Subject Representation. An Activity-theoretical approach to Information Science*. Westport, CT & London, UK: Greenwood Press.
13. Brookes B.C. (1969). Bradford's law and the bibliography of science. *Nature, 224*: 953–956.
14. Diodato, V. (1994). *Dictionary of Bibliometrics*. Binghamton, NY: Haworth Press.
15. Nisonger, T.E. (1998). *Management of Serials in Libraries*. Englewood, CO: Libraries Unlimited.
16. White, H.D. (1981). "Bradfordizing" search output: How it would help online users. *Online Review*, 5: 47-54.
17. Sandstrom, P.E. (2001). Scholarly communication as a socioecological system. *Scientometrics, 51*(3): 573-605.
18. Evans, G.E. (2000). *Developing Library and Information Center Collections*. 4th ed. Englewood, CO: Libraries Unlimited.
19. Hjørland, B. (2002). Epistemology and the socio-cognitive perspective in Information Science. *Journal of the American Society for Information Science and Technology, 53*(4): 257-270.
20. Greenwood, J.K. (1991). *Relations and Representations: An Introduction to the Philosophy of Social Psychological Science*. New York, NY: Routledge, Chapman & Hall.
21. Bradford, S.C. (1948). *Documentation*. London, UK: Crosby Lockwood.
22. Bradford, S.C. (1953). *Documentation*. 2nd ed. London, UK: Crosby Lockwood.
23. Bradford, S.C. (1934). Sources of information on specific subjects. *Engineering, 26*: 85-86.
24. Carnap, R. (1938). Logical Foundations of the Unity of Science. In: Neurath, O., Carnap, R. & Morris, C. (eds.), *International Encyclopedia of Unified Science*. Chicago, IL: University of Chicago Press.
25. Kuhn, T. (1962). *The Structure of Scientific Revolutions*. Chicago, IL: University of Chicago Press. [Also issued as Vol. II, No. 2, of the International Encyclopedia of Unified Science].
26. Andersen, H. (2000). Influence and reputation in the social sciences - how much do researchers agree? *Journal of Documentation, 56*(6): 674-692.

27. Bernier, C.L. (1980). Subject Indexes. In: Kent, A.; Lancour, H. & Daily, J.E. (eds.), *Encyclopedia of Library and Information Science: Volume 29.* New York, NY: Marcel Dekker, Inc.: 191-205.
28. Hood, W. & Wilson, C.S. (2001). The scatter of documents over databases in different subject domains: How many databases are needed? *Journal of the American Society for Information Science and Technology, 52*(14): 1242-1254.
29. Hjørland, B. (2001). Towards a theory of aboutness, subject, topicality, theme, domain, field, content . . . and relevance. *Journal of the American Society for Information Science and Technology, 52*(9): 774–778.
30. Hjørland, B. & Sejer Christensen, F. (2002). Work tasks and socio-cognitive relevance: A specific example. *Journal of the American Society for Information Science and Technology, 53*(11): 960-965.
31. Nicolaisen, J. (2004). *Social Behavior and Scientific Practice – Missing Pieces of the Citation Puzzle.* Copenhagen, DK: Royal School of Library and Information Science. PhD Thesis.
32. Urquhart, D. (1986). Librarianship is an experimental science. In: Allen, G.G. & Exon, F.C.A. (eds.), *Research and the Practice of Librarianship: An International Symposium. Western library studies,* 7. Perth: The Library, Western Australian Institute of Technology: 21-28.

The Instrumentality of Information Needs and Relevance

Olof Sundin and Jenny Johannisson

Swedish School of Library and Information Science,
Göteborg University & University College of Borås,
SE-50190 Borås, Sweden
{olof.sundin, jenny.johannisson}@hb.se

Abstract. An important question in Library and Information Science (LIS) is for what purpose information is sought; information seeking is not carried out for its own sake but to achieve an objective that lies beyond the practice of information seeking itself. Therefore, instrumentality could be seen as an overarching principle in the LIS field. Three different epistemological approaches to information needs and relevance, and the views on instrumentality that goes with them, are presented: the structure approach, the individual approach and the communication approach. The aim of the paper is to show how a communication oriented, neo-pragmatist epistemology enables research that in a dialogic manner highlights both the social contexts that information users are part of, and positions users as active contributors to the shaping of these contexts. The power relations that permeate these processes of negotiation between users and contexts are highlighted by introducing a Foucauldian perspective on power.

1 Introduction

The aim of CoLIS 5 is to explore different conceptions of *context* in Library and Information Science (LIS). This paper aims to contribute to this discussion by introducing neo-pragmatism as an epistemological tool to understand how and why context matters in LIS practices. In this paper, we focus on the practice of information seeking. An important and recurrent research theme in LIS is for what purpose information is sought. This theme is fundamentally instrumental in character; information seeking is not carried out for its own sake but to achieve an objective that lies beyond the practice of information seeking itself. This assumption clearly points to the necessity of including those social practices and institutions – that is, the contexts – where these objectives are formed, in the academic study of how people seek information. In fact, instrumentality could be seen as an overarching principle in a discipline that is so often assessed in relation to its ability to improve information systems and services. Having made this observation, it is important to recognize that there are different views on instrumentality expressed in LIS research. Therefore, one of the questions we explore in this paper is what these different conceptions of instrumentality entail when related to information seeking practices.

F. Crestani and I. Ruthven (Eds.): CoLIS 2005, LNCS 3507, pp. 107–118, 2005.
© Springer-Verlag Berlin Heidelberg 2005

In exploring instrumentality in relation to information seeking practices, we particularly focus on different conceptions of "information needs" and "relevance".[1] In highlighting information needs, we deal with one of the most central concepts in LIS. The ways in which the LIS community relates to this concept have consequences for how it relates to many other phenomena in the field. One example is the assessment of the relevance of information – a practice that, in LIS, is rarely studied from a social perspective. The concept of relevance has in LIS mainly been explored in the context of information retrieval research (IR). We wish to supplement this perspective by focusing on relevance from the perspective of information seeking research (IS). The second question that we address in this paper, therefore, is the question of how different conceptions of information needs and relevance in LIS could be characterized. In answering this question, we present three epistemological approaches: the structure approach, the individual approach and the communication approach. We argue that the communication approach, which we prefer, contributes to an understanding of information needs and relevance that takes social context into serious account, while simultaneously appointing an important role to individual agency.

Thirdly and finally, we introduce our version of what a communication-oriented approach to information needs and relevance could look like. This version takes a neo-pragmatist epistemology as its point of departure, mainly as this is expressed by Richard Rorty [e.g. 1]. Neo-pragmatism is an epistemological position that has lately attracted increased attention in the social sciences. The neo-pragmatist view of instrumentality, which we promote in this paper, emphasizes the positive aspects of instrumentality and opens up for an improved dialogue between LIS and other academic disciplines, as well as between LIS research and other professional practices within this field. We particularly focus on the neo-pragmatist concept of *community of justification* as a way of illustrating context. But since neo-pragmatism provides a somewhat insufficient tool when dealing with questions of power [e.g. 2], we turn to the works of Michel Foucault [3] in order to develop a deepened understanding of how power and power relations work in information seeking practices. We conclude by outlining some of the implications of this epistemological and theoretical approach for LIS in general, and IS in particular.

We mainly draw on a theoretical discussion in order to provide a more nuanced understanding of the multifarious social practices through which information seeking is carried out. We believe that our discussion contributes to making visible the often implicit epistemological claims that all empirical studies are based on. Such clarifications are especially important in LIS as an inter-disciplinary endeavor. In making this claim, we continue an on-going discussion that is exemplified also in the proceedings of previous CoLIS conferences.

---

[1] We have put quotation marks around "information needs" and "relevance" so as to indicate that our focus is on how these concepts are *used* in different LIS practices, and not on providing any absolute or essentialist definitions. To improve readability, we only use quotation marks the first time the concepts are introduced, but the reader should bear this remark in mind.

2   Three Approaches to Information Needs, Relevance and Instrumentality

Concerning the question of the purpose of information seeking, the answer is usually given that this purpose is an expression of the user requiring information in some way, which often includes both the user's explicitly stated wishes – her *wants* – and those wishes that the user possesses, albeit not consciously recognizes – her *needs*. A search in LISA on information needs reveals that this concept has drawn a lot of both empirical and theoretical attention in LIS. Already in 1981, Tom Wilson states in his frequently cited article *On user studies and information needs*, that since the institutionalization of user studies in 1948 through the Royal Society Scientific Information Conference, the development of a theoretical understanding of information needs has not been attained. The concept of need connotes a psycho-logical way of describing the reason for which users decide to seek information and why they prefer certain resources over others. This psychological framework includes how the issue of relevance is dealt with. What has happened since Wilson wrote his article is that the psychological approach has become dominant.

Tom Wilson [4] showed, in spite of his interest in primarily psychological aspects of the concept and even though he wanted to avoid the concept of information need itself, how both socially and individually oriented aspects of information needs should be considered. In Wilson's own writing, social aspects could be exemplified by his deployment of the concept of "dominance". Wilson stated that:

> *Because the situations in which information is sought and used are social situations, however, purely cognitive conceptions of information need are probably inadequate for some research purposes in information science, but not for all.* [4, p. 9]

Despite Wilson's argument that was presented so many years ago, social aspects of information needs and relevance assessments have not been explored to any great extent. As a symptomatic indication of this state of affairs, individual aspects are very prominent when Donald Case [5] in his recent book summarizes IS literature. For example, Case's book does not include any discussion at all of the social aspects of relevance assessments. This exclusion is not stated explicitly. Still, different epistemological approaches always – explicitly or implicitly – mediate specific views on how information needs are formed and satisfied by information, which is assessed as relevant from this specific viewpoint.

In the following, we briefly and schematically describe how information needs and relevance are dealt with in LIS. In this presentation, we use the mediated view on the origin of an information need in order to illustrate three different approaches: the structure approach, the individual approach and the communication approach. These approaches are based on different epistemological claims concerning how information needs and relevance should be defined, and they include different views on instrumentality. The three approaches can be labeled as metatheories, and have as such been described in LIS research literature [6], [7], [8], [cf. 9]. Our categorization differs from the one commonly applied in LIS which takes the research perspective (that is, user or system) as its point of departure. We wish to emphasize that our application of these approaches to the issues of information needs and relevance should be regarded as ideal types, that is, as abstracted simplifications of what is in fact various, nuanced and seminal research approaches.

When we refer to specific researchers in exemplifying these ideal types, it is important to note that we do not intend to identify the individual researcher with the ideal typical definitions given.

2.1 The Structure Approach

The structure approach builds upon a distinction between expressed wants and unconscious collective needs, a distinction which is made against the backdrop of an epistemology that gives precedence to social *structures*. This realist epistemology emphasizes the shaping of human behavior as the result of social structures in society, such as class, education, gender or ethnicity. The structure approach entails a collectivist view of knowledge as something that is defined socially, for example as the result of the division of labor in society.

The structure approach often views information needs as "objective" in relation to a specific knowledge domain, academic discipline or profession [e.g.10], [e.g. 11]. There are always given solutions to the problems specific for a certain practice, from which it follows that it is possible to more or less objectively define information needs and, thus, relevance. Concerning empirical studies, the approach, as traditionally applied in user studies, usually prefers large surveys where relations between structural factors and behaviors, alternatively experiences, can be "discovered" [12], [13]. This can be exemplified with one of the research questions in Maurice Line's report from the, at that time ground breaking, INFROSS project: "/.../ did the basic pattern of information need divide according to discipline, or according to environment, or what?" [13, p. 415]. Individual information seeking practices can from this perspective be supported by information systems or by the working methods of LIS professionals, which primarily contribute to making the basically "objective" information needs of the user visible. The user can thus be more or less aware of her/his own needs.

From the point of view of the structure approach, information seeking is portrayed as something that is enacted in practices whose rationality is defined at the collective, and not at the individual level. Information is often treated – in accordance with the conduit metaphor – as something that represents an external reality. Accordingly, information seeking is seen as the transferring of facts or opinions from information systems to individuals. If the information need is regarded as something objective, it follows that relevance can be assessed in an objective[2] manner. The important point to make here, is that the kind of *instrumentality* which this approach illustrates goes beyond the objectives of single individuals. Instead, it portrays socially oriented objectives produced within different contexts as something that determines the actions of the individual. To oversimplify, context is here defined as

---

[2] However, when objective relevance is discussed in research on relevance, it is from the point of departure of a *system* driven approach where relevance is seen as a relation between query representation and "content" of retrieved information. A system driven approach is out of scope for this paper. See Borlund [14] for a thorough discussion of this issue. When we use the term "objective" in this paper, we instead refer to a specific view on the relation between human knowledge and the world.

social structures that determine the individual's range of action. In IS research, this approach has not been dominant since the 1970's.

2.2 The Individual Approach

Towards the end of the 1970's and in the beginning of the 1980's, research based on the structure approach increasingly received criticism from the international research community. A recurrent theme in this critique was that a research focus on structures positioned the information system ahead of the user [e.g. 15], [e.g. 16]. With this critique as its point of departure, a user-centered epistemological approach, which gave precedence to the individual, grew stronger. Instead of measuring the information needs, seeking and use of different groups, like the structure approach recommends, the individual approach mediates an interest in how single individuals construct meaning through more or less dynamic information seeking processes. A prominent tradition in this approach, among others, is the cognitive viewpoint [17]. With this viewpoint in mind, an information need can, somewhat simplified, be seen as an expression of a "deficiency" in the cognitive structures of an active individual when faced with a problem solving situation, for example the solving of a specific work task. An observation to be made in connection to this is that the cognitive viewpoint positions structures in a cognitive framework instead of a societal one.

The kind of instrumentality that develops from this viewpoint focuses on individually formed objectives, created in relation to specific tasks solved in specific and, from our point of view, narrowly defined situations. Hence, information seeking is regarded as the expression of a rational practice, in the sense of being founded in the individual's ability to apply the faculty of reason when solving a task. With this said, it is important to recognize research in this approach that has also included affective aspects [18]. Furthermore, another theme in the individual approach is how individuals' information needs and relevance assessments develop dynamically over time in the process of information seeking [e.g. 19]. As in the structure approach, information seeking tends to be illustrated and analyzed with the conduit metaphor as point of departure, but the content of the information is assessed according to the effect it has on the cognitive structures of the active user, rather than according to external and objective criteria. The individual approach thus relies on idealist assumptions about the relation between human knowledge and the world.

The individual's information seeking process can be supported by information systems or the working methods of LIS professionals, which primarily help to make the individual aware of the character of her information need. Relevance is from this perspective defined and assessed by the individual user in relation to task solving. Such a view on relevance has been dominant since the 1990's and it has been presented in the form of different types where each type includes a particular focus [20]. A recent trend can be exemplified by Pia Borlund [14] who highlights "situational relevance" as the most fruitful type, building on the writings of Patrick Wilson. Context is by Borlund positioned in the mind of the user and it is narrowly defined in the following manner:

The context, i.e. the user's perception of a (work task) situation, is a psychological construct that represents the user's assumptions about the world at a given moment. [14, p. 922]

We will now proceed to what we regard as an important and complementary perspective to the two already introduced.

2.3 The Communication Approach

The third approach gives precedence to *communication*. This approach argues that different knowledge claims and, hence, information needs and relevance, are formed through linguistically communicated processes of negotiation. There are several more specific theoretical traditions which would agree with this assumption, for example discourse analysis [21], [22], but we want to make a case for neo-pragmatism. Pragmatism and neo-pragmatism has been touched upon before in IS research [23, p. 3], [24, p. 89], [8, p. 278] and recently, it has been more thoroughly introduced by Sundin and Johannisson [25]. Neo-pragmatism, which is dealt with in more detail in the next section, proceeds from the linguistic turn in the human and social sciences and, in addition, it acknowledges a fundamental instrumentality in the sense that all human beings always act with a specific objective in mind. While the individual and structuralist approaches encompass instrumentality as an implicit assumption, neo-pragmatism makes this assumption explicit. In doing so, neo-pragmatism provides a helpful tool when dealing with the kind of instrumentality that characterizes LIS practices, and, in this case, information seeking practices.

From a neo-pragmatist viewpoint, information seeking (including the shaping of information needs and relevance assessments) is a social practice. A social practice is defined here as an institutionalized activity that consists of more or less formal sets of rules concerning, among other things, what should be considered "proper" information seeking. The institutionalization of social practices takes place in different communities of justification. This is where the sets of rules are negotiated and become formalized. These processes of negotiation are enacted through the linguistic use that individual agents/groups of agents make of different social interests. In other words, the significance of information seeking, information needs and the relevance of information should be regarded as formed through negotiations within different communities of justification. For example, in the nursing profession, professional information and information seeking practices have proven to be useful tools in the professional project of nursing [26]. The professional information of nursing symbolizes the maturity of nursing as a profession in its own right, based on a knowledge system of its own. The new professional identity of nursing, which is negotiated and mediated through the nursing literature and training, constructs the nurse as an "information seeking professional" who uses nursing research as a foundation for her work.

The communication approach shares the interest in the social aspects of information seeking practices that is emphasized in the structure approach. But we argue that the neo-pragmatist tool is more suitable in order to illustrate the contingent character of the social, that is, the possibilities for a single individual, or for groups of individuals to, in historically and geographically specific situations, influence the shaping of the social. It also enables a different and complementary view on the role of information. Instead of seeing information as something that is transferred from one person or information system to another, information is a tool for the mediation of the rules that apply within different communities of justification [25].

The communication approach proposes a dialogic view of identity, knowledge formation and other social practices that unites an interest in the social aspects of information seeking practices with an interest in how individuals act upon the social by using linguistic and physical tools. It is in order to create such a deepened understanding of the interplay between individuals and the contexts that these individuals contribute to creating, while at the same time being regulated by them, that we want to introduce a neo-pragmatist approach inspired by Foucault. Such an approach also has consequences for the working methods of LIS professionals; in user education, for example, it emphasizes that one of the most important elements of such practices is to mediate an understanding of how information is assessed as relevant within different communities of justification. User education carried out along these lines creates an awareness of cognitive authorities [cf. 27] concerning the assessment of information resources within these communities. In the following, we will briefly introduce our deployment of a communication approach, that is, a neo-pragmatist approach supplemented with a Foucauldian notion of power.

3 Neo-pragmatism, Communities of Justification and Governmentality

According to neo-pragmatism, the question we should be interested in is not whether a specific knowledge claim is "true" or not, but whether it is useful, for whom and for what purpose; knowledge is a tool for action and not something waiting to be discovered. Humans actively interact with their environment in order to obtain their goals by using the tools that this environment offers, which illustrates the basic instrumentalist assumption of pragmatism. These tools are developed within so-called communities of justification that give them meaning, and the same tools can have different meanings within different communities of justification. Rorty [28, pp. 24, 35] argues that language is the most important tool available to human beings. He wants to override the traditional and unfruitful dichotomy between reality and linguistic representations of this reality and focus on how knowledge of the world is given legitimacy. Neo-pragmatism could thus perhaps best be described as a post-epistemology [29].

To Rorty, different knowledge claims are given legitimacy within different communities of justification. It is in these arenas that the validity of specific knowledge claims is decided upon, an assumption that also entails a view of how relevance is assessed in LIS practices:

> [J]ustification is not a matter of a special relation between ideas (or words) and objects, but of conversation, of social practice. /---/ The crucial premise of this argument is that we understand knowledge when we understand the social justification of belief and thus have no need to view it as accuracy of representation. [1, p. 170]

From a neo-pragmatist standpoint, information seeking practices are always enacted against the backdrop of different knowledge claims, negotiated in different communities of justification. If specific knowledge claims are judged in different, and sometimes conflicting, communities of justification, it means that information needs and relevance should be regarded as the results of linguistically communicated processes of negotiation. Hence, if we want to understand how information needs and relevance are shaped, we have to explore how different communities of justification – the different contexts – that surround information seeking practices work. An understanding of users' information needs and relevance assessments should, from this perspective, start in an understanding of the communities of justification the users participate in. Such a view gives priority to the study of the individual user as an active agent, positioned in different communities of justification that provide the tools by which the user gives meaning to different tasks and situations.

Rorty's neo-pragmatist approach acknowledges the instrumental character of all human action. We regard communities of justification as a fruitful way of visualizing those discursive arenas – that is, those contexts – where the criteria against which instrumentality is judged are negotiated. The concept therefore provides an important tool when trying to understand the formation of information needs and relevance. But as we have already pointed out, Rorty's approach is somewhat insufficient when you want to identify and explore the potential conflicts of interest both within and between different communities of justification. As a remedy for this weakness, we want to explore power issues with the help of Foucault.

The individual approach, where the solving of narrowly defined tasks is put at the fore, runs the risk of not recognizing conflicts and, hence, the power relations that permeate the construction of the task and its possible solutions [e.g. 6, p.761]. Therefore, a discussion of power can contribute to an understanding of why certain information resources are considered more useful than others, why certain information is considered more relevant than other, and the criteria against which such assessments are made. Research performed with the structure approach has already shown that, for example, professions, academic disciplines and knowledge domains play an importing part in establishing those criteria. To explore how competing epistemologies and methodologies of research are used as instruments in this respect is therefore an interesting research question when dealing with information seeking practices. But we argue that it is important not to reproduce the view that, for example, academic disciplines determine the conduct of individuals in an "objective" manner, thereby manifesting a realist epistemological approach.

Rorty [28, p. 69] himself refers to Foucault when he argues that power is not to be considered as something always oppressive and negative. We agree with Rorty in acknowledging that Foucault's greatest contribution concerning power issues is precisely that he shows that power can be enacted in various ways, in various situations, and by various people; power relations permeate our life worlds and are productive in that they create social practices. In spite of his wide definition of power, Foucault has been criticized for not allowing single individuals any agency as to influencing the disciplinary mechanisms that regulate their life worlds. Foucault has met this critique by defining power, as opposed to mere physical violence or dominance, as something that can only be exercised over individuals with the potential to act freely in a number of ways [30, p. 97ff.]. We find that this conceptualization of power nicely illustrates the dialogic character of the relation between individuals and the contexts that simultaneously form and are formed by those individuals. It also illustrates the importance of language in these processes of negotiation.

Both theoretically and empirically, Foucault has explored how different power relations are shaped and enacted. From the perspective of the social sciences we find, like many others, that Foucault's [3] way of dealing with power in terms of *governmentality* provides the most fruitful approach. According to Nikolas Rose, Foucault provided methodological recommendations that

> */.../ defined their problemspace in terms of government, understood, in the words of Foucault's much cited maxim, as 'the conduct of conduct'. Government, here, refers to all endeavours to shape, guide, direct the conduct of others, whether these be the crew of a ship, the members of a household, the employees of a boss, the children of a family or the inhabitants of a territory. And it also embraces the ways in which one might be urged and educated to bridle one's own passions, to control one's own instincts, to govern oneself.* [31, p. 4]

The quote above illustrates a methodological approach to power which both emphasizes that governing practices are heterogeneous and that those who are governed are active contributors to these practices, just as those who govern. To the list of examples of groups that are involved in governing practices it is easy to add users of information. How different users engage in information seeking practices is partly dependent on how information needs and relevance are shaped by those who provide the conditions for those practices. This could be exemplified by how text books on information seeking mediate views on the professional expertise of librarians and the position of the user [c.f. 32]. By studying these different agents – users, mediators and producers – in relation to each other, a deeper understanding of the governing practices at work when information needs and relevance are created, sustained and transformed can be obtained.

In the governing of information needs and relevance it is not only the users of information who shape the objectives of their information seeking practices. The objectives of the producers and the mediators of the conditions for information seeking are equally influential; "Practices of government are deliberate attempts to shape conduct in certain ways in relation to certain objectives" [31, p. 4]. Governing practices are thus always instrumental, regardless of which agent that enacts them [3, p. 93], [30, p. 147]. In LIS, instrumentality is inherent both in the individual and the structure approach but focus has been put either on individual objectives or on objectives of social institutions. This means that emphasis has been put *either* on the experienced wants or unconscious needs of individual users *or* on the social structures that are portrayed as governing the wants and needs of individual users. Instead we wish to emphasize the dialogic relation between these two analytical levels. It is through such a double analysis that the conflicts between different objectives, shaped in different communities of justification, can be identified and explored.

We will now conclude with some remarks on the implications of this approach for LIS research.

4 Concluding Remarks

Research with an individual approach to information needs and relevance has produced significant contributions to our understanding of how individual human beings, actively engaged in information seeking activities, construct meaning from information. The instrumentality of information needs and relevance is in this approach based on objectives formed in the individual mind. In this paper, though, we argue that the dominant view of today on information needs as an expression of a deficiency in individual cognitive structures in relation to the solving of a specific task in specific and narrowly defined situations is insufficient. This insufficiency includes how the issue of relevance is dealt with, even when developed and labeled as situational relevance. The definition of context that follows from this approach is too narrow to include power relations. Instead, we argue that a certain task or situation is given meaning when it is seen as part of a specific community of justification.

Research with a structure approach emphasizes the importance of the social level in information seeking practices, but the relation between social structures and individuals are, from our point of view, given far too determining a character. In this approach, social structures – that is, contexts – force individuals to act in a certain way. Furthermore, it entails the realist assumption that both information needs and relevance can be assessed in a more or less objective way. The formation of objectives lies beyond the control of individual agency, thereby positioning the instrumentality of information needs and relevance in social structures alone. Instead, we argue that a more nuanced understanding of human' information needs and relevance assessments can be reached by focusing on information needs and relevance assessments as elements of a simultaneously regulated and regulating practice. The governing practices through which this regulation is enacted take place in different communities of justification. Thinking of contexts in terms of communities of justification positions instrumentality in the dialogic interplay between individual agency and social interests.

A methodological consequence of our approach would be to focus on how governing practices are enacted within specific communities of justification. Here, what is considered to be the expertise within this community, and which cognitive authorities that are considered to possess this expertise, is of utmost importance. Concerning information needs and relevance, various cognitive authorities contribute with different kinds of expertise. For example, in health care an expertise built on a biomedical perspective often conflicts with a psychodynamic one in the practice of diagnosing mental illness. In line with this, there are specific sets of tools that create information needs and the criteria against which the relevance of information is assessed; thus, tools both embody and mediate governing practices. Such tools can be exemplified by articles in scientific journals, classification systems and thesauri that mediate the above mentioned conflicting forms of expertise, including a preferred hierarchical ordering and "objectification" of different knowledge claims. A methodological focus on tools and governing practices helps to illustrate the dialogic relation between individuals who actively make use of the tools and the environment that offers these tools.

By including the social level, we also want to further the possibilities for LIS researchers to increasingly transgress the boundaries of other social sciences in dealing with important empirical questions. LIS emanates from instrumental concerns, that is, the creation and continuing improvement of information services and systems. In order to further these aims it is important to have a dialogue with other social sciences so that LIS does not run the risk of trying to invent the wheel again. But it is equally important to recognize that LIS entails exclusive issues and in order to create a deeper understanding of these it is crucial to improve the dialogue with LIS professionals. To them the importance of the social level that we have argued for in this paper is already evident since knowledge of users and information systems is always imbedded in those different institutional settings where these professionals work. Thus, an improved dialogue between LIS researchers and practitioners would help to show the necessity of including the social and communicative aspects of information seeking practices, no matter if these practices are carried out in the professional field or the field of research.

References

1. Rorty, R.: Philosophy and the Mirror of Nature. Princeton University Press, Princeton, N.J. (1979)
2. Mouffe, C.: Deconstruction, pragmatism and the politics of democracy. In: Mouffe, C. (ed.): Deconstruction and Pragmatism. Routledge, London (1996) 1-12
3. Foucault, M.: Governmentality. In: Burchell, G. et al. (eds.): The Foucault Effect: Studies in Governmentality. The University of Chicago Press, Chicago (1991) 87-104
4. Wilson, T.: On user studies and information needs. Journal of Documentation 37 (1981) 3-15
5. Case, D.: Looking for Information: A Survey of Research on Information Seeking, Needs, and Behavior. Academic Press, Amsterdam (2002)
6. Talja, S., Keso, H., Pietiläinen, T.: The Production of 'Context' in Information Seeking Research: A Metatheoretical View. Information Processing and Management 35 (1999) 751-763
7. Talja, S., Tuominen, K., Savolainen, R.: "Isms" in Information Science: Constructivism, Collectivism and Constructionism. Journal of Documentation 61 (2005) 79-101
8. Tuominen, K., Talja, S., Savolainen, R.: Discourse, Cognition and Reality: Towards a Social Constructionist Metatheory for Library and Information Science. In: Bruce, H., Fidel, R., Ingwersen, P., Vakkari, P. (eds.): Proceedings of the Fourth International Conference on Conceptions of Library and Information Science (CoLIS): Emerging Frameworks and Methods. Libraries Unlimited, Greenwood Village (2002) 271-283
9. Pettigrew, K.E., Fiedel, R., Bruce, H.: Conceptual Frameworks in Information Behaviour. In: Williams, M. (ed.): Annual Review of Information Science and Technology, Vol. 35. Information Today Inc., Medford, N.J. (2001) 43-78
10. Hjørland, B., Albrechtsen, H.: Toward a New Horizon in Information Science: Domain-Analysis. Journal of the American Society for Information Science 46 (1995) 400-425
11. Taylor, R.S.: Information Use Environments. In: Dervin, B. (ed.): Progress in Communication Sciences, Vol. 10. Ablex. P., Norwood, N.J. (1991) 217-255
12. Marcella, R., Baxter, J.: The Information Needs and the Information Seeking Behaviour of a National Sample of the Population in the United Kingdom, with Special References to Needs Related to Citizenship. Journal of Documentation 55 (1999) 159-183
13. Line, M.B.: The Information Uses and Needs of Social Scientists: an Overview of INFROSS. Aslib Proceedings 23 (1971) 412-434

14. Borlund, P.: The Concept of Relevance in IR. Journal of the American Society for Information Science and Technology **54** (2003) 913-925
15. Belkin, N.: Anomalous States of Knowledge as a Basis for Information Retrieval. Canadian Journal of Information Sciences **5** (1980) 133-143
16. Dervin, B.: Useful Theory for Librarianship: Communication, not Information. Drexel Library Quarterly **13** (1977) 16-32
17. Ingwersen, P.: Cognitive Perspectives of Information Retrieval Interaction: Elements of a Cognitive IR Theory. Journal of Documentation **52** (1996) 3-50
18. Kuhlthau, C.C.: Inside the Search Process: Information Seeking from the Users' Perspective. Journal of the American Society for Information Science **42** (1991) 361-371
19. Schamber, L., Eisenberg, M.B., Nilan, M.S.: A Re-examination of Relevance: Toward a Dynamic, Situational Definition. Information Processing & Management **26** (1990) 755-775
20. Saracevic, T.: Relevance Reconsidered '96. In: Ingwersen, P., Pors, N.O. (eds.): Proceedings of CoLIS 2, Second International Conference of Library and Information Science: Integration in Perspective. Royal School of Librarianship, Copenhagen (1996) 201-218
21. McKenzie, P.: Positioning Theory and the Negotiation of Information Needs in a Clinical Midwifery Setting. Journal of the American Society for Information Science and Technology **55** (2004) 685-694
22. Talja, S.: Constituting "Information" and "User" as Research Objects: a Theory of Knowledge Formations as an Alternative to the Information Man-Theory. In: Vakkari, P., Savolainen, R., Dervin, B. (eds.): Information Seeking in Context (ISIC). Proceedings of an International Conference on Research in Information Needs, Seeking and Use in Different Contexts. Taylor Graham, London (1997) 67-80
23. Hjørland, B.: Information Seeking and Subject Representation: an Activity-Theoretical Approach to Information Science. Greenwood Press, Westport, Conn. (1997)
24. Tuominen, K., Savolainen, R.: A Social Constructionist Approach to the Study of Information Use as Discursive Action. In: Vakkari, P., Savolainen, R., Dervin, B. (eds.): Information Seeking in Context (ISIC). Proceedings of an International Conference on Research in Information Needs, Seeking and Use in Different Contexts. Taylor Graham, London (1997) 81-96
25. Sundin, O., Johannisson, J.: Pragmatism, Neo-pragmatism and Sociocultural Theory: Communicative Participation as a Perspective in LIS. Journal of Documentation **61** (2005) 23-43
26. Sundin, O.: Towards an Understanding of Symbolic Aspects of Professional Information: an Analysis of the Nursing Knowledge Domain. Knowledge Organization **30** (2003) 170-181
27. Wilson, P.: Second-Hand Knowledge: an Inquiry into Cognitive Authority. Greenwood Press, Westport, Conn. (1983)
28. Rorty, R.: Philosophy and Social Hope. Penguin Books, London (1999)
29. Malachowski, A.: Richard Rorty. Princeton University Press, Princeton, N.J. (2002)
30. Hindess, B.: Discourses of Power: From Hobbes to Foucault. Blackwell, Oxford (1996)
31. Rose, N.: Powers of Freedom: Reframing Political Thought. Cambridge University Press, New York (1999)
32. Tuominen, K.: User-Centered Discourse: an Analysis of the Subject Positions of the User and the Librarian. Library Quarterly **67** (1997) 350-371

Lifeworld and Meaning - Information in Relation to Context

Janne Backlund

Library & Information Science,
Department of Archives, Libraries and Museums,
University of Uppsala
Janne.Backlund@abm.uu.se

Abstract. This paper proposes a concept of information defined as semantic links to a meaning external to the information, located in the structure of the lifeworld. In building upon Habermas' *Theory of Communicative Action*, the progress of linguistically coordinated action in the lifeworld through speech acts connected with claims of validity is briefly described. The claim is put forward that the meaning of a statement or an artefact can only be determined through communicative action since all information is semantically contextualized in the lifeworld, the basic structure of society within which the reproduction of world views and cultural traditions occurs. However, communicative rationality shapes social institutions into a system of growing complexity that exerts pressure on the lifeworld, increasing the need for communicative action. The function of facilitating the evaluation of validity claims makes access to information necessary for consensus formation and action coordination, thereby emphasizing the significance of IS. The paper presents a model of contextualized praxis as it concludes that information specialists must act communicatively.

1 Introduction

There are indications that a paradigm shift is underway in the social science and, to some extent, in the humanities as well. Over roughly the last two decades the empirical/positivist influence seems to have given way to theoretical perspectives grounded on different presuppositions of reality, which has suddenly become a much more *social* reality. The trend is even visible in the philosophy of science (Bryant, 2000). Postmodern theories paved the way for this change, followed by renewed versions of such older views as pragmatism, critical theory, speech act theory, and so forth. A majority of these new enrichments share a body of basic epistemological assumptions that influence their theoretical frameworks more or less radically. Some of these common assumptions are that truth is an inter-subjective acceptance, (social) reality is a construct, and language is the central, structural element in culture and society. In addition, interpretation has come to the fore as the main method for reaching an understanding of (social) reality. In comparison with the relatively uncomplicated objective conception of facts in positivist thinking, the more realistic

F. Crestani and I. Ruthven (Eds.): CoLIS 2005, LNCS 3507, pp. 119 – 140, 2005.
© Springer-Verlag Berlin Heidelberg 2005

views of society that have emerged from the new perspectives are far more complex, with relativistic meanings, discourse dependent explanations, etc. It is not surprising, therefore, that concepts such as meaning and context draw a great deal of attention today. In this respect, I intend to illuminate the context dependency of information and indicate its relation to meaning in the following discussion.

In addition, the interest in social context and in new theoretical perspectives appears to be growing in IS and related sciences. This trend is visible even in such a technology driven area as information systems and management. For example, the *Journal of Information Technology* dedicated two special issues in 2002 to what they term "critical approaches to information systems research," while a great deal of critical theory has been explored in reference to a wide variety of thinkers, including Habermas, Foucault, Latour, Heidegger, and others (Brooke 2002, p. 179). The contributions in question may all be characterized as attempts to establish a social viewpoint for a variety of problems concerning management, communication, and information. Varey, Wood-Harper and Wood, in their somewhat confusing article concerning information systems and critical communication theory, criticize positivist approaches in the field for applying purposive rational views to the design of systems that are communicatively oriented. They instead propose "a recursive system for understanding" based on communicative action (2002, pp. 229-239). Andrew Basden introduces a Dutch philosopher with critical ambitions and applies a set of criteria developed by Klein to test whether this philosopher in fact fits into the critical approach that originates with Habermas. Basden is coherent in his presentation, but he unfortunately demonstrates a poor grasp of the Habermasian universe, a deficiency that is perhaps easy to overlook in light of his enthusiasm and evident interest in social matters (2002, pp. 257-269).

While these two brief examples, more or less randomly chosen, are of poor quality when viewed as applications of social theory, they nevertheless represent an undertaking in a field where the type of social awareness they represent may not be expected.

Moreover, the interest that has been demonstrated in social matters raises the issue of whether it is possible to integrate the field of IS with a complete social theoretical framework, a task which the present paper addresses. Internally developed, specific theoretical foundations are, as a rule, absent from young and relatively immature fields like IS, not to mention many traditional disciplines, too. However, while older scholarly fields that have no specific theoretical ground can rely on tradition, this shortcoming is felt to be a problem in younger ones. Although many fields and disciplines when scrutinized carefully can indeed be seen to have no solid foundation in the sense of a rationally constructed system of beliefs that exclusively guides the majority of the activities in that particular field, it is the case that fields and disciplines within the social sciences and humanities are in fact often based on either a single or a many faceted theme. My position is that IS, as a young science, should focus on certain themes such as information, libraries, documents, etc., and not waste energy on developing an exclusive theory of its own. We ought to do as many of the other disciplines have done, namely, find proper theories elsewhere, which is in fact what most of us are already doing. My contribution in this regard will be an attempt to connect IS to Jürgen Habermas' *Theory of Communicative Action* (*TCA*). This will be done by means of a not overly complicated elaboration of the concept of information such that it can take its place as an element of that theory. Since in this short paper there is obviously no room for a thorough investigation of this matter, I will confine myself to only a few important themes relevant to IS. In particular, meaning and context will together comprise the main theme of the discussion, and I intend to shed light on this issue by means of the concept of lifeworld in *TCA*.

It can be said with a certain justification that the development of a contextual view has already been underway in IS for quite some time. It is well known that information retrieval research initially focused on machines with an almost total disregard of even the slightest hint of surroundings. User studies then evolved such that computers were supplied with at least a system environment, if not a context, and certain approaches took up the issue of an interface between the personality system and the IR-system. But since IS was deeply rooted in the meagre soil of positivism, the advancement of an articulated recognition of the context proceeded slowly. In parallel with this progress, however, there has always existed research with other perspectives in IS, perhaps especially within knowledge organization. An early but still modern example with an articulated semantic point of view is an article by Bernard Frohman in which he utilizes CRG:s classificatory principles in order to critique Derek Austin's proposal concerning the difference between machine-compatible classifications and traditional ones. Insofar as Frohman's theoretical framework is based on the later Wittgenstein's theory of language games, the complex relation between meaning and context more or less by itself moves into the argumentative framework (1983, pp. 11-27).

More recently, context has attracted renewed interest in an area of research within IS that deals with information need, seeking, and use, which at times is shortened to INSU. This field is sometimes applying pedagogical views probably because the role of an information service is to be a mediators in a fashion that resembles the mediating properties of education. The perspective of the user may be either individualistic, collectivist, or both. To a certain extent it is relevant to say that the the interest in the tools in information services is secondary to the user. The overall goal is however to improve services by means of better knowledge on users and their needs. An early proponent of this view is Carol Kuhlthau, and the very title of her principal publication in this regard, *Seeking Meaning*, reveals the change of perspective of the approach in question. Even though she does not use the term "context," it is evident that the typically individual user is located within an environment that influences her/his quest, not for information, but meaning (1993, pp. 1-13). Bruces *Seven faces of information literacy* discusses the competences necessary in the information society and points out the pedagogical issue of mediating them (1997).

An overview by Barbara Wildemuth of articles presented at a symposium on methods in 'information seeking and use' clearly illustrates that the six articles presented all use methods that involve an elaborated recognition of the dependency on context. Some are more advanced in this respect, such as the one that applies participatory action research in a project to improve health information services, while another is basically a quantitative mass study of web use with prepared search questions. Nevertheless, even the latter utilizes interviews as well. From Wildemuth's review it appears that none of the articles explicitly thematizes the problematic of context dependency, although this may well be the case in the full texts (2002, pp. 1218-1219).

In Sweden, too, the new theoretical views are gaining ground in IS, both in information seeking and use, and in other approaches. For example, Limberg investigates the ways in which high school students acquire and use information during a special assignment. Her study reveals how their cognitive views of the problematic they are faced with steer them towards matching *types* of information, which are concise and authoritative when view is factual, and narrative and argumentative when view is analytical. The interpretative method used is, of course, situated in respect to the context (1998; 1999, pp. 116-135). Sundin examined the strategies in information use among a specific professional group (nurses), using discourse analysis with a social constructivist perspective (2003). It is also necessary to mention Hansson's thorough investigation of the SAB Swedish classification system, in which he employed an approach that takes meaning to be embedded in a social and historical context (1999).

Birger Hjørland has developed the context oriented view into the domain analytic perspective, which provides a framework for theory and practice in IS. He differs in many ways from the former approaches mentioned, one of which involves his direct interest in improving IS tools. Hjørland claims that the use and production of information take place in groups of individuals with more or less shared knowledge interests. The collectives they form constitute knowledge domains, which should be studied in IS in respect to the underlying theories, the structure, and the content of the knowledge representations produced. Hjørland's aim is to improve the tools used in information seeking and, consequently, information services themselves. This view is certainly oriented towards the context, and one basic conception is that information acquires its meaning within the domains, or context, a notion that Hjørland outlines under the influence of pragmatic semantic theory. He explicitly refers to the later Wittgenstein, but also points to Peirce and Dewey as forerunners (1997, pp. 20-22). Hjørland states that Wittgenstein later theory constitutes an abandonment of his earlier empirical/positivist position in which he maintained that words gain their meaning from the things they represent. He instead advanced a theory of language games proceeding from the philosophy of language and pragmatism. Briefly stated, Wittgenstein's later theory implies that the meaning of words is not fixed in a simple object—designation relation, but rather evolves and changes through the use of language. Hjørland states that Wittgenstein's earlier views are common in IR, not least of all because it is more convenient to create tools for information seeking when the meanings of words are fixed, but he is also careful to indicate that the principles based on such a view are not wrong. On the contrary, these principles have been used successfully by many information seekers. Nevertheless, IS will be able to create more sophisticated principles for IR if it recognizes the need for a more elaborated semantic theory (1997, pp. 18-19).

In *TCA* Habermas formulates a description and explanation of the modern society on formal pragmatic grounds that relies greatly on the later Wittgenstein's semantic theory and on an intersubjective concept of truth (Reese-Schäfer 1991, pp. 25-44). Building upon the theory of speech acts, Habermas formulates what I find to be a convincing explanation of how mankind understand the world, themselves, and others through language. Through a critical reconstruction of both previous and con-temporary thinkers, *TCA* leads to a theory that explains society from a dual perspective; the *lifeworld* with the concrete side of socal life, linguistic communication, interpretation and the creation of meaning; and the *system* with the abstract, general, and formal side of society. An important point of departure for Habermas is the conviction that the Enlightenment is not an historically exhausted phenomenon that only explains the development of Western society up to a certain point. In opposition to such postmodern thinkers as Derrida and Foucault, the Enlightenment idea of a rationally acting human being capable of building and developing society is still vivid with Habermas, and he considers it to be a project worthy of preservation and enhancement. His contribution resides in the formulation of formal pragmatics and communicative rationality, which I take as meaning that mankind in the lifeworld can reach mutual understanding through reason and on common rational grounds also make the decisions necessary to steer events in a certain direction.

There are some features in the domain analytic perspective connecting it with TCA. In addition to the pragmatically influenced and context-oriented semantic basis, Hjørland makes several references to interpretation, an action-based view of knowledge, rationalization through the division of labor, value dependency, etc (1995, 2003b). I view his discussion as pointing towards a notion of IS that has ambitions far beyond making contributions "to the process of identifying those documents that can be of most value to the user's tasks" (Hjørland 1997, p. 27). Moreover, Hjørland together with Capurro in their critical of the concept of information broaden the task at hand such that "[t]he most important thing in IS [...] is to consider information as a constitutive force in society" (2003a, p. 345). Not only do I sympathize with both of these general goals of IS as they have been formulated by Hjørland, I do not see that there is any necessary opposition between them.

My intention in the present discussion is to utilize Habermas' theory to further illuminate the relation between information and context, partly through an investigation of the function fullfilled by information in the lifeworld, and partly through an effort to reveal the structures of meaning within it. *TCA* also offers the opportunity to critically examine information systems through the dual perspective of lifeworld and system, although the systems view is only touched upon in this paper. In my view, an integration of the views presented in *TCA* with IS reinforces the inherently emancipatory and socially critical relevance of the latter.

2   An Action Oriented Concept of Information

Traditionally, and in spite of certain early attempts to widen the perspective in documentation, IS has typically connected information with documents containing texts. In recent years this view has changed considerably, due first and foremost to the digital revolution, although the greater part of the IS domain remains occupied with text-based documents. This is not surprising insofar as the targets of the most important information services relevant for (L)IS, such as schools, universities, research institutes, large commercial organizations, culturally interested private citizens in the public domain, and so forth, are text producing and hence text consuming domains of action. In line with the majority of the many propositions for concepts of information in IS and elsewhere, the concept I wish to advance here is not restricted to documents carrying text. On the contrary, I maintain that virtually every entity in reality can take on the form of information when certain conditions are fulfilled.

Buckland accounts for a variety of views of what a document may be, and he is largely positive towards the broad definitions he presents (1997, pp. 804, 808; 1991, pp. 46-49). For example, he has uncovered connections with the ways signs are recognized in modern semiotics (1997, p. 805-808) in the definitions Paul Otlet and Suzanne Briet proposed in the early decades of the 20th century that treat as documents almost anything that represents ideas, concepts, objects, or phenomena, and he concludes that the evolving use of digital documents indeed calls for a broad definition of the concept. In many ways digital documents are even more difficult to grasp than some of the more problematic entities put forward as documents by Otlet and Briet, such as when the latter declare that the famous Zebra in the Zoo was a document (1997, p. 808).

I view information as constituting links to a meaning that is embedded in a context. Different types of artefacts, such as books, pictures, items, films, natural objects under specific conditions, and verbal utterances or gestures, may function as information by providing a link to a meaning in some given sequence of action. The meaning linked to is necessary in order to evaluate validity claims connected with speech acts raised in the action sequence. Speech acts can thus emanate from either a human participant or, virtually, from an artefact. The meaning the information links up with can only be reachable through action (interpretation, argumentation, and activity such as observation directed to physical or other objects and entities in reality) within the context of the lifeworld. This way of viewing information, which is inspired by Habermas, has the advantage of providing IS with access to a fully developed and powerful theoretical tool.

Case (2002) and Capurro & Hjørland (2003a) present comprehensive overviews of the concept of information in IS and other disciplines. Since the former is a textbook, it proceeds in a more practical way, with a critical attitude and precision suitable for our present needs, while the latter illuminate their inventory with a thorough etymology of the word information as well as an epistemological perspective. For example, Case states that the various attempts to define the concept fall into two categories, namely, those which are more specific and formally restricted, and those which are rather typologies of information than definition. The former are usually restricted to five basic premises: uncertainty, physicality, structure/process, intentionality, and truth. Case points out that placing emphasis upon a single premise tends to render the use of the concept more problematic. Stated otherwise, when the definition is overly restricted, either its space of execution is narrowed, or its explanatory power is weakened (2002, p. 50).

The view of information I propose falls into the first category and is, of course, restricted by the premise that Case terms structure/process. However, the loose definition utilized, i.e., links used for evaluating validity, focuses more on the function in action contexts than on the structures or processes themselves. It is true that the structure of the lifeworld and the communicative action in which information fulfills its function do restrict the use of the concept to a certain extent, and must do so, since everything is not always information. Knowledge in this regard is evidently not information even though it can function as information, and I reject perspectives that treat the structural relation to knowledge in a non-mediated fashion such that the latter is taken to constitute simple building blocks within the structure of the former. Such a view is not uncommon in cognitively informed orientations of IS. For example, not only does Brooke's famous mathematical expression of information in the form of an equation clearly define this reduction to structural similarity, it also demonstrates the affiliation to hard science and positivism typical of his time, and not only in IS.[1] The impact and enticement of this view can be demonstrated with Ingwerssen's elaboration of the equation. Despite his explicit remark that the mathematical expression should be seen as a model and that knowledge and information do not have the same dimension, the lingering impression to the reader is that of potential information as something which in a calculable way will build up a structure of knowledge (1996 s.96). It is evident, however that information plays a central role in actions in which knowledge is created, and this relation also manifests itself in the fact that intentionally produced knowledge representations comprise the most common information carrier dealt with in information services. The other premises Case mentions, including physicality, are also relevant in various ways since a book or other object may certainly be designated as information when it takes on the function of a link. In my view, however, the premises for and the properties of the proposed concept do not restrict the use of it in any problematic way. Among the many researchers in IS Case presents, C.J. Fox and Tor Nörrestrander seems to have touch upon context dependent views with some resemblance of mine (2002, p. 55).

Case's impressive inventory seems to have intimidated him since he ends up pleading that the concept of information should be left undefined as a primitive term (2002, pp. 42-59).

Capurro & Hjørland (2003) tackle the great number of proposed concepts of information with great scepticism, but they do indicate that for "a science like information science (IS), it is of course important how fundamental terms are defined" (p. 345). In principle, they state that one may define the concept as one wishes, but many different definitions make it more difficult to communicate relevant themes within the discipline. They also stress the importance of not using definitions that are too distant from the everyday use of words (p. 345).

From their etymology it appears that the oldest meaning is molding something with your hands from clay, i.e. to give form to something (p. 352). Cicero, they say, used the term "[...] in order to describe the active and a posteriori action of the mind depicting something unknown or helping memory, as part of the *ars memoriae*, to better remember a past situation through the pictorial representation of a sentence (*sententiae informatio*)." (Ibid.). A view in a sense similar with information as links. The meaning is not in the information but rather pointed out by it.

After some arguments for a wide definition, opening up for possible use in all areas of IS, they finally present their own view of the concept:

> Information is any thing that is of importance in answering a question. Anything can be information. In practice, however, information must be defined in relation to the needs of the target groups served by the information specialists, not in a universalistic or individualistic, but rather in a collectivist or particularistic fashion. Information is what can answer important questions related to the activities of the target group. (p. 390).

---

[1] The origins of this view is a theory that uses stochastic probability to calculate entropy in transmissions of information, developed by Shannon in the 1940s with the purpose of estimating needed capacity in signal cables.

They explicitly rejects the view of information as a thing, the reason being that information must be seen as something subjective, depending on interpretation of what they call a "cognitive agent", and continues: "The interpretative view shifts the attention from the attributes of things to the 'release mechanisms' for which those attributes are of importance" (pp. 396-397).

Capurro & Hjørland presents a concept with many characteristics in common with the one I have proposed. From their definition it's clear that the meaning of information is not fixed but determined from the use in a context. It is also clear that interpretation is the only way possible for reaching the meaning, in my view a kind of communicative activity. The function of answering questions, is not to distant from evaluating claims to validity either and as I will show below, Hjørland describes the function elswhere with even closer resemblance. They also reveal a social awareness close to the view of TCA.

3 Communicative Action and Speech Acts

The central idea of *TCA* is that man as a social being strives to understand and to be understood for the purpose of coming together in common actions in the world. Habermas identifies it as communicative action when we aim at mutual understanding by saying what is *true* in relation to the objective world, *right* in respect to norms and rules in the social world, and *truthful* in relation to our own subjective world. When these premises are fulfilled common actions anchored in communicative rationality may come to be. With common forces institutions is created which in a rational way facilitate production, distribution, consumption and so on in parallel with the reproduction of the lifeworld. A social machinery of growing complexity emerges with institutions, organizations and enterprises which at the same time facilitate the conditions for man as it threatens to capture her. From a systems perspective, Habermas' diagnosis is that the sub-systems of the social system colonize the lifeworld, distort the processes of reaching understanding, and threaten to medialize human relations. Indeed, never before has the need for as well as the demands placed upon communicative action been greater than in our modern society. The hope that we have resides in the fact that the possibilities for communication, including cognitive and cultural assets as well as technical prerequisites, are also greater. The outcome of the process is open-ended. Mankind always have a choice in respect to their possibilities for communication and the coordination of action, at least as long as the lifeworld does not collapse.

TCA is a normative theory and does not confine itself to a description and explanation of society, but rather *prescribes* what society should be, although not in a deterministic fashion like historical materialism. It is communicative action upon the basis of communicative rationality that constitutes the norm within the theory, or the universalistic claim prescribing the ways in which we as human beings should proceed when we act. We act in other ways as well, putting mutual understanding aside when we act strategically and manipulate our fellow human beings for the sake of our own self-interests. However, we always reorientate ourselves to communicative action in an intact lifeworld since such action is rational.

As stated above, it is in connection with the validity claims following every speech act that the concept of information put forward here hooks into the theory. A validity claim may be seen at one and the same time as a guarantee of as well as a demand for information, which reveals that this concept differs greatly from other definitions that consider anomalies and uncertainty to be central properties of information since *each and every* speech act is accompanied by claims to validity. The amount of information needed in even a simple conversation would thereby be enormous. But even if that were true to some extent, the difference in practice from other views need not be as great as it first might seem since most such claims are eliminated discretely, without the need for explicit references to some artefact, through the shared fond of cultural tradition and world views that create a common interpretative horizon of meaning in the lifeworld (Habermas 1981a, pp. 335-337). It's only in problematic situations when hearer rejects claims connected with speakers utterance, the   guarantee for information must be fulfilled to enable continuation of interaction(1981b, 125-126).

A few words about speech acts may be in order at this point before we proceed to a further elaboration of the concept of information proposed here.

The theory of speech acts utilizes three concepts to group such acts in respect to their aims, namely, locution for propositional speech (that S), illocution for speech that expresses an action (I hereby confess to you that S), and perlocution for unintended effects of speech of the other two types (ibid., p. 288). Habermas focuses on the group of illocutionary speech acts, stating that "I count as communicative action those linguistically mediated interactions in which all participants pursue illocutionary aims, and *only* illocutionary aims, with their mediating acts of communication" (ibid., 1981a, p. 295). Moreover, he criticizes Austin's view of perlocutionary effects as being too narrow since it actually includes another type of speech as well insofar as an illocutionary speech act may be used to conceal the strategic aims of action, such as when the speaker tries to manipulate the listener. The reason for this deficiency was that Austin was inclined to mix acts of communication with the interactions coordinated by speech acts. Habermas concludes that acts of communication are not the same as what the concept of communicative action is all about, which is action in the three worlds coordinated by communication (ibid., pp. 288-295).

Habermas also criticizes Searle's elaboration of Austin's classification of speech acts. Searle's underlying ontology, here presented in a simplified manner as reality understood as the totality of all states of affairs along with the actor/speaker standing beside it and acting against it, permits only two linguistically mediated relations between actor and world, namely, "the cognitive relation of ascertaining facts and the interventionist relation of realizing a goal of action" (ibid., p. 323). Speech acts representing institutional facts and expressions of psychological states has no place in this view since the ontology does not include the worlds in which they are anchored. In typically critical and re-constructive manner Habermas proposes that:

> We can avoid the difficulties of Searle's attempts at classification, while retaining his fruitful theoretical approach, if we start from the fact that illocutionary aims of speech acts are achieved through the inter-subjective recognition of claims to power or validity, and if, further, we introduce normative rightness and truthfullness as validity claims ana-logous to truth and interpret them too in terms of actor/world relations (ibid., p. 325).

Habermas finally reaches his own classification of speech acts on the basis of the three worlds ontology. He presents the following schema of linguistically mediated interaction in which the types of speech acts are accompanied by other formal pragmatic features. As can be seen, there are three types of action that are oriented towards understanding: conversation, normatively regulated action, and dramaturgical action. These three merge together into communicative action in the lifeworld, thereby setting free the power of communicative rationality.

Formal-pragmatic feature/ Types of action	Characteristic speech acts	Functions of speech	Action Orientation	Basic Attitudes	Validity Claims	World Relations
Strategic action	Perlocutions imperatives	Influencing one's opposite number	Oriented to success	Objectivating	(Effectiveness)	Objective world
Conversation	Constatives	Representation of states of affairs	Oriented to reaching understanding	Objectivating	Truth	Objective world
Normatively regulated action	Regulatives	Establishment of interpersonal relations	Oriented to reaching understanding	Norm-conformative	Rightness	Social world
Dramaturgical action	Expressive	Selfrepresentation	Oriented to reaching understanding	Expressive	Truthfullness	Subjective world

Fig. 1. Pure Types of Linguistically Mediated Interaction. Source: Habermas 1981a, p. 329

The concept of information proposed above states that information constitutes links to a meaning and is used to evaluate claims to validity. Habermas' schema categorizes each type of claim in relation to one of the three worlds, from which follows that the particular meaning indicated by a specific item of information as it fulfills its function is also related to a corresponding world. However, the information itself, taking the form of an artefact or some verbal utterance, cannot be related to any specific world. A reference in a text to another text may be conceived of as a kind of generalized claim to validity, such as an assurance that a proposition in the first text is true and thus linked to a meaning embedded in the objective world. But the very text that is cited may also be used as reference by virtue of the fact that its author is a highly esteemed scientist. In this case the purpose of the citation is to raise the status of the first text by linking it to a meaning in the social world. This clearly demonstrates not only the contextual dependency of information, but also, in my view, the character of the link. From this follows that it is simply not possible to establish the exact meaning of some item that might come in use as information. Another conclusion that may be drawn is that there is a potentially huge need for information linking up with meaning anchored in the social world. This point is perhaps somewhat neglected in information services, which usually focus on truth-related knowledge.

4 Validity Claims, Meaning, and Context

Since validity claims play an important role for the concept of information proposed here, along with its relation to context, a legitimate question that arises is What constitutes such a claim and how is it related to meaning? Hjørland draws attention to the function of information for the evaluation of knowledge claims (2002, p. 450), and the question is whether this is the same as a validity claim in the way Habermas uses the term? Other relevant questions concerns the context: What can be said of the structure of the context? How is meaning embedded in the context?

In respect to the term "reaching understanding," Habermas states that it is far more complex to understand even an elementary expression than first appears to be the case. There are at least two acting subjects involved, and "[the] meaning of an elementary expression consists in the contribution it makes to the meaning of an acceptable speech act." Moreover, the listener has to know the conditions under which the speech act can be accepted. He adds that, "[i]n this respect, understanding an elementary expression points beyond the minimal meaning of the term" (Habermas 1981a, p. 307). I take this statement as referring to the context and to the shared interpretative horizon of a cultural tradition and world views. That is to say that reaching understanding about the simplest thing involves access to and evaluation of knowledge from three worlds at the same time. Habermas formulates this as follows:

> When a hearer accepts a speech act, an agreement [Einverständnis] comes about between at least two acting and speaking subjects. However, this does not rest only on the intersubjective recognition of a single, thematically stressed validity claim. Rather, an agreement of this sort is achieved simultaneously at three levels. […] It belongs to the communicative intent of the speaker (a) that he perform a speech act that is *right* in respect to the given normative context, so that between him and the hearer an intersubjective relation will come about which is recognized as legitimate; (b) that he make a *true* statement (or *correct* existential presuppositions), so that the hearer will accept and share the knowledge of the speaker; and (c) that he express *truthfully* his beliefs, intentions, feelings, desires, and the like, so that the hearer will give credence to what is said (ibid.).

Even if speech acts gain their binding force in this way through validity claims anchored in each of the three worlds at the same time, there is always one aspect or theme which the speaker primarily seeks acceptance for, as the citation indicates. Perhaps one way of viewing this is that the speaker presents a particular facet of validity to the listener. In scientific contexts, for instance, the theme is normally related to the objective world, which is also the case to a lesser degree for pedagogical situations, at least at the University level. Reaching understanding is of great importance in both scientific and pedagogical communication, where the goal is typically to establish mutual understanding about a fact or state of affairs in the objective world. Habermas points out, however, that it is not enough that validity claims concerning the truth be accepted. In order for there to be mutual understanding, it is also necessary to accept claims that the proposition was put forward by the speaker at the proper moment and in the proper environment, and that the speaker was entitled to do so. Furthermore, the speaker must also be sincere in what s/he is saying.

Habermas' produces an example illuminating the complex character of the relation between speaker and listener:

> A murderer who makes a confession can mean what he says and yet, without intending to do so, be saying what is untrue. He can also, without intending to do so, speak the truth although, in concealing his knowledge of the facts of the case, he is lying. A judge who had sufficient evidence at his disposal could criticize the truthful utterance as untrue in the one case, and the true utterance as untruthful in the other (Habermas 1981a, p. 313).[2]

My position is that it is permissable to generalize speech acts and validity claims, collect them in a sort of array, and treat them as if they were rudimentary as long as the logic of the theory is not violated. In this way we can use a scientific paper as an example to illustrate the significance of Habermas' view. For instance, if a paper proposes something about diseases of the blood and the claims made are true in relation to the objective world, hardly no one would understand it if the paper were published in a journal of Chinese art. And if the paper were written in such a way that the author occasionally stated that his findings were false and the experiments were conducted improperly, even if that was not the case in fact, a competent reader would probably not understand the truth of findings that were so untruthfully presented, even if the paper had found its way into a proper journal.

Speech acts, utterances, arguments, or longer segments of speech may of course be seen as information. The validity claims connected with a speech act are not themselves information, but rather a type of guarantee for the validity of the utterance. By providing such an assurance, the speaker makes the listener accept what is said, thereby providing for continuation of the communication. The validity claim thus says nothing about the validity of the utterance itself. Habermas argues in this way that the validity of an expression cannot be established independently from the fulfillment of the validity claim raised by the expression. The validity in what is said is attached to the inter subjective recognition of the corresponding claims to validity (ibid., p. 316). I take this as meaning that the validity claim is an assurance that the meaning of an utterance may be tested and that the speaker, if needed, can refer to either discrete knowledge in the fond of the lifeworld, or to some representation of knowledge that makes it possible to establish the meaning intersubjectively. Consequently, the listener's rejection of a validity claim becomes a demand for information.

---

2 This citation may need some explanation: The murderer says "I shot the man because he slept with my wife." (a) The murderer shot the man in the belief that the victim had slept with his wife, which was not the case. (b) The murderer shot the man because the victim had stolen money from him, but he does not know that the man had also slept with his wife.

The provisional conclusion to this point is that information, either in the form of shared knowledge in the fond of the lifeworld or as representations of knowledge in the form of artefacts, points to a meaning that must be intersubjectively recognized by the participants in communication. This suggests that when a demand for information is fulfilled, the process of communication continues until the meaning it links up with is established. Also, my claim above that it is possible to generalize validity claims, probably equate these with the knowledge claims Hjørland mentions. This raises two questions: What happens when the information is an artefact? and Where is the context located?

To interpret an artefact is basically the same as reaching understanding with fellow participants in communicative action. If the definition of an artefact is that it represents knowledge, then it must be kept in mind that the knowledge has been created through communicative practices somewhere in the lifeworld. In a wider sense, moreover, the represented knowledge shares to a certain extent the cultural tradition and world view common for the context. Although the limits of the present discussion do not permit an examination of the various types of artefacts, I would like to observe that pictures, films, items in general, and even natural objects under certain conditions share the common property of a meaning based in linguistic structures (Buckland 1997, p. 805-808). Documents containing text are however more easily grasped as knowledge representations suitable for communication since their contents more directly mimic verbal speech.

Habermas' position is clear when he discusses the possibilities of interpretation, namely, the only way for an observer to understand the meaning of what he or she observes is to assume a location in the contexts for action in the lifeworld. Otherwise, if "the interpreter confines himself to observations in the strict sense, he perceives only the physical substrata of utterances without understanding them [...] he must adopt a performative attitude and participate, be it only virtually." Habermas further states that the interpreter "can understand the meaning of communicative acts [speech acts] only because they are embedded in contexts of *action* oriented to reaching understanding – this is Wittgenstein's central insight" (Habermas 1981a, pp. 114-115). This means that even when it comes to the interpretation of a document, communicative action is the only way to reach the meaning of the knowledge it represents. By virtue of the "performative attitude," the interpreter can take on the role of a virtual participant, ask questions, evaluate the validity claims connected with the speech acts, and so forth. There is a difference, of course, between being a virtual participant and participating in real action contexts insofar as a higher degree of temporal and spatial distance hampers the efficiency of communication and the risk of distortion is thereby heightened. In addition, the interpreter can only take part in the act of reaching understanding.

The second question concerning the location of the context has in fact already been broached in that I have already referred to the context as the "lifeworld," although I have not described it in any great detail. Habermas provides this brief description of the concept of the lifeworld:

> What this expression means can be clarified intuitively by reference to those symbolic objects that we produce in speaking and acting, beginning with immediate expressions (such as speech acts, purposive activities, and cooperative action), through the sedimentations of these

expressions (such as texts, traditions, documents, works of art, theories, objects of material culture, goods, techniques, and so on), to the indirectly generated configurations that are self-stabilizing and susceptible of organization (such as institutions, social systems, and personality structures) (ibid., p. 108).

Almost everything thus seems to be included in the lifeworld, but it is important to keep in mind that what belongs to the lifeworld is not restricted merely to objects in reality. The lifeworld rather consists of symbolically structured objects, which I understand to mean that everything is pre-interpreted. That is to say that the lifeworld is the human world, not some metaphysical reality existing in its own right. It thereby provides an interpretative horizon for all communication, or a kind of implicit background knowledge that is almost impossible to dispute. This implicit knowledge, which Habermas refers to as cultural tradition and world view, is necessary to make communicative action possible (ibid., pp. 335-337).

Habermas elaborates the concept of the lifeworld further, proceeding from Alfred Schutz' and Thomas Luckmann's theoretical framework of action. A given event of communicative action take place in a *situation* that is consensually recognized by the participants. And while such situations are not defined or even informally demarcated,

> [t]hey always have a horizon that shifts with the theme. A *situation* is a segment of *lifeworld contexts of relevance* [*Verweisungszusammen-hänge*] that is thrown into relief by themes and articulated through goals and plans of action; these contexts of relevance are concentrically ordered and become increasingly anonymous and diffused as the spatio-temporal and social distance grows (Habermas 1981b, p. 122).

This context of relevance supports the participants with a stock of shared, unquestionable knowledge, which comprises a taken-for-granted common meaning that facilitates mutual understanding in communication. Habermas describes the lifeworld in this respect "as represented by a culturally transmitted and linguistically organized stock of interpretive patterns," and he further refines the specification of the relevance structures

> as interconnections of meaning holding between a given communica-tive utterance, the immediate context, and its connotative horizon of meanings. Contexts of relevance are based on *grammatically regulated* relations among the elements of a *linguistically organized* stock of knowledge (ibid., p. 124).

However, every state in the lifeworld is unproblematic. None of its elements are characterized as facts, norms, or experiences about which we must come to an understanding, not even when the situation is shared with other people. By definition, the lifeworld cannot be problematic, although it is possible for it to collapse.

> The lifeworld is the intuitively present, in this sense familiar and transparent, and at the same time [a] vast and incalculable web of presuppositions that have to be satisfied if an actual utterance is to be at all meaningful, that is, valid *or* invalid (ibid., p. 131).

This background knowledge remains discrete, or even invisible, for the participants as long as the theme of the situation fits within the horizon. The lifeworld is always there for us, always ready to support our interpretation of whatever life brings to us. This knowledge, or the meaning within the horizon of a given situation, is not questionable in the way that what belongs to the three worlds is:

> Together with criticizable validity claims, these latter [the three worlds] concepts form the frame or categorial scaffolding that serves to order problematic situations – that is, situations that need to be agreed upon – in a lifeworld that is already substantively interpreted. With the formal world-concepts, speakers and hearers can qualify the possible referents of their speech acts so that they can relate to something objective, normative or subjective (ibid., pp. 125-126).

The elements of the action situation about which the participants want to come to an understanding are always questionable, and they are exposed to evaluation concerning their relevant validity claims. But that which can be thematized and problematized is restricted to the action situation encompassed by the lifeworld horizon (ibid., pp. 130-131). If a situation develops through communicative action into something that no longer fits into the actual segment of the lifeworld, the horizon will recede and preserve a safe, pre-interpreted context of relevance for the participants. Something that had been intuitively well-known and pre-interpreted then suddenly becomes subject to criticism and evaluation from a new situation embedded in another segment of the lifeworld. Only then do we begin to realize that there was something that we had conceived to be safe, well-known, and pre-interpreted (ibid., pp. 132-133). This is also the mechanism for the reproduction of cultural knowledge in the lifeworld:

> Every step we take beyond the horizon of a given situation opens up access to a further complex of meaning, which, while it calls for explication, is already intuitively familiar. What was until then 'taken for granted,' is transformed in the process into cultural knowledge that can be used in defining situations and exposed to test in communicative action (ibid., p. 133).

It should now be clear that the meaning of all linguistically structured utterances – be they verbal arguments or discussions, or captured in the form of texts, images, or other types of artefacts – is located in the lifeworld and accessible through communicative action. The physical objects themselves, such as books, documents, or other types of media we usually connect with information and information services, are naturally not placed in the lifeworld *as is*. But the knowledge they represent, or the narratives that the signs and symbols of texts, images, and other items stand for, is sedimented in the lifeworld. Now, it may seem like a complex and difficult process to reach the meaning of even the most tiny little document, obviously demanding a perhaps exhausting engagement in communicative action. This is indeed at times the case. But as I indicated above, it is only the problematic situations, or those in which expressions in speech acts are rejected, that call for further action in order to reach an understanding of the meaning. Even the central part of the most voluminous book will to a great degree have a meaning that is perfectly clear to us, provided we understand the language in it, because of the shared horizon of relevance in the lifeworld.

The lifeworld in its totality is impractical as an analytical category in IS, at least in research directed to the improvement of tools and electronic systems, in investigations intended to elaborate information services as part of organizations, or from an organizational point of view, i.e., for libraries. However, I consider it to be reasonable to use *action contexts* as a loose concept for the realms in which information is used, produced, and managed. These action contexts, which are of course located in the lifeworld, consists of a variety of themes that, whenever actualized, take the form of a vast variety of situations of communicative action. Depending on the orientation and interest of the research in question, such action contexts should likely be subject to further description and perhaps formal definition as well.

Hjørland arrives in his writings at the concept of domain, which is closely related to this type of action context. Together with Albrechtsen he states that

> The domain-analytic paradigm in information science (IS) states that the best way to understand information in IS is to study the knowledge-domains as thought or discourse communities, which are parts of society's division of labor (Albrechtsen and Hjørland 1995, p. 400).

It seems reasonable that a knowledge domain is a larger entity than an action context insofar as it is formed by generalized themes and also comprised of a large number of ever changing contexts of action. I would also argue that knowledge domains are subject to change at a slower pace by virtue of their semi-institutional or systems character, whereby change is brought about by the processes underway in the action contexts in which these domains are institutionalized. Hjørland makes remarks concerning the division of labor as constitutive for knowledge domains, and he also identifies the use of information as a function for knowledge claims (2002, p. 450). This supports the semi-institutional or systems character of these domains.

In order to clarify this concept, it may be appropriate to present certain provisional examples of action contexts relevant to IS. For instance, an action context in higher education could be the master degree courses of a certain discipline. In the field of research, a larger project involving several participants or a doctoral project with a single participant may both be considered contexts of action. An example from a different domain would be a local environmental protection association planning a demonstration against the building of a sea-side luxury apartment complex. And in respect to libraries, user instruction is a typical action context in which communicative action is aimed directly at the heart of IS. Carrying out reference services, cataloguing, and the indexing of new items in the library are other central activities.

All these activities are typical human pursuits that depend on communicative action. Providing information to the groups mentioned is obviously important, and if this may be said to consist of matching the meaning of certain artefacts with the meanings indicated by validity claims made in utterances within the contexts in question, then it is at least possible to describe the task in general terms. This task certainly constitutes a challenge for the information expert, and the artefact, which is a representation of knowledge sedimented in some segment of relevance in the lifeworld, must be grasped through communicative action. Fortunately, the expert will in most cases intuitively share large amounts of knowledge with the lifeworld segments in which the possibly useful artefacts were created, as was stated above. The other part of the task is in a certain sense easier in that structures of meaning are readily available in the action contexts that are the targets for the service, possibly residing within the service organization itself. Our information expert can simply visit these contexts and take part in the interactions aimed at understanding without sharing the ultimate goals of the action orientations. It goes without saying that this will not be as easy as it sounds in light of considerations considering time, space, background knowledge, etc. This is however a strong case for better integration of information services with the target contexts, in organizations where it is possible, for instance in schools and at Universities.

5 The System Side of Society

Habermas makes clear at the beginning of volume two of *TCA* that the lifeworld perspective taken together with communicative action is not capable of explicating the reproduction of society in its totality.

> The limits of a communication-theoretic approach of this sort are evident. The reproduction of society as a whole can surely not be adequately explained in terms of the conditions of communicative rationality, though we can explain the symbolic reproduction of the lifeworld of a social group in this way, if we approach the matter from an internal perspective (Habermas 1981b, p. 2).

From the internal perspective of the lifeworld it is possible to understand the meaning of people's actions and of the changing social reality they create. The relevance structures that remain hidden from a systems perspective can be grasped from the internal viewpoint of a participant in the communicative interactions that are oriented to mutual understanding. The external systems view is only capable of interpreting actions as functional requirements for a system as viewed from the outside by an observer. The internal perspective is, in contrast, incapable of grasping actions steered by systems features, such as how the market system balances the consequences of the strategic actions of several actors. Habermas' solution involves a dual perspective that conceives of society as lifeworld and system at the same time. He states that, "Thus I have proposed that we distinguish between *social integration and system integration*: the former attaches to action orientations, while the latter reaches right through them" (ibid., p. 150).

A very important aim of *TCA* is to both explain and resolve the problematic of reification in modern society, which arises in the work of Marx and Weber as a consequence of the rationalization of society. Marx discussed reification in terms of the division of labor and proletarianization, which finally results in labor becoming a commodity that workers sell on the market. He went so far as to claim that the objectification of human labor was the reason for the alienation of man in modern society. Weber views the rationalization of society, with an ever growing complex of administrations, institutions, organizations, industries, and commercial enterprises, as having led, on the one hand, to secure material conditions and better lives for mankind, but, on the other, to a loss of meaning as well. In his image of modern society, man was trapped in an iron cage, circumscribed by rules and fulfilling seemingly meaningless tasks. Simply stated, Weber's explanation for this state of affairs was that administration, government, and private enterprises became increasingly anonymous and steered by impersonal rules. In addition, while the process of rationalization left no room for religious belief systems in society, bureaucratic and secularized modern society failed to replace the meaning that had once emanated from the will of God.

Reification means both the objectification of a human being and treating something abstract as if it were material. Habermas identifies the problem with reification as treated by Marx, Weber, and their followers as their inclination to view rationalization as the reification of consciousness. Purposive rational action in the objective world, i.e. material manipulations, was seen as projections of the mind.

The structure of the lifeworld as presented above is basically coherent with the finalized concept Habermas arrives at after necessary adjustments were made to fit it into the dual perspective of *TCA*. These adjustments involve adding the components of society and person in order to eliminate the initially one-sided cultural feature of the lifeworld. Not only is cultural reproduction thereby incorporated into the premises of communicative action, but the reproduction of society and personality as well (ibid., p. 138). The resulting three structural components of culture, society, and the person correspond to the processes of cultural reproduction, social integration, and socialization, and the reproduction of each of these components supports the preservation of the other two. For example, the reproduction of culture supplies the existing social institutions with legitimization, while disturbances in the reproduction of one the components will have analogous repercussions for the others. If the reproduction of culture is disturbed, for instance, not only will there be a loss of meaning, but the legitimization of social institutions will also suffer (ibid., pp. 141-144).

The lifeworld has, of course, changed through history. Habermas claims in this regard that the worldview in ancient times made no particular distinction between the sources of meaning for each of the three components, primarily because of the strength of the force with which it was gripped by myth and religion. Over time, however, religion gradually lost its grip, leading to a linguistification of society and a decentered worldview (ibid., pp. 145-147). Habermas makes the point that,

> the further the structural components of the lifeworld and the processes that contribute to maintaining them get differentiated, the more interaction contexts come under conditions of rationally motivated mutual understanding, that is, of consensus formation that rests *in the end* on the authority of the better argument (ibid., p. 145).

The differentiation of the lifeworld increases communicative action, which in turn releases the potential of rationality, leading to an increasingly complex society. Habermas maintains that system and lifeworld become differentiated in a second order process that gives rise to an increased complexity in the former and to rationalization in the latter. They are also simultaneously further differentiated from each other (ibid., p. 153). The growing complexity of the system also directs pressure upon the lifeworld since all systems mechanisms must be anchored in the lifeworld, which means, in Habermas' words, that "they have to be institutionalized" (ibid., p.

154). That is to say that the contents of the system, which are institutions, organizations, etc., result from the ongoing rationalization that is supposed to facilitate the lives we live.

However, through the uncoupling of system and lifeworld, i.e., the differentiation *between* them, sub-systems of action are released from institutionalization in the lifeworld, which in turn is releaved of the burden of having to steer them through communicative action. Such sub-systems are instead then steered by the media of money or power, and they come to constitute *"formally organized domains of action"* (ibid., p. 307). As long as this concerns domains of action that are distinct from the symbolic reproductive structures, such as those that deal with material reproduction, a certain weight is in fact lifted from the lifeworld. But there is a risk that,

> In the end, systemic mechanisms suppress forms of social integration even in those areas where a consensus-dependent coordination of action cannot be replaced, that is, where the symbolic reproduction of the lifeworld is at stake. In these areas, the *mediatization* of the lifeworld assumes the form of a *colonization* (ibid., p. 196).

In this way Habermas explains the problematic of reification from a formal pragmatic perspective, which is informed by communicative rationality, instead of the perspective of purposive rationality utilized by Marx and Weber. Instead of becoming bogged down in the dilemma of having to face a dark future because of positive accomplishments in the past, as Weber and Adorno did, Habermas is thus in the position of being able to envisage ways around the problematic, thereby turning it into an open-ended question. Since systems are anchored in the lifeworld, and are thereby steered by the processes of mutual understanding, *we* are capable of deciding whether or not they should become medialized domains of formally organized action. This is, of course, much easier to say than to do. However, my claim is that IS plays an important role in this process by virtue of the varities of research concerning information that are aimed to find ways of improving access to information as much as possible.

In the concluding chapter of *TCA* Habermas diagnoses certain areas of concern in light of the dangers that arise from the system's colonization of the lifeworld. In addition to such threatened areas as health care, social services, and other typical welfare topics, he also argues that the educational system is vulnerable to colonization. I find this worth noting for two reasons. The first involves the increasing focus on formal, possibly normative, accomplishments at all levels in the educational system. Grades, evaluations, and quantitative examinations appear to occupy ever more space at the same time that economics is tightening its grip in both public and private educational institutions. This draws attention away from the central action orientaion in all pedagogical pursuits, which is the creation of knowledge. As I have tried to demonstrate in an earlier paper, this also has a bearing on IS insofar as it effects how students evaluate the artefacts they create within their educational contexts (2003).

The second reason involves the more general affiliation between a large segment of information services and all types of schools and universities. Those areas of research within the field of IS that are oriented towards the pedagogical realm are therefore dealing with a relevant theme. If this orientation is intuitively constituted or not is of less importance; it should of course be seen as challenge for other to identify urgent areas of research.

6 The Dual Challenge for Information Science

The acceptance of *The Theory of Communicative Action* as a framework for IS is, in my view, of secondary importance for the future development of the field. But whether or not Habermas' critical theory is used for this purpose, I view IS as being challenged in two ways. The first instance involves the need to apply an underlying semantic theory more in line with how knowledge and meaning is actually created and used in society. The implications of this challenge to determine what may be termed a more realistic underpinning for IS reach in the first instance into research, where, as was discussed above, they have already begun to inform investigation concerning the meaningful structures embedded in contexts of both individual and collective users. The second instance involves the information services themselves, influencing the creation of improved tools, work methods, and organizational structures. This is a process that will certainly be gradual, lengthy, and undoubtedly cause some degree of pain.

The investments in time and money in existing tools and organization are huge in the information services and extend over long periods of time. Resistance to change and conservatism are thus to be expected, especially since they can readily be supported by economic arguments. However, the heart of the challenge, whether for the researcher or the information expert, resides in the learning process that is needed to internalize new ways of understanding meaning. The positivist approach to the world that was mentioned aboved is in many way easier to accept, in science and elsewhere as well, insofar as the various methods used are often straightforward and rewarding in their seemingly exact and relevant response to research questions. In contrast, the variety of interpretative methods associated with the hermeneutic understanding, along with the results obtained, can be difficult to present, and often appear to be imprecise or ambiguous. The learning process involved with this challenge has more to do with understanding that interpretation is in fact what we have already been doing intuitively, than with mastering specific methods.

The Polish historian Jerzy Topolski discusses in length what he terms "tacit knowledge" in his methodology for historical research, emphasizing the important role it plays in a research community (1976). For example, when a researcher set a specific method in action, such as a statistical investigation in IR, all the factors and variables expressed in relation to the task are obviously utilized when evaluating and presenting the result. In the background, however, tacit knowledge will help to interpret what is seen and to correct any hasty, perhaps even thoughtless, conclusions. In a similar way an information expert, such as a librarian, intuitively uses tacit knowledge when interpreting a search result (see Hjørland's example above) or trying to assign the best possible index term to a new catalogue item. And both the researcher and the librarian will no doubt take the possibility to discuss problems with colleagues.

I view such tacit knowledge as not only being of the same type as background knowledge in the lifeworld that was examined above, but also reproduced in the same manner. It should be obvious at this point that my claim that understanding meaning necessarily relies on communicative action is not as radical as it might at first seem to be. That is to say that IS is challenged to make the use of "realistic" semantic theories explicit, not least of all among information experts in the various types of information services. If the learning process mentioned above is put into motion, then knowledge of the relational character of meaning and context will be made explicit, serving to improve information services.

The second challenge concerns the social significance of our field, which it has acquired by virtue of the crucial role information plays in all communication structures in contemporary society. Capurro and Hjørland have also stressed this point. I maintain that the integration of *TCA* with IS will both make possible a structural explanation of the crucial role of information today, and also highlight the way in which our field can contribute to the emancipation of threatened discourse communities in society through the provision of better access to information.

In many ways these two tasks stands in close relation to each other in respect to the general goal of improving information services. Why, then, is there a need for a social theoretical framework? I would first say that there is a danger that the social perspective will be lost without such a framework when research initiatives in IS orient themselves to specific, perhaps even traditional, areas of interest. And this is something which they certainly will do. Now, such initiatives may well be both highly relevant as well as informed by new semantic theories with useful conceptions of context. But both the selection of research areas and the formulation of research questions require input from a larger, social theoretic framework.

Furthermore, the type of theory represented by *TCA*, which employs both an internal interpretative perspective and an external observational perspective, makes it possible to examine more closely particular regions within society, study them as systems, and determine the formalized actions they generate. The results obtained may in turn inform other studies that examine various lifeworld contexts as they are affected by the system. This way of proceeding may be useful in investigating how various sub-systems in society may in fact hamper access to information.

We should not be too modest within our field, shyly hiding behind our theme. On the contrary, we should argue for the ever increasing importance of access to information in a globalized world, where the complexity of society more than ever before has placed the underlying structures of discourse in democracy to the test, where an unbridled consumism is invading all areas of life in the name of the free market and economic growth, and where breakdowns in communication are all too often announced in outbursts of sheer violence.

References

Bruce, Christine (1997) *The Seven Faces of Information Literacy.* Adelaide: Auslib Press.
Bryant, Rebecca (2000) *Discovery and Decision. Exploring the Metaphysics and Epistemology of Scientific Classification.* London: Associated University Presses.

Backlund, J., (2003) "How to claim knowledge: The use of information in the lifeworld of the educational context.", *HERDSA Annual Conference Proceedings* Vol 26

Buckland, Michael (1991) *Information and Information Systems.* New York: Praeger.

Buckland, Michael (1997) "What is a 'Document'?" *Journal of the American Society for Information Science*, 48(9).

Case, D. O. (2002) *Looking for Information. A Survey of Research on Information Seeking, Needs, and Behavior.* New York: Academic Press.

Capurro, R. and B. Hjørland (2003a) "The Concept of Information." *Annual Review of Information Science and Technology*, vol. 37.

Frohman, B. (1983) "An Investigation of the Semantic Bases of Some Theoretical Principles of Classification Proposed by Austin and the CRG." *Cataloging and Classification Quarterly*, vol. 4(1)

Habermas, J. (1981a) *Theorie des kommunikativen Handels*, Band 1. Frankfurt am Main: Suhrkamp. English translation: *The Theory of Communicative Action,* vol 1. Oxford: Polity Press, 1984.

Habermas, J. (1981b) *Theorie des kommunikativen Handels*, Band 2. Frankfurt am Main: Suhrkamp. English translation: *The Theory of Communicative Action*, vol. 2. Oxford: Polity Press, 1987.

Hansson, Joacim (1999) *Klassifikation, bibliotek och samhälle : en kritisk hermeneutisk studie av "Klassifikationssystem för svenska bibliotek."* Göteborg: Valfrid.

Hjørland, B. and H. Albrechtsen (1995) "Toward a New Horizon in Information Science: Domain-Analysis." *Journal of The American Society for Information Science*, 46 (6).

Hjørland, B. (2002) "Domain Analysis in Information Science. Eleven approaches – Traditional as well as Innovative." *Journal of Documentation*, 58:4.

Hjørland, B. (2003b) "Social and Cultural Awareness and Responsibilty in Library, Information and Documentation Studies." In R. Boyd, J. Hansson, V. Suominen, and M. D. Lanham (eds.) *Aware and Responsible.* Lanham, MD: Scarecrow Press.

Hjørland, B. (1998) "Information Retreival, Text Composition, and Semnatics." *Knowledge Organization*, 25.

Ingwersen, Peter (1995) "Information and Information Science in Context." In J. Olaisen, E. Munch-Petersen, and P. Wilson. *Information Science: From the Development of the Discipline to Social Interaction.* Oslo: Scandinavian University Press.

Kuhlthau, Carol (1993) *Seeking Meaning: A Process Approach to Library and Information Services.* Norwood, NJ: Ablex.

Limberg, Louise (1998) *Att söka information för att lära. En studie av samspel mellan informationssökning och lärande.* Borås: Valfrid.

Limberg, Louise (1999) "Three Conceptions of Information Seeking and Use." In T. D. Wilson and D. K. Allen (eds.) *Exploring the Contexts of Information Behaviour.* London: Taylor Graham.

Reese-Schäfer, W. (1991) *Jürgen Habermas.* Frankfurt and New York: Campus.

Sundin, Olof (2003). *Informationsstrategier och yrkesidentiteter: en studie av sjuksköterskors relation till fackinformation vid arbetsplatsen.* Borås: Valfrid.

Topolski, Jerzy (1976) Methodology of history, Dordrecht : Reidel, cop.

Wildemuth, Barbara M. (2002) "Effective Methods for Studying Information Seeking and Use." *Journal of the American Society for Information Science and Technology*, 53(14).

Personometrics: Mapping and Visualizing Communication Patterns in R&D Projects

Morten Skovvang[1], Mikael K. Elbæk[2], and Morten Hertzum[3]

[1] Corporate Library & Information Center, Ferring Pharmaceuticals,
Copenhagen, Denmark
[2] Copenhagen Business School Library, Copenhagen, Denmark
[3] Computer Science, Roskilde University, Roskilde, Denmark
mos@ferring.com, mke.lib@cbs.dk, mhz@ruc.dk

Abstract. People such as R&D engineers rely on communication with their colleagues to acquire information, get trusted opinion, and as impetus for creative discourse. This study investigates the prospects of using bibliometric citation techniques for mapping and visualizing data about the oral communication patterns of a group of R&D engineers. Representatives of the R&D engineers find the resulting maps – we term them personometric maps – rich in information about who knows what and potentially useful as tools for finding people with specific competences. Maps of old projects are seen as particularly useful because old projects are important entry points in searches for information and the maps retain information indicative of people's competences, information that is otherwise not readily available. Face-to-face communications and communications via phone, email, and other systems are more ephemeral than scholarly citations, and (semi-)automated means of data collection are critical to practical application of personometric analyses.

1 Introduction

Interpersonal communication is of key importance in knowledge-intensive organizations such as those in research and development (R&D). Studies have repeatedly found that engineers rely more on oral communication with organizational colleagues than on written communication such as project documentation, textbooks, and research papers [2, 14, 20]. Conversely, research in Library and Information Science (LIS) has primarily concerned itself with search behaviour related to retrieval of information from documents [8, 24]. Given its practical significance there is an urgent need for additional research on how to represent people as information objects, as a means to assist effective identification of people who are capable of providing information, advice, and trusted opinion. This study investigates the prospects of adapting techniques originally developed for citation analysis to visualizing communication and competence patterns in R&D projects.

Within bibliometrics, authors are related to each other by means of their citation patterns; thereby providing information about the intellectual structure of a domain [4, 22, but see also 16]. There are potentially exciting possibilities for using bibliometric

F. Crestani and I. Ruthven (Eds.): CoLIS 2005, LNCS 3507, pp. 141–154, 2005.
© Springer-Verlag Berlin Heidelberg 2005

techniques in other domains and for other purposes than the study and evaluation of scholarly writing. In this study, we aim to outline how such techniques can be utilized for investigating, mapping, and visualizing the competences of individual employees in organizations, based on the patterns of communication they exhibit in accomplishing their tasks. We term this *personometrics*, a field of study intended to advance our understanding of people as information sources and, thereby, inform the design of people-finding systems.

We conducted an exploratory empirical study in which the participants in an R&D project were asked to indicate the personal communications they engaged in as part of their day-to-day project activities. Data were collected by means of a questionnaire and validated by interviews. If individuals can be viewed as information objects it should be possible to represent project participants visually through mapping. We aim to investigate:

- Whether such maps can be constructed by applying bibliometric citation techniques to data about project participants' interpersonal communication patterns
- How project participants react to these maps and whether they consider them indicative of people's competences and of potential value as a people-finding tool.

We expect that personometric maps will visualize information that is partially tacit and not fully known by some project participants. This way personometric mapping is inscribed in and adds to a collective cognitive perspective on information seeking [12]. Further, personometric mapping entails that users are presented with and considered capable of interpreting fairly large amounts of data (whereas computer power is directed at visualizing the information space). This accords with humans' greater ability to browse and thereby recognize what is wanted over being able to describe it by means of queries.

2   People as Information Sources

With the reference interview as a prominent exception, LIS studies of collaborative aspects of information seeking tend to focus on collaboration among peers – often engineers – and on how technology may enable such collaboration. The most well-known example of collaborative information seeking is probably Allen's [2] description of the gatekeeper phenomenon. A gatekeeper takes the responsibility to look for information and, when consulted by colleagues, forwards it to people in her team or organization. This way, the recipient of the information and the gatekeeper collaborate to find information useful to their work. In relation to this study, the key contribution of the gatekeeper phenomenon is its attention to collaboration and communication because this attention entails that people are recognized as central sources of information. Though many studies have investigated communication among engineers [14, 20], we still lack a solid understanding of what it is that makes people such good information sources. Elements of such an understanding are, however, emerging [9, 10]:

- Engineers are involved in a construction process and for that reason they need a *synthesis* of the prospective product and use situation and are only *analysing the present* as a way of getting at the future. The ability to transcend current practice, identify underlying needs, and envision new products and ways of working is specific to people – though they find it difficult.
- Engineers are involved in an applied process and for that reason they are often looking just as much for *experiences* with certain tools or work tasks as they are looking for *facts*. Such experiences are seldom available in writing because such explication is a difficult and time-consuming activity, because other activities compete for experienced people's time, and because the experienced people themselves gain little from committing their experiences to writing.
- Engineers are involved in a cooperative process and for that reason they often need *commitment* to future actions as much as they need *information*. The capacity to make commitments is specific to people. In many situations the distinction between information and commitment is, in fact, blurred because people thought capable of providing information may instead commit to investigate the issue in question, or vice versa.

In many if not most organizations, few organizational mechanisms are in place to manage the flow of communications among people. A good few prototype systems do, however, attempt to support people in finding other people with specific competences. These include Referral Web [13] which helps find research experts based on co-occurrences of names, Yenta [7] which matches people based on textual analysis of personal profiles, Expertise Browser [17] which uses data from a change-management system for software engineering to locate software engineers with desired knowledge, and Answer Garden [1] which routes users to recorded information, if available, and otherwise to knowledgeable people. Whereas these prototype systems hide the data upon which the systems base their suggestions for people to contact, we explore the prospects of visualizing these data by means of personometric maps.

3 Personometrics

Personometrics is a field of study in which quantifiable data about the relations between individual persons serve as the basis for mapping intellectual structures in an organizational environment. Personometrics is inspired by bibliometrics, in particular scientometrics, which attempts to map the intellectual structures in a domain or discipline by means of citation data [19, 23, 24]. Further, personometrics resembles certain branches of social network analysis [18, 21]. In personometrics, data are collected about the colleagues with whom people communicate when they are in need of information. These data comprise what could be termed *social reference lists* to emphasize that personometrics is based on representations of *persona*, not *biblos*. As we outline it, personometrics is specifically targeted at the actual patterns of communication that ensue in response to employees' information needs. That is, formal organizational structures with nominated specialists are only recognized if the nominated specialists are actually consulted by their colleagues.

The peer communications represented on social reference lists to some extent resemble scholarly citations but also exhibit distinctive characteristics. First, people communicate with their colleagues to acquire and explore a web of information from different domains and therefore familiar to people with different professional backgrounds. Normally, no single R&D engineer knows all the domains involved in an R&D project in the necessary detail. Second, whereas engineers sometimes communicate with their colleagues to get factual information they regularly seek feedback on their ideas or designs, either as trusted opinion or as impetus for creative discourse [25]. Third, engineers' close working relationships with their colleagues often enable them to select the person to approach in a given situation based on such fine details and informal distinctions as the person being very helpful, too slow, or inefficient due to lack of recent experience with this particular topic. Fourth, people frequently combine sources when they look for information and thus intertwine looking for informing documents with looking for informed people [11].

Personometrics borrows from bibliometric methods in which citation data are aggregated into condensed descriptions that acquire robustness from the large amounts of data they bring together as well as from the scientific tradition that scientists cite each other and, thereby, contribute to an inter-subjective qualification of scientific results [23, 24]. With respect to amounts of data, work in organizations abounds in communication among colleagues, providing plenty of data for personometric analyses, see Fig. 1. Previous research suggests that people also communicate with each other in ways that could, over time, be accumulated into inter-subjectively qualified descriptions of their colleagues as information sources [2, 5, 6, 8]. This is, however, a critical precondition for personometric analysis and rather than merely assuming it we address this issue explicitly in our empirical study.

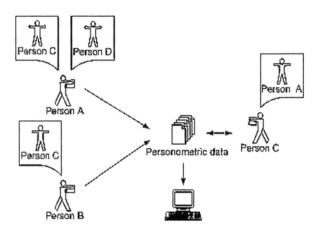

Fig. 1. Collecting data about interpersonal communications for use in personometric analyses

The empirical results presented in this article are based on data collected via questionnaires. Questionnaires are, however, unsuited for real-world applications of personometrics to the design of people-finding systems because questionnaires must be filled in manually and this is a resource-demanding activity that easily gets postponed or glossed over, especially as the questionnaire must be administered regularly to keep the personometric data up to date. Thus, automated means of data collection are needed. Multiple possibilities present themselves, including extraction of sender and recipient information from emails and phone calls, extraction of information about meeting participants from electronic calendars, and extraction of visitor information from employees' web pages [see, e.g., 5, 6]. In addition to information about the parties engaged in communicating it should be noted that email, web sites, and other forms of computer-mediated communication also provide opportunities for extracting keywords describing the topics about which people are consulted.

Data such as sender and recipient information for emails and phone calls are often recorded already, but reusing them for new purposes requires careful consideration of privacy issues. These issues may concern (a) the raw data extracted from, for example, emails and (b) the aggregated data presented to users of the people-finding systems. For the raw data, one approach is to automate both the extraction and the processing of them, and thereby make the raw data invisible to humans [7]. Another approach is to provide each employee with the data that involve him or her and the opportunity to make deletions in these data before they are included in the next update of the people-finding system. The aggregated data presented to users of people-finding systems may vary from detailed personometric maps, such as those in the empirical study below, to none at all. If no aggregated data are presented the system merely suggests people to contact but provides no clues as to the basis of its suggestions. This is the approach adopted by most extant people-finding systems [e.g., 1, 5, 7].

4   Empirical Study

Oticon A/S, which develops, produces, and sells hearing aids and other communication products, has a flat organizational structure, an open office landscape that emphasizes informal communication, and is characterized by self-organizing projects. The project in which our empirical study took place concerned the development of platforms for hearing aids targeted at the low-end segment of the market. The project had 22 participants spread across two sites that were several hundred kilometres apart. The project participants were mainly engineers (in the fields of electro acoustics, integrated circuits, applied digital processing, and quality management) but also audiologists and people from marketing and creative communications. As a self-organizing team the project had its own budget and was to a large extent autonomous, although supported by a set of staff functions. This gave the project group a wide range of contacts with people external to the project group.

4.1 Methods of Data Collection

We collected data from the project at Oticon by means of a questionnaire administered to all project participants and two validation interviews. The purpose of the *questionnaire* was to provide survey data about the informal communication patterns in the project. Apart from general information such as professional group respondents were asked to indicate the persons they communicated with in accomplishing their project tasks. The names of all project participants were listed in the questionnaire to jog the respondents' memory, and empty slots were available for indicating communication with people external to the project. For each person with whom they communicated the respondents were asked three questions:

1. Who typically initiates communications? Categories: you, her/him, or equally split.
2. How often do you communicate with this co-worker? Categories: every day, several times a week, several times a month, or up to once a month.
3. What professional knowledge does this co-worker represent? No pre-specified categories.

Following pilot testing with employees external to the project, the project manager sent an email to all project participants asking them to respond to the questionnaire. With this managerial recognition of the questionnaire as an extra motivation to respond, 77% of the 22 project participants responded to the questionnaire.

After the questionnaire survey, two project participants were selected for *validation interviews*. The interviews followed a general recommendation in bibliometrics by validating the quality and practical potential of the personometric maps against the domain knowledge of selected project participants [19]. The selection of the two interviewees was based on three criteria: (a) position on the personometric maps, (b) frequency of communications with colleagues, and (c) experience with R&D projects. Thus, one interviewee had a central position on the maps, the other a peripheral position. Both interviews concerned the general information-seeking behaviour of the project participants and their perception of the accuracy and practical potential of the personometric maps, which were shown to and discussed with the interviewees during the interviews. The interviews, which lasted about an hour each, were audio recorded and subsequently transcribed.

4.2 Production of Personometric Maps

The questionnaire data, which form the basis for the personometric maps, are collected at one point in time, whereas data in conventional bibliometric analyses are accumulated over time. This means that we cannot count the frequency of communications in the same way as the frequency of citations is normally counted. As frequency provides a rough estimate of importance, we believe that assigning frequency weights to communications will substantially improve personometric maps by bringing out more differences and details. We used questions 1 and 2 from the questionnaire for this purpose:

1. Initiation of communications. We assigned double weight to self-initiated communications because people are likely to have a more valid memory of their own enquiries and to avoid that employees inflate their own position on the maps.
2. Frequency of communications. We assigned higher weights to more frequent communications, see Table 1. The weights convert the response categories into an approximate number of monthly communications.

Question	Response category	Weight
1. Who typically initiates communications?	You	x2
	Her/him	x1
	Equally split	x1
2. How often do you communicate with this co-worker?	Every day	20
	Several times a week	8
	Several times a month	4
	Up to once a month	1

Inspired by White and McCain [24], the answers to question 3 (What professional knowledge does this co-worker represent?) were converted into slightly generalized competence descriptions and all persons on the personometric maps were labelled with the generalized competence most frequently ascribed to them.

The personometric maps were generated with *Bibexcel* (www.umu.se/inforsk/ Bibexcel), which uses multidimensional scaling to determine the layout of the maps. Multidimensional scaling is restricted to data sets of limited size, so whereas multidimensional scaling can handle the number of members in most project groups it will typically not be possible to make maps of entire organizations. Computationally this limitation can be overcome by choosing other visualization techniques [see, e.g., 3] but as maps become large they also become increasingly difficult to make sense of. Thus, for large data sets there may be a need for alternatives to maps.

4.3 Within-Project Communication Patterns

Fig. 2 is a map of the communication structure *within* the project. Each circle represents a person and each line represents communications between persons. The size of a circle indicates the accumulated number of times the person has been mentioned in the questionnaires, while the thickness of a line indicates the frequency of communications between the two persons connected by the line. The thicker the line, the more they communicate. Further, circles clustered close to each other indicate that these persons have similar communication patterns in the sense that they tend to communicate with the same people and to about the same extent.

The map shows a strong central person, the project manager (no. 21). As indicated by the size of her circle, the project manager is the project participant involved in the largest number of within-project communications. Her position close to the centre of the map indicates that she communicates with most of the other project participants. The map suggests that the project manager along with an electro-acoustics engineer (no. 10) and a mechanical engineer (no. 4) form the centre of the project. They are all three involved in lots of communications, and there are strong similarities in their communication patterns. Continuing the exploration of the map, the project participants seem to form two rings around the centre. The inner ring (participants 1, 5, 8, 14, 16, 20, 22, and possibly 11 and 17) includes people from the more peripheral site as well as recently hired people. This sets the inner ring apart from the centre, which consists of three longstanding employees from the main site. The outer ring (participants 2, 3, 6, 7, 9, 12, 13, 15, 18, 19, and possibly 11 and 17) is, however, similar to the inner ring in its mix of people from the two sites and in its mix of recently hired and longstanding employees. To further explore differences between the inner and outer ring we will look at the competences represented by the project participants.

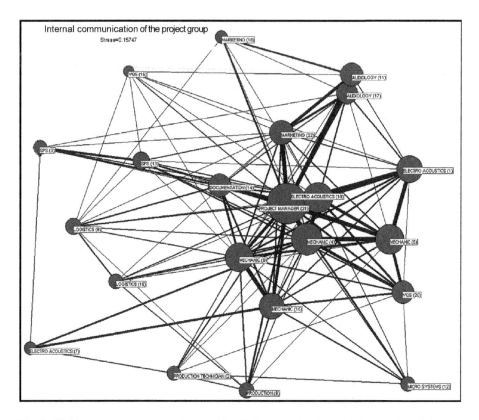

Fig. 2. Within-project personometric map. The fit between the data and the map is satisfactory, Kruskal's [15] stress measure gives a *badness of fit* of 0.16 (0 indicates a perfect fit)

Fig. 3 shows the project participants grouped by the competence most frequently ascribed to them. The project participants in most of the eleven competence groups are quite close together, indicating similar communication patterns. Group 8 on the map exemplifies that personometric analyses may reveal similarities between persons who are at different sites and in different organizational units (here, production and R&D). However, a few groups (4 and 6) contain project participants far apart on the personometric map. This reflects differences in the involved project participants' secondary competences and the separation between the two physical sites. As an example, the project participant in the lower left corner of group 4 is at the more peripheral site whereas the other participants in the group are at the main site. Several competence groups (2, 4, and 6) span both the inner ring and the outer ring. These groups could be seen as having a representative in the inner ring who acts as an intermediary between the group and the centre of the project. Finally, *Audiology* and

Marketing (groups 2 and 3) are somewhat removed from the centre of the map although the total weighted communications of the participants in these two groups are high. The synergy between these two groups as well as within the *Audiology* group results in *Audiology* and *Marketing* standing out as relatively autonomous and, consequently, as somewhat removed from the centre of the map.

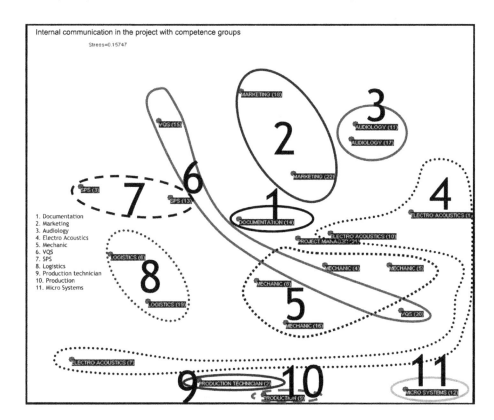

Fig. 3. Project participants divided into competence groups

4.4   Communications with People External to the Project

The project participants' total weighted communications are evenly split between within-project communications and communications with people external to the project. The vast majority of the communications with people external to the project are with other colleagues in the organization. Only 2% of the project participants' weighted communications are with people external to the organization. This suggests a competitive industrial setting in which small advancements in knowledge may have substantial commercial value [26]. In such settings project participants must carefully balance the capacity of their organization to exploit exclusive knowledge against the faster progress that may result from collaboration with outsiders.

Fig. 4 shows communications among all persons – both project participants and people external to the project – who were involved in ten or more communications. This personometric map provides strong evidence that the competences brought to bear on the project are not limited to those of the project participants. The map is characterized by a strong centralisation around what conceivably constitutes the core of the project with respect to persons as well as competence areas, but it extends into a complex network of interpersonal connections within the organization, and outside of it. This emphasizes the importance of having a well-developed personal network and, just as importantly, a good grasp of the network in general. There may be considerable strategic potential in using personometric maps to get an overview of where project participants turn for information as well as to identify important competences not sufficiently covered internal to the organization.

4.5 Validation

The objective of the validation interviews was to have project participants (a) assess the accuracy and understandability of the personometric maps and (b) discuss their practical potential as a means of supporting people finding.

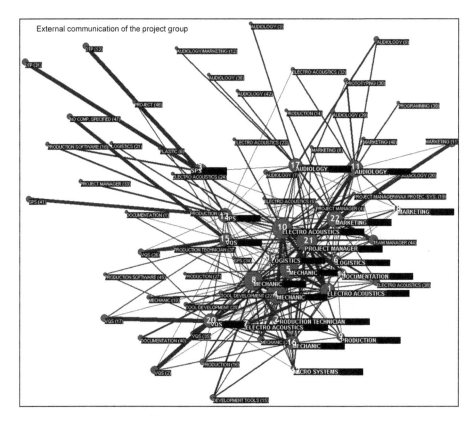

Fig. 4. Personometric map for both project-internal and project-external communications. The fit between the data and the map is good, Kruskal's [15] stress measure gives a *badness of fit* of 0.06

Prior to introducing the personometric maps, the interviewees were asked to name the project participants they considered most knowledgeable of who knows what. Both interviewees named project participants 4, 8, and 21. On the personometric maps participants 4 and 21 are two of the three persons in the centre of the project, and participant 8 is located in the inner ring. When shown the maps, both interviewees found them in accordance with their own image of the project, and they were readily able to interpret the general structure of the maps and provide explanations for various details. For example, the distance between some project participants on the maps was explained by their physical dissociation owing to the two separate sites, and a group of participants located close to each other on the maps was recognized as a subgroup responsible for the development of a new component. This suggests that the personometric maps were both sufficiently accurate and sufficiently easy to understand to provide the basis for a system supporting project participants in identifying colleagues to approach in different situations.

Interviewee A (R&D engineer, central position, two years in Oticon) found the maps very informative and was particularly positive toward using personometric maps as a way of visualizing the communication and competence patterns of old projects. Maps of old projects would retain information about project participants' communications and competences, and keep a record of important information sources external to the project group. Interviewee A emphasized that old projects are an important entry point in searches for information within the organization and that personometric maps appear to provide useful information that is otherwise not readily available. Further, interviewee A believed automated data collection was necessary for personometric maps to remain up to date, and he mentioned the privacy and status/power issues involved in making communication and competence patterns explicitly visible.

Interviewee B (production engineer, peripheral position, less than a year in Oticon) had more doubts about the potential of the maps. Due to her role in the project, interviewee B did not interact much with the other project participants and, consequently, she did not perceive that the personometric maps would ease her day-to-day work. She suggested that the maps would be more relevant for project participants who communicated more or were closer to R&D, and that they might relieve the project manager from many communications where she is merely asked for the name of the most appropriate project participant to contact. Nevertheless, the maps made interviewee B aware of project participants she had hitherto been unaware of, because "I'm not sitting down there, and I'm very bad at names."

4.6 Limitations

Our empirical study has several limitations, which should be remembered in interpreting our results. First, the study is based on data collected at one point in time. People's competences and their roles in projects are, however, not static but evolve over time. This suggests that data should be collected continuously or at regular intervals. Second, in this study data were collected by means of a questionnaire. In practical applications of personometric maps, (semi-)automated data collection appears necessary to keep the maps up to date over longer periods of time. Extracting data about communication patterns directly from, for example, logs of phone calls and emails will also provide data sufficiently fine-grained to count actual frequencies of communications, rather than have people estimate them, as in this study. Third, the project consisted of 22 participants. While very many projects are this size or smaller it remains unknown whether personometric maps scale to considerably larger projects. For larger projects interactive maps may be superior to the static maps studied in this paper. Fourth, the personometric maps have only been validated by people internal to the project. People external to the project will lack project participants' contextual knowledge and it is unknown to what extent this makes the maps less useful to them. These limitations suggest important areas of future work on personometric mapping.

5 Conclusion

Multi-site projects are prevalent in R&D, and engineers increasingly experience that information pertinent to their work is held by remote co-workers external to the group of colleagues with whom they regularly meet face to face. Personometrics, as put forward in this study, intends to advance our understanding of people as information objects by mapping and visualizing the intellectual structures embedded in interpersonal communication patterns. An important practical application of personometrics is to provide a conceptual basis and feasible techniques for the design of systems that support engineers in ad hoc identification of distributed colleagues with specified competences.

By equating the co-occurrence of interpersonal communications with co-citations in scholarly writings, personometrics extends the scope of bibliometric citation techniques to the investigation, mapping, and visualization of project participants' communication and competence patterns. In this study we have demonstrated how personometric maps can be constructed from empirical data about the interpersonal communications made by a group of R&D engineers. These personometric maps, which project participants find accurate and easy to understand, show that communications in the project centre around the project manager and two other longstanding employees, all at the main site. The other project participants form two rings around the centre. Participants with identical primary competences are frequently distributed across sites but mostly appear close to each other on the maps, indicating similar communication patterns. However, three competence groups span both the outer and inner ring, suggesting that these groups have a representative who mediates between the group and the centre of the project.

Half of the project participants' communications are with colleagues external to the project and intended to complement the expertise available in the project and avoid rework. Project participants see personometric maps of old projects as particularly useful because old projects are important entry points in searches for information and the maps retain information that is indicative of people's competences and otherwise not readily available. By also including communications with people external to the organization, in this project only 2% of the communications, personometric maps may identify strategically important competences not sufficiently covered within an organization.

In relation to practical application of personometric maps, (semi-)automated data collection appears necessary but an occasional, supplementary questionnaire may provide additional data about face-to-face communications and improve the possibilities of removing noise in the data by triangulation. The use practices that emerge when personometric maps become an established means of people finding in an organization should be examined to assess and refine this type of analysis. While exploratory, this study suggests that personometric analysis holds promise.

Acknowledgements

This paper is based on Morten Skovvang and Mikael Elbæks's Master's thesis from the Royal Danish School of Library and Information Science. Birger Larsen and Peter Ingwersen are acknowledged for their support and inspiration in writing the Master's thesis. Morten Hertzum was supported, in part, by the IT University of Copenhagen and the Contextual Models of Trust project. Olle Persson is acknowledged for providing free access to *Bibexcel* (www.umu.se/inforsk/Bibexcel), the tool used for producing the personometric maps. Special thanks are due to our informants who generously devoted their time to this study in spite of their busy schedules.

References

1. Ackerman, M.S.: Augmenting organizational memory: A field study of Answer Garden. *ACM Transactions on Information Systems*, 16, 3 (1998) 203-224
2. Allen, T.J.: *Managing the flow of technology: Technology transfer and the dissemination of technological information within the R&D organization*. MIT Press, Cambridge, MA (1977)
3. Börner, K., Chen, C., Boyack, K.W.: Visualizing knowledge domains. In: Cronin, B. (ed.): *Annual Review of Information Science and Technology*, Vol. 37. Information Today, Medford, NJ (2003) 179-255
4. Cronin, B.: *The citation process: The role and significance of citations in scientific communication*. Taylor Graham, London (1984)
5. Dunlop, M.D.: Development and evaluation of clustering techniques for finding people. In: Reimer, U. (ed.): *Proceedings of the Third International Conference on Practical Aspects of Knowledge Management*. CEUR, Technical University of Aachen, Aachen, Germany (2000) 9-1 - 9-7
6. Fisher, D., Dourish, P.: Social and temporal structures in everyday collaboration. In: *Proceedings of the CHI 2004 Conference on Human Factors in Computing Systems*. ACM Press, New York (2004) 551-558
7. Foner, L.N.: *Political artifacts and personal privacy: The Yenta multi-agent distributed matchmaking system*. MIT, Cambridge, MA (1999) [PhD Thesis]. Available from: http://foner.www.media.mit.edu/people/foner/PhD-Thesis/Dissertation (consulted January 3, 2005)
8. Grosser, K.: Human networks in organizational information processing. In: Williams, M.E. (ed.): *Annual Review of Information Science and Technology*, Vol. 26. Knowledge Industry Publications, White Plains, NY (1991) 349-402

9. Hertzum, M.: Six roles of documents in professionals' work. In: Bødker, S., Kyng, M., Schmidt, K. (eds.): *Proceedings of the Sixth European Conference on Computer Supported Cooperative Work*. Kluwer, Dordrecht (1999) 41-60
10. Hertzum, M.: People as carriers of experience and sources of commitment: Information seeking in a software design project. *New Review of Information Behaviour Research*, 1 (2000) 135-149
11. Hertzum, M., Pejtersen, A.M.: The information-seeking practices of engineers: Searching for documents as well as for people. *Information Processing & Management*, 36, 5 (2000) 761-778
12. Ingwersen, P.: Cognitive perspectives of information retrieval interaction: Elements of a cognitive IR theory. *Journal of Documentation*, 52, 1 (1996) 3-50
13. Kautz, H., Selman, B., Shah, M.: Referral web: Combining social networks and collaborative filtering. *Communications of the ACM*, 40, 3 (1997) 63-65
14. King, D.W., Casto, J., Jones, H.: *Communication by engineers: A literature review of engineers' information needs, seeking processes, and use*. Council on Library Resources, Washington, DC (1994)
15. Kruskal, J.B., Wish, M.: *Multidimensional scaling*. Sage, Newbury Park, CA (1978)
16. MacRoberts, M.H., MacRoberts, B.R.: Problems of citation analysis: A critical review. *Journal of the American Society for Information Science*, 40, 5 (1989) 342-349
17. Mockus, A., Herbsleb, J.D.: Expertise browser: A quantitative approach to identifying expertise. In: *Proceedings of the 24th International Conference on Software Engineering*. ACM Press, New York (2002) 503-512
18. Mueller-Prothmann, T., Finke, I.: SELaKT – Social network analysis as a method for expert localisation and sustainable knowledge transfer. *Journal of Universal Computer Science*, 10, 6 (2004) 691-701
19. Noyons, E.: Bibliometric mapping of science in a science policy context. *Scientometrics*, 50, 1 (2001) 83-98
20. Pinelli, T.E., Bishop, A.P., Barclay, R.O., Kennedy, J.M.: The information-seeking behavior of engineers. In: Kent, A., Hall, C.M. (eds.): *Encyclopedia of library and information science*, Vol. 52. Marcel Dekker, New York (1993) 167-201
21. Scott, J.: *Social network analysis: A handbook*. Sage, London (1991)
22. Small, H.: Co-citation in scientific literature: A new measure of the relationship between publications. *Journal of the American Society for Information Science*, 24, 4 (1973) 265-269
23. van Raan, A.F.J.: In matters of quantitative studies of science the fault of theorists is offering too little and asking too much. *Scientometrics*, 43, 1 (1998) 129-139
24. White, H.D., McCain, K.W.: Visualizing a discipline: An author co-citation analysis of information science, 1972-1995. *Journal of the American Society for Information Science*, 49, 4 (1998) 327-355
25. Zipperer, L.: The creative professional and knowledge. *Special Libraries*, 84, 2 (1993) 69-78
26. Zucker, L.G., Darby, M.R., Brewer, M.B., Peng, Y.: Collaboration structure and information dilemmas in biotechnology: Organizational boundaries as trust production. In: Kramer, R.M., Tyler, T.R. (eds.): *Trust in Organizations: Frontiers of Theory and Research*. Sage, Thousand Oaks, CA (1996) 90-113

Annotations as Context for Searching Documents

Maristella Agosti and Nicola Ferro

Department of Information Engineering – University of Padua,
Via Gradenigo, 6/B – 35131 Padova (PD) – Italy
{maristella.agosti, nicola.ferro}@unipd.it

Abstract. This paper discusses how to exploit annotations as a useful context in order to search and retrieve relevant documents for a user query. This paper provides a formal framework which can be useful in facing this problem and shows how this framework can be employed, by using techniques which come from the hypertext information retrieval and data fusion fields.

1 Introduction

Digital Library Management Systems (DLMSs) are currently in a state of evolution: today they are simply places where information resources can be stored and made available, whereas for tomorrow they will become an integrated part of the way the user works. For example, instead of simply downloading a paper and then working on a printed version, a user will be able to work directly with the paper by means of the tools provided by the DLMS and share their work with colleagues. This way, the user's intellectual work and the information resources provided by the DLMS can be merged together in order to constitute a single working context. Thus, the DLMS is no longer perceived as something external to the intellectual production process nor as a mere consulting tool, but as an intrinsic and active part of the intellectual production process, as pointed out in [1].

Annotations are effective means in order to enable the paradigm of interaction between users and DLMSs envisioned above, since they are very well-established practice and widely used. Annotations are not only a way of explaining and enriching an information resource with personal observations, but also a means of transmitting and sharing ideas in order to improve collaborative work practices. Furthermore, annotations allow users to naturally merge and link personal contents with the information resources provided by the DLMS in order to create a common context that unifies all of these contents.

In fact, annotations allow the creation of new relationships among existing contents, by means of links that connect annotations together and with existing content. In this sense we can consider that existing content and annotations constitute a hypertext, according to the definition of hypertext provided in [2]. This hypertext can be exploited not only for providing alternative navigation and browsing capabilities, but can also offer advanced search functionalities. Furthermore, [3] considers annotations as a natural way of creating and increasing

F. Crestani and I. Ruthven (Eds.): CoLIS 2005, LNCS 3507, pp. 155–170, 2005.

hypertexts that connect information resources in a DLMS by actively engaging users. Finally, the hypertext existing between information resources and annotations enables different annotation configurations, that are *threads of annotations*, i.e. an annotation made in response to another annotation, and *sets of annotation*, i.e. a bundle of annotations on the same passage of text [4, 5].

Thus, annotations introduce a new content layer aimed at elucidating the meaning of underlying documents, so that annotations can make hidden facets of the annotated documents in a more explicit way. In conclusion, we can consider that annotations constitute a special kind of context, that we call *annotative context*, for the documents of a DLMS, because they provide additional content which is related to the annotated documents. This viewpoint about annotations covers a wide range of annotations, ranging from personal jottings in the margin of a page to scholarly comments made by an expert in order to explain a passage of a text. Thus, these different kinds of annotations involve different scopes for the annotation itself and, consequently, different kinds of annotative context. If we deal with a personal jotting, the recipient of the annotation is usually the author himself and so this kind of annotation involves a *private annotative context*; on the other hand, the recipients of a scholarly annotation are usually people who are not necessarily related to the author of the annotation, which thus involves a *public annotative context*; finally, a team of people can work together on a shared topic and can exchange annotations related to the topic in question: thus, in this case we have a *collaborative annotative context*.

In this paper, we aim at exploiting the annotative context in order to use annotations as an effective means for searching and retrieving the documents managed by a DLMS. The presentation is structured as follows: Section 2 introduces an overview of our approach; Section 3 describes our reference architecture; Section 4 presents our framework, which enables the annotations to be effectively employed to search for the documents, and describes an example of data fusion strategy applied to the framework; finally, Section 5 draws some conclusions and gives us an outlook for the future.

2   Search Strategy Overview

Despite all of the research in modelling annotations and providing annotation–enabled systems, there is much less study regarding the usage of annotations for retrieving documents. Golovchinsky et al. [6] compare queries based on annotations with relevance feedback, and considers annotation–based queries as an automatic technique for query construction, since queries are automatically generated from annotated text, e.g. from highlighted text. Frommholz et. al [7] consider annotations – specifically annotations threads – as an extension of the document they belong to, creating a discourse context, in which not only the annotation itself but also its position in the discourse and its type, are exploited for searching and retrieving documents; this approach is revised and extended upon in [8] to probabilistic datalog.

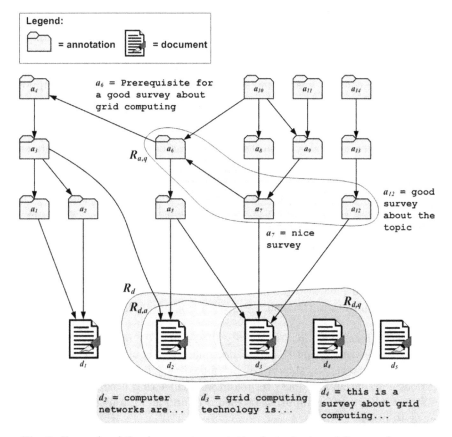

Fig. 1. Example of the document–annotation hypertext used for search purposes

We need to develop a search strategy which is able to effectively take into account the multiple sources of evidence which come from both documents and annotations. In fact, the combining of these multiple sources of evidence can be exploited in order to improve the performances of an information management system. Our aim is to retrieve more documents that are relevant and to have them ranked in a way which is better than a system that does not makes use of annotations.

We will now introduce our search strategy by means of illustrating an example. It is important to note that this is not an exhaustive example, however it will help the reader to familiarize themselves with our search strategy. Figure 1 shows a possible hypertext which could exist among documents and annotations, and which we have called document–annotation hypertext. Suppose that we have the following query: $q =$ "good survey grid computing".

Firstly, we can start by searching the set of documents for this query. Let us suppose that we obtain the first result set $R_{d,q} = \{d_4, d_3\}$ ($R_{d,q}$ stands for: Result Documents by Query) where, intuitively, d_4 is ranked higher than d_3 because three query terms out of four are contained in d_4 while d_3 contains only two terms out of four. However, none of these two documents explains anything about how good the survey is and d_3 does not specify whether the document is a survey or not. Moreover, d_2 is not retrieved because it is concerned with computer networks in general and not with grid computing in particular.

Secondly, we can also search the set of annotations for this query. Suppose that we obtain the second result set $R_{a,q} = \{a_6, a_{12}, a_7\}$ ($R_{a,q}$ stands for: Result Annotations by Query) where, intuitively, a_6 has the highest rank because it contains all of the query terms; a_{12} is ranked lower than a_6 because it contains only two query terms; finally, a_7 has the lowest rank because it contains only one query term. It is worth noting that neither a_7 nor a_{12} explains what the topic of the survey is about, even if they provide additional information about the document they annotate; in a certain sense, it is the symmetric problem with respect to d_3 and d_4, that do not specify that much about the "survey side" of the query. At this point, we have two distinct sources of evidence on hand – the one which comes from the document set and the one which comes from the annotation set – and therefore we should exploit both of them in order to better satisfy the user's information need. Thus, we can exploit them with a twofold aim: firstly, to add new relevant documents to the result set and, secondly, to re-rank the documents in the result set. With this in mind, we can note that:

– the annotations thread $a_6 \rightarrow a_5 \rightarrow d_2$ allows us to connect annotation a_6 to document d_2, suggesting that also document d_2 should be included in the result set. However, d_2 should not be ranked very high because, intuitively, it does not contain any query term and we deduce that it could be related to a survey about grid computing by means of an annotation that is two steps away from d_2;
– the annotations set a_7 and a_{12} regarding document d_3 allows us to understand that d_3 is a survey about grid computing, which is probably a good one. Therefore, we could consider ranking it higher.

Thus, we can identify a third result set $R_{d,a} = \{d_3, d_2\}$ ($R_{d,a}$ stands for: Result Documents by Annotation) where d_3 is ranked higher than d_2 for the reasons explained above. Note that we identified $R_{d,a}$ by means of $R_{a,q}$, that is we found the documents contained in $R_{d,a}$ using the annotations contained in $R_{a,q}$ and the document–annotation hypertext permitted us to pass from annotations ($R_{a,q}$) to documents ($R_{d,q}$).

We can conclude this line of reasoning with the final result set $R_d = \{d_3, d_4, d_2\}$ (R_d stands for: Result Documents). Intuitively, d_3 has the highest rank because it is strongly supported by its own evidence and the evidence provided by the annotations a_7 and a_{12}; in fact, $d_3 \in R_{d,q} \cap R_{d,a}$, as depicted in Figure 1. d_4 keeps its former rank, which is now lower than the rank given to d_3, due to the fact that it is not supported by any further evidence except its own; indeed, $d_4 \in R_{d,q} \setminus R_{d,a}$, as depicted in Figure 1. Finally, we add d_2 which has the lowest rank, due to the fact that it is supported only by the annotation a_6 which, as mentioned above, is not so close to d_2; indeed, $d_2 \in R_{d,a} \setminus R_{d,q}$, as depicted in Figure 1.

In conclusion, annotations provide us with an additional context which can be exploited with the ultimate goal of retrieving more documents that are relevant and better ranked. Furthermore, the document–annotation hypertext is the basic infrastructure which enables us to combine the sources of evidence which derive from documents and annotations. Thus, we face this research problem in the context of *data fusion* [9], because we need to combine the source of evidence which comes from annotations with the one which comes from documents. Moreover, also *Hypertext Information Retrieval (HIR)* techniques [10] are suitable in order to support the search strategy described above, because we need to deal with an hypertext in order to combine the different sources of evidence.

2.1 Search Strategy Issues

The search strategy introduced above presents some issues concerning how to use the document–annotation hypertext in order to identify the annotated documents, specifically regarding how to map $R_{a,q}$ to $R_{d,a}$.

In our previous example, we started from $R_{a,q} = \{a_6, a_{12}, a_7\}$ and we mapped it to $R_{d,a} = \{d_3, d_2\}$; this mapping is not the only possibility: we could also add d_1 to $R_{d,a}$, if we follow the path $a_6 \rightarrow a_4 \rightarrow a_3 \rightarrow a_1 \rightarrow d_1$.

The first issue is that the mapping between $R_{a,q}$ and $R_{d,a}$ is not univocally determined. The second issue concerns the cardinality of R_{d_a}: there is the risk, as shown above, that all the documents that have one or more annotations will be included in the $R_{d,a}$ set, through either a long or a short path. Worst case scenario, we could obtain $R_{d,a} = D$ or, in any case, $|R_{d,a}| \gg |R_{d,q}|$, even though we started with a few annotations retrieved for the query.

Thus, we should add some constraints to the document–annotation hypertext, so that the $R_{d,a}$ set can be unambiguously determined and its cardinality does not increase too much. We will discuss how to overcome these issues in Section 4.

3 Reference Architecture

As explained in the Section 1, annotations create an hypertext that allows users to merge their personal content with the information resources provided by diverse DLMSs: this hypertext can span and cross the boundaries of a single DLMS, if users need to interact with diverse DLMSs. The possibility of having a hypertext that spans the boundaries of different DLMSs is quite innovative because up to now DLMSs do not normally have a hypertext connecting information resources with each other and, if present, such a hypertext is usually confined within the boundaries of a single DLMS. In particular, annotations exploit the hypertext in order to provide users with a *distributed annotative context*, which connects the documents managed by different DLMSs.

We aim at designing and developing a system which is able to carry out the annotative context and the search strategy, previously discussed. We face this problem from an abstract point of view: we do not fully specify how each component of the system works but we describe and define how these components interact with each other. Thus, our architectural approach is based on *flexibility*,

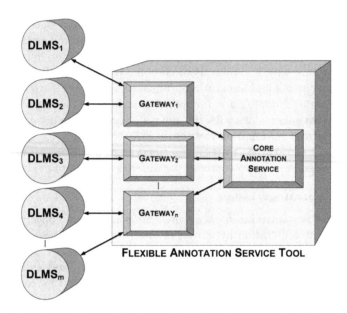

Fig. 2. Overview of the architecture of FAST with respect to different DLMSs

because we need to adopt an architecture which is flexible enough to support a wide range of different DLMSs; thus, we named our target system *Flexible Annotation Service Tool (FAST)*. Figure 2 shows the general architecture of the FAST system and its integration with different DLMSs: the *Core Annotation Service (CAS)* provides annotation management functionalities, and is able to interact with different gateways, that are specialised for integrating the CAS into different DLMSs. From the standpoint of a DLMS the FAST system acts like any other distributed service of the DLMS, even if it is actually made up of two distinct modules, the gateway and the CAS; on the other hand, the FAST system can be made available for another DLMS by creating a new gateway.

As a consequence of this architectural choice, the FAST system knows everything about annotations, however it cannot make any assumption regarding the information resources provided by the DLMS, being that it needs to cooperate with different DLMSs. This architectural choice influences the way in which our search strategy is carried out. Indeed, we aim at combining multiple sources of evidence which come from both documents and annotations. Since the source of evidence concerning the documents is completely managed by the DLMS, FAST has to query the DLMS in order to obtain it. Only after that FAST has acquired this information from the DLMS, it can be combined with the source of evidence which comes from annotations in order to create a list of result documents that better satisfies the user's information needs. In conclusion, we can now deal with a distributed search problem.

4   Search Strategy Framework

In order to carry out the introduced search strategy, we need to deal with two kinds of *Digital Objects (DOs)*, that are documents and annotations. Let D be the *set of documents* and $d \in D$ is a generic document; let A be the *set of annotations* and $a \in A$ is a generic annotation; let $DO = D \cup A$ be the set of digital objects and $do \in DO$ is a generic digital object, which can be either a document or an annotation. Finally, let Q be the *set of user queries* and $q \in Q$ is a generic query. The *Unified Modeling Language (UML)* [11, 12, 13] sequence diagram of Figure 3 summarizes our search strategy:

1. the user submits a query $q \in Q$ to FAST;
2. FAST forwards the query to the DLMS, which searches for documents to retrieve for the query q.
   We call $R_{d,q} \subseteq D$ the result set returned by the DLMS, $s_{d,q} \in [0,1]$ the similarity score of the document d with respect to the query q. According to our architecture, $R_{d,q}$ is completely defined and managed by the DLMS and FAST has no control over $R_{d,q}$. Thus, the DLMS has the function of providing $R_{d,q}$ and a similarity score $s_{d,q}$ for each document $d \in R_{d,q}$ to FAST;
3. FAST searches for annotations to retrieve for the query q.
   We call $R_{a,q} \subseteq A$ the result set returned by FAST, $s_{a,q} \in [0,1]$ the similarity score of the annotation a with respect to the query q. According to our architecture, $R_{a,q}$ is completely defined and managed by FAST;
4. FAST determines the documents associated to the annotations contained in $R_{a,q}$, by using a *mapping function* $M : A \rightarrow D$, that associates an annotation $a \in A$ to a document $d \in D$.
   We call $R_{d,a} \subseteq D$ the set containing the documents associated to the annotations in $R_{a,q}$, i.e. $R_{d,a} = M(R_{a,q})$; $s_{d,a} \in [0,1]$ is the similarity score of a document $d \in R_{d,a}$;
5. FAST combines the two sets $R_{d,q}$ and $R_{d,a}$ into one set $R_d = R_{d,q} \cup R_{d,a} \subseteq D$ in order to obtain only one list of retrieved documents. $s_d \in [0,1]$ is the similarity score of a document $d \in R_d$, obtained combining $s_{d,q}$ and $s_{d,a}$;
6. FAST returns the list of retrieved documents to the user.

We can point out some interesting characteristics of this search strategy. Firstly, in the fourth step FAST needs to employ both HIR and data fusion techniques: indeed, the different paths in the hypertext allow FAST to associate annotations to documents, which are necessary to determine $R_{d,a}$ from $R_{a,q}$; furthermore, FAST has to exploit also data fusion techniques in order to compute the similarity score $s_{d,a}$ of a document d from the similarity scores $s_{a,q}$ of the annotations linked to d. Secondly, in the fifth step we need to combine the similarity scores $s_{d,q}$ computed by the DLMS with the similarity scores $s_{d,a}$ computed by FAST, which is a data fusion problem. Finally, the sequence diagram of Figure 3 further highlights that we are dealing with a distributed search problem.

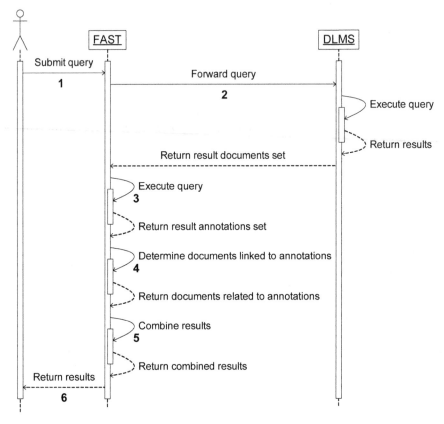

Fig. 3. Search strategy

Note that, as introduced in Section 3, we will face our problem from an abstract point of view. Thus, in the following sections we will not go into a lot of detail on how annotations and documents are indexed and searched, but instead we will assume that there is a component of the system designated with providing such functionalities.

In the next section, we will formally define the basic structure needed to perform our search strategy, which is the document–annotation hypertext; we will also point out some properties of the document–annotation hypertext relevant for our search strategy.

4.1   Document–Annotation Hypertext

Annotations can be linked to DOs with two main types of links, as pointed out in [5]:

– *annotate link*: an annotation annotates a DO, which can be a document or another annotation. The "annotate link" is intended only to allow an annotation to annotate one or more parts of a given DO. Thus, this kind of link lets the annotation express *intra–DO relationships*, meaning that the annotation creates a relationship among the different parts of the annotated DO;

– *relate-to link*: an annotation relates to a DO, which can be a document or another annotation. The "relate-to link" is intended only to allow an annotation to relate to one or more parts of other DOs, but not the annotated one. Thus, this kind of link lets the annotation express *inter–DO relationships*, meaning that the annotation creates a relationship between the annotated DO and the other DOs that it is related to.

With respect to these two main types of link, we introduce the following constraint: an annotation must annotate one and only one DO, which can be either a document or another annotation, that is an annotation must have one and only one "annotate link". In other words, this constraint means that an annotation can be created only for the purpose of annotating a DO and not exclusively for relating to a DO. Moreover, an annotation can annotate one and only one DO, because the "annotate link" expresses intra–DO relationships and thus they cannot be mutual to multiple DOs which are different from the annotated one. Finally, this constraint does not prevent the annotation from relating to more than one DO, i.e. from having more than one "relate-to link". We can associate to these links a *set of allowed link types* $LT = \{\text{Annotate}, \text{RelateTo}\}$; an element $lt \in LT$ corresponds to one of the link types.

Definition 1. *The **document–annotation hypertext** is a labeled directed graph $H_{da} = (DO, E_{da} \subseteq A \times DO)$ where DO is the set of vertices and E_{da} is the set of edges. Let $l_{da} : E_{da} \rightarrow LT$ be the labelling function. For each $e = (a, do) \in E_{da}$ there is a $l_{da}(e)$-labeled edge from the annotation a to the generic digital object do. The following constraints must be satisfied:*

1. *each annotation a must annotate one and only one digital object[1]:*

$$\forall a \in A \; \exists! \, e = (a, do) \in E_{da} \mid l_{da}(e) = \text{Annotate}$$

2. *the graph does not contain loops:*

$$\forall a \in A \; \nexists e = (a, do) \in E_{da} \mid a = do$$

3. *the graph does not contain cycles:*

$$\nexists C = a_0 a_k a_{k-1} \cdots a_1 a_0 \mid$$
$$e_0 = (a_0, a_k), e_k = (a_k, a_{k-1}), \ldots, e_1 = (a_1, a_0) \in E_{da},$$
$$l_{da}(e_0) = l_{da}(e_k) = \ldots = l_{da}(e_1) = \text{Annotate}$$

---

[1] $\exists!$ is the *unique existential quantifier*, and it is read "there exists a unique ... such that ...".

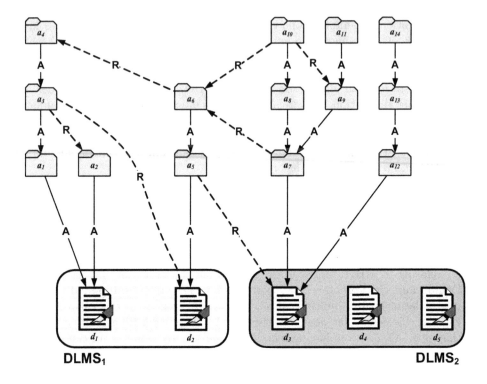

Fig. 4. Example of document–annotation hypertext H_{da}, corresponding at the hypertext shown in figure 1

Note that each $e \in E_{da}$ always starts from an annotation, while $e \in E_{da}$ that starts from a document does not exist. Each annotation is constrained to be incident with one and only one edge with link type "Annotate", thus formalizing the notion of link type mentioned above. The constraint related to loops prevent us from creating self-referencing annotations, which have no use for our purposes. Finally, annotations involve a temporal dimension, since each annotation has to annotate an already existing DO. Thus, the last constraint about cycles of annotations prevents us from creating cycles where the oldest annotation a_0 annotates the newest annotation a_k; note that this is not an issue for document vertices, since "Annotate" links can start only from annotations.

Figure 4 shows an example of document–annotation hypertext, which corresponds to the hypertext show in Figure 1, where the "Annotate links" are represented with a continuous line labeled "A", while the "RelateTo links" are represented with a dotted line labeled "R". Figure 4 also points out another important feature of the document–annotation hypertext: it can span and cross the boundaries of the single DLMS, as discussed in Section 3. The DLMS$_1$ manages d_1 and d_2, while the DLMS$_2$ manages d_3, d_4, and d_5. There are annotations that act as a bridge between two DLMSs: for example, a_5 annotates d_2, which is managed by $DLMS_1$, and refers to d_3, which is managed by $DLMS_2$. This is a quite an innovative characteristic of the document–annotation hypertext. This characteristic further highlights the distributed nature of our search strategy, which is not only distributed between the DLMS and FAST, but it may also involve more DLMSs.

The following proposition will show that each annotation a belongs to a unique tree rooted in a document d.

Proposition 1. *Let $H'_{da} = (DO', E'_{da})$ be the subgraph of H_{da}, such that:*

- $E'_{da} = \{e \in E_{da} \mid l_{da}(e) = \text{Annotate}\}$
- $DO' = \{do \in DO \mid \exists\, e' \in E'_{da}, e' = (a, do)\}$

H'_{da} is the subgraph whose edges are of kind Annotate and whose vertices are incident with at least one of such edges. Let $H''_{da} = (DO'', E''_{da})$ be the underlying graph of H'_{da}, that is the undirected version of H'_{da}.

The following properties hold: H''_{da} is a forest[2] and every tree in H''_{da} contains a unique document vertex d.

Proof. Ab absurdo: if H''_{da} was not a forest, then it would be a cyclic graph. The only way of obtaining a cycle in H''_{da} is that in H_{da}:

$$\exists\, a \in A,\ \exists\, e_1 = (a, do_1)\,, e_2 = (a, do_2) \in E_{da}, do_1 \neq do_2\ |$$
$$l_{da}(e_1) = l_{da}(e_2) = \text{Annotate}$$

i.e. an annotation exists in H_{da} from which two *Annotate* edges start from, but this contradicts the definition 1 given for the graph H_{da} and thus, H''_{da} is a forest.

Since H''_{da} is a forest, its components are trees. Ab absurdo suppose that there is a tree T whose vertices are only annotations. A tree T with n vertices has $n-1$ edges but, for the item number 1 of definition 1 each annotation a must be incident with one and only one Annotate edge, then for n annotations there are n edges in H''_{da}; so T can not be a tree. Therefore, every tree in H''_{da} contains, at least, a document vertex d. Suppose now that there is a tree T which contains two document vertices d_1 and d_2, $d_1 \neq d_2$. Being that for every two vertices in a tree there is a unique path connecting them, in the path $P = d_1 a_1 \ldots a_i \ldots a_k d_2$ there must be an annotation a_i from which in H_{da} two edges of kind Annotate start, since by definition of H_{da} the are no edges of the type $e = (d_m, d_n) \in E_{da}$. But the annotation a_i contradicts the definition of H_{da} and thus, there is a unique document vertex d in T. □

Proposition 1 assures us that for each document there is a unique tree T_d that can be rooted in d. Remembering that in a tree any two given vertices are linked by a unique path, for each annotation $a \in R_{a,q}$ we can determine the unique path to the root d of the tree to which the annotation belongs. In this way we can figure out the mapping function M between $R_{a,q}$ and $R_{d,a}$. Finally, we are

---

[2] A forest is an acyclic graph. A forest is a graph whose components are trees [14].

sure that each annotation $a \in A$ belongs to a tree T_d in H''_{da}, since by definition of H_{da} each annotation must be an incident with one and only one edge e with $l_{da}(e) =$ Annotate and thus each annotation $a \in A$ also belongs to H''_{da}.

Note that if we had not removed the "RelateTo link" edges from the graph H''_{da}, it could have contained cycles; consider Figure 4: for example, a cycle would be $C = a_7 a_6 a_{10} a_8 a_7$, because in H''_{da} we do not consider the direction of the edges.

Finally it is worth noting that the document-annotation hypertext of definition 1 lets the mapping function M and the set $R_{d,a}$ overcome the issues described in Section 2.1: firstly, $R_{d,a}$ is unambiguously identified, since proposition 2 ensures us that each annotation $a \in A$ belongs to a unique tree rooted in a document $d \in D$; secondly, the cardinality of $R_{d,a}$ is not too high, since each annotation is connected to only one document and so $|R_{d,a}| \leq |R_{a,q}|$.

Our search strategy consists of several steps: we assume that we have already determined both $R_{d,q}$ and $R_{a,q}$ (respectively, the second and third step of the search strategy), by using the proper information retrieval techniques for indexing and retrieving both documents and annotations; for the fourth and fifth steps it is necessary to define proper algorithms, which are discussed in the following sections.

4.2   Search Strategy Step 4: Hypertext-Driven Data Fusion

We call *hypertext-driven data fusion* the fourth step of our search strategy, because it needs to exploit the document–annotation hypertext in order to compute the similarity scores $s_{d,a}$ for the documents in $R_{d,a}$, that are the documents determined by using, by combining the similarity scores $s_{a,q}$ of the annotations linked to them.

Proposition 1 ensures us that each annotation belongs to a tree rooted in a document. Thus, we can carry out the mapping function M between $R_{a,q}$ and $R_{d,a}$ by simply associating each annotation $a \in R_{a,q}$ to the document d at the root of the tree the annotation belongs to. In this way, $R_{d,a}$ can be unambiguously determined starting from $R_{a,q}$.

Before we can compute $s_{d,a}$ for each document $d \in R_{d,a}$, we need to introduce the notion of *compound similarity score*. To this end, consider the graph $H''_{da} = (DO'', E'')$, a tree T_d rooted in a document $d \in DO''$ and a subtree T_a of T_d rooted in an annotation a. Let $s^c_{a,q}$ be the *compound similarity score* between an annotation $a \in DO''$ and a query $q \in Q$, defined as follows:

$$s^c_{a,q} = \begin{cases} \alpha s_{a,q} & \text{if } a \text{ is a leaf} \\ \alpha s_{a,q} + \dfrac{(1-\alpha)}{|\text{succ}(a)|} \displaystyle\sum_{a_k \in \text{succ}(a)} s^c_{a_k,q} & \text{if } a \text{ is not a leaf} \end{cases} \tag{1}$$

where $\text{succ}(v_j)$ is a function that returns the set of successors of a vertex v_j and $\alpha \in [0, 1]$ is a parameter. In the following we assume that $s_{a,q}$ is zero for annotations that do not belong to $R_{a,q}$.

$s^c_{a,q}$ recursively computes the weighted average between the similarity score $s_{a,q}$ of an annotation a and the average of the compound similarity scores of its successors. Furthermore $s_{a,q}^c$ penalizes scores which come from lengthy paths, because for a path $P = a_0 \ldots a_k$ the similarity score $s_{a_k,q}$ of a_k is weighted $\alpha(1-\alpha)^k$. Thus $s_{a,q}^c$ satisfies the requirement, expressed in Section 2, that the similarity scores should not be influenced by annotations that are too far apart from the document. Remember that $s_{a,q}$ is not null only for those annotations that belong to $R_{a,q}$; thus annotations, that belong to a path but not to $R_{a,q}$, do not contribute to $s_{a,q}^c$, even if they are taken into account during the averaging by the $|succ(a)|$ term, thus further penalizing long paths. Equation (1) resembles the CombANZ strategy of [15], proposing a recursive version of this strategy, even if CombANZ averages only on non-zero similarity scores. In this sense we entitled this section graph-driven data fusion strategy. Example of functions similar to $s_{a,q}^c(a,q)$ can be found in [7, 8, 16], but [7, 8] exploit a probabilistic framework and chooses the path with the maximum probability of the relevance of a document, while [16] does not average the similarity scores and has an iterative approach to the problem.

At this point, for each document $d \in R_{d,a}$ FAST needs to compute its similarity score $s_{d,a}$. If we consider the graph H_{da}'', and for each document $d \in R_{d,a}$ we identify the tree T_d rooted in d, then the similarity score $s_{d,a}$ is given by:

$$s_{d,a} = \frac{1}{|succ(d)|} \sum_{a \in succ(d)} s_{a,q}^c \qquad (2)$$

where $succ(v_j)$ is a function that returns the set of successors of a vertex v_j. $s_{d,a}$ simply averages the compound similarity score of the annotations belonging to the tree rooted in d.

4.3   Search Strategy Step 4: Traditional Data Fusion

We call *traditional data fusion* the fifth step of our search strategy, because in this step we compute a similarity score s_d for a document by combining the evidence which comes from $R_{d,q}$ and $R_{d,a}$, as in a usual data fusion problem. With this in mind, we can apply the CombMNZ strategy, proposed by [15], as follows:

$$s_d = \begin{cases} 2\,(s_{d,q} + s_{d,a}) & \text{if } d \in R_{d,q} \cap R_{d,a} \\ s_{d,q} & \text{if } d \in R_{d,q} \cap \overline{R_{d,a}} \\ s_{d,a} & \text{if } d \in \overline{R_{d,q}} \cap R_{d,a} \end{cases} \qquad (3)$$

If the similarity score $s_{d,q}$ is not normalized, before applying equation (3), we can normalize it according to the expression proposed by [17]:

$$\bar{s}_{d,q} = \frac{s_{d,q} - \min_{d \in R_{d,q}} s_{d,q}}{\max_{d \in R_{d,q}} s_{d,q} - \min_{d \in R_{d,q}} s_{d,q}} \qquad (4)$$

4.4   Example of the Search Strategy

Consider the example discussed in Section 2 and shown in Figure 1. Suppose that: $R_{d,q} = \{d_4, d_3\}$ with $s_{d_3,q} = 0.40$, and $s_{d_4,q} = 0.85$; $R_{a,q} = \{a_6, a_{12}, a_7\}$ with $s_{a_6,q} = 0.90$, $s_{a_{12},q} = 0.25$, and $s_{a_7,q} = 0.10$.

In order to carry out the fourth step of our search strategy, i.e. the hypertext-driven data fusion strategy, we start mapping $R_{a,q} = \{a_6, a_{12}, a_7\}$ into $R_{d,a} = \{d_2, d_3\}$. Then, we choose $\alpha = 0.50$, as an example, and, by applying equations (1) and (2), we obtain:

$$s_{d_2,a} = s^c_{a_5,q} = \alpha s_{a_5,q} + (1 - \alpha)s^c_{a_6,q} = \alpha(1 - \alpha)s_{a_6,q} = 0.23$$

$$s_{d_3,a} = \frac{1}{2}\left(s^c_{a_7,q} + s^c_{a_{12},q}\right) = \frac{\alpha}{2}\left(s_{a_7,q} + s_{a_{12},q}\right) = 0.09$$

In order to carry out the fifth step of our search strategy, i.e. the traditional data fusion strategy, we apply equation (3), obtaining $R_d = \{d_3, d_4, d_2\}$ with:

$$s_{d_2} = s_{d_2,a} = 0.23$$

$$s_{d_3} = 2\left(s_{d_3,q} + s_{d_3,a}\right) = 0.98$$

$$s_{d_4} = s_{d_4,q} = 0.85$$

In conclusion, equations (1), (2), and (3) fit well with the search strategy discussed in Section 2. Indeed, the initial ranking provided the DLMS was d_4, d_3, while the final ranking is d_3, d_4, d_2. Thus, we re-ranked the documents, giving a better rank to d_3 which benefits from the evidence of both documents and annotations, and we also added the new document d_2 to the result list, without ranking it too high, since it has been only added on the basis of the annotations which it is linked to.

5   Conclusions and Future Work

We presented a framework in which annotations can be exploited as a useful context in order to retrieve documents relevant for a user's query. Then, we showed how this framework can be effectively employed for developing search strategies, that adopt techniques which come from the HIR and data fusion fields.

Future research work will be concerned with the application of the proposed search strategy to a real application in order to assess the performances of the proposed search strategy. An obstacle to the evaluation of these kinds of systems is the lack of an experimental test collection with annotations, that would allow us to test and quantitatively compare different search strategies.

Acknowledgements

Sincere thanks are also due to Luca Pretto for the time he spent in discussing the aspects related to document-annotation hypertext.

The work reported in this paper has been conducted in the context of a joint program between the Italian National Research Council (CNR) and the Ministry of Education (MIUR), under the law 449/97-99. The work is also partially supported by the DELOS Network of Excellence on Digital Libraries, as part of the

Information Society Technologies (IST) Program of the European Commission (Contract G038-507618).

References

1. Agosti, M., Ferro, N.: An Information Service Architecture for Annotations. In Agosti, M., Schek, H.J., Türker, C., eds.: Digital Library Architectures: Peer-to-Peer, Grid, and Service-Orientation, Pre-proceedings of the 6th Thematic Workshop of the EU Network of Excellence DELOS, Edizioni Libreria Progetto, Padova, Italy (2004) 115–126

2. Agosti, M.: An Overview of Hypertext. In Agosti, M., Smeaton, A., eds.: Information Retrieval and Hypertext. Kluwer Academic Publishers, Norwell (MA), USA (1996) 27–47

3. Marshall, C.C.: Toward an Ecology of Hypertext Annotation. In Akscyn, R., ed.: Proc. 9th ACM Conference on Hypertext and Hypermedia (HT 1998): links, objects, time and space-structure in hypermedia systems, ACM Press, New York, USA (1998) 40–49

4. Agosti, M., Ferro, N.: Annotations: Enriching a Digital Library. In Koch, T., Sølvberg, I.T., eds.: Proc. 7th European Conference on Research and Advanced Technology for Digital Libraries (ECDL 2003), Lecture Notes in Computer Science (LNCS) 2769, Springer, Heidelberg, Germany (2003) 88–100

5. Agosti, M., Ferro, N., Frommholz, I., Thiel, U.: Annotations in Digital Libraries and Collaboratories – Facets, Models and Usage. In Heery, R., Lyon, L., eds.: Proc. 8th European Conference on Research and Advanced Technology for Digital Libraries (ECDL 2004), Lecture Notes in Computer Science (LNCS) 3232, Springer, Heidelberg, Germany (2004) 244–255

6. Golovchinsky, G., Price, M.N., Schilit, B.N.: From Reading to Retrieval: Freeform Ink Annotations as Queries. In Gey, F., Hearst, M., Tong, R., eds.: Proc. 22nd Annual International ACM SIGIR Conference on Research and Development in Information Retrieval (SIGIR 1999), ACM Press, New York, USA (1999) 19–25

7. Frommholz, I., Brocks, H., Thiel, U., Neuhold, E., Iannone, L., Semeraro, G., Berardi, M., Ceci, M.: Document-Centered Collaboration for Scholars in the Humanities – The COLLATE System. In Koch, T., Sølvberg, I.T., eds.: Proc. 7th European Conference on Research and Advanced Technology for Digital Libraries (ECDL 2003), Lecture Notes in Computer Science (LNCS) 2769, Springer, Heidelberg, Germany (2003) 434–445

8. Frommholz, I., Thiel, U., Kamps, T.: Annotation-based Document Retrieval with Four-Valued Probabilistic Datalog. In Baeza-Yates, R., Maarek, Y., Roelleke, T., de Vries, A.P., eds.: Proc. 3rd XML and Information Retrieval Workshop and the 1st Workshop on the Integration of Information Retrieval and Databases (WIRD2004), http://homepages.cwi.nl/~arjen/wird04/wird04-proceedings.pdf [last visited 2004, November 22] (2004) 31–38

9. Croft, W.B.: Combining Approaches to Information Retrieval. In Croft, W.B., ed.: Advances in Information Retrieval: Recent Research from the Center for Intelligent Information Retrieval. Kluwer Academic Publishers, Norwell (MA), USA (2000) 1–36

10. Agosti, M., Smeaton, A., eds.: Information Retrieval and Hypertext, Kluwer Academic Publishers, Norwell (MA), USA (1996)

11. OMG: OMG Unified Modeling Language Specification – March 2003, Version 1.5, formal/03-03-01. `http://www.omg.org/technology/documents/formal/uml.htm` [last visited 2004, November 22] (2003)
12. Booch, G., Rumbaugh, J., Jacobson, I.: The Unified Modeling Language User Guide. Addison-Wesley, Reading (MA), USA (1999)
13. Rumbaugh, J., Jacobson, I., Booch, G.: The Unified Modeling Language Reference Manual. Addison-Wesley, Reading (MA), USA (1999)
14. Diestel, R.: Graph Theory. Springer-Verlag, New York, USA (2000)
15. Fox, E.A., Shaw, J.: Combination of Multiple Searches. In Harman, D.K., ed.: Proc. 2nd Text REtrieval Conference (TREC 2), NIST Special Publication 500–215 (1994) 243–252
16. Savoy, J.: Citation Schemes in Hypertext Information Retrieval. In Agosti, M., Smeaton, A., eds.: Information Retrieval and Hypertext. Kluwer Academic Publishers, Norwell (MA), USA (1996) 99–120
17. Lee, J.H.: Analyses of Multiple Evidence Combination. In Belkin, N.J., Narasimhalu, A.D., Willett, P., Hersh, W., Can, F., Voorhees, E., eds.: Proc. 20th Annual International ACM SIGIR Conference on Research and Development in Information Retrieval (SIGIR 1997), ACM Press, New York, USA (1997) 267–276

Conceptual Indexing Based on Document Content Representation

Mustapha Baziz, Mohand Boughanem, and Nathalie Aussenac-Gilles

IRIT, Campus universitaire ToulouseIII, 118 rte de Narbonne,
F-31062 Toulouse Cedex 4, France
{baziz, boughane, aussenac}@irit.fr

Abstract. This paper addresses an important problem related to the use of semantics in IR. It concerns the representation of document semantics and its proper use in retrieval. The approach we propose aims at representing the content of the document by the best semantic network called *document semantic core* in two main steps. During the first step concepts (words and phrases) are extracted from a document, driven by an external general-purpose ontology, namely WordNet. The second step a global disambiguation of the extracted concepts regarding to the document leads to build the best semantic network. Thus, the selected concepts represent the nodes of the semantic network whereas similarity measure values between connected nodes weight the links. The resulting scored concepts are used for the document conceptual indexing in Information Retrieval.

Keywords: Information Retrieval, Semantic Representation of Documents, Similarity Measures, Conceptual Indexing, ontologies, WordNet.

1 Introduction

Information Retrieval (IR) is concerned with finding representations and methods of comparison that will accurately discriminate between relevant and non-relevant documents. The *retrieval model* for an information retrieval system specifies how documents and queries are represented, and how these representations are compared to produce relevant estimates [1]. Many information retrieval systems represent documents and queries with a bag of single words. Several scientists have reported on the limits of these models and systems. This is mainly due to the ambiguity and limited expressiveness of single words. As a consequence, a the representation of the documents in the collection may result inaccurate, as well as the user's queries may seem imprecise. Various approaches have been developed to overcome this restriction, including one that has received much attention in recent years, ontology-based IR, or the use of semantics for representing documents and queries.

Ontology-based information retrieval approaches are promising to increase the quality of responses since they aim at capturing some parts of the semantics of documents. In document representation, known as semantic indexing and defined by [2] and [3], the key issue is to identify appropriate concepts that describe and

F. Crestani and I. Ruthven (Eds.): CoLIS 2005, LNCS 3507, pp. 171 – 186, 2005.

characterize the document content. The challenge is to make sure that irrelevant concepts will not be kept, and that relevant concepts will not be discarded.

This paper addresses an important problem related to the use of semantics in IR. It concerns the representation of document semantics and its proper use in retrieval. The approach that we propose aims at representing the content of a document by the "best" semantic network, which we call the *document semantic core*. This approach is an extension of the one introduced in a previous paper [4]. The main extension is the global disambiguation method of the extracted concepts regarding the context of the document, and the evaluation of its contribution. Here, the best known similarity measures proposed in literature are used to compute relatedness between concepts. Each similarity measure has an impact on the selection of the best semantic network (semantic core), thus on the document representation. Roughly, the resulting semantic networks could be used either for conceptual indexing , for document classification or to identify the document focus. Especially in this paper, we propose to evaluate the approach by using the disambiguated concepts (nodes) of the resulted semantic cores for conceptual indexing in IR.

The paper is organized as follows. First, we describe related works on using semantics in information retrieval (section 2). In Section 3, our approach for matching ontology with a document is presented and then detailed in (3.1). First of all, we describe the concept extraction and weighting methods (3.1.1). Then in section (3.1.2), we explain how the document semantic core is built up: we justify why and how using similarity measures to disambiguate the extracted concepts (3.1.1.1) and to (3.1.1.2) select the best concepts for building the best semantic network. In section (3.2), we describe the four similarity measures used in (3.1.1.1). An evaluation of the approach is reported in section 4. Conclusions and prospects are drawn in section 5.

2   Using Semantics in Information Retrieval

Over the last 15 years, several approaches have attempted to use semantics in IR. In semantic-based IR, sets of words, names, noun phrases are mapped into the concepts they represent [5]. In these approaches, a document is represented as a set of concepts. To achieve this, external semantic structures for mapping document representations to concepts are needed. Such structures may be dictionaries, thesauri and ontologies [6]. They can be either manually or automatically generated or they may pre-exist. WordNet and EuroWordNet are examples of (thesaurus-based) lexical data-bases including a semantic network. As such, they are close to ontologies. They are widely used to improve the effectiveness of IR systems although they do not always bring major gains. Techniques involving word sense disambiguation (WSD) rather than key-words have been investigated with mixed results. According to [1] and [7], even perfect word sense information may be of only limited utility. For Oakes and colleagues in [8], using a sense based information retrieval improves retrieval over traditional TF.IDF techniques. Gonzalo and colleagues in [9] reported that indexing with WordNet synsets can improve information retrieval. They measured up to +29% improvements when using synsets as indexing space comparing to simple key-word indexing. Being given that our aim in this work is not especially Word Sense Disambiguation (WSD) -- even though we proposed a global disambiguation algorithm by using similarity measures for selecting concepts senses in our document semantic cores building process--, we refer the interested reader to [10] for a state of the art about the use of WSD in IR. About the use of ontology, Khan in [2] proposed a method for connecting concepts from an ontology to those in the documents. Sub-trees "regions" of an ontology are defined to represent different concepts. The concepts that appear in a given region are mutually disjoint from the concepts of other regions. The region containing the largest number of document concepts is selected. Then, all the selected concepts that also appear in other regions are pruned. Inside a region, the selection is tuned using a path-based "semantic distance" taking into account paths between concepts in the ontology. Thus the concepts that correlate with the higher number of other concepts are selected. Woods [11] proposed a conceptual indexing method by mapping words and phrases onto conceptual taxonomies. Navigli and colleagues [12] proposed in their system (OntoLearn) a method called structural semantic interconnection to disambiguate words in text using WordNet glosses (definitions). Disambiguation is achieved by intersecting the semantic networks built for each word to be disambiguated. This technique is used in query expansion too.

In our case, we propose to match a document with an ontology to produce the "best" semantic network that represents the document content. This approach carries out a global disambiguation method by scoring most of the similarity measures known in literature, between all possible extracted concept senses regarding the document. Concept extraction and disambiguation are not evaluated for themselves here, but in term of retrieval accuracy in the overall process, as the objective is not so much disambiguation but rather conceptual indexing.

3   The Semantic Core Based Approach for Document Representation

In this section, we describe our semantic representation approach based on document-ontology matching. The approach consists of building, from a given document, the best semantic network, called *document semantic core*, which better represents the document content. Roughly, two main steps are carried out. The first step, ((1) in Figure1), concerns concept extraction. Here, single and multi words from a document which are identified in at least one node in the ontology are detected. A frequency according to CF.IDF (a kind of TF.IDF) is then computed for each concept. Only the words having a frequency greater than a certain threshold are kept. At this stage of the process, each extracted concept could have several meanings (or senses) as it could belong to more than one node in ontology (WordNet Synsets in our case). So, we need to disambiguate them in order to select the adequate nodes (second step (2)). Here, various similarity measures known in literature are used in order to compute relatedness between concepts. These measures have an impact on scoring and then selecting the semantic core nodes. At the same step (2), the best concept senses are selected, and then de facto, the best semantic network is built up using such concepts senses as nodes and the similarity measures between them as weights for the links. In this paper we evaluate the impact of using such selected and weighted concepts for conceptual indexing in IR.

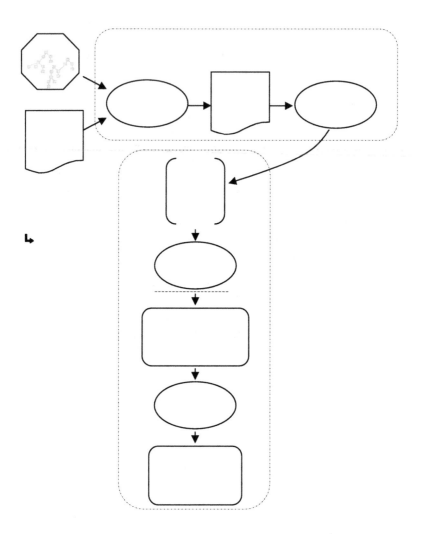

Fig. 1. Description of the completely automated method for building semantics cores from documents

3.1 Summary of the Approach

We will describe in the next sections the main steps of the method to build the document semantic cores as schematized in Figure1. The similarity measures that we used are described in section 3.2.

3.1.1 Concepts Detection and Extraction

Two alternative ways can lead to concept detection in documents. The first one consists in projecting the ontology on the document by extracting all multiword concepts (compound terms) from the ontology and then identifying those occurring in the document. This method has the advantage to be fast and to make it possible to have a reusable resource even though the corpus changes. Its drawback is the possibility to omit some concepts which appear in the source text and in the ontology with different forms. For example if the ontology contains a compound concept *solar battery*, a simple comparison with the text does not recognize the same concept appearing in its plural form *solar batteries*. The second way, which we adopt in this paper, follows the reverse path, projecting the document onto the ontology: for each concept candidate formed by combining adjacent words in text sentences, we first question the ontology using these words just as they are, and then we use their base forms, if necessary to resolve the problem of word forms. A third means could be to combine both ways to benefit from the rapidity of the first but we did not investigate this possibility in this paper.

Concerning word combination, we select the longest term for which a concept is detected. If we consider the example shown on Figure2, the sentence contains three (3) different concepts: *external oblique muscle, abdominal muscle* and *abdominal external oblique muscle*.

Fig. 2. Example of text with different concepts

The first concept *abdominal muscle* is not identified because its words are not adjacent. The second one *external oblique muscle* and the third one *abdominal external oblique muscle* are synonyms. So, they belong to the same WordNet synset also labelled by the term node, and their definition is:

external oblique muscle, musculus obliquus externus abdominis, abdominal external oblique muscle, oblique -- (a diagonally arranged abdominal muscle on either side of the torso)

The selected concept is associated with the longest multiword *abdominal external oblique muscle* which corresponds to the correct meaning in the sentence. Note that in word combination, the order must be respected (left to right) otherwise we could be confronted to the syntactic variation problem (*science library* is different from *library science*).

The extracted concepts are then weighted according to a kind of TF.IDF that we called CF.IDF. Thus, global frequency of a concept c_i in a document d_j is:

$$Weight(c_i, d_j) = cf_{d_j}(c_i).\ln(N / df) \tag{1}$$

where N is the total number of documents and df (document frequency) is the number of documents a concept occurred in. If the concept occurs in all documents, its frequency is null. We have used 2 as a frequency threshold value.

Such that the local frequency cf of a concept c_i composed of n words (n≥1) in a document d_j, depends on the number of occurrences of the concept itself, and the one of all its sub-concepts. Formally:

$$cf(c_i) = \underset{d_j}{count(c_i)} + \sum_{sc \in sub\_concepts(c)} \frac{Length(sc)}{Length(c_i)} \cdot \underset{d_j}{count(sc)} \qquad (2)$$

where *Length(c)* represents the number of words and *sub_concepts(c$_i$)* is the set of all possible sub-concepts derived from c_i. For example, frequency of the *"elastic potential energy"* concept the label of which is composed of 3 words is computed as follows:

f("elastic potential energy") = count("elastic potential energy") + 2/3 count("potential energy") + 1/3 count("elastic") + 1/3 count("potential") + 1/3 count("energy").

Other methods for concept frequencies are proposed in the literature, they use in general statistical and/or syntactical analyses [13], [14]. In short, they add single words frequencies, multiply them or multiply the number of concept occurrences by the number of single words belonging to this concept.

3.1.2 Building the Best Semantic Network: Document Semantic Core

After the first stage, each document is represented as a set of concepts. At this second stage, two steps are required to build the document semantic core. First, similarity measures are computed between all possible concept senses as each concept could have several senses (3.1.2.1), and then a global disambiguation method is carried out (3.1.2.2). Here, the selected sense of each concept depends on its similarity measure values (score) with all the remaining concept senses occurring in the same document.

3.1.2.1 Computing Similarity Between Concepts

Let $$D_c = \{C_1, C_2, ..., C_m\} \qquad (3)$$

be the set of selected concepts from a document D using concept detection and CF.IDF as described in section 3.1.1. Concepts could be mono or multiword and each C_i could have a certain number of senses represented by WordNet synsets noted S_i:

$$S_i = \{S_1^i, S_2^i, ..., S_n^i\} \qquad (4)$$

such that a concept C_i has $|S_i| = n$ senses. So the problem is how to select the best sense for each extracted concept from D_c.

Example: let suppose we have in the source text of a given document the noun *atmosphere*. When projecting the document onto the ontology, *atmosphere* is detected as a candidate concept. So, it could have six different senses, i.e., it could belong to six nodes. In WordNet, the six nodes/synsets with their glosses (definitions) between brackets are:

1. atmosphere, ambiance, ambience -- (a particular environment or surrounding influence; "there was an atmosphere of excitement")
2. standard atmosphere, atmosphere, atm, standard pressure -- (a unit of pressure: the pressure that will support a column of mercury 760 mm high at sea level and 0 degrees centigrade)

3. atmosphere, air -- (the mass of air surrounding the Earth; "there was great heat as the comet entered the atmosphere"; "it was exposed to the air")

4. atmosphere, atmospheric state -- (the weather or climate at some place)

5. atmosphere -- (the envelope of gases surrounding any celestial body)

6. air, aura, atmosphere -- (a distinctive but intangible quality surrounding a person or thing; "an air of mystery"; "the house had a neglected air"; "an atmosphere of defeat pervaded the candidate's headquarters"; "the place had an aura of romance")

When we choose one sense for each concept from D_c, we will always have a set $SN(j)$ of m elements, because we are sure that each concept from D_c has at least one sense, given the fact that it belongs to the ontology semantic network. We define a semantic net $SN(j)$ as:

$$SN(j)=(S_{j1}^{1}, S_{j2}^{2}, S_{j3}^{3},..., S_{jm}^{m})$$
(5)

It represents a jth configuration of concept senses from D_c. $j_1, j_2, .., j_m$ are sense indexes between 1 and all possible senses for respectively concepts $C_1, C_{2,...} C_m$.

For the m concepts of D_c, different semantic networks could be constructed using all sense combinations. The number of possible semantic networks Nb_SN depends on the number of senses of the different concepts from D_c:

$$Nb\_SN = |S_1| . |S_2| ... .|S_m|$$
(6)

For example, Figure3 represents a possible semantic network $(S_2^{1}, S_7^{2}, S_1^{3}, S_1^{4}, S_4^{5}, S_2^{m})$ resulting from a combination of the 2nd sense of the first concept, the 7th sense of C_2, the 2nd sense of C_m (we suppose that null links are not represented). Links between concepts senses (P_{ij}) in Figure3 are computed using similarity measures as defined in formula (7) below.

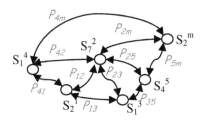

Fig. 3. A semantic network built from one configuration of concept senses

Thus, similarity measures are used to select, for each extracted concept, the best synset (node) which represents its sense in the context of a document. We propose a global disambiguation method where the selected sense of a concept depends on the similarity measure values (score) it has with all the remaining concepts senses occurring in the same document as described in formulas (8) and (9) of the next section. In literature, there are about a dozen of similarity measures, mostly used for disambiguating words in text (WSD). A complete state of the art about the use of

semantic networks for disambiguating words could be found in [15] and [16]. We have evaluated four of these measures in our semantic core building system (step 2 in Figure1): the Leacock and Chodorow (Lch) measure, the Lin measure, the Resnik measure and the gloss overlaps measure (noted Lesk) from Banerjee and Pedersen [16]. To select measures, we focused on those that used WordNet as their knowledge source (to keep that as a constant) and those with an acceptable computing time.
Formally, given two concepts, C_k and C_l with assigned senses j_1 and j_2: S_{j1}^k and S_{j2}^l. The semantic similarity/relatedness between the two concepts senses, S_{j1}^k and S_{j2}^l, noted $P_{kl}(S_{j1}^k, S_{j2}^l)$ is defined as follows:

$$P_{kl}(S_{j1}^k, S_{j2}^l) = Sim\_x(S_{j1}^k, S_{j2}^l) \qquad (7)$$

where Sim_x is one of the four semantic similarity measures $\{Sim_{\_Lch}, Sim_{\_Resnik}, Sim_{\_Lesk}, Sim_{\_lin}\}$ described in section 3.2.

In our system, we used the two perl packages named WordNet::QueryData2.0[1] and WordNet::Similarity0.07[2] [17] to compute these measures.

After this first step of stage (2) (Figure1), we have computed all the similarity measures between the different concept senses. Now, we have to keep the best concept senses to build the best semantic network.

3.1.2.2 Selecting the Best Semantic Network
To build the best semantic network, we have to carry out a global disambiguation. Therefore, for each concept, we have to compute the scores of all its senses (C_score). The score of a concept sense equals the sum of semantic relatedness computed with all the remaining concepts senses except those sharing with him the same synset. Thus, for a concept C_i, the score of its sense number k is computed as:

$$C\_score(S_k^i) = \sum_{\substack{l \in [1..m], l \neq i \\ j \in [1..n]}} P_{i,l}(S_k^i, S_j^l) \qquad (8)$$

where m is the number of concepts from D_c and n represents the number of WordNet senses which is proper to each C_l as defined in equation (5). Then, the best concept sense to retain is the one which maximizes C_score:

$$Best\_score(C_i) = \max_{k=1..n} C\_score(S_k^i) \qquad (9)$$

where n is the number of possible senses of the concept C_i. By doing so, we have disambiguated the concept C_i which will be a node in the semantic core. The final semantic core of a document is $(S_{j1}^1, S_{j2}^2, S_{j3}^3,..., S_{jm}^m)$ where nodes correspond respectively to those having $(Best\_Score(C_1), Best\_Score(C_2), ... , Best\_Score(C_m))$.

3.2 Description of the Used Similarity Measures

Four semantic similarity measures were evaluated in our approach: the Leacock and Chodorow (Lch) measure, the Lin measure, the Resnik measure and the Pederson and

---

[1] http://search.cpan.org/dist/WordNet-QueryData/.
[2] http://sourceforge.net/projects/wn-similarity/ (last visited 02/03/05).

colleagues' measure (also noticed Lesk). The three first are *is-a* based measures while the fourth one is based on gloss (WordNet definition) overlaps. We describe them in the next sections.

3.2.1 The Leacock and Chodorow Measure

The measure of Leacock and Chodorow [18] is path-based. It depends on the length of the shortest paths between noun concepts in an *is-a* hierarchy. The shortest path is the one which includes the smallest number of intermediate concepts. This value is scaled by the depth D of the hierarchy, where depth is defined as the length of the longest path from a leaf node to the root node.

This similarity measure is defined as follows:

$$Sim\_{lch}(c_1,c_2) = \max[-\log(length(c_1,c_2)/(2.D))] \tag{10}$$

where $length(c_1,c_2)$ is the shortest path length (ie., having a minimum number of nodes) between the two concepts and D is the maximum depth of the taxonomy (equals to 16 in WordNet 1.7).

Example: in Figure4 below, *Sim_lch(credit card, medium of exchange)=-log(1/2x16)*

3.2.2 The Resnik Measure

Resnik [19] introduces the notion of informational content (IC) of noun concepts as found in the WordNet *is-a* hierarchy. The main idea behind this measure is that two concepts are semantically related proportionally to the quantity of information they share. This quantity is determined by the informational content of their lowest common subsumer (lcs). It is defined as follows:

$$Sim\_{resnik}(c_1,c_2) = IC(lcs(c_1,c_2)) \tag{11}$$

The informational content of a concept is estimated by counting the concept frequency in a large corpus and thereby determining its probability via a maximum likelihood estimate. The informational content of a concept is defined as the negative log probability of the concept:

$$IC(concept) = -\log(P(concept)) \tag{12}$$

Fig. 4. Fragment of the WordNet taxonomy. Solid lines represent IS-A links; dashed lines indicate that some intervening nodes have been omitted. Example from Resnik [19]

The frequency of a concept includes the frequency of all its subordinate concepts since the count we add to a concept is added to its subsuming concepts as well. As a result, the higher a concept is up in the hierarchy the higher is his count and associated probability . Such high probability concepts will have low informational content since they are associated with more general concepts.

Example: in Figure4, *lcs((dime, credit card)= medium of exchange.*

Thus, *Sim_Resnik(dime, credit card)=-log p(medium of exchange),* where *p(medium of exchange)* represents the number of occurrences of the concept *medium of exchange* in a training corpus.

3.2.3 The Lin Measure

The *Similarity Theorem* of Lin [20] states that the similarity of two concepts is measured by the ratio of the amount of information needed to state the commonality of the two concepts on the amount of information needed to describe them.

The commonality of two concepts is captured by the informational content of their lowest common subsumer and the informational content of the two concepts themselves. This measure turns out to be a close cousin of the Jiang-Conrath measure [21] (not used here), although they were developed independently:

$$Sim_{-lin}(c_1, c_2) = \frac{2.IC(lcs(c_1, c_2))}{IC(c_1) + IC(c_2)} \tag{13}$$

This can be viewed by taking the informational content of the intersection of the two concepts (multiplied by 2) and divided by their sum, which is analogous to the well-known Dice coefficient.

3.2.4 The Pederson's and Colleagues Measure

Pederson and colleagues measure [16] is based on an adapted Lesk algorithm. The original Lesk algorithm [22] disambiguates a target word by comparing its definition with those of its surrounding words. Two hypotheses underlie this approach. The first one follows the intuition that words that appear together in a sentence must be related in some way, since they are normally working together to communicate some idea. The second hypothesis is that related words can be identified by finding overlapping words in their definitions.

Thus, the Pederson and colleagues measure represents the number of common words which is squared in the case of successive words.

Example: the WordNet glosses of sense 1 of *applied science* and sense 1 of *computing* are:

Gloss(*applied science#1*)= (the discipline dealing with the art or **science** of applying scientific knowledge to practical problems; "he had trouble deciding which **branch of engineering** to **study**")

Gloss(*computing#1*)= (the **branch of engineering science** that **studies** (with the aid of computers) computable processes and structures).

Here, *Sim_lesk (applied science#1, computing#1)=* 1x "science" +1x "branch of engineering" + 1x "study" $=1 + 3^2 + 1 = 11.$

4 Experiments

4.1 Evaluation Method

We evaluated our approach in Information Retrieval. We used a vector model based IRS [23] which uses a kind of BM25 TF.IDF formula, a porter stemmer with a standard stop-word list [24]. However, modifications were added namely to support multiword concept indexing as well as the proposed CF/IDF and *C_score* weighting. A test collection is issued from the MuchMore project[3] [25]. This collection includes 7823 documents (papers abstracts) obtained from the Springer Link web site whith 25 topics from which the queries are extracted and a relevance judgment file established by domain experts from Carnegie Mellon University, LT Institute. We chosed to use this "small" collection because of computing complexity. The calculation of similarity measures between all concepts senses extracted from one document takes about one minute in average.

Only concept detection and extraction using CF.IDF are applied to queries (except in the classical indexing) because they are shorter. This is an example of query labeled 109:

> *Query 109: Treatment of sensorineural hearing loss (SNHL)*

after the identification of a multiword concept *sensorineural_hearing_loss* in the query defined in WordNet as:

> sensorineural hearing loss, nerve deafness -- (hearing loss due to failure of the auditory nerve)

and CF.IDF weighting, the final query will be as follows:

```
109      treatement  1
109      sensorineural_hearing_loss  2      /*  =1+1/3+1/3+1/3  */
109      sensorineur  1
109      hear  1
109      loss  1
109      snhl  1
```

The collection deals with medical domain, however, the vocabulary is rather general and almost covered by WordNet (the cover rate equals to about 87% for the documents and 77% for the queries). The experimental method follows the one used in TREC's campaigns [8]. For each query, the first 1000 retrieved documents are returned by the search engine and precisions are computed at different points.

The document semantic cores built using the four measures (Sim_{Lch}, Sim_{Resnik}, Sim_{Lesk}, Sim_{lin}) are used for a semantic indexing. We compared search results obtained with this semantic indexing to those obtained when using a classical key-words indexing. Six cases were experimented:

- Baseline *Classical*: the classical keyword indexing is used. Here no multiword is used and TF.IDF, which is a kind of Okapi [23], is used for weighting all single words.
- *CO_W*: only extracted concepts (nodes of semantic cores) are used for indexing documents with their CF.IDF as weights.

---

[3] http://muchmore.dfki.de/ (last visited 02/03/05).

- *CO_W + Classical*: extracted CF.IDF concepts are added to those resulting from a classical indexing. Two cases could then arise: either a concept sense is a multiword then it is directly added to the inverted file with *CF.IDF* as a weight, or a concept sense is a single word (i.e. it is already indexed by the first classical indexing method) and in this case, its weight based on TF.IDF is changed by the CF.IDF one.
- *C_scores + Classical*: this case is similar to the *CO_W + Classical* case, but here *C_scores* are used in turn of CF.IDF. Two cases as in the above measure may arise while adding concepts senses from semantic core nodes. Either a concept sense is a multiword then it is added directly to the inverted file with *C_score* as a weight, or a concept sense is a single word and in this case, we change only its weight based on TF.IDF by its *C_score* .
- *E_C_scores1 + Classical*: idem with *C_scores + Classical,* but here concepts from semantic cores are expanded by their synonyms ie., by those belonging to the same Wordnet synset. Here, original and added concepts have log (*C_score*) as weight.
- *E_C_scores2 + Classical*: the same with the above case, but the weight of added concepts is lower than the one of original concepts: 0.5* log (*C_score*) (according to [8]).

4.2 Results and Discussion

The results for the five cases are summarized in Figure 5. In [graph1], we can see that using concept senses (nodes) of semantic cores for a pure conceptual indexing does not improve the searching results when compared to the baseline indexing. This could be explained by the fact that, while classical indexing is supposed to cover the overall document, our proposed CF.IDF tries to capture the most important concepts. But when combining the two methods (*CO_W +Classical*), we can see clearly that accuracy retrieval is improved at all precision points. For example, the precision is 0,3360 for the top five retrieved documents while the baseline brings only 0,2672 (+26%). We can conclude that combining our CF.IDF conceptual representation of document contents with a classical representation enhances retrieval accuracy. We will consider this last case for the remaining experiments, as this is the best way to bring better results.

In [graph2] (*C_scores + Classical*), contrary to *CO_W + Classical* case, the concepts are "semantically" weighed with their *C_score* values that resulted from the four similarity measures instead of CF.IDF. Here, all the measures except Lesk enhance precision. The weak result of Lesk could be explained by the fact that its measures are too disparate comparing to the others. Below, we have an example of similarity values returned by the four measures between sense 1 of *dog* and sense 1 of *cat Sim_x*(dog#n#1, cat#n#1):

$Sim\_Lch=1.85629$ $Sim\_Lesk = 83$ $Sim\_Lin = 0.89835$ $Sim\_Resnik=8.09797$

Indeed, the Lesk measure value seems to be too large regarding to the remaining measures.

Now in *E_C_scores1+Classical* [Graph3, *C_scores* are passed to log to attenuate a too large variation. Then, concepts from document semantic cores are expanded with the remaining concepts from the synsets they belong to (ie., with their synonyms).

According to Gonzalo and colleagues [10], because the synonyms of a word – concept-sense were part of the same synset, the representation would be richer. Here, the added concepts and the original ones are weighed in a similar way using log (*C_score*). Results show a short improvement for the three measures *Resnik*, *Lch* and *Lin* while a significant improvement in retrieval accuracy is reported for the Lesk measure (+30% in AvgPr: from 0.1693 to 0.2210).

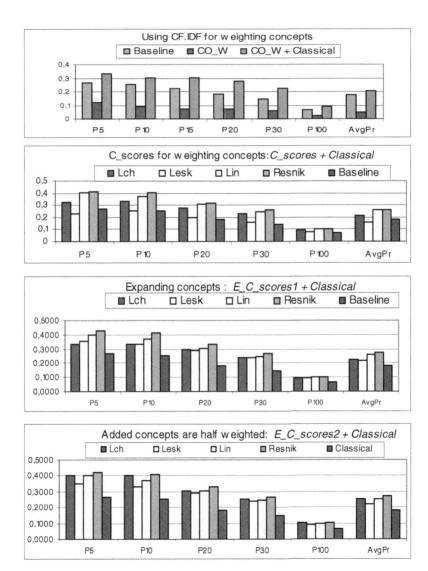

Fig. 5. Results of searching for the 5 cases using CF.IDF and the four measures

The short improvement of the three measures from *Resnik*, *Lch* and *Lin* could be explained by the expansion method while the large improvement of Lesk should be partially due to the expansion but especially to the passage of its measurement values to the log.

In the last run (*E_C_scores2+Classical*), which is the same as the above *E_C_scores+Classical*, but where the added concepts are half-weighed, we have the best and most homogeneous results. This confirms in general the fact that weighing is very important in IR. Results show also that these "semantic" weighing using similarity measures, brings better results than CF.IDF which is encouraging. We can also conclude that in our disambiguation method, the best measure is the *Resnik* one, followed by *Lin*, *Lch*, and *Lesk*.

Thus, assigning lower weights to the added concepts seems to enhance retrieval accuracy. This is in keeping with Voorhees [8] where an α factor between 0 and 1 is used for weighing added terms (it was reported that the optimal value for α is 0.5). This seems to be valid also in document expansion.

5   Conclusion

In this paper, we have shown an approach that represents document contents by the best semantic network called *document semantic core*. We have demonstrated that it is possible to use the resulted documents semantic cores for conceptual indexing. Conceptual indexing used alone does not improve accuracy, but when mixed with classical keyword indexing, it enhances retrieval accuracy. Four similarity measures known in literature are used for selecting and weighting concepts senses. These "semantic" weights (*C_scores*) are also successfully merged with the classical indexing, namely, when they are passed to log in order to bring back the different similarity values to the same scales.

Our short-term goal is to investigate the impact of one important factor that we neglected here: the collection size. The number of documents in the used collection was quite small. We are aware that the evaluation carried out in this paper can be only used as a rough indication of the methodology because of the collection size. We have chosen to use this collection because of the constraint of time computing (running the four similarity measures for the overall collection took about six days). To deal with this problem, we plan to pre-compute the similarity measures between all WordNet concept senses, constituting thus, a reusable resource. We plan to use it on larger collections, by participating to the robust track of the next TREC campaign.

References

1. Krovetz, R., and W B Croft Lexical ambiguity and information retrieval ACM Transactions on Information Systems, Vol. 10(2), pp. 115-141, 1992.
2. Khan, L., and Luo, F.: Ontology Construction for Information Selection In Proc. of 14th IEEE *International Conference on Tools with Artificial Intelligence*, pp. 122-127, Washington DC, November 2002.
3. Mihalcea, R. and Moldovan, D.: Semantic indexing using WordNet senses. In Proceedings of ACL Workshop on IR & NLP, Hong Kong, October 2000.

4. Baziz, M., Boughanem, M., Aussenac-Gilles, N., Chrisment, C., "Semantic Cores for Representing Documents in IR". In Proceeding of the 2005 ACM Symposium on Applied Computing, vol2 pp. 1011-1017, Santa Fe, New Mexico, USA, March 2005.
5. Haav, H. M., Lubi, T.-L.: A Survey of Concept-based Information Retrieval Tools on the Web. In Proc. of 5th East-European Conference ADBIS*2001, Vol 2., Vilnius "Technika", pp 29-41.
6. Guarino, N., Masolo, C., and Vetere, G. "OntoSeek : content-based access to the web". *IEEE Intelligent Systems*, 14:70-80, 1999.
7. Voorhees, E. M. Using WordNet to Disambiguate Word Sense for Text Retrieval. In Proceedings of the 16th Annual International ACM/SIGIR Conference on Research and Development in Information Retrieval, pages 171-180, Pittsburgh, PA, 1993.
8. Stokoe, C., Oakes, M. P., Tait, J. "Word sense Disambiguation in Information Retrieval Revisited". Proceed. of the 26th Annual International ACM/SIGIR Conference on Research and Development in Information Retrieval, pages 159-166, Toronto, Canada, 2003.
9. Gonzalo, J., Verdejo, F., Chugur, I., Cigarrán, J., Indexing with WordNet synsets can improve text retrieval, in *Proc. the COLING/ACL '98 Workshop on Usage of WordNet for Natural Language Processing*, 1998.
10. Sanderson, M., "Retrieving with good senses". In Information Retrieval, Vol. 2(1), pp. 49-69, 2000.
11. Woods, W., 97: Conceptual Indexing: A Better Way to Organize Knowledge. Technical report SMLI TR-97-61, Sun Microsystems Laboratories, Mountain view, CA.
12. Cucchiarelli, Navigli, R., Neri, F., Velardi, P., Extending and Enriching WordNet with OntoLearn, Proc. of The Second Global Wordnet Conference 2004 (GWC 2004), Brno, Czech Republic, January 20-23rd, 2004.
13. Croft, W. B., Turtle, H. R. & Lewis, D. D. (1991). The Use of Phrases and Structured Queries in Information Retrieval. In Proceedings of the 4th Annual International ACMSIGIR Conference on Research and Development in Information Retrieval, A. Bookstein, Y. Chiaramella, G. Salton, & V. V. Raghavan (Eds.), Chicago, Illinois: pp. 32-45.
14. Huang, X. and Robertson, S.E. "Comparisons of Probabilistic Compound Unit Weighting Methods", Proc. of the ICDM'01 Workshop on Text Mining, San Jose, USA, Nov. 2001.
15. Budanitsky A., Lexical Semantic Relatedness and its Application in Natural Language Pro-cessing, technical report CSRG-390, Department of Computer Science, University of Toronto, August1999..
16. S.Patwardhan,S.Banerjee,andT.Pedersen.2003.Using measures of semantic relatedness for word sense disambiguation. In Proceedings of the Fourth International Conference on Intelligent Text Processing and Computational Linguistics CICLING, Mexico City, 2003.
17. Jason Rennie, WordNet::QueryData: a Perl module for accessing the WordNet database, http://people.csail.mit.edu/~jrennie/WordNet, 2003.
18. Claudia Leacock and Martin Chodorow. 1998. Combining local context and WordNet similarity for word sense identification. In Fellbaum 1998, pp.265–283.
19. Philip Resnik, "Using Information Content to Evaluate Semantic Similarity in a Taxonomy" Proceedings of the 14th Intern. Joint Conference on Artificial Intelligence (IJCAI), 1995.
20. Dekang Lin. An information theoretic definition of similarity. In Proceedings of the 15 th International Conference on Machine Learning, Madison, WI. 1998.
21. Jay J.Jiang and David W. Conrath. 1997. Semantic simi-larity based on corpus statistics and lexical taxonomy. In Proceedings of International Conference on Research in Computational Linguistics,Taiwan.

22. Lesk M.E., Automatic sense disambiguation using machine readable dictionaries: How to tell a pine cone from a nice cream cone. In Proceedings of the SIGDOC Conference. Toronto, 1986.
23. Boughanem M., Dkaki, T. Mothe J and C. Soulé-Dupuy "Mercure at TREC-7". In Proceeding of Trec-7, (1998).
24. Salton G The SMART Retrieval System. Englewood Cliffs, NJ, Prentice Hall 1971.
25. Buitelaar, P., Steffen D., Volk, M., Widdows, D., Sacaleanu, B., Vintar, S., Peters, S., Uszkoreit, H., *Evaluation Resources for Concept-based Cross-Lingual IR in the Medical Domain In Proc. of LREC2004*, Lissabon, Portugal, May 2004.

What's the Deal with the Web/Blogs/the Next Big Technology: A Key Role for Information Science in e-Social Science Research?

Mike Thelwall[1] and Paul Wouters[2]

[1] School of Computing and Information Technology, University of Wolverhampton,
Wulfruna Street, Wolverhampton WV1 1SB, UK
m.thelwall@wlv.ac.uk
[2] Networked Research and Digital Information - Nerdi, NIWI-KNAW,
Joan Muyskenweg 25, PO Box 95110, 1090 HC Amsterdam,
The Netherlands
paul.wouters@niwi.knaw.nl

Abstract. Since many nations have provided substantial funding for new e-social science and humanities investigations, there is now an opportunity for information scientists to adopt an enabling role for this new kind of research. Logically, a more information-centred environment should be more conducive to information science and to information scientists taking part in other types of research. In this article it is argued that information scientists can play a valuable role by evaluating new information *sources* in a meta-disciplinary context, developing tools and methods to analyse the data and, crucially, contributing to the prediction of the kinds of research questions that the data may usefully help address. It is argued that this is both an essential service for social science research and one that information science is uniquely placed to provide. A timely response to this challenge may also generate novel research problems within information science itself.

1 Introduction

There have been so many changes to our lives enabled by computing technologies that it seems inadequate to refer to a single computer/information/communication revolution. Governments have recognised the potential advances that the technologies may facilitate in many ways, including the funding of large e-science programmes and infrastructures. Recently, the term e-science has been adopted for initiatives that have taken advantage of Grid infrastructures for shared computing power [1]. Following e-science, and often explicitly seeking to imitate it, funding has been provided for e-social science and humanities research (e.g., the UK's ESRC National Centre for e-Social Science[1]; the Netherlands' Virtual Knowledge Studio for the Humanities and Social Sciences[2]; and the USA's ACSL-sponsored Commission on

---

[1] http://www.ncess.ac.uk/
[2] http://www.virtualknowledgestudio.nl

F. Crestani and I. Ruthven (Eds.): CoLIS 2005, LNCS 3507, pp. 187–199, 2005.
© Springer-Verlag Berlin Heidelberg 2005

Cyberinfrastructure for the Humanities & Social Sciences[3]). We use the phrase e-social science research to describe research that is enabled by the new electronic technologies (e.g., digital media creation; Grid-enabled social science research, e.g. [2]) or studies their social impacts. Logically, the new funding should give challenges and opportunities to those who study information in various ways, and information scientists in particular. Yet there does not seem to be an explicit debate over this issue within the journals of information science, perhaps because practitioners are already struggling to cope with managing continuous changes in core activities such as information retrieval, effective (mainly digital) search strategies, and library services.

One of the by-products of the digital revolutions and the Internet has been the creation of huge informal repositories of public access, easily discoverable information including the web and newsgroups. An advantage of Internet sources is that it is often possible to use tools to automatically retrieve and process information in large quantities. A second advantage is that large sections of the information come from genres that have previously been inaccessible to researchers in any quantity, and may therefore help to address research questions that have been previously left unanswered. This may even create new research areas. There is a precedent for this in the creation of the field of bibliometrics largely in response to the availability of the Institute for Scientific Information's databases [3,4].

The central thesis of this paper is that there is an opportunity for information science as a discipline to take on the role of assessing new *information sources* for use in social science research, including the development of appropriate *methods*. There is a theoretical basis for this in the novel roles that information is starting to play in scientific and scholarly research. This has been captured in the notion of the "informational turn" in research [5,6]. We argue that information science is uniquely positioned to most effectively develop each new potential data source from a social science perspective. First, however, we review three case studies of large-scale Internet phenomena/information sources that have attracted research interest: web links, newsgroups, and blogs; contrasting computer science, information science and social sciences approaches. We also discuss current e-social science initiatives and examine their possible roles in developing new data sources.

2   New Data Sources

2.1   Web Links

Link analysis has produced significant findings that underpin the potential for the academic Web to be used as an information source, a potential that was recognised once commercial search engines introduced facilities that could be used for link counting [7,8]. Results have shown that university Web site links are influenced by a combination of geographic [9] and research-related [10] factors, confirming that significant patterns can be mined from this kind of link data. Mapping techniques have also been developed to visualise the flow of information between national educational systems [11]. Colinks have been used to map patterns of interlinking between universities in Europe [12]. In contrast to the above university-wide

---

[3] http://www.acls.org/cyberinfrastructure/cyber_charge.htm

studies, some link analysis research has analysed the Web pages relating to a single subject within a country (e.g., [13-17]).

In the social sciences, Social Network Analysis [18] has been the perspective from which some hyperlink analyses have been developed, particularly in communication and Internet studies. Often, the existence of a hyperlink is taken as an indicator of either a social connection or a communication channel. Links have been used to map online connections between the web sites of political movements [19], to track individual issues [20,21], and as indicators of business connections [22]. Linking has also been investigated for its own sake: as a phenomenon that is important in its own right, although as part of wider investigations into web use [23,24].

Computer scientists tend to use links as the basis of new algorithms or to improve the functioning of existing ones. The name web structure mining is often given to computer science link analysis. A high profile example is Google's link-based PageRank algorithm, designed to help identify the most authoritative pages in the web [25]. Another common computer science use of links is as the raw data for automatically-generated web site navigation aids [26]. There are also many descriptive link analyses, although these tend to be justified in terms of future benefits for improved algorithm design. Examples include a topological analysis of the link structure of the web, as crawled by AltaVista [27], and investigations into the relationship between links and text in web pages [28,29].

2.2 Newsgroup Postings

Newsgroups are themed discussion lists that allow anyone to contribute although some are moderated. They are sources of relatively informal opinions even though contributions probably typically vary in tone between the relatively informal communications such as personal e-mails and relatively more formal documents such as personal home pages (which are more visible to general users). For social sciences research, they provide a non-intrusive, though possibly ethically problematic [30], source of information about the informal opinions of a section of the population. Intuitively, they may help to address many social science research questions, especially because of their topic-structured nature. For example, researchers into sport attitudes may visit the sporting groups. Intuitively also, newsgroups participants are likely to come from a small segment of society: the more IT literate and perhaps the more expressive or opinionated.

Information scientists have analysed newsgroups from the perspective of demonstrating that bibliometric laws apply to them [31] and analyzing their influence on scholarly communication and the invisible college [32]. The former has a more information centred approach, concerned with mathematical modelling of the data. Caldas [32], in contrast, addresses a more social sciences type question focussing on the impact of technology upon scholarly communication, a recurrent theme in information science (e.g., [33]). Outside of information science, social scientists have analysed newsgroups from various disciplinary perspectives: as an example of computer mediated communication in communication science by researchers seeking to investigate social aspects of its use (e.g., [34]), also an information science theme [35].

Computer science newsgroup research tends to be characterised by the development of algorithms to extract particular types of information, such as which articles are likely to be of interest to an individual user. One typical and highly cited example is a paper describing a new approach for constructing newsreader software [36].

2.3 Blog Postings

Web logs or blogs, are a newer development than the web itself. They are based around software that makes it easy for non-technical web users to maintain a frequently updated collection of online information, which is typically presented in the form of an online log or diary. The software automatically moves old postings into an archive, accessible by following links from the main page, and formats the postings in an attractive style. Many other features make blogs easy to use and integrate blogs with each other, such as permalinks (link to a particular post, even after it has been archived), trackback (to find who links to a blog post), and blogrolls (collections of links to recommended blogs).

Blogs were a hot topic at the 2004 Association of Internet Researchers conference, a multidisciplinary conference mainly reflecting sociology, media and cultural studies, and social sciences [37,38]. The excitement centred around the potential for public glimpses into the private lives of individuals on a scale not previously possible [39]. For example, one presentation examined anti-war blogs to see how mainstream mass media could be challenged online [40]. Bloggers are probably a wider social group than newsgroup posters because a lower technical competence is needed. Most likely the IT skills of the average blogger are typically significantly lower than that of newsgroup posters. A disadvantage is the lack of an 'official' topic organisation of blogs, although blogrolls make an unofficial substitute. At the 2004 ASIST conference, representing here the information science angle, there were two blog discussions: "Blogs for information dissemination and knowledge management" and "Beyond the sandbox: Wikis and blogs that get work done" and a paper on the value of blogs for information dissemination [41]. The themes here are information dissemination and communication. Information science seems to be a latecomer to blog research, with no papers at all at any previous ASIST conference, nor any blog papers published in JASIST before 2005.

Computer scientists have quietly found one very interesting blog application: using blogs as a source of information about the public reaction to large-scale marketing campaigns. IBM's WebFountain project continually monitors thousands of blogs, creating a large, real time database of public opinions [42]. The underlying belief is that even if only a very small percentage of blogs happen to give any reaction to an advertising campaign, as long as there are a few responses then these can give instant feedback to advertisers. This is a commercial rather than scientific application, but has been reported in an academic forum, centring on quantitative descriptions of aspects of blog evolution such as time series for word usage in blogs. Perhaps the commercial applications found by IBM for social context information explain the interesting mix of computer science and other approaches found in the blog workshop within the traditionally computer science-dominated World Wide Web series of conferences (http://www.blogpulse.com/www2004-workshop.html). The computing presentations in 2004 included a descriptive, structure-seeking contribution (Implicit structure and the dynamic of blogspace, by Adar and Zhang) and an initiative similar to IBM's (BlogPulse: Automated Trend Discovery for weblogs, by Glance, Hurst &

Tomokiyo). The non-computer science contributions reported on where bloggers live (Mapping the blogosphere in America, by Lin & Halavais), and the social and psychological background to blogging (Blogs as "Protected Space", by Gumbrecht), as well as one aiming at social context (How can we measure the influence of the blogosphere? by Gill).

2.4 Overview of Data Sources and Research Areas

The above examples illustrate the approaches that different research areas take to new Internet information formats. Table 1 summarizes the discussion. The categories are generalizations and there will be exceptions. This is unavoidable because fields are ultimately defined by human factors rather than solely by objective considerations of content. In particular, journal and conference reviewers may accept work that might objectively be considered to be part of a different field than the journal/conference, particularly if the authors are associated with the normal field of the journal or if the referees are unaware of more directly relevant fields. Moreover, computer science is a very large field that incorporates a range of disciplinary backgrounds and overlaps (e.g. with psychology), and there are intersections and grey areas between different fields.

Table 1. Research into new data sources

Source	Social Science	Information Science	Computer Science
Web links	Descriptive analysis of user communities; descriptive web mapping; analysing linking as a social phenomenon; using links as indicators for social relations	Mapping scholarly communication	Algorithms to build web navigation and information retrieval tools; descriptive modelling
Newsgroups	Social organisation of newsgroups; newsgroups as a new communication form	Modelling of information in newsgroups.	Algorithms to help individuals to discover of relevant postings
Blogs	Social context of creators and users; new communication forms; new insights into existing social issues.	Blogs for communication and information dissemination	Algorithms to extract social information; descriptive modelling
Overall	Social impact and context, tools to analyse society	Scholarly communication, libraries, information dissemination	Algorithm development, descriptive modelling

The discussions so far have primarily treated research areas as separate entities. In practice, however, for decades there has been a trend towards problem solving research involving increasingly large and increasingly interdisciplinary teams of investigators [43]. Nevertheless, disciplines are still important both as focal points for training and research [44,45]. It seems clear that some types of social science problems will have the computational complexity to require computer scientists to be engaged as part of interdisciplinary research teams, but this does not seem to be a dominant paradigm in social sciences research yet, perhaps because of its relatively individualistic nature [44,45].

3 E-Social Science Research Initiatives

Significant funding has been allocated by many national governments to various forms of e-social science research. The UK has taken the lead with its ESRC National Centre for e-Social Science. This programme "aims to stimulate the uptake and use by social scientists, of new and emerging Grid-enabled computing and data infrastructure, both in quantitative and qualitative research"[4]. In its initial stage, which was set to start in April 2005, the ESRC's e-social science strategy is made up of three components: a training and awareness programme, pilot demonstrator projects and the National Centre for e-Social Science (NCeSS). NCeSS has a distributed structure, comprising a co-ordinating hub, based at the University of Manchester in collaboration with the UK Data Archive at the University of Essex, and a set of research-based nodes distributed across the UK. The research has a two-fold goal. It will focus either on the application of Grid technologies to generate new solutions to social science research problems, or on the social shaping and socio-economic impact of e-science. At the time of writing, it was not yet clear how the balance between these two aims would be struck.

In the Netherlands, the Royal Netherlands Academy of Arts and Sciences has taken the lead together with the Dutch national science foundation (NWO). In the course of 2005, a new research centre was set to start, the Virtual Knowledge Studio for the Humanities and Social Sciences[5]. This will be accompanied by a reorganisation of existing data archives for the social sciences and humanities in a new initiative called DANS: Digital Archive and Networked Services. This data archive, comparable to the UK Data Archive[6], should also harness R&D to further develop the technical expertise needed to archive social science and humanities data sets, including non-textual sources. The new Virtual Knowledge Studio has a multi-tiered goal. It aims to contribute to the design and conceptualisation of novel scholarly practices in the humanities and social sciences; to support scholars in their experimental play with new ways of doing research and emerging forms of collaboration and communication; to facilitate the travel of new methods, practices, resources and techniques across different disciplines; and to contribute to a better understanding of the dynamics of knowledge creation [46].

---

[4] http://www.esrc.ac.uk/esrccontent/researchfunding/esciencecentre.asp
[5] http://www.virtualknowledgestudio.nl
[6] http://www.data-archive.ac.uk/home/

In the US, the natural sciences and engineering are still central to initiatives in "cyberinfrastructures", which is the key concept in e-science initiatives. The closest parallel to the British and Dutch initiatives is the national Commission on Cyberinfrastructure for the Humanities & Social Sciences, which was initiated by the American Council of Learned Societies[7]. The Commission was set to report in early 2005, and was charged to "describe and analyze the current state of humanities and social science cyberinfrastructure; articulate the requirements and the potential contributions of the humanities and the social sciences in developing a cyberinfrastructure for information, teaching, and research; and recommend areas of emphasis and coordination for the various agencies and institutions, public and private, that contribute to the development of this cyberinfrastructure"[8]. It is not yet clear to what extent this will lead to substantial initiatives in e-social science research in the US.

4   A New Information Science Approach

Recall that the central thesis of this paper is that there is an opportunity for information science as a discipline to take on the role of *assessing new information sources* for use in social science research, including the development of appropriate *methods*. Traditional boundaries between information sharing and social communication have become blurred in the new Internet based information environments. Moreover, the distinctions between communication and collaboration are often more difficult to uphold in digital collaboratories (i.e., electronic environments for collaborative research between geographically distant partners: [47]). This is the case, for example, in collaborative annotation tools that are developed by scholars in literary research. An example of this is the Dutch e-laborate project[9]. The emergence of digital information, embedded in information and communication technologies, has enabled a radical lowering of the costs related to many types of information dissemination. At the same time, new research technologies have affected the process of data generation itself. They have enabled new types of experiments (e.g., sequencing technologies in bioinformatics), measurements (e.g., statistical pattern recognition in astronomy), imaging (e.g., body scanning in medical sciences) and data visualisation (e.g. using modelling software to visualise complex protein structures). These have in their turn vastly increased the level of data production in research. Where this happens, scientific research is becoming more dependent on information and communication technologies [48]. In the social sciences and humanities, this development leads to specific configurations. Because the implications of *e*-research for the humanities and social sciences are still far from clear, these configurations have not yet stabilised. A systematic and critical interrogation of the potential of *e*-research paradigms and methodologies for the humanities and social sciences has been hampered by disciplinary boundaries between fields, by a relative lack of resources and research infrastructures, and by the

---

[7] http://www.acls.org/
[8] http://www.acls.org/cyberinfrastructure/cyber_charge.htm
[9] www.e-laborate.nl

dominance of particular computational approaches in the world of *e*-science. Our claim is that precisely because the informatisation of academic research in the social sciences and humanities has not yet been blackboxed in stable socio-technical configurations (see [45]), information scientists can play an exploratory and supportive role. We also expect that this will generate research puzzles for the information scientists that are different from the ones that have emerged in the context of the natural sciences and engineering. This is related to both the data sets and the research questions in humanities and social science research. In the remainder of this paper, we focus on the characteristics of the data sets and the assessment of the methods to analyse these data.

Assessing New Information Sources for Social Science Research. The Internet is characterised by the rapid evolution of new communication forms. Aside from e-mail and newsgroups, this is true for the web alone. To give some examples of revolutionary parts of the web: commercial search engines are themselves a mass media [49]; blogs have been discussed; chat rooms are a new communication form [35]; and the web has spawned many new document genres [50]. Perhaps each newly identified genre or publishing/communication form should be assessed to see what new insights it can give into aspects of human behaviour. For example, Herring [51] claims that each new communication technology gives rise to research into how it helps to shape social practices.

Whilst many social scientists wish to and do explore emerging Internet phenomena enthusiastically, there is an obvious danger that in the rush to explore and exploit, many researchers in different fields will develop largely similar techniques. An example is Hyperlink Network Analysis [52], derived from Social Networks Analysis, and Link Analysis, derived from bibliometrics [53]. Whilst each subject specialist can ask whether the new source can provide new answers, for their concerns and develop new methods, the information scientist can step back and attempt to identify the research areas for which the data source would be appropriate, and develop a generic methodology and tools that each subject could adopt or adapt. In practice, of course, social sciences research fields and methods are too diverse for any researcher to be able to match new data sources to research areas in a comprehensive way. It would also be impossible and undesirable to ask social scientists to avoid new data sources until someone else has first assessed them. In practice, however, it may be possible for information scientists to combine the roles of data evaluator/method developer with brokering organically growing social science methods so that the information science approach incorporates the best of the best of a range of social science initiatives and also plays the role of disseminating the developed methods to a wider social science audience, perhaps through books, chapter in social science methods books and presentations at social sciences methodologies conferences.

Creating Programs to Mine New Information Sources. Given that future new information sources will be almost exclusively digital and predominantly Internet-based, part of the task of developing tools to effectively exploit them is likely to involve developing computer programs to automatically process large volumes of online data. A previous example of this is a suite of link analysis programs [53]. Such development requires programming skills or the services of a programmer (e.g., in a collaborative project). Information science as a field does seem to contain many programmers, so this is not necessarily an obstacle, and information science must be one of the better-furnished fields in this regard amongst the social sciences. Computer science is an alternative choice as the centre of new information tools development, however, as the home of computer programming. It has played an increasing role in many research areas as they harness its data processing capabilities to their needs (e.g., computational linguistics, bioinformatics, medical visualisation, data mining). Disciplinary contributions to each field, in addition to processing power, seem to be in relatively portable data processing algorithms, often highly mathematical ones. Computational linguistics, for example employs the generic Expectation Maximisation and Viterbi Search algorithms [54]. It does not seem to contribute developed methodologies for extracting meaning from data types, in the same way that information science has contributed Author Cocitation Analysis [55], Link analysis [53] and citation analysis [56]. Perhaps this distinction is partly phenomenological: very application-oriented research by computer scientists may not be labelled as computer science research. Nevertheless, it seems that what computer scientists excel at is producing software and systems to match certain goals rather than producing computer centred methodologies for tackling research questions.

The blog case study above shows that computer scientists can develop tools for the extraction of social information from data source, when there is a market for them. It seems to be the case that computer scientists do not tend to independently create tools designed for research outside of computer science, so this is a role that information science may fill. In fact computer scientists have a rich tradition of giving software for free, exemplified by the open source community, and these are sometimes used in others' research (e.g., [57]) but this is typically not the computer scientists' primary purpose. There are also some examples of research tools developed by computer scientists and used by social scientists including the Pajek and VisOne network drawing software packages. But there are also many examples (more, we believe) of programs created and used by social scientists. Examples in the field of network analysis include UCINET, NetMiner, SocSciBot and, in bibliometrics, BibExcel.

Developing Methods Suitable for New Information Sources. Information scientists already contribute to research in other disciplines by applying information science methods to analyze specific data sources. For example, bibliometrics researchers with the expertise to analyse the Institute for Scientific Information's data can contribute to subject-specific investigations in any academic field. Others analyse the same data but orient towards applying the techniques to make advances in theory outside of information science. For example, Leydesdorff has developed a suite of tools for the co-word analysis of bibliographic records, investigating questions typically grounded in Luhmann's sociology of communicative systems [58,59].

The development of methods to analyse a particular type of data is not peculiar to information science; arguably research fields are defined by their methods and practices rather than just the content of their object of study [60, p.8-12] so the whole of science is much more methods-oriented than is apparent from a surface perspective. Statisticians perhaps deserve a special mention as specialists in information analysis methods, but there are other information methods specialists such as data miners. Nevertheless, because methods are so central to disciplines, it is unlikely that one generic research method for a new data source would be appropriate to a wide range of different fields. Hence any method developed by information scientists for social scientists would have to be *customisable* so that individual researchers could adapt it to suit local needs.

5 Conclusion

We have argued that information science, as a field, is particularly well placed to assess new information sources for their use in social sciences research, including large scale and hybrid or fuzzy data sets. This includes developing appropriate general methods and programs in addition to identifying the types of research questions that the data may support. In practice, since information science is a large and varied field, this argument will apply to a minority of researchers, perhaps those with access to programming skills and an interest in social sciences research. The payoff for our field is an increased profile within the social sciences. One lesson that we will need to learn, however, is the need to react faster to new developments, because the blog examples suggest that other fields have been quicker to respond.

Acknowledgements. We thank Matt Ratto for useful comments on an earlier draft on this article, and the referees for their very useful suggestions. The work was supported by a grant from the Common Basis for Science, Technology and Innovation Indicators part of the Improving Human Research Potential specific programme of the Fifth Framework for Research and Technological Development of the European Commission. It is part of the WISER project (Web indicators for scientific, technological and innovation research, contract HPV2-CT-2002-00015, www.webindicators.org).

References

1. NCeSS, *What is the Grid?* 2004: p. http://www.ncess.ac.uk/grid/index.shtml.
2. NCeSS, *Frequently asked questions.* 2004: p. http://www.ncess.ac.uk/resources/faqs/.
3. Garfield, E., *Citation indexing for studying science.* Nature, 1970. 227(669-671).
4. Wouters, P., *The creation of the SCI*, in *Proceedings of the 1998 Conference on the History and Heritage of Science Information Systems*, M.E. Bowden, T.B. Hahn, and R.V. Williams, Editors. 1999. p. 127-136.
5. Wouters, P. *Cyberscience: The informational turn in science.* in *Lecture at the Free University.* 2000. Amsterdam.
6. Beaulieu, A., *From brainbank to database: the informational turn in the study of the brain.* Studies in History and Philosophy of Biological and Biomedical Sciences., 2004.
7. Ingwersen, P., *The calculation of Web Impact Factors.* Journal of Documentation, 1998. 54(2): p. 236-243.
8. Rodríguez i Gairín, J.M., *Valorando el impacto de la información en Internet: AltaVista, el "Citation Index" de la Red.* Revista Española de Documentación Científica, 1997. 20(2): p. 175-181.
9. Thelwall, M., *Evidence for the existence of geographic trends in university web site interlinking.* Journal of Documentation, 2002. 58(5): p. 563-574.

10. Thelwall, M. and G. Harries, *Do better scholars' Web publications have significantly higher online impact?* Journal of American Society for Information Science and Technology, 2004. 55(2): p. 149-159.
11. Thelwall, M. and A.G. Smith, *A study of interlinking between Asia-Pacific university web sites.* Scientometrics, 2002. 55(3): p. 335-348.
12. Polanco, X., et al., *Clustering and mapping Web sites for displaying implicit associations and visualising networks.* 2001, University of Patras.
13. Chen, C., et al., *How did university departments interweave the Web: A study of connectivity and underlying factors.* Interacting With Computers, 1998. 10(4): p. 353-373.
14. Thomas, O. and P. Willet, *Webometric analysis of departments of Librarianship and information science.* Journal of Information Science, 2000. 26(6): p. 421-428.
15. Chu, H., S. He, and M. Thelwall, *Library and Information Science Schools in Canada and USA: A Webometric Perspective.* Journal of Education for Library and Information Science, 2002. 43(2): p. 110-125.
16. Li, X., et al., *The relationship between the WIFs or Inlinks of computer science departments in UK and their RAE ratings or research productivities in 2001.* Scientometrics, 2003. 57(2): p. 239-255.
17. Tang, R. and M. Thelwall, *US academic departmental web-site interlinking in the United States disciplinary differences.* Library and Information Science Research, 2003. 25(4): p. 437-458.
18. Wasserman, S. and K. Faust, *Social network analysis: Methods and applications.* 1994, Cambridge, NY: Cambridge University Press.
19. Garrido, M. and A. Halavais, *Mapping networks of support for the Zapatista movement: Applying Social Network Analysis to study contemporary social movements*, in *Cyberactivism: Online activism in theory and practice*, M. McCaughey and M. Ayers, Editors. 2003, Routledge: London. p. 165-184.
20. Rogers, R., *Operating issue networks on the Web.* Science as Culture, 2002. 11(2): p. 191-214.
21. Rogers, R., *Information Politics on the Web.* 2004, Massachusetts: MIT Press.
22. Park, H.W., G.A. Barnett, and I. Nam, *Hyperlink affiliation network structure of top web sites: Examing affiliates with hyperlink in Korea.* Journal of American Society for Information Science and Technology, 2002. 53(7): p. 592-601.
23. Foot, K.A., et al., *Analyzing linking practices: Candidate sites in the 2002 US electoral web sphere.* Journal of Computer Mediated Communication, 2003. 8(4): p. http://www.ascusc.org/jcmc/vol8/issue4/foot.html.
24. Hine, C., *Virtual Ethnography.* 2000, London: Sage.
25. Brin, S. and L. Page, *The anatomy of a large scale hypertextual Web search engine.* Computer Networks and ISDN Systems, 1998. 30(1-7): p. 107-117.
26. Wheeldon, R. and M. Levene. *The best trail algorithm for assisted navigation of Web sites.* in *1st Latin American Web Congress (LA-WEB 2003).* 2003. Sanitago, Chile: IEEE Computer Society.
27. Broder, A., et al., *Graph Structure in the Web.* Journal of Computer Networks, 2000. 33(1-6): p. 309-320.
28. Chakrabarti, S., et al., *The structure of broad topics on the Web.* 2002, WWW2002.
29. Menczer, F., *Lexical and semantic clustering by web links.* Journal of the American Society for Information Science and Technology, 2004. 55(14): p. 1261-1269.
30. Ess, C. and A.E.W. Committee, *Ethical decision-making and Internet research. Recommendations from the aoir ethics working committee.* 2002.

31. Bar-Ilan, J., *The 'Mad Cow Disease', Usenet Newsgroups and bibliometric laws.* Scientometrics, 1997. 39(1): p. 29-55.
32. Caldas, A., *Are newsgroups extending 'invisible colleges' into the digital infrastructure of science?* Economics of Innovation and New Technology, 2003. 12(1): p. 43-60.
33. Kling, R., *The Internet and unrefereed scholarly publishing.* Annual Review of Information Science and Technology, 2004. 38: p. 591-631.
34. MacKinnon, R.C., *Searching for the Leviathan in Usenet*, in *Cybersociety: Computer-mediated communication and community*, S. Jones, Editor. 1995, Sage: Thousand Oaks, CA. p. 112-137.
35. Herring, S.C., *Computer-mediated communication on the Internet.* Annual Review of Information Science and Technology, 2002. 36: p. 109-168.
36. Konstan, J., et al., *GroupLens: Applying collaborative filtering to usenet news.* Communications of the ACM, 1997. 40(3): p. 77-87.
37. Rall, D.N., *Exploring the breadth of disciplinary backgrounds in internet scholars participating in AoIR meetings, 2000-2003.* Proceedings of AoIR 5.0, 2004: p. http://gsb.haifa.ac.il/~sheizaf/AOIR5/399.html.
38. Silver, D., *Internet/cyberculture/digital culture/new media/fill-in-the-blank studies.* New Media & Society, 2004. 6(1): p. 55-64.
39. Schaap, F. *Multimodal interactions and singular selves: Dutch weblogs and home pages in the context of everyday life.* in *AoIR 5.0.* 2004. Brighton, UK.
40. Gorgura, H. *The war on the terror consensus: Anti-war blogs as an online sphere of dissensus.* in *AoIR 5.0.* 2004. Brighton, UK.
41. Bar-Ilan, J., *Blogarians – A new breed of librarians*, in *Proceedings of the American Society for Information Science & Technology.* 2004.
42. Gruhl, D., et al. *Information diffusion through Blogspace.* in *WWW2004.* 2004. New York, http://www.www2004.org/proceedings/docs/1p491.pdf.
43. Gibbons, M., et al., *The New Production of Knowledge.* 1994, London, UK: Sage.
44. Whitley, R., *The Intellectual and Social Organization of the Sciences.* 2 ed. 2000, Oxford: Oxford University Press.
45. Fuchs, S., *The Professional Quest for Truth: A Social Theory of Science and Knowledge.* 1992, Albany, NY: SUNY Press.
46. Wouters, P., *The Virtual Knowledge Studio for the Humanities and Social Sciences.* 2004, The Royal Netherlands Academy of Arts and Sciences: Amsterdam.
47. Finholt, T., *Collaboratories.* Annual Review of Information Science and Technology, 2002. 36: p. 73-107.
48. Lenoir, T. *Shaping Biomedicine as an Information Science.* 1998.
49. Van Couvering, E. *New media? The political economy of Internet search engines.* in *Annual Conference of the International Association of Media & Communications Researchers.* 2004. Porto Alegre, Brazil.
50. Rehm, G. *Towards automatic web genre identification.* in *the 35th Hawaii International Conference on System Sciences.* 2002.
51. Herring, S.C., *Slouching toward the ordinary: Current trends in Computer-Mediated Communication.* New Media & Society, 2004. 6(1): p. 26-36.
52. Park, H.W., *Hyperlink network analysis: A new method for the study of social structure on the web.* Connections, 2003. 25(1): p. 49-61.
53. Thelwall, M., *Link Analysis: An Information Science Approach.* 2004, San Diego: Academic Press.
54. Mitkov, R., *The Oxford handbook of computational linguistics.* 2003, Oxford: Oxford University Press.

55. White, H.D. and K.W. McCain, *Visualizing a discipline: An author co-citation analysis of information science, 1972-1995.* Journal of the American Society for Information Science, 1998. 49(4): p. 327-355.

56. Garfield, E., *Citation indexing: its theory and applications in science, technology and the humanities.* 1979, New York: Wiley Interscience.

57. Goodrum, A.A., et al., *Scholarly publishing in the Internet age: a citation analysis of computer science literature.* Information Processing and Management, 2001. 37(5): p. 661-676.

58. Hellsten, I. and L. Leydesdorff, *Measuring the meaning of words in contexts: An automated analysis of controversies about 'Monarch butterflies,' 'Frankenfoods,' and 'stem cells.'* in preparation, 2005: p. http://users.fmg.uva.nl/lleydesdorff/meaning/measuring%20meaning.pdf.

59. Leydesdorff, L., *Words and co-words as indicators of intellectual organization.* Research Policy, 1989. 18: p. 209-223.

60. Hyland, K., *Disciplinary discourses: social interactions in academic writing.* 2000, Harlow: Longman.

Assessing the Roles That a Small Specialist Library Plays to Guide the Development of a Hybrid Digital Library

Richard Butterworth[1] and Veronica Davis Perkins[2]

[1] Senate House Library, University of London,
Malet Street, London. UK
rbutterworth@shl.lon.ac.uk
[2] Interaction Design Centre, Middlesex University,
Trent Park, London. UK
v.davis-perkins@mdx.ac.uk

Abstract. A case study of the development of a hybrid digital library system for a small, specialist library is discussed. It is proposed that small, specialist libraries play different roles for their stakeholders than academic or commercial libraries do, and therefore different models of digital library systems are required. It is primarily shown that the community building and supporting roles are much stronger and more important and that financial resources are even more scarce than for academic and commercial libraries. Although the findings are based on an in-depth analysis of one library, a semi-formal interview study with librarians from similar institutions was undertaken. This demonstrates that the arguments presented here have a good level of generality.

1 Introduction

This work analyses the roles that libraries play for their stakeholder communities, in particular focussing on small, specialist libraries (SSLs) as they play different roles to the more general academic or commercial libraries that are typically considered in the digital library literature.

This work is based on the results of the requirements gathering and analysis phase of a project to develop a digital library (DL) system to complement the traditional services offered by the Vaughan Williams Memorial Library (VWML): a London library specialising in British folk arts. The results of the requirements analysis showed that in several important ways the VWML operated differently to the commercial and academic libraries that the authors were used to studying and developing.

1.1 Models and Conceptualisations of DL Systems

Chowduhury and Chowdhury [7] and Borgman [4] discuss different conceptions of DL systems, in essence making a distinction between techno-centric models where it is emphasised that DLs are systems for delivering digital information, and 'library centric' models in which DLs are about delivering library services.

It was clear that techno-centric conceptions of DL systems as collections of digital content were very inappropriate for the VWML. Furthermore even though the more

F. Crestani and I. Ruthven (Eds.): CoLIS 2005, LNCS 3507, pp. 200–211, 2005.
© Springer-Verlag Berlin Heidelberg 2005

'library-centric' conceptions were much better, they were still based on large academic and commercial libraries or libraries that had the possibility of becoming entirely virtual.

It was obvious that one of the VWML's stengths was its archive materials (and very rare published materials), and therefore it would always be a hybrid library. There will always be a need for library clients to access the physical archival primary source materials, which need to be housed and maintained using traditional library practice. Therefore models of DL systems that are principally aimed at creating an entirely virtual library were not appropriate. However the emphasis that SSLs place on their archival (and very old) holdings can generate public interest in these artefacts and their delicate nature means that they are actually prime candidates for digitisation.

We also found that even the most sophisticated DL models (eg [20]) which describe online services, digital content, and community building and maintenance were adequate in coverage, but not in emphasis. It is the intangible work of the librarian in building and maintaining a vibrant research community which makes the VWML such a well respected and important library, probably more so than it tangible assets in the form of books and archive materials. One of the most striking observations we made at the VWML was that library clients left the library with their queries fully answered, but not that many of them came into contact with the books; the librarians were dealing directly with most queries. Whereas most DL models put content 'centre stage' (e.g. Fox and Urs, [11] pg. 523) we believe that a better approach for small, specialist libraries would be to put community centre stage with design decisions being made about how to best allow the content to support the community.

We also found that once we became involved in thinking about the community of researchers who used the VWML it became useful not to think of small, specialist libraries as ends in themselves, but to examine them within the context of both their user groups and the parent organisations that house and fund them. In this sense we are moving towards a broader model of libraries (and hence DLs), in the tradition of Checkland's [6] 'systems thinking' or more recently Nardi and O'Day's [13] 'information ecologies'. This view is not novel, but is underrepresented in the literature.

1.2 A Unique Library?

Given that we saw the VWML as a different class of library needing a different class of DL system, we also undertook a semi-formal interview study with librarians in similar institutions to see if the VWML was a genuine 'one off' or whether our findings in the VWML had any generality. We found that the librarians in the other institutions, despite a wide variety of domains, shared many of the issues and problems exposed at VWML. This paper, therefore, draws on examples gained from observing users at the VWML and interviewing librarians.

1.3 Related Work

There is little work explicitly addressing the issues of building DL systems for SSLs. Julie M. Still [18] edited a collection of pieces about developing DLs and online databases for 'libraries, museums and other non-profits'. These are generally practitioner reports about enthusiasts developing DL systems on very tight, or non existent budgets. This work is interesting in that it makes it evident that a lot of crucial work is done in non-profits by teams of determined but unsung volunteers. However as a collection of practitioner reports, it does not set out to discuss a general agenda for DL development for non-profits.

Our work is certainly not unique in identifying the need for community support and development roles to be explicitly designed for in DL systems. Related work in this field [15, 16] is still broadly experimental and typically on a different scale than we could reasonably expect SSLs to afford to implement and maintain. However much of the motivation for these larger scale projects – that information seeking users prefer interacting with human rather than automated intermediaries, and get better 'value' by doing so – clearly also applies the context of SSLs.

2   What Are Small, Specialist Libraries?

Broadly speaking SSLs are established to serve some intellectual or artistic specialism by a learned society, guild, etc. The libraries themselves are therefore closely allied to a learned society and are established to implement and support the aims of that parent society. Although many have public access as part of their mission, and are currently under pressure from funding agencies to widen public access, they are primarily aimed to serve a specific group of library clients, which may be made explicit by membership to the parent society, or simply be implicit by title and role.

'Small' and 'specialist' are comparative terms, which obviously lie on continua. The VWML is very small: it houses about 20,000 items (compared to half a million for a typical academic library in the UK) and is very specialist, concentrating on British folk arts. In comparison, the Institute of Electrical Engineers (IEE) library, is rather larger and specialises in a broader domain. As the IEE library is the largest and least specialised library that we would still feel comfortable classifying as a SSL, we did not consider such libraries as (for example) the Association of Computing Machinery DL, because even though it could be argued that it is specialised, its scale and funding is of a very different order to the libraries discussed here.

3   Methodology

As described in the introduction the examples used in this paper come from two sources: a requirements analysis of the VWML, and semi-formal interviews with librarians in SSLs.

3.1   Requirements Gathering for the VWML

The Vaughan Williams Memorial Library is run by the English Folk Dance and Song Society. (See http://www.efdss.org/library.htm). We initially began work with the VWML as an example of user-centred design for DL systems, in the style of Theng [19] or Allen [3].

As part of the requirements gathering exercise the librarians were interviewed extensively, and users of the library were observed and informally interviewed over a six month period. We also became involved in developing a wider IT strategy for the library, and liaised with other similar online folk arts projects that were being developed.

As the requirements for the VWML DL system have emerged we have also rapidly prototyped DL systems and tested them with small sets of folk music researchers and experts.

3.2 Interviews with SSL Librarians

We also conducted semi-formal interviews with librarians from the following institutions:

- The Women's Library.
  See http://www.thewomenslibrary.ac.uk
- The Poetry Society Library.
  See http://www.poetrylibrary.org.uk and http://www.poetrymagazines.org.uk.
- The Geological Society Library.
  See http://www.geolsoc.org.uk
- The Institute of Electrical Engineers Library.
  See http://www.iee.org/TheIEE/Research/LibSvc

4   Properties of Small, Specialist Libraries

The results of the interview study showed that despite a wide variety in their domains, the librarians shared very similar problems. The IEE librarian stated:

> "Publishers in particular don't know how to deal with membership libraries. There are well established models of how an academic library works and how commercial company libraries work, but every time I speak to publishers I have to start from the very beginning. I spend years having to explain what we are, what we do, how and why we do it differently to other libraries. Whenever I speak to other librarians in similar institutions to us they say that they have exactly the same experience."

A description of the major properties that we found distinguished SSLs from other libraries are described below.

4.1 The Librarian Plays a Crucial Role

In several cases the librarians we interviewed were true domain experts, and were highly regarded not only for their librarianship skills, but also for their domain knowledge, and are active members in the research community the SSL serves. This means that the librarian not only mediates between library clients and the resources in the library but can also play a mediating role between the library clients and resources external to the library and, possibly more importantly, to other key researchers (who may be in a better position to answer the client's questions). We discuss these roles in more detail below.

Intermediating Between Library Clients and Library Resources. A library client asked the VWML librarian for a biography of Cecil Sharp; one of the foremost folk-song collectors. There does not exist an authoritative modern biography of Sharp and therefore the librarian furnished the client not only with an old biography, but also with several modern academic works, criticising or defending Sharp's work and legacy. This meant that the librarian supplied the client with a much richer picture of Sharp and his work than was actually asked for: the librarian supplied what the client implicitly wanted, rather than what they explicitly asked for.

Nardi and O'Day [13] describe the intangible but considerable value that librarians supply to clients via reference interviews. We observed exactly the same process, where librarian mediation put clients onto the most appropriate library resources, in a more efficient way than the clients themselves would have managed on their own. Our observations however were that this process in SSLs was both more profound and subtle. Just about every library client who entered the library had a reference interview, and the interviews were not explicitly flagged as such, but more as interesting conversations.

Interpreting the Library Resources for the Library Clients. We observed a student enter VWML and ask for some information on morris dancing for an essay. The librarian then proceeded to give a potted history of morris dancing, describing different styles and its history. He also made an effort to counter some of the more common misunderstanding typically held about morris dancing.

In this example the main information source is the librarian, rather than the library resources. There are unlikely to be physical library resources that give such a well honed description of morris dancing. Given the canonical texts on morris dancing the student would have taken several days of reading to come as good an understanding of the art, as the librarian delivered in half an hour.

We have observed many cases where the client's main interaction with the library is not with the library resources, but with the librarian. In several cases the only interaction was with the librarian, and in most cases the majority of the interaction was with the librarian, with the library resources being used as a 'colour' to the discussion.

That said, the IEE and Geological Society employ library staff predominantly on their librarianship skills rather than their aptitude in geology or engineering and in that way are not domain experts in the way that we observed in other libraries. The opinion was expressed that library clients in these two libraries value strict objectivity (probably more highly than the clients in the other more humanities/arts libraries we investigated) and would not appreciate the librarians adding their own explicit interpretation to the resources held in the library.

Mediation Within Research Communities. The librarian can also act as a mediator between researchers, putting researchers in contact with each other. For highly expert researchers the content of the libraries is likely to be well known to them, and therefore a trip to visit the library is as much a 'social' visit to have discussions with the librarians or other researchers who happen to be there.

Looked at in this light the librarian plays another role than that normally associated with librarians: they facilitate communications between the research communities that build up around the library, and in doing so they in effect establish, maintain and develop those communities. These communities can be broader and informationally much richer than the information simply gleaned from the library resources themselves.

Again we argue that these roles that we have observed SSL librarians performing, are even more intangible and valuable than those described by Nardi and O'Day.

Adams and Blandford [2] argue that information mediators have extremely positive effects, and also show [1] that removing librarians from hybrid libraries has negative effects. Our work suggests an even stronger, but equally invisible role for librarians, as mediators between clients and intangible information resources, such as research communities. Furthermore suggesting that librarians are information 'mediators' also implies a certain passivity in the librarians' role. The librarians we have observed take an extremely active role, establishing and propagating the communities themselves.

Librarians also described part of their role as not only being a mediator between clients and library resources, but between clients and the parent organisations: clients with questions to be answered typically interact with the library staff in the first instance, even if the question is not a 'library' question, and the library staff will direct the clients to the appropriate place or people in the parent organisation.

4.2 Quirky Legacy Issues

The libraries may have developed unsystematically, and therefore cataloguing and housing can be eccentric. A reliance on voluntary manpower means that cataloguing may not have been done to a professional standard, or may be incomplete. Nowadays the libraries are aware that voluntary labour can be a mixed blessing and vet volunteers rather more carefully than previously. Even so there may be large backlogs of erratically organised materials. Commercially available DL management systems expect standardised cataloguing procedures, and the first stage of any digitisation project is typically to fully catalogue holdings in a standard way, and this may be a prohibitively expensive exercise. If it is not possible or desirable to rationalise out these quirks, then this again makes the librarians' role more important, as a casual user is going to need an experienced guide to lead them around the confusing information structure of the library.

4.3 An Active 'Political' Role

We observed a teacher who entered the VWML ostensibly to look at photographs of dancers in the 1930s. The informal reference interview that the librarian conducted discovered that the school at which the teacher worked was founded in the 1930s and wanted to put on a show to celebrate its anniversary with students dressed in period costume. The teacher spent several hours in the library researching her topic, and by the end of the visit the librarian had discussed the folk dances and local customs and had convinced her to add these to the show. The teacher became very enthusiastic about this, promising to return to do further research.

Many of the parent organisations that control the SSLs have built into their mission a public role to improve the general public's perception and understanding of their domain. The English Folk Dance and Song Society (VWML's parent organisation) puts this colourfully: 'to put English tradition into the hearts and minds of the people of England'. This mission is about actively externalising knowledge and awareness to the public, and in that sense is political. The libraries also play a part in this outreach exercise, taking their specialism out to the public, and so have a more active role than more general libraries, which can be seen as being more passive information stores which clients come to. Their size can also belie their influence: the Women's Library is active in determining UK schools' gender studies curricula.

Related to this political role SSLs can have very strong relationships with some of the artists or researchers who actually generate the library content. In many cases there is no division between library clients and content generators: many library clients in the Poetry Library are poets, etc. Indeed in the case of VWML the librarians are content producers too (compare this to Brier's [5] conceptualisation of an information system, where originators, users and human mediators are all separated). Through this relationship with content generators the libraries can influence the way that its own potential content is produced and hence fulfill the outreach role described above.

4.4 Summary

Given that SSLs are a distinct class of libraries to academic and commercial libraries, and that their difference is not simply one of scale, it is important to know their value. The IEE librarian argued that academic libraries make high quality information available to academics and commercial libraries supply the information needs of the employees of the (usually) large organisations that run the libraries, but his library supplied high quality resources to small to medium enterprises or individual workers. There is therefore considerable value in science/engineering SSLs as they can fill this small business/self employed need. Similarly the arts/humanities SSLs play a unique and valuable role by being a reservoir of cultural artefacts and knowledge that are considered too small scale by the larger libraries.

Our work is very strongly at odds with Atkins' (summarised in Fox and Urs [11, page 518]) distinctions between traditional and digital libraries where it is claimed that traditional libraries support 'slow and usually one way interactions' whereas DLs support 'two way communication with real time and rich interactions'. Our observations of client/librarian interactions in SSLs is that they are very rich, thoroughly two-way, and can support very large increases in understanding in a very short time.

5   A Model for the Development of DL Systems for Small, Specialist Libraries

A small specialist library setting out to augment its services with a digital library system faces a difficult set of issues. When it comes to the bottom line cost is the main motivating factor and based on this it would natural for a SSL to purchase off-the-shelf DL systems, so that they do not have to pay for the much more expensive development and maintenance of a custom made DL system.

5.1 Development Using Off the Shelf Technology?

Currently most off-the-shelf DL systems are more techno-centric than user-, task- or organisation-centric, and therefore according to the arguments presented in the previous section are inappropriate for SSLs. Generic digital library[1] software does not provide shrink wrapped digital library functionality. To instantiate a working digital library system from the software, the developers need to complete extensive configu-

---

[1] e.g. Greenstone (http://www.greenstone.org), DSpace (http://www.dspace.org), etc.

ration or even further programming code. This approach may be suitable to large institutions with dedicated IT support, but the skill set necessary to perform this configuration is unlikely to be available in SSLs. Once again the problem is made more acute by the variation in the formats and cataloguing of the source materials typical in SSLs. For example in a standard academic DL system (which generic DL software is primarily designed for) the ingest process needs to deal with at most half a dozen document formats, whereas in SSLs no predictions can be made about the different formats that content authors and publishers may supply.

What is actually happening in these institutions, as demonstrated by Still [18] is that the systems are being put together by teams of volunteers, working in their own time and with little or no funding. As we discussed above, volunteer labour is a mixed blessing, and just as the VWML is having to deal with eccentrically catalogued materials due to relying on well meaning volunteer cataloguers in the past, it is just as likely that SSLs will have to deal with eccentrically implemented but well meaning DL systems in the future.

5.2 Community Support

Establishing, maintaining and propagating the research communities is a human task: there is no real possibility that such a subtle, diplomatic role could be automated, and librarians are the prime candidates for performing this task.

Other writers (eg [12]) have vigorously argued for the retention of librarians in DL systems, exhorting librarians to redefine their roles to that of digital librarians in order to ensure their survival. This must be put against claims such as those quoted by Choudhury and Choudhury [7] that DLs 'presuppose the absence of human intermediaries, and hence appropriate mechanisms should be put in place to support users with all different levels of IT, subject and linguistic skills.' (pg. 9). What is apparent in this assertion is a belief that intermediary roles firstly can be automated, and maybe so automating them can improve the library clients' experience. Our work has exposed roles that cannot be automated, and Adams and Blandford [2] have shown that disintermediation is largely detrimental to the library clients. Plenty of community support and CSCW tools which can support the role of client/librarian interaction are available and in some cases (eg. [17]) have been put to DL-like roles.

Sonnenwald *et al* [16] in particular describe a design for a large scale and ambitious project to incorporate user participation into a DL system. Although we share many of the aims of this project cost restrictions necessarily mean that we need to work towards a much more modest implementation. We therefore based our implementation around asynchronous communication methods, as they are cheaper and more reliable to implement. Furthermore guaranteeing the availability of an online synchronous communication channel between users and librarians would impose unsustainable demands on the running of the library.

5.3 A Proposed Implementation

Many of the VWML's catalogues have already been digitised and therefore it has been a simple step to put these indexes online. Our next step is to allow each of those index entries to be linked to a potentially unbounded number of 'representations' of the indexed artefact. These representations maybe a digitised scan, a sound recording, a transcription and so on. However in order to facilitate community building a representation may also be a comment submitted by the librarian or users about the artefact. These comments are then treated by the system as artefacts themselves which can in turn be commented upon or linked to representations.

The ability to comment upon comments in effect gives us a threaded discussion system, but in this case the discussion is fully integrated with the content of the DL system. The comments themselves will be as searchable as the content, and ultimately we would wish to end up with a system where the dividing line between the content and the discussion about it is invisible, and the discussion can have as much authority as the content.

We believe such a system would be specifically beneficial to the VWML, whose domain is the folk arts. The folk arts are studied for how they show cultural artefacts such as songs being processed and changed through performance, and the sharing and reuse of repertoire [14]. One of the problems that has emerged in other projects to put folk art archives online is that a single representation of an artefact may have several relationships (and kinds of relationships) with other artefacts. For example a song tune transcribed by a folksong collector may be related to a recording of the song, and to recordings of variations of the same song by different performers, photographs of the performers, critical commentary of the song words, and so on. Allowing users to contribute representations of an artefact allows for these relationships between artefacts to build up in the DL system.

We also believe that this integration of discussion facilities with content is generally beneficial to DL systems. These tools can add a huge amount of value to the digitised artefacts on the site, as they promote investigation, and understanding of the artefacts by promoting debate about them. They also allow annotations, whereby contextualising information can be added by to the site by users, which again promotes a much richer understanding of the artefacts. They move us in effect to a system designed to capture and surrogate information as 'practice' as discussed by Cornelius [8].

When we proposed a design for a DL system for VWML where users were allowed to annotate and pose questions about the online resources, several of the library stakeholders expressed concern about offering users this level of freedom, until we made it clear that all the user input would be moderated by the librarian to ensure that the user input added value to the online resources. Thought of in this way the proposed system effectively allows the librarian to play many of the same roles online that were observed being played in the physical library. We also argue that the small size of SSLs becomes a clear strength, as the throughput of user annotations and questions is not expected to be large, dealing with the online interactions should not add dramatically to the librarians' workload. SSLs could therefore provide a much richer, more personalised online service to their clients, which larger libraries would find very difficult to match.

Fox and Urs [11, page 523] describe how 'content has moved to center stage in the DL field.'. Our work has demonstrated that for SSLs at least, content should share centre stage with community building and discussion resources, as it is this communal role that gives SSLs their particular value. We have shown that librarians are the prime candidates for continuing in their role as community establishers and builders, and that putting resources online makes librarians more, not less, important. Developing DL systems where community tools are integrated into the centre of the system allow librarians to continue to play the mediation roles they already play in the physical libraries, as well as the active political roles required by their parent organisations.

5.4 A Framework Approach

Typically digitisation funding is granted over a short term (one or two years), the belief apparently being that all the 'work' can be done in those two years, and a self maintaining DL system delivered as the product, which can sit on a server without much intervention being needed. Some of the funding bodies are now explicitly advising hosting institutions to consider continuation strategies, but the ways they suggest of doing this – advertising, subscription, etc – are not well tested.

We believe this product centred approach is misguided. Davis Perkins *et al*'s [9, 10] study of archive custodians has shown that there are significant problems in funding DL systems as one off, short term projects. Tangible results, such as the number of items digitised, are given more priority than less obvious outcomes such as adequate cataloguing, and as a result many projects have produced in effect a 'fixed' DL system that represents the state of the hosting library or archive at the time that the project, but with no consideration of sustainability built in. In many cases these systems rapidly go out of date and are either quietly dropped, or become an extra burden to the hosting institution who try to update and maintain them without explicit funding.

This idea of developing lightweight 'frameworks' into which it is cheap to add DL resources (or if not cheap, at least adding resources is explicitly costed) should be the primary model for SSL DL development. Our proposed system for the VWML is in effect a framework: initially we are placing the existing electronic catalogues online with the commenting and annotation system described above. The catalogues form a 'skeleton' content, and the annotation system gives the ability to cloth that skeleton with richer content. We can foresee the DL system developing in two parallel ways:

– by systematic efforts by the library staff to put digitised content online (for example by digitising a photograph archive, or by adding scholarly annotations to a collection of songs). The cost of doing so should be fairly stable and predictable, so that (for example) when a new collection is accessioned the costs of putting a digitised surrogate of it online would be as predictable as the costs of cataloguing and housing it, and therefore digitising collections can become core library practice; and
– by the efforts of users to add comments and queries to the artefacts. The librarians play a moderating role in this process, making sure that the annotations added are reasonable comment and useful, and winnowing out those comments that may have become out of date and so on.

In effect these two processes are enabled by the same underlying technology: once we have developed and tested a system that allows the librarians to add representations, we can simply make a moderated form of that system available online to users.

A useful implication of this approach is that the library staff can digitise materials in accordance with user requests (rights issues and finances permitting) and therefore may be able to make very well evidenced selection decisions about which resources there is a need for.

5.5 Summary

Our proposed VWML system is based around two principles:

- that discussion and interaction is given as much priority as content is, and that the librarian is perfectly placed to mediate that discussion,
- that sustainability is explicitly designed for by producing a framework for holding content and a costed process for populating it, rather than aiming for a DL product that is 'finished'.

As it happens, designing the discussion and annotation system to support the first principle also results in a system that supports the second. Also note that technology wise we have not proposed anything expensive that requires large amount of development time, so hopefully our development is a sensible half way house between using inappropriate one size fits all, off the shelf software, and expensive custom made systems.

6 Conclusions and Further Work

This paper has set out a collection of properties that are common to a class of libraries that are neither the academic or commercial libraries usually discussed in the literature. While these properties are not all unique to small, specialist libraries we believe that the combination of them and the 'intensity' of them (i.e. one would be hard pressed to find a library that did not feel itself to be under-funded, but SSLs are *particularly* under-funded) makes them a class alone and worth studying in their own right. An analysis of what actually happens in a SSL exposes the wider roles that they play in supporting communities of researchers and promoting the political roles of their parent organisations.

Given this set of properties we have then given a broad agenda for designing a DL system which deals with the inherent problems of SSLs, and also plays to their strengths.

The VWML system is currently under development, and once it is working there is then wide scope for evaluation to see if it does indeed encourage and support the sorts of in depth discussion online that we see in the physical library.

Acknowledgements

The authors acknowledge the time and help freely given by the librarians and library clients who participated in this study. We are also grateful to colleagues from Middlesex University's Interaction Design Centre, Senate House Library, University of London and George Buchanan and Ann Blandford from University College London Interaction Centre who commented on, contributed to, and supported the development of this work, and the comments of the anonymous reviewers who helped improve this paper.

References

1. Adams, A. and Blandford, A. Acceptability of Medical Digital Libraries. Health Informatics Journal. 8(2), Sheffield Academic Press (2002) 58–66.
2. Adams, A., Blandford, A. and Lunt, P. Social empowerment and exclusion: a case study on digital libraries. To appear in ACM transactions on CHI. (in press).
   See: www.uclic. ucl.ac.uk/annb/DLUsability
3. Allen, B. From research to design: a user-centered approach. In Ingersen and Pers (Eds) CoLIS 2: Second international conference on library and information science. Copenhagen, Denmark. (1996) 45–59.
4. Borgman, C. L. What are digital libraries? Competing visions. Information Processing and Management. 35 (1999) 227–243.
5. Brier, S. Cybersemiotics: a new paradigm in analyzing th eproblems of knowledge organization and document retrieval in information science. In Ingersen and Pers (Eds) CoLIS 2: Second international conference on library and information science. Copenhagen, Denmark (1996) 23–42.
6. Checkland, P. Systems thinking, Systems practice. John Wiley. (1981)
7. Chowdhury, G. G. and Chowdhury, S. Introduction to digital libraries. Facet publishing. (2003)
8. Cornielius, I., Information and interpretation. In Ingersen and Pers (Eds) CoLIS 2: Second international conference on library and information science. Copenhagen, Denmark. (1996) 11–21.
9. Davis Perkins, V., Butterworth, R., and Curzon, P. Don't forget the STAGES: Searching for values in digital surrogates of historical photographs. To be presented at IS&T Archiving Conference. Washington DC, USA. (2005)
10. Davis Perkins, V., Butterworth, R., Curzon, P., and Fields, B. A study into the effect of digitisation projects on the management and stability of historic photograph collections. Submitted to European Conference on Digital Libraries. (2005).
11. Fox, E. and Urs, S. Digital libraries. Annual Review of Information Science and Technology, ed. Blaise Cronin, Vol. 36, Ch. 12 (2002) 503-589.
12. Lipow, A. 'In Your Face' Reference Service. Library Journal, August 1999, (1999) 50–52.
13. Nardi, B. A., and O'Day, V. Information Ecologies. MIT Press. (2000).
14. Russell, I. Stability and change in a Sheffield singing tradition. Folk Music Journal, 5 (1987) 317 – 358
15. Sánchez, J., Proal, C., Carballo, A., and Pérez, D. Personal and group spaces: Integrating resources for users of digital libraries. Proceedings of the 4th Workshop on Human factors in Computer Systems (2001).
16. Sonnenwald, D. H., Marchionini, G., Wildemuth, B. M., Dempsey, B. J. Viles, C. L., Tibbo, H. R., and Smith, J. B. Collaboration services in a participatory digital library: an emerging design. In Aparac, T., Saracevic, T., Ingersen, P., and Vakkari, P. CoLIS3: Third international conference on conceptions of library and information science. Zagreb, Croatia. (1999) 141–152.
17. Spasser, M. Realistic activity theory for digital library evaluation: conceptual framework and case study. Computer Supported Co-operative Work. 11. Kluwer Academic Publishers. (2002) 81 – 110.
18. Still, J. (Ed) Creating Web Accessible Databases: Case Studies for Libraries, Museums and Other Non-Profits. Information Today, Inc. (2001).
19. Theng, Y. L. Framework for an application development model to build user-centred digital libraries. CoLIS '99. Croatia.
20. UCLA-NSF Social Aspects of Digital Libraries Workshop. Social aspects of digital libraries. http://is.gseis.ucla.edu/research/dl/ (1996).

Power Is Information: South Africa's Promotion of Access to Information Act in Context

Archie L Dick

Department of Information Science, University of Pretoria,
Pretoria, 0002 Republic of South Africa
archie.dick@up.ac.za

Abstract. Information professionals in some developing countries are likely to view 'context' differently from those in developed countries. 'Context' becomes even more problematic when the searchers for information are ordinary citizens and the retrieval tool is a piece of national legislation that promotes access to information held by the state and the private sector. These and other difficulties become apparent in a case study of South Africa's Promotion of Access to Information Act (PAIA), of 2000. Using this legislation, 'context' is examined from the perspective that power is access to information, which focuses on tensions in the struggle for access. The paper argues that an enabling context or culture of access is just as important as progressive information access legislation in developing countries. And it comments on the 'remote contexts' of Ingwersen and Jarvelin's nested model of context stratification. Ways of extending this model and promoting a culture of access are recommended.

1 Introduction

Information professionals and scholars in some developing countries are likely to view 'context' differently from those in developed countries. And 'context' becomes even more problematic when the searchers for information are ordinary citizens and the retrieval tool is a piece of legislation that provides access to information held by the state and the private sector. In other words, information seeking and retrieval is placed in wider contexts than found in recent research literature.

In 1990 there were information access laws in just a handful of countries. By 2004, access to information legislation had been introduced in more than 50 countries, including the Republic of South Africa – a middle-income developing country (See figure 1). And it was under consideration in 15 to 20 countries [1], [2]. This spurt of growth signals a growing global recognition of the empowering role of information in open and democratic governance, in civil society and in personal development.

But the increase in the number of countries with information access laws obscures government motives for their introduction and an assessment of their effective implementation and use by citizens. Governments that pass such laws to satisfy

F. Crestani and I. Ruthven (Eds.): CoLIS 2005, LNCS 3507, pp. 212–225, 2005.
© Springer-Verlag Berlin Heidelberg 2005

conditions for a grant or aid from international financial institutions like the World Bank and the International Monetary Fund, for example, are unlikely to have the same level of commitment to implementation as a government in transition from an oppressive past towards a democracy. But even a transition government like South Africa is subject to contradictory tensions that influence the balance of forces between secrecy and transparency.

An ambivalent picture emerges in a case study of South Africa's Promotion of Access to Information Act (PAIA), of 2000, which examines the context of its implementation from the perspective that **power is information**. This reverses the more familiar phrase that **information is power**. So the emphasis falls on the secular terrain of politics and of power over information instead of the belief in information's power over everything else [3]. This perspective draws on the growing awareness of a sense of responsibility for library and information studies (LIS), and the 'importance of social, cultural, and even political orientations to research in the discipline'- as articulated at a recent Nordic-International Colloquium [4]. The results of this case study are used to comment on the 'remote contexts' of Peter Ingwersen and Kalervo Jarvelin's [5] nested model of context stratification for information seeking and retrieval, and to recommend ways of promoting a culture of access to information.

Access to Information Laws Around the World

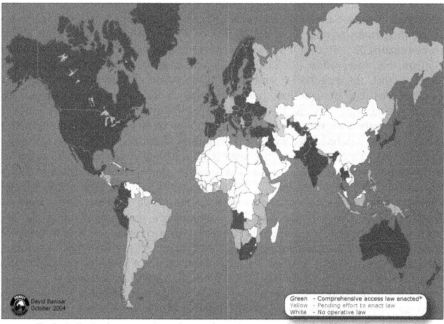

Fig. 1. (Source: http://www.privacyinternational.org/issues/foia/foia-laws.jpg)

2   Power Is Information and the PAIA in South Africa

Whereas an '**information is power**' outlook generally signifies a democratic ethos for expanding access, a '**power is information**' perspective focuses on an authoritarian spirit for blocking access. But it refers also to a countercheck to such restriction. In other words, access to information in this perspective always involves a power struggle between opposing social forces to expand and to restrict access. But what is power? When put very simply, there is **behavioural power** that is the ability to obtain desired outcomes, and there is **resource power** that is the possession of resources to achieve the desired outcomes [6]. It is the degree of possession or deprivation of resource power - like information and communication technologies (ICTs) - that defines the kind of access to and the quality of information accessed. But power is not just restricted to one or the other side or one scale of a balance, as it were. Power is diffuse and porous, and may be exercised by both protagonists and antagonists in the struggle for access to information. This case study will illustrate the point.

In December 2003, the World Summit on the Information Society (WSIS) held in Geneva expressed its vision [7] of an information society that would function as people-centred, equitable, inclusive and development-oriented. Yet it overlooks structural obstacles and fails to explain how inclusiveness, for example, would be achieved in an extremely unequal society like South Africa where the political-economic situation has shifted from the old *systemic exploitation* of mainly black South Africans to their new *systemic exclusion* from the economy. Or, as South African economist Sampie Terreblanche [8] says in a historical study of inequality in South Africa: 'poverty is worse than in 1970, and probably also more deeply institutionalised'. Recent analyses of poverty and inequality in South Africa confirm this observation [9], [10]. They join a growing body of research that suggests that the negotiated settlement brokered in the early 1990s involved compromises with the apartheid regime that led to dramatic political changes, but little meaningful poverty and inequality changes in South Africa [11], [12], [13].

This poverty and inequality are carried over to South Africa's information society. **The Global Information Technology Report** of 2004, for example, shows South Africa as having the second largest disparity among 102 countries between individual readiness (ranked 67) and business readiness (ranked 33) to benefit from and participate in ICT developments [14]. Since most of the selected countries have a much smaller gap between these two indicators, this Network Readiness Index reveals the business community's over-preparedness and the average South African's under-preparedness to participate in the information society. But the PAIA, according to Richard Calland [15] of the Open Democracy Advice Centre (ODAC) in Cape Town, is an example of pro-poor legislation that involves issues of socio-economic justice for all South African citizens.

The PAIA of 2000 is a landmark for access to information and is internationally admired. The Act can be found on the Internet at www.law.wits.ac.za/rula.docu-ments. html. And there is a useful recent overview of the Act by legal scholar, Iain Currie [16]. This progressive piece of legislation is especially significant because it seeks to give effect to the South African constitutional right of public access to information following the control of information and the secrecy that was at the heart of the anti-democratic character of the apartheid system [17]. But it should be noted that secrecy also characterised the resistance against apartheid [18]. There are of course reasonable limitations and exemptions stipulated in the Act to protect a variety of interests, although these can be challenged in court. But its poor implementation track record so far deserves less admiration because it effectively denies a fundamental human right and the tool needed to empower South African citizens and to fight corruption. Examples from the context of implementing the PAIA demonstrate how **power is information** works in South African society.

3   The Power to Deny and Defer

In October 2004, the ODAC laid a formal complaint with the Public Protector after a five-country pilot study on access to information placed South Africa last in ignoring requests for access to information held by the state. The ODAC believes that high levels of silence in response to requests for information under the PAIA amounts to maladministration. ODAC monitored 100 information requests by a diverse group of requesters to a range of government institutions. The study showed that 17% of requests could not be submitted at all for a variety of reasons (See figure 2).

It also found that South African deputy information officers simply ignored 52% of the requests and performed worse than their counterparts in the other transitional democracies, namely, Armenia, Macedonia, Bulgaria and Peru [19]. The study showed that an illiterate woman was given the run-around and was harassed by officials with questions like why she wanted this information. According to the PAIA, the motivation for a request is completely immaterial, and its consideration is in fact illegal. A blind requester also failed to submit many requests for information, which makes nonsense of the equality and inclusiveness claims made by information society advocates.

Requesters for information routinely meet with non-compliance, bureaucratic arrogance and hostility. The Presidency was among those that fared worst in the study, and is embarrassing to the President who played a leading role in this act, and who zealously advocates the information society for Africa. The Provincial departments did better, and the departments of defence and education answered half of all the requests within the 30-day period required by the act [20]. The Open Society, which conducted the study, said that follow-up interviews with South African officials revealed that many felt that information released would be abused or used against the government. State suspicion, it would seem, still takes precedence over the right of public access to information.

The power to deny can also be coupled with the power to defer, as South Africa's Human Rights Commission (HRC)'s 2004 Annual Report confirms. The HRC must include in its Annual Report to the National Assembly statistics regarding the PAIA compliance for each public body. But it was only after reminders in four major newspapers and pleas to the Minister of Justice, the President's Office and the Speaker of the National Assembly that 62 out of all the public bodies eventually submitted reports to the HRC [21].

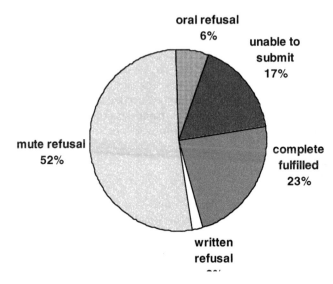

oral refusal
6%

unable to
submit
17%

mute refusal
52%

complete
fulfilled
23%

written
refusal

Fig. 2. ODAC study of PAIA – 2003 (Source: http://www.opendemocracy.org za/ index.htm)

And the statistics for 2003 collected by the South African History Archives (SAHA), a human rights archives, are 'statistics of refusal' (See Appendix). These statistics support the ODAC.'s findings and provide a snapshot of the national situation on public access to information, and the implications for scientific work [22].

4 The Power to Destroy and Delay

The apartheid government destroyed state documents over a number of years in order to deny the new government access to incriminating evidence and to sanitise the history of the apartheid era [23]. And the new government's National Intelligence Agency (NIA) was caught destroying records of former bantustan intelligence agencies in 1996 [24]. But South Africa's Truth and Reconciliation Commission (TRC) collected a large amount of valuable information about the apartheid security establishment and the violation of human rights.

The TRC report recommended that upon completion of its work all TRC records be transferred to the National Archives, and that they should be accessible by the public. However, 34 boxes and two folders that contained information on apartheid regime informers, the Civil Cooperation Bureau, the Dulcie September case, Wouter Basson's Project Coast on chemical warfare, and confidential military intelligence submissions by the African National Congress, went missing. In early 2001 the SAHA, submitted a PAIA request to the Department of Justice for a list of the missing files.

Full access to these files however is still impossible, which shows how determined government departments and politicians are to hide sensitive information. Some of these files could indeed have been destroyed already, as archivists from the National Archives suspected when they discovered that some of the records were returned to the government departments from which they had been originally accessed. McKinley [23] explains that the SAHA's efforts show the 'extremely limited nature of realising the right of access to a body of information that rightfully belongs to the people of South Africa but that has been effectively hijacked by government officials and politicians for their own purposes and reasons'.

Former Minister of Justice Penuell Maduna granted the NIA, where the missing files were located, an exemption until 2008 from compliance with the PAIA disclosure provisions. The former Minister also announced that the missing TRC records would be subject to re-classification by a NIA-based classification review committee. And this shows the state's **power to define** what information qualifies as accessible by the public. Curiously enough, the file containing a list of apartheid-era informers is missing [24], which affirms the state's power of surveillance and access to information about its citizens, and the difficulties faced by citizens to access state information. The point is that full access to all the missing files dealing with sensitive information around human rights violations committed during the apartheid era now seems more remote than ever.

5 The Power to Defy and Disregard

On 19 November 2003, the South African Cabinet announced its operational plan on Comprehensive Care and Treatment for HIV and Aids. This gave hope to the 5.6 million people living with Aids in South Africa, which includes a 15.7% HIV prevalence rate among nurses in four provinces according to a survey by the Human Sciences Research Council, the Medical Research Council and the Medical University of South Africa [25]. The operational plan committed government to roll out antiretroviral treatment, improve the public health system by hiring 22 000 more health care workers over a five-year period, provide nutritional programmes and improve accessibility to counselling and testing.

The implementation of this treatment plan would proceed according to a timetable that appeared as 'Annexure A' of the operational plan. The Treatment Action Campaign (TAC), a non-government organisation that campaigns for greater access to HIV treatment for all South Africans, sought access to this timetable in order to assist government with its implementation by ascertaining dates, locations and numbers of clinics, hospitals and numbers of patients to be treated and additional health care workers that would be hired.

Requests were directed at the Minister of Health since 20 February 2004, and letters were addressed to the African National Congress (ANC) and the Parliamentary Portfolio Committee on Health appealing for intervention. All of this in vain! The Department of Health's behaviour was not surprising. The ODAC survey revealed that it failed to respond to any requests filed with it. When the TAC finally took the Minister of Health to court on 18 June 2004 to compel access under the PAIA, the department responded in September 2004 that 'Annexure A' was in fact a draft, and that references in the operational plan to this annexure were errors that should have been corrected [26]. So it took the department about a year to realise and announce that a poorly edited document was officially released to the public!

The TAC asked the Pretoria High Court to award legal costs for taking the case so far before being informed that 'Annexure A' was just a draft. And in December 2004 the Minister of Health was ordered to pay punitive costs [27]. According to the High Court judgement, the Minister had had eleven opportunities to inform the TAC of the true situation but failed to do so. The TAC is also considering proceeding with separate litigation to compel the government to make the timetable available. On 4 November 2004 thousands of TAC members marched and demonstrated in six cities around the country to demand access to information [28]. Possible litigation could be ended if the Minister of Health simply provides the information [29]. But the Minister remains defiant and still refuses to make an implementation timetable publicly available.

6   The Power to Demand and Promote a Culture of Access

These examples provide evidence that public access to information is not automatically guaranteed by a constitution, a bill of rights and a piece of legislation like the PAIA. Moreover, the right of access needs to be defended more strenuously in a post-911world with more and more countries passing anti-terrorism legislation that threatens to roll back information access rights. In South Africa today, there are also signs of a retreat from the openness and transparency of the early 1990s towards greater secrecy. The ANC records of the exile settlements in Tanzania, for example, were transferred to Fort Hare University archives in September 1992 for open public perusal. But records of overseas ANC offices were subsequently sent to ANC headquarters at Luthuli House (formerly Shell House) in Johannesburg. And public access to these archives is now more difficult [30].

Success with implementing the PAIA thus far has come mostly through pressure and struggle, and from pressing for public access to information. The most notable achievements came through the SAHA as a result of both its experience and resources. In October 2003, for example, the Department of Defence released to the SAHA 'the first official record documenting South Africa's nuclear weapons programme to be released since the apartheid government's pre-1994 disclosures' [31].

But this kind of success comes at a price that ordinary South Africans cannot afford. In another case, for example, the SAHA was charged more than R5000-00 for access to 30 files [32]. The charges were for the access fee, search and preparation fees and copying fees. There have also already been instances of organisations requiring payment of fees much higher than provided in the PAIA [33]. Ordinary South Africans therefore work through organisations like SAHA to have any hope of success. Some of the other NGOs committed to make the PAIA work are ODAC, the Freedom of Expression Institute (FXI), Khulumani Support Group for victims of apartheid, which seeks access to information about the Department of Justice's policy on reparations, and the Institute for the Advancement of Journalism.

Confronting state and private power requires a coordinated effort from civil society organisations committed to strengthening the public sector, and enforcing compliance with the PAIA. The power to demand is based on South Africa's constitutional right of access to information and the democratic responsibility of holding power to account. It is in a collective and integrated effort that demands will yield results. There is already talk of the need for a coalition of civil society forces and a broader strategy of engagement in the struggle for public access to information [23] – a **public access to information front**, as it were, to promote a culture of access and disclosure.

Such a culture will strengthen the political will to provide access, test existing legislation, challenge refusals in court, secure funding and resources for implementation, and empower the public sector. Such a culture recognises that public access to information is a human right that gives effect to the achievement of all other human rights. Self-informed HIV-Aids patients can, for example, take some responsibility for their own care and treatment as information actors. And because it also drives progress in science and technology, the LIS research community should monitor public access to information and help make it work. This activity should be guided by the perspective that **power is information**.

7   Implications for the Nested Model of Context Stratification

This case study indicates at least five things about the context of implementing access to information legislation in a developing country, and about information seeking and retrieval by its citizens:

- The professional context of information seeking and retrieval is more complex and varied than just the restricted interaction environment widely assumed in the LIS research literature. This warrants a disciplinary interest also, for example, in information access legislation, and in other social sites of information seeking and retrieval;
- The political context of implementing information access legislation in the case of South Africa is a negotiated settlement that broke the deadlock of apartheid, but involves several key compromises between the old and new orders;
- The economic context is influenced by the forces of globalization and a neo-liberal consensus, and means that there are limited resources and a reduced state capacity in South Africa to implement information access legislation, and worsening poverty and inequality;
- Disclosure of information by the South African state is uneven. There is a marked difference, for example, between the Department of Defence and the Department of Health; and
- Sustained pressure by some civil society organisations is improving affordable and successful access to information.

Whether all the rich complexity of context can be captured at all in any model is doubtful. Models of context themselves originate and are constructed in given contexts, and abstracted away from others. And they promote certain perspectives and viewpoints either consciously or unconsciously. The Ingwersen and Jarvelin nested model of context stratification for information seeking and retrieval [5] explicates the cognitive perspective, whose shortcomings have been critiqued elsewhere [34], [35]. Most significant among them are the restrictive view of the information seeker and limited recognition of the influences of culture, time and place on the information seeking and retrieval process. The Ingwersen and Jarvelin model, however, now attempts to introduce and theorise these and other 'remote contexts' for information seeking and retrieval (See figure 3), and it deserves constructive comment in order to enlarge its scope of application.

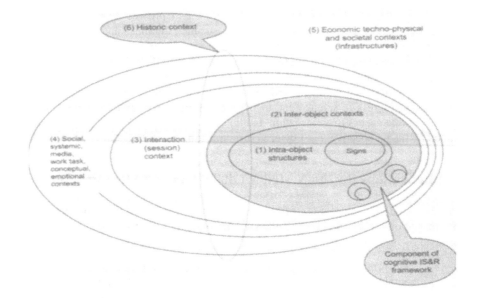

Fig. 3. Nested model of context stratification (Source: Ingwersen & Jarvelin 2004: 305)

In an application to the model's 'remote contexts', the findings of this case study:

- Extend some aspects of Ingwersen and Jarvelin's model of context;
- Question the arrangement of specified contexts; and
- Widen the meaning of the historic context.

First, the model identifies but does not yet elaborate the content of societal, economic and political contexts (infrastructures) as remote contexts. Several case studies are necessary to provide the content to extend and develop the model's remote contexts. A country's information access legislation, as this case study shows for example, belongs to the societal-economico-politico context. Its impact on information seeking and retrieval deserves analysis to discover the extent of its influence on actors, components and interactive sessions in information retrieval processes. This case study found that in a developing country it often trumps other 'immediate contexts' in achieving success. Also, matters of globalization and post-colonialism that feature in the South African case can be explored further. This may enrich the model with an additional context that is relevant to other developing countries.

Second, there are implications of this case study for the model's arrangement of contexts. Whereas the surrounding of a current context of a component by others suggests flexibility, this quality is in fact sacrificed in the modeling of that component in a fixed stratification of contexts. In this way, sensitivity to the uneven and often variable impact of different contexts in actual information seeking and retrieval situations is not a feature of the model. Whatever happens to be nested at the core, whether objects, searchers or interface, determines which other framework components act as further context, and their immediacy and/or remoteness.

But this case study underscores instead the need for and value of greater flexibility. In a middle-income developing country like South Africa with deep structural inequalities, information seeking and retrieval operate at both the typically advanced level described in Ingwersen and Jarvelin's model, and at the more basic level illustrated by the PAIA case study. In other words, some sections of South African society would comply with the model, as it would apply in the mature and stable democracies of Europe and the United States. But other sections of South African society would not.

At the more basic level, the layers of context will nest themselves differently because of the power dynamics associated with the inferior socio-economic circumstances of many information seekers. The historical legacy of apartheid and its damaging personal and social impact mean that matters of self-confidence, literacy levels and financial status rank as critical success factors for many information seekers, and are decisive for simply getting involved in any systematic search for information.

It is unsurprising that wealthy South African citizens and organisations have had greater success with the PAIA than poorer citizens. In general therefore, this would imply a less rigidly stratified nested model of context to allow a flexible interplay of the several layers of context, more sensitive to time, place and circumstances. Ingwersen and Jarvelin's 'remote' historical and economic and socio-cultural contexts are in fact more 'immediate' and salient in respect of their influence on a large number of information seekers in a developing country like South Africa.

Third, the case study widens the meaning of the historic context. It is commendable that the historic context operates across all the model's other contexts and affects all information seeking and retrieval processes and activities. But it needs to be more explicit in terms of its content and meaning. Currently, it emphasizes the information seeker's personal experiences. This case study suggests that foregrounding politico-historical content would include the collective historical experience of denied access to information, as was the case in apartheid South Africa [36]. This would make the model more historically specific and widely applicable.

If the politico-historical aspect is implicit in the historic context, then it needs to become explicit. This is necessary especially given the model's cognitive emphasis on the individual information seeker, and hence on personal experiences and expectations. The South African case elicits the collective and socio-cultural dimensions of information seeking and retrieval where groups of citizens, assisted by skilled mediators, undertake access to information projects. But whereas socio-cultural and political factors in developing countries may explain the social dimension in information seeking and retrieval, a growing emphasis on social cognition and its implications more universally, merit the model's attention.

In conclusion, the model needs to:

- Take on board recent challenges of social epistemology to the traditional individualist epistemological position of its cognitive outlook [37], [38];
- Take a wider view of the social contexts in which information seeking and retrieval take place, and hence enlarge its scope of application;

- Clarify how contexts can nest themselves differently. The reference to 'context stratification' implies an unfortunate rigidity of the model;
- Elaborate its remote historical, economic, societal and political contexts to affirm the secular dimensions of information seeking and retrieval, and so underscore also a social responsibility orientation; and
- Grapple with ways of connecting an improved understanding of social, cultural and political contexts of information seeking and retrieval with programmes of action to improve access for information seekers.

This case study concludes that promoting a culture of access in a developing country like South Africa is just as important as enacting information access legislation. It urges the linking of information seeking and retrieval research with civil society projects to produce an enabling context for information seekers. And it challenges LIS researchers and information professionals to consider how an understanding of how power and information access works, should make a difference.

References

1. Calland, R. Turning right to information into a living reality: access to information and the imperative of effective implementation (2003) Available Online: http://64.233.183.104/ search?=cache:jMQ6pWM9eI4J:www.humanrightsinitiative.org/p (Accessed December 2004)
2. World Bank. Legislation on freedom of information: trends and standards. Prem notes: public sector, October 2004, no. 93. Available Online: http://64.233.183.104/ search? q=cache:6kUsIQcP8CsJ:www1.worldbank.org/prem/PREM... (Accessed December 2004)
3. Black, A.: Information society: a secular view. In: Hornby, S., Clarke, Z (eds.): Challenge and change in the information society. Facet, London (2003) 18-41
4. Boyd Rayward, W. Introduction. In: Boyd Rayward, W. (ed.): Aware and responsible: Papers of the Nordic-International colloquium on social and cultural awareness and responsibility in library, information and documentation studies (SCARLID). Scarecrow Press, Inc., Lanham, Maryland (2004) v-vii
5. Ingwersen, P. and Jarvelin, K.: Context in information retrieval. In: Bothma. T., Kaniki, A. (eds.): ProLISSA 2004: Proceedings of the third biennial DISSAnet Conference, 28-29 October 2004, Farm Inn, Pretoria, South Africa. Infuse, Pretoria (2004) 301-10
6. Keohane, R.O., Nye.: J.S. Power and interdependence in the information age. Foreign Affairs, **77: 5** (1998) 81-94
7. WSIS Executive Secretariat. Report of the Geneva phase of the World Summit on the Information Society, Geneva-Palexpo, 10-12 December 2003. Document WSIS-03/GENEVA/9(Rev.1)-E.   (2004)   Available   Online: http://www.tac.org. za/newsletter/2004/ns17_11_2004.htm (Accessed November 2004)
8. Terreblanche, S.: A history of inequality in South Africa, 1652-2002. University of Natal Press, Pietermaritzburg (2002)
9. South Africa Human Development Report. Poverty and inequality. In: The challenge of sustainable development in South Africa: *Unlocking People's Creativity*. United Nations Development Programme. Oxford University Press, Cape Town (2003) 69-96
10. Roberts, B.: 'Empty stomachs, empty pockets': poverty and inequality in post-apartheid South Africa. In Daniel, J., Southall, R., Lutchman, J. (eds.): State of the Nation; South Africa 2004-2005. Human Sciences Research Council, Cape Town (2005) 78-91

11. Marais, H.: South Africa: limits to change; the political economy of transition. University of Cape Town Press. Cape Town (1998)
12. Bond, P.: Elite transition: from apartheid to neoliberalism in South Africa. Pluto Press, London (2000)
13. Saul, J. S.: Cry the beloved country: the post-apartheid denouement. Review of African political economy **89** (2001) 429-460
14. Dutta, S., Lanvin, B., Paua, F. (eds.): The Global Information Technology Report: towards an equitable information society. Oxford University Press, New York, Oxford 2004
15. Calland, R., Tilley, A. (eds.): The right to know, the right to live: access to information and socio-economic justice. The Open Democracy Advice Centre (ODAC), Cape Town (2002)
16. Currie, I.: Scrutiny: South Africa's Promotion of Access to Information Act. European public law **9: 1** (2003) 59-72
17. Mathews, A.S.: The darker reaches of government: access to information about public administration in the United States, Britain and South Africa. University of California Press, Berkeley (1979)
18. Herbstein, D.: White Lies: Canon Collins and the secret war against apartheid. Human Sciences Research Council Press, Cape Town (2004)
19. South Africa fails the right to know. 23 September 2004. Available Online: http://archive. mg.co.za/nxt/gateway. dll/PrintEdition/MGP2004/31v00269/41v00320/51v00 (Accessed October 2004)
20. South Africa denied knowledge. 24 September 2004. Available Online: http://archive.mg. co.za/nxt/gateway. dll/PrintEdition/MGP2004/31v00269/41v00320/51v00 (Accessed October 2004)
21. Sorenson, R.: Statistics with respect to Promotion of Access to Information Act (PAIA): Report to National Assembly by Human Rights Commission pursuant to Section 84(b) of PAIA (2004) Available Online: http://66.102.9.104/search? q=cache:wfzyDWq1vu8J: www.wits.ac.za/saha/ publications/F (Accessed November 2004)
22. South African History Archives.: Annual Report 2003. Appendix B: Freedom of Information Programme Statistics (2004) Available Online: http://www.wits. ac. za/saha/publications/ann_rep_2003.pdf (Accessed November 2004)
23. McKinley, D.T.: The state of access to information in South Africa. Report prepared for the Centre for the Study of Violence and Reconciliation (2003) Available Online: http://66.102.9.104/search?q=cache:xajL0amYBukJ:www.   apc.org/apps/imgupload/697 (Accessed October 2004)
24. Harris, V.: NIA: a friendlier Big Brother? (2004) Available Online: http://www.wits.ac. za/saha/publications/FOIP_6_1_Harris.pdf (Accessed November 2004)
25. Shisana, O. **et al**.: The impact of HIV-AIDS on the health sector: National Survey of health personnel, ambulatory and hospitalised patients and health facilities. HSRC, MRC, MEDUNSA (2002)
26. Why the TAC is going to court tomorrow and holding country-wide demonstrations: we need a treatment timetable now! (2004) Available Online: http://www.tac.org.za/ Documents /AccessToInfoCourtCase/WhyTACGoingtoCourt4Nov (Accessed November 2004)
27. TAC awarded punitive costs in case against Minister of Health. TAC electronic newsletter (2004) Available Online: http://www.tac.org.za/newsletter/2004/ns14_12_2004.htm (Accessed December 2004)
28. Brief Note: TAC demonstrations for access to information on 4 November. TAC electronic newsletter (2004) Available Online: http://www.tac.org.za/newsletter/2004/ns 17_11_2004.htm (Accessed November 2004)

29. Achmat, Z.: HIV-AIDS and human rights: a new South African struggle. John Foster lecture – 10 November 2004 Available Online: http://www.tac.org.za/Documents/John GalwayFosterLecture-finalVersion-20041116.pdf (Accessed November 2004)
30. Morrow, S., Wotshela, L.: State of the archives and access to information. In: Daniel, J., Southall, R., Lutchman, J. (eds.): State of the Nation; South Africa 2004-2005. Human Sciences Research Council Press, Cape Town (2005) 313-35
31. Harris, V., Hatang, S., Liberman, P.: Unveiling South Africa's nuclear past. Journal of Southern African studies, **30: 3** (2004) 457-475
32. Harris, V.: Using the Promotion of Access to Information Act. (2002) Available Online: http://www.wits.ac.za/saha/publications/FOIP_1_1_Harris.pdf(Accessed November 2004)
33. Sorenson, R.: Paying for access to information (2004) Available Online: http://www.wits. ac.za/saha/publications/FOIP_2_2_Sorensen.pdf(Accessed November 2004)
34. Frohmann, B.: The power of images: a discourse analysis of the cognitive viewpoint. Journal of documentation **48: 4** (1992) 365-386
35. Hjorland, B.: Det kognitive paradigme i biblioteks- og informationsvidenskaben (The cognitive paradigm in library and information science). Biblioteksarbejde **33** (1991) 5-37
36. Merrett, C.: A culture of censorship: secrecy and intellectual repression in South Africa. David Philip, Cape Town (1994)
37. Fallis, D. (ed.): Social epistemology **16: 1** (2002) [Special issue]
38. Zandonade, T.: Social epistemology from Jesse Shera to Steve Fuller. Library trends **52: 4** (2004) 810-832

Appendix: SAHA 2003 STATISTICS OF PAIA

Requestee	Carried Over requests	No. of requests	Requests granted	Refusals	Pending, or Inadequate Response	Retracted	Internal appeals	Court action	Average Response Time
PUBLIC BODIES - NATIONAL									
ARMSCOR	2	11		11[1]	2				94 days
Central Firearms Register		1		1					70 days
Dep. of Health	1			1					665 days
Dept. of Agriculture	1	1	1	1					90 days
Dept. of Defence	40	10	33	10	6	1	1	1	137 days
Dept. of Environmental Affairs	2		1		1				333 days
Dept. of Finance		1	1						123 days
Dept. of Foreign Affairs	1	10	3	3	5				26 days
Dept. of Justice	15	10	8	15	2		13	3[2]	119 days
Dept. of Trade and Industry		3		3					46 days
George Magistrate's Court		2	2						75 days
Health Professions Council of South Africa	6		2	4					10 days

Requestee	Carried Over requests	No. of requests	Requests granted	Refusals	Pending, or Inadequate Response	Retracted	Internal appeals	Court action	Average Response Time
National Archives	13	9	7	10	5		2	4	209 days
National Intelligence Agency	3	4	1	3	3				80 days
Nuclear Energy Corporation of South Africa	1	6		1	6				177 days
Nuclear Fuels Corporation of South Africa		1		1					2 days
Office of the Auditor General	1	1		1	1				177 days
Office of the President		2			2				241 days
South African Council for Non-proliferation of Weapons of Mass Destruction	1	1			1	1			167 days
South African Police Service	11	4	4	7	4				197 days

PUBLIC BODIES - PROVINCIAL

KwaZulu-Natal Parks Board	2			2					34 days
Limpopo MEC Finance Economic Affairs, Tourism and Environment	7			7					159 days
Mpumalanga MEC Agriculture, Conservation, and Environment	4			4					159 days

Requestee	Carried Over requests	No. of requests	Requests granted	Refusals	Pending, or Inadequate Response	Retracted	Internal appeals	Court action	Average Response Time
Western Cape National Conservation Board	3			3					166 days

PRIVATE BODIES

Denel		2		2					24 days
Eskom		2	1	1					13 days
i Themba Labs		1	1						12 days
ISCOR	1			1					75 days
Ithala Development Finance Corporation Limited		1		1					23 days
Legal Transcriptions cc/bk		1	1						51 days
South African Breweries Limited		1	1						12 days
Telkom		2	2						43 days
Total	115	87	69	93	38	2			

1. All refused but are pending reconsideration
2. Three of the appeals resulted in one single court action

(Source: http://www.wits.ac.za/saha/publications/ann_rep_2004.pdf)

A Bibliometric-Based Semi-automatic Approach to Identification of Candidate Thesaurus Terms: Parsing and Filtering of Noun Phrases from Citation Contexts[*]

Jesper W. Schneider and Pia Borlund

Department of Information Studies,
Royal School of Library and Information Science,
Aalborg Branch, Sohngaardsholmsvej 2, 9000 Aalborg, Denmark
{jws, pb}@db.dk

Abstract. The present study investigates the ability of a bibliometric based semi-automatic method to select candidate thesaurus terms from citation contexts. The method consists of document co-citation analysis, citation context analysis, and noun phrase parsing. The investigation is carried out within the specialty area of periodontology. The results clearly demonstrate that the method is able to select important candidate thesaurus terms within the chosen specialty area.

1 Introduction

A basic characteristic of thesaurus construction is the collection of a set of candidate terms (words or phrases) [1]. Selection of candidate thesaurus terms usually implies scanning 'exemplary documents' for potential terms, and a review of the subject matter by domain experts, who then suggest potential terms [2, 3]. The manual process of term collection is labour intensive [1]. Accordingly, more or less sophisticated automatic methods have been devised in order to alleviate the collection of candidate thesaurus terms [1]. Automatic methods range from simple extraction of single words from various data fields in bibliographic records, to sophisticated extraction methods based on term distributions in full text documents [1, 4]. Nevertheless, automatic extraction of terms from full text documents typically relies on flawed term distributions [5]. Little attention is given to the role of schematic, discourse and thematic structures within documents, and how they influence term distributions [e.g., 6]. To distinguish the specific semantic nature of extracted terms is therefore usually beyond the scope of automatic methods. Most often, too many contextually irrelevant and semantically unreliable terms are extracted. However, recent research indicates the 'burstiness' of term distributions, and how semantically related terms thereby tend to 'clump' together in special contextual areas of documents [e.g., 7, 8]. The latter research suggests that document structures should be utilized to identify these small contextual text windows within full text documents.

---

[*] The present paper is sponsored by NORSLIS (Nordic Research School in Library and Information Science).

F. Crestani and I. Ruthven (Eds.): CoLIS 2005, LNCS 3507, pp. 226–237, 2005.
© Springer-Verlag Berlin Heidelberg 2005

The small text windows most likely contain related terms that refer to some common subject matter and should be the target for term extraction. As a result, fewer candidate terms are probably extracted, though it is assumed that these terms, since they are extracted from contextual surroundings, are semantically more reliable and thus more relevant.

When automatic approaches are used as a tool for thesaurus constructers, and not as a mean in itself, then we speak of semi-automatic thesaurus construction [1]. The present study introduces a bibliometric based semi-automatic method that identifies and selects important candidate thesaurus terms from citation contexts. Citation contexts are seen as a special form of document structure. A citation context is the loosely defined text window in scientific works that surrounds reference markers[1]. The assumption is that terminology used in the citation contexts of citing works reflects upon *concepts* in a specialty area due to the notion of *concept symbols* [9].

Small [9] established that highly cited documents symbolize concepts to those who cite them. While it has long been known that when references are made into citations they can be construed as subject headings [e.g., 10], different people may construe the same cited document differently. However, Small [9] showed that citing authors in chemistry tended to be both specific and highly uniform in the meanings they assign to cited documents, as revealed by the contexts of the references. Scientists tend to give earlier works consensual meaning by 'piling up' identical or similar words and phrases in the sentences in which their citation markers are embedded [9]. Consequently, when citation contexts show that citing authors have used a cited document to stand for a given idea more or less uniformly over many papers, the document attains the status of a concept symbol [9]. For that reason, the highly cited document communicates a specific topic or concept and resembles a subject heading.

Former research by Rees-Potter [11] verifies that citation contexts can be used to identify candidate thesaurus terms within two disciplines of the social sciences. However, the investigated citation contexts primarily concern monographs, and the manual process applied in the study for selecting conceptual phrases is exceedingly labour intensive [11]. Conversely, in the present study we wish to verify whether selection of candidate thesaurus terms can be satisfactorily accomplished on a lower disciplinary level in a scientific domain where scholarly knowledge is primarily mediated through journal papers. The assumption is that the behaviour of terminology here may be different to that of the social sciences. The scientific domain chosen is *periodontology*, a specialty area of dentistry within the life sciences. The choice of dentistry within the life sciences is governed by funding whereas the choice of periodontology is coincidental.

Further, a key premise in citation context analysis is the use of conceptual phrases as they represent more meaningful concepts than individual words [e.g., 12]. Unfortunately, automatic extraction of coherent conceptual phrases is much more complicated than extraction of single words. As a result, former citation contexts analyses have typically extracted conceptual phrases manually [9, 11]. In the present study however, we parse citation contexts with a natural language parsing tool in order to extract coherent noun phrases. Noun phrases are believed to be content bearing units and thus good indicators of concepts in a text. Automatic parsing of

---

[1] A citation context closely resembles the anchor-text in hyperlink document structures.

noun phrases alleviates the otherwise labour intensive process of extracting candidate thesaurus terms through citation context analysis.

Our semi-automatic method comprises a number of filtering steps that warrant selection of *important* candidate thesaurus terms. The steps are: 1) creation of *concept groups* by use of document co-citation analysis, 2) citation context analysis, which include *parsing* of noun phrases and identification of *concept symbols*, 3) *filtering* of noun phrases within a concept group to identify primary and secondary candidate thesaurus terms. Consequently, the aim of the present study is to investigate the ability of the bibliometric based semi-automatic method to select important candidate thesaurus terms. Neither of the steps are applied in a vigorous automatic manner. They are explored and utilized in a semi-automatic approach to thesaurus construction based on bibliometric methods [5, 13]. The purpose of the method is to collect a restricted set of important candidate thesaurus terms that can be used as a basis for manual thesaurus construction.

The paper is composed of four main sections. Section two presents the basic steps of the semi-automatic method. Section three outlines the validation of the method. Finally, section four summarises the main findings.

2   Method

The present study and its results derive from a comprehensive dissertation work that investigates the applicability of bibliometric methods for thesaurus construction [5]. Only the basic methodical steps for extraction and validation of candidate thesaurus terms are outlined here. Readers are referred to Schneider [5] for detailed description, analysis, and validation of the proposed method.

In the present section, we present the basic methodical steps of document co-citation analysis, citation context analysis, and noun phrase parsing.

2.1   Document Co-citation Analysis

A central notion of the present study is the creation of coherent *concept groups*. A concept group is defined as a cluster of subject related co-cited references that act as concept symbols [11]. Clusters of co-cited references serve as the 'intellectual base knowledge' to citing papers in more recent research fronts [14]. The cited references within the clusters are comparable to the notion of 'exemplary documents' suggested by Blair and Kimbrough [3], in that they represent key concepts, methods, or experiments, which researcher build on in a research front of a specialty area [9].

As stated in the introduction, a cited reference that symbolizes the same content to a majority of later citing authors acts as a concept symbol [9]. In the present application, a coherent concept group makes sure that semantically related concept symbols are clustered under a common concept. The link between a concept symbol and its reference marker in the citation context of later citing papers ensures that we can select terminology from the citation contexts and attach it to the concept symbol and its parent concept group. Thus, semantically related terminology used in citation contexts to describe the individual concept symbols in a concept group is likewise joined under the common concept.

It is the assumption that when terminology is related to the usage of references in small text windows of citing documents, then we can expect the terminology to be contextual and subject specific, similar to the notion of term 'burstiness' and term 'clumping' mentioned above [7, 8]. It is assumed that such terminology is important as it reflects special characteristics in relation to the concept symbol and more broadly to the common concept(s) of the concept group. Thus, joining semantically related terminology in a concept group further strengthens its conceptualization. Consequently, citation contexts of concept symbols are interesting sources for selection of candidate thesaurus terms.

We know from bibliometrics that document co-citation analysis is an appropriate bibliometric method for clustering of topically related cited documents [15]. The clustering algorithm chosen for the present study is complete linkage due to its strong cluster criterion, and its ability to create 'clique-like' clusters [16]. This is deemed advantageous in connection with concept group creation, where the aim is to maximize intra-cluster similarity and minimize inter-cluster similarity [17]. Concept groups are defined as solid clusters of 'significantly' co-cited reference pairs. Similar to Small and Greenlee [18], the Jaccard proximity measure is invoked to compose a co-citation matrix of cited references participating in at least one 'significant' co-citation relation above a predefined threshold.

2.2   Citation Context Analysis and Noun Phrase Parsing

The main assumption behind the present study is that terminology used in citation contexts of citing papers reflects upon concepts in a specialty area due to the notion of concept symbols [9]. It is assumed that focus on recent citation contexts within the structure of citing documents makes it possible to identify current, contextual, and agreed upon candidate thesaurus terms. The terms are expected to reflect aspects of their concept symbol, and more generally, the common subject matter of the concept group. Consequently, a prerequisite for the present study is that highly cited references within periodontology to a large extent act as concept symbols.

The basic purpose of the citation context analysis is to identify and select a sample of citation contexts, which constitute the basis for extraction of candidate thesaurus terms. However, the citation context analysis is also used to validate whether the cited references act as concept symbols, as well as to identify the common concepts expressed by the concept groups in accordance with the concept symbols they contain. The present application of citation context analysis includes identification of citation contexts, identification of 'consensus passages', parsing of citation contexts, validation of concept symbols, validation of concept groups, and finally selection and validation of candidate thesaurus terms. The steps are briefly outlined below.

A necessary preliminary step is the selection of a sample of citation contexts for each of the cited references. Since our study is exploratory, we want to be sure that the contexts indeed reflect upon the content of the cited reference. Thus, we apply a less rigid citation context limitation than normal, as citing documents from the 2001 set are available in electronic form. The electronic format makes the manual process of citation context selection less cumbersome and swifter. We aim at citation contexts with the least possible number of sentences, but still sufficient for construction of meaningful citation contexts. Most of the time, one to three sentences suffice. In order to establish a sample of citation contexts, *at least five* citation contexts for each of the cited references are chosen. We suppose that a minimum of five citation contexts may be a sufficient number for identification of concept symbols. Further, we expect that the majority of cited references eventually will attain more than five citation contexts due to multiple citing of references within a document.

In order to apply noun phrases from the citation contexts, we need to verify whether the cited references act as concept symbols within periodontology. For this purpose, we apply a modified version of the 'consensus passage' procedure introduced by Small [19]. The 'consensus passage' procedure identifies the citation context that best expresses the 'consensus' terminology in the sample of contexts to an individual cited reference. Traditionally, an agreed upon conceptual phrase that denotes the concept symbol is extracted from the 'passage' [19]. The 'consensus passage' procedure is quantitative, which implies that all citation contexts are given a score that reflects their use of consensus terminology. In the present application, the 'passage' with the highest score is compared to the list of extracted commonly used noun phrases in order to determine the phrasal expression of the concept symbol. This ensures that the expression of the concept symbol will resemble the potential consensus usage of the noun phrases.

Frequently occurring noun phrases are the basis for candidate thesaurus terms and are needed in combination with the 'consensus' passages' for the concept symbol analysis. Novel to citation context analysis is the introduction of natural language parsing of noun phrases from the citation contexts. We use the advanced noun phrase parser *Connexor* (www.connexor.com) to select noun phrases from the citation contexts of citing documents. *Connexor* is a shallow syntactic parser based on a functional dependency grammar.

In order to do frequency analysis, a normalization procedure is applied to compensate for slightly different morphological, lexical, and syntactical expressions of phrasal concepts [6]. Notice, the main purpose of the present step is to identify agreed upon terminology in the citation contexts. This implies that the degree of normalization has to be low in order not to impose a deduced 'superficial' consensus terminology upon the citation contexts.

As indicated above, the concept symbol analysis consists of a combined investigation of 'consensus passages' and extracted noun phrases attached to the cited references. The purpose is to establish whether the references act as concept symbols. The phrasal expression of a potential concept symbol is determined from terminology in the 'consensus passage', in combination with the extracted noun phrases. If a cited reference acts as a concept symbol, a *portfolio* of prevalent noun phrases is created and attached to the concept symbol. Consequently, the portfolio of noun phrases denotes the concept symbol. Eventually all portfolios of identified concept symbols within a concept group are compared in order to determine the candidate thesaurus terms appropriate for the particular concept group.

The purpose of concept groups in the present methodology is to strengthen the conceptualization of their member concept symbols. We believe this leads to a further contextualization of the noun phrases characterizing the group of individual concept symbols, and eventually it ensures a more solid basis for selection of candidate thesaurus terms. We evaluate the semantic coherence [20] of the concept groups to verify their common conceptual meaning. Subsequently, we name the groups in accordance with the common conceptual meaning expressed by their member concept symbols, and the portfolios attached to the latter.

The previous steps of concept group creation, citation context analysis, and noun phrase parsing, leads to identification of important candidate thesaurus terms. A final filtering procedure makes it possible to select between primary and secondary candidate thesaurus terms from the portfolio of noun phrases. The selected candidate thesaurus terms are subsequently evaluated by investigating their overlap with possible corresponding subject headings in the MeSH® vocabulary.

3 Results

This section presents the main results of the investigation of the semi-automatic method for identification of candidate thesaurus terms.

The study is based on bibliographic data retrieved and downloaded from Science Citation Index® (SCI®) hosted by Dialog®. The bibliographic data contain 801 citing papers published within periodontology in 2001. For pragmatic reasons, an arbitrary citation threshold value of 13 is decided upon. As a result, the 64 most highly cited references within periodontology in 2001 are selected for the subsequent co-citation analysis. The Jaccard proximity measure is imposed to estimate the 'significance' of the co-citation relations among the 64 cited references. The threshold value is set to 0.16, which reduces the co-citation matrix to 45 co-cited references. Accordingly, the remaining cited references participate in at least one 'significant' co-citation relation on or above the 0.16 threshold value. The reduced co-citation matrix forms the basis for the subsequent complete-link cluster analysis. The cluster analysis reveals 13 clusters, or rather concept groups within periodontology, as reflected in the citing literature for the year 2001.

Eventually, 88 citing documents were needed to obtain at least five citation contexts for each of the 45 cited references. Note that the sampling procedure deliberately does not take into account multiple citing of a reference within a document. The threshold value of *at least* five implies a larger probability of highly co-cited references to emerge in several 'extra' citation contexts, contrary to 'lower' co-cited references. Thus, the rationale behind the threshold is twofold. First, we expect that the majority of cited references eventually will attain more than five citation contexts due to the sampling procedure. Secondly, we suppose that a minimum of five citation contexts may be a sufficient number for identification of concept symbols. The 88 citing documents produced a sample of 580 citation contexts. That is an average of 12.9 citation contexts per cited reference (median 11). The highest number of contexts to one cited reference is 34 and the lowest is five. Further, only two cited references ended up having the minimum number of five citation contexts attached to them [5].

The concept symbol analysis investigates the contextual and consensus usage of terminology in relation to individual highly cited references within periodontology. The concept symbol analysis is performed manually by comparing the statistically derived 'consensus passage' for a cited reference, with the parsed list of commonly agreed upon noun phrases. A mean 'consensus score' is often used to characterize the degree of consensus usage of terminology in the citing sample investigated [19]. The mean 'consensus score' for the present study is 0.52 (median 0.56) [5, p. 255]. We consider this a good score that indicates consensual usage of terminology, as it corresponds to the exemplary result of 0.48 from the study of *leukaemia viruses* by Small [19, p. 102]. The result indicates that highly cited references within periodontology show an inclination to act as concept symbols to the citing papers in the research fronts of 2001.

Nonetheless, the 'consensus scores' and the selected 'consensus passages' are compared with the lists of frequently occurring noun phrases, parsed from the citation contexts of the individually cited references. In order for a noun phrase to be selected for the frequency list, we apply a 'citation context frequency threshold value' of around ⅓ of the sample size, thus a phrase must occur at least in ⅓ of the citation contexts to a cited reference. The determination of whether a cited reference act a concept symbol is therefore based on a complimentary analysis between the 'consensus passage' and the list of commonly agreed upon noun phrases.

The concept symbol analysis of the 45 cited references identifies 42 concept symbols, which means that three cited references are excluded from the remaining analysis. However, the excluded cited references do share a common terminology with the fellow members of their parent concept groups; though it is not possible from the extracted data to designate them unequivocally as concept symbols [5]. Thus, we end up with 42 concept symbols in 13 concept groups; and each concept symbol has a portfolio of prevalent noun phrases attached to it. What remains before selection of candidate thesaurus terms, is to name the concept groups, and to evaluate the semantic coherence within the groups.

The purpose of the concept groups is to strengthen the conceptualization of their attached concept symbols. Evaluation of concept groups ensures a further contextualization and consensus usage of noun phrases, this time at the aggregate group level, provided that there exists a semantic coherence within the group. In a semantically coherent concept group, all members must unequivocally refer to some common conceptual meaning. Lack of semantic coherence means that the expected solid basis for selection of candidate thesaurus terms is disrupted.

The sum of meanings reflected by concept symbols in a concept group, defines the common conceptual meaning for the parent concept group. Thus, concept symbols and their portfolios are used to name their parent concept groups.

The evaluation and naming of the concept groups are done manually and substantiated by the quantitatively derived similarity measure of semantic coherence. The main results are presented in Table 1 below.

The results of the manual evaluation and naming of the concept groups are unambiguous. All groups are semantically coherent [5]. This implies that the concept symbols within the concept groups unequivocally refer to some common concept.

The unambiguous result of the evaluation and naming of the concept groups is substantiated by the semantic coherence scores, developed by Braam, Moed and van Raan [20] for related purposes. The degree of semantic coherence is measured by comparing the individual portfolios of noun phrases attached to the concept symbols in a group, with an 'aggregate portfolio' of noun phrases that represents the entire concept group. The 'aggregate portfolio' is represented as a vector that comprises all

Table 1. Name of concept groups and the semantic coherence scores

Concept group no.	Name of concept groups	Semantic coherence
1	Enamel matrix proteins	0.620
2	Guided tissue regeneration	0.902
3	Complications of periodontal disease	0.650
4	Furcation involvement	0.548
5	Risk factors for periodontal disease	0.585
6	Periodontitis progression, p. gingivalis	0.762
7	Periodontal pathogen, p. gingivalis	0.787
8	Cytokines	0.707
9	Periodontal pathogens	0.623
10	Classification of bacteria	0.774
11	Periodontal pathogen, A. actinomycetemcomitans	0.638
12	Periodontal index	0.707
13	Risk factor of smoking	0.592

different noun phrases appearing in the individual portfolios of the group's concept symbols. The individual portfolios are likewise represented as vectors with a length that corresponds to their number of different noun phrases. A binary count is used to indicate whether a noun phrase is present or absent in the vector representations. Notice, that the 'aggregate portfolio' representing the concept group only contains presence counts, as it is a representation of all different noun phrases in the group. A binary variant of the cosine measure is used to determine the similarity between the individual portfolios and the 'aggregate portfolio' of the concept group. This implies that a similarity result is obtained for each portfolio attached to a concept symbol within a concept group. The *average value* of the individual similarities indicates the semantic coherence within the concept group. In their study, Braam, Moed and van Raan [20, pp. 240-241] obtained average similarity scores in the range of 0.36 to 0.44, which they considered sufficient in order to conclude that their groups were coherent. We use their results as a baseline for evaluating the average similarities computed for the present concept groups. The semantic coherence scores in the present analysis, ranging from 0.585 to 0.902, are far above the results obtained by Braam, Moed and van Raan [20]. Thus, compared to their results and subsequent conclusions, the present quantitative coherence results are very convincing and confirms the manual evaluation.

The aforementioned successive steps ensure that potential candidate thesaurus terms are contextual, agreed upon, and therefore assumed to be important. The final step in the process of term selection is the actual selection between primary and secondary candidate thesaurus terms. A filtering procedure is applied, which separates the noun phrases from the individual portfolios in two categories, primary and secondary phrases. Table 2a presents concept group 1, its four concept symbols, and their attach portfolios of noun phrases and their citation context frequencies. The filtering procedure is applied to select primary and secondary candidate thesaurus terms from concept group 1. The filtering procedure is based on a simple 'portfolio frequency analysis'. The diverse number of citation contexts appended to the individual concept symbol influences the frequency count of noun phrases in the portfolios, as indicated in Table 2a. Hence, the application of 'portfolio frequency' normalizes for the variances in frequencies of noun phrases between the portfolios. Consequently, primary phrases have higher frequencies across the portfolios than secondary phrases. This implies that primary phrases most likely appear in several portfolios within a concept group. Primary phrases are therefore expected to reflect upon the common concept of the group. Conversely, secondary phrases are likely to reflect upon specific aspects of the common concept within a group. The result of the filtering procedure for concept group 1 is illustrated below in Table 2b.

Table 2a. Concept symbols of concept group 1 and their attached portfolios of important noun phrases

Concept group 1: Enamel matrix proteins	
Concept symbol	**Portfolio of noun phrases**
HAMMARSTROM_97a	5 enamel_matrix_protein 4 enamel_matrix_derivative 3 periodontal_regeneration
HAMMARSTROM_97b	7 enamel_matrix_protein 2 regenerative_therapy
HEIJL_97a	7 enamel_matrix_protein 3 periodontal_regeneration
HEIJL_97b	16 enamel_matrix_derivative 14 clinical_attachment_level 11 treatment

Table 2b. Selected primary and secondary candidate thesaurus terms for concept group 1 after invoking the filtering procedure

Primary:	3	enamel_matrix_protein
	2	periodontal_regeneration
	2	enamel_matrix_derivative
Secondary:	1	treatment
	1	regenerative_therapy
	1	clinical_attachment_level

From Table 2b, we can infer that *enamel matrix protein*, *periodontal regeneration*, and *enamel matrix derivative*, indeed reflect upon the common concept of group 1, that is *enamel matrix proteins*, see [5] . Eventually, the filtering step selects a total of 60 candidate thesaurus terms, 21 primary and 39 secondary terms [5].

The selected candidate thesaurus terms are evaluated by use of a quantitative validation procedure. The procedure consists in matching the selected primary and secondary terms with possible corresponding descriptors in the MeSH® vocabulary, the standard authority in relation to index terms concerning periodontology. It is assumed that the presented selection method is able to put forward a significant proportion of important candidate thesaurus terms among the selected primary terms. If the assumption is true, primary candidate thesaurus terms should acquire high overlap scores. The selected terms are coded to determine the level of match acquired. Four different categories are decided upon; these are: Exact match, entry term match, partial match, and no match. The former two categories are considered relevant matches, as they refer to immediate matches between the selected term and a MeSH® descriptor. The latter two categories are considered non-relevant matches, as they either indicate a partial or no-match between the select term and the MeSH® vocabulary; for an elaborate description of the coding see [5, p. 269].

As stated above, a total of 60 candidate thesaurus terms are investigated, 21 primary and 39 secondary terms [5]. Table 3 below shows the overlap scores for primary and secondary candidate thesaurus terms.

Table 3. Overlap scores between selected primary and secondary terms and MeSH® descriptors

Primary candidate terms		Secondary candidate terms	
Relevant matches	0.76	Relevant matches	0.38
Non-relevant matches	0.24	Non-relevant matches	0.59

The results are very promising. The scores indicate a high representativeness of selected primary candidate thesaurus terms in the MeSH® vocabulary. Overall, the categories deemed relevant obtain a total score of 0.76 for primary terms and 0.38 for secondary terms [5, p. 270]. The results indicate that approximately three primary terms out of every four match a MeSH® descriptor, and approximately two secondary terms out of every five match a MeSH® descriptor. The results imply that the proportion of important index terms among the selected primary candidate thesaurus terms is higher compared to the selected secondary terms. The high relevant overlap score for the selected primary candidate thesaurus terms suggest that the method selects a considerable number of important index terms in this category.

The chi-square statistic is used to determine whether there is a significant difference in the proportion of overlap scores between primary and secondary terms: $\chi^2(1) = 6.35 \, p < 0.01$ (one-tailed) [5, p. 271]. Thus, we can infer that the proportional difference of relevant selected terms between primary and secondary candidate thesaurus terms is significant. Consequently, a significantly higher proportion of the selected primary candidate thesaurus terms are represented in the MeSH® vocabulary compared to the selected secondary terms [5].

The validation results, the high relevant overlap score and the significance test, confirm the assumption, that the special selection procedures of the bibliometric based semi-automatic method produce important index terms among the selected primary and secondary terms. More importantly, the selection procedures enable the selection of a significantly higher number of important index terms among the selected primary terms. As a result, at least for the specialty area of periodontology, we can expect the method to identify a significant number of important and highly relevant candidate thesaurus terms among the selected primary terms.

4 Summary

The exploration of the bibliometric based semi-automatic method within the specialty area of periodontology clearly demonstrates that the applied bibliometric methods are able to select important candidate thesaurus terms. We believe that the special selection procedures inherent in the methodical steps ensure that a significant number of the selected primary candidate thesaurus terms turn out to be important index terms. The conclusion therefore is that the applied bibliometric methods are suitable for selection of candidate thesaurus terms.

The key to this result is the focus on cited references as the primary unit of analysis. The citation context of a cited reference, acting as a concept symbol, is very interesting in relation to semi-automatic thesaurus construction. The terminology in the text window is most likely highly contextual as it reflects special characteristics in relation to the concept symbol. Likewise, consensus terminology is most likely found in the text window, as the cited reference acts as a concept symbol. These features are very important in relation to selection of important index terms. Consequently, the proposed methodology establishes literary warrant for a significant number of important contextual and agreed upon primary candidate thesaurus terms. This is an excellent basis for further manual thesaurus construction.

The results produced by the citation context analysis extend the findings of Rees-Potter [11]. We demonstrate the usefulness of citation context analysis for thesaurus construction purposes in a specialty area within the life sciences, dominated by journal papers. We can conclude that it is possible to identify concept symbols in citing journal papers in periodontology, and to extract noun phrases from their citation contexts. These procedures are useful for thesaurus construction.

The investigation also demonstrates the usefulness of noun phrase parsing in citation context analysis. Noun phrase parsing alleviates the time consuming process of phrase identification. In the present approach, noun phrase parsing is especially suitable, as it extracts agreed upon terminology from which candidate thesaurus terms are eventually selected. However, refinements of the method are still needed. The most obvious next step is to devise an algorithm, based on the experiences from this study that can identify suitable citation contexts automatically.

There are some deficiencies too. Document co-citation clustering as applied in the present study only focuses on a small number of the core intellectual base references for the 2001 citing papers. This produces few concept groups. Nevertheless, the groups reflect the most visible research areas within periodontology, as reflected in the bibliographies of the 2001 citing papers.

References

1. Soergel, D. (1974). *Indexing languages and thesauri: construction and maintenance.* Los Angeles, CA: Melville.
2. Aitchison, J., Gilchrist, A. and Bawden, D. (2000). *Thesaurus construction and use: A practical manual* (4th ed.). London: Aslib.
3. Blair, D.C. and Kimbrough, S. O. (2002). Exemplary documents: foundation for information retrieval design. *Information Processing and Management,* 38, 363-379.
4. Salton, G.and McGill, M. (1983). *Introduction to modern information retrieval.* New York: MaGraw-Hill.
5. Schneider, J.W. (2004) *Verification of bibliometric methods' applicability for thesaurus construction.* PhD dissertation. Aalborg: Royal School of Library and Information Science. Available: http://biblis.db.dk/uhtbin/hyperion.exe/db.jessch04
6. Moens, M. F. (2000). *Automatic indexing and abstracting of document texts.* Dordrecht, The Netherlands: Kluwer Academic Publishers.
7. Katz, S. (1996). Distribution of content words and phrases in text and language modelling. *Natural Language Engineering,* 2(1), 15-60.
8. Bookstein, A., Klein, S. T. and Raita, T. (1998). Clumping properties of content-bearing words. *Journal of the American Society for Information Science and Technology,* 49(2), 102-114.
9. Small, H. (1978). Cited documents as concept symbols. *Social Studies of Science, 8*(3), 327-340.
10. Garfield, E. (1974). The citation index as a subject index. *Current Contents, May*(18), 5-7.
11. Rees-Potter, L. K. (1989). Dynamic thesaural systems: a Bibliometric study of terminological and conceptual change in sociology and economics with the application to the design of dynamic thesaural systems. *Information Processing and Management, 25*(6), 677-691.
12. Anick, P. G. and Vaithyanathan, S. (1997). Exploiting clustering and phrases for context-based information retrieval. *Proceedings of the ACM/SIGIR Conference on Research and Development in Information Retrieval, Philidelhia, PA, 1997,* 314-323.
13. Schneider, J.W. & Borlund, P. (2004). Introduction to bibliometrics for construction and maintenance of thesauri: methodical considerations. *Journal of Documentation,* 60(5), 524-549.
14. Persson, O. (1994) The intellectual base and research front of JASIS 1986-1990. *Journal of the American Society for Information Science,* 45(1), 31-38.
15. Small, H. (1973). Co-citation in the scientific literature: a new measure of the relationship between two documents. *Journal of the American Society for Information Science,* 24(4), 265-269.
16. Sneath, P. and Sokal, R. (1973). *Numerical taxonomy : The principles and practice of numerical classification.* San Francisco, CA: W. H. Freeman.
17. Sparck Jones, K. (1971). *Automatic keyword classification for information retrieval.* London: Butterworths.
18. Small, H. and Greenlee, E. (1980). Citation context analysis of a co-citation cluster: Recombinant DNA. *Scientometrics, 2*(4), 277-301.
19. Small, H. (1986). The synthesis of specialty narratives from co-citation clusters. *Journal of the American Society for Information Science, 37*(3), 97-110.
20. Braam, R. R., Moed, H. and van Raan, A. F. J. (1991). Mapping of Science by combined Co-Citation and Word Analysis. I. Structural aspects. *Journal of the American Society for Information Science, 42*(4), 233-251.

Context Matters: An Analysis of Assessments of XML Documents

Nils Pharo and Ragnar Nordlie

Oslo University College, Faculty of Journalism, Library and Information Science,
Postboks 4 St. Olavs plass, N-0130 Oslo, Norway
{nils.pharo, ragnar.nordlie}@jbi.hio.no

Abstract. The paper analyses searchers' assessments of usefulness and specificity on different levels of granularity in XML-coded documents. Documents are assessed on 10 usefulness/specificity combinations and on the granularity levels of article, section, and subsection. Overlapping judgements show a remarkable lack of consistency between searchers. There is an inverse relationship between articles and sections both in the assessment of specificity and of usefulness, indicating that retrieval on different granularity levels are a useful feature of a retrieval system. Searchers find the full article more useful when they assess the same document both on the article and section level indicating that there is a need to provide context to the sections and subsections when presenting result list of XML-documents.

1 Introduction

The eXtensible Markup Language (XML) is increasingly becoming the standard for content representation on the Web. In this paper the focus is on XML used for representing semi-structured documents, i.e., documents with a certain amount of systematically occurring elements mixed with longer bits of unstructured full text. Scientific articles represent good examples of semi-structured documents, where the content partly consist of specific formally defined elements such as titles, captions, footnotes, headings, formulas etc, as well as elements representing unstructured sections of full text such as abstracts, subsections, paragraphs etc. These elements are for a large part used in order to serve publishing and presentation purposes, but to exploit these structural elements in information retrieval is an appealing idea, e.g., by developing ranking algorithms that combine element names and content.

One of the presumed advantages of XML-based information retrieval is that the XML coding will enable retrieval systems to present searchers with search results consisting of the document elements presumed to be most relevant to their problem [1]. The underlying assumption is that searchers should retrieve as much, but not more of the document than is necessary to satisfy their information need. We wish to investigate the validity of this assumption. In this paper we present a study of searchers' relevance assessments of different levels of granularity in XML documents. Our main research question has been to investigate how different levels of

F. Crestani and I. Ruthven (Eds.): CoLIS 2005, LNCS 3507, pp. 238–248, 2005.
© Springer-Verlag Berlin Heidelberg 2005

granularity influence searchers' evaluation and their ability to evaluate. In this study the lowest level of granularity is sections and subsections of articles.

2 Previous work

Both outside of and particularly within the framework of the INEX family of experiments, much has been written on various aspects of information retrieval in structured documents, and a particular focus within INEX has been on metrics for retrieval evaluation in such settings, see for instance [5], but there are few investigations of searcher behaviour in this connection. [2] analyze which parts of structured documents searchers access (in their case a structured collection of Shakespeare texts), but their focus is on task performance and interface design, not on relevance assessments. A brief summary of findings from the INEX interactive track is presented in [9]. Our investigation elaborates some of the general findings referenced here. There are a number of investigations which discuss the problems connected with such aspects of user assessments as for instance the use of graded relevance assessments, e.g. [3], and an extensive literature on the problems of consistency in relevance judgements, see for instance [8].

3 Method

At present the largest set of available data on how searchers evaluate XML documents on different levels of granularity stems from the international Initiative for the Evaluation of XML retrieval (INEX). We chose to use data collected from this initiative, thus limiting our ability to control factors such as participants and tasks. In this chapter, we first describe the INEX initiative, which is followed by a part presenting how we analysed the data.

3.1 The INEX Initiative

INEX was established in 2002 in order to provide "an infrastructure to evaluate the effectiveness of content-oriented XML retrieval systems" [4]. INEX builds its experimental design on the TREC model, with a test collection which consists of topics/tasks (submitted by the participating groups), documents (approximately 12 000 articles from a selection of IEEE Computer society's journals) and relevance assessments provided by the participants, thus making it possible to compute the retrieval effectiveness of different matching algorithms.

A new interactive track was introduced in INEX in 2004 [9] which aimed at focusing on how searchers performed when solving the tasks (which for this experiment were formulated following Borlund's [1] simulated work task procedure). The INEX 2004 Interactive Track (http://inex.is.informatik.uni-duisburg.de:2004/tracks/int/) is a collective effort by ten different research groups at sites in Asia, Australia and Europe. The data are collected at the different sites from searchers who were each given two search tasks of different complexity and performed searches following precise guidelines from the track organizers:

- The Hyrex experimental IR system was used with a specific interface developed for the INEX interactive track [7]
- Searchers were allowed to spend a maximum of 30 minutes working on each task
- Searchers were requested to assess all document elements they chose to view on a ten-point relevance scale (see Table 1 for the relevance scale)

Table 1. Relevance scale

Grade	Description
A	Very useful & Very specific
B	Very useful & Fairly specific
C	Very useful & Marginally specific
D	Fairly useful & Very specific
E	Fairly useful & Fairly specific
F	Fairly useful & Marginally specific
G	Marginally useful & Very specific
H	Marginally useful & Fairly specific
I	Marginally useful & Marginally specific
J	Contains no relevant information
U	Unspecified

The system is designed with a simple search interface where searchers can input queries to the system. The result list contains four different granularity levels of documents: whole articles, sections, subsection level 1, and subsection level 2. When selecting a (part of an) article the searcher also is presented with a table of contents to the other parts (sections/subsections) of the article. The system provides searchers with the opportunity to assess the relevance level of the different entries in the result list. The relevance levels are based on two dimensions of relevance, "usefulness" and "specificity". Usefulness has to do with the exhaustiveness of the documents' treatment of the question topic, in fact in the other tracks at INEX 04 "exhaustiveness" has been used to signify this dimension rather than usefulness. Specificity deals with the extent to which the retrieved article (part) is focussed on the topic of the searcher's task. The ten-point relevance scale combined three different levels (from "marginally" via "fairly" to "very") of specificity and exhaustiveness in addition to the option of judging the document (part) non-relevant.

There were ten research institutions around the world participating in the study, each site was required to collect data from at least eight volunteers. The data were collected following the guidelines from the INEX Interactive Track organisers: participants were first given a brief introduction to the experiment and the Hyrex system, before and after the experiment they were asked to fill out general questionnaires, the searchers selected one task from each of two task categories, before and after each task they were asked to answer task-related questionnaires. The search tasks were formulated as simulated work task situations [1], meaning that the tasks were also placed in a more specific context, giving the searchers more information about why the information is needed.

Two tasks belonged to the Background category (*B*), the other two to the Comparison category (*C*). Table 2 contains the four tasks as they were presented to the searchers.

All transaction in the systems are logged in XML and plain text format, including queries, viewed document element, search paths, assessments, time spent etc.

We have analysed transaction logs from the search sessions in order to look at the distribution of different levels of relevance assessments at the various document levels.

Table 2. Simulated work tasks in INEX Interactive track 2004

Task ID: B1 You are writing a large article discussing virtual reality (VR) applications and you need to discuss their negative side effects. What you want to know is the symptoms associated with cybersickness, the amount of users who get them, and the VR situations where they occur. You are not interested in the use of VR in therapeutic treatments unless they discuss VR side effects.	**Task ID: B2** You have tried to buy & download electronic books (ebooks) just to discover that problems arise when you use the ebooks on different PC's, or when you want to copy the ebooks to Personal Digital Assistants. The worst disturbance factor is that the content is not accessible after a few tries, because an invisible counter reaches a maximum number of attempts. As ebooks exist in various formats and with different copy protection schemes, you would like to find articles, or parts of articles, which discuss various proprietary and covert methods of protection. You would also be interested in articles, or parts of articles, with a special focus on various disturbance factors surrounding ebook copyrights.
Task ID: C1 You have been asked to make your Fortran compiler compatible with Fortran 90, and so you are interested in the features Fortran 90 added to the Fortran standard before it. You would like to know about compilers, especially compilers whose source code might be available. Discussion of people's experience with these features when they were new to them is also of interest.	**Task ID: C2** You are working on a project to develop a next generation version of a software system. You are trying to decide on the benefits and problems of implementation in a number of programming languages, but particularly Java and Python. You would like a good comparison of these for application development. You would like to see comparisons of Python and Java for developing large applications. You want to see articles, or parts of articles, that discuss the positive and negative aspects of the languages. Things that discuss either language with respect to application development may be also partially useful to you. Ideally, you would be looking for items that are discussing both efficiency of development and efficiency of execution time for applications.

3.2 Data Analysis

In our study we have used the transaction logs from nine sites, in all 140 sessions. The sessions contained 1835 relevance assessments, out of which 1259 were between A and I, i.e. the article element was considered relevant to some degree. We have only made limited use of the data collected from the various questionnaires since our aim has been to look at the general distribution of relevance assessments over article elements rather than taking into account individual factors affecting the assessments. We are, however, aware that factors such as search experience and task knowledge influence the choices of individual searchers.

Table 3. Excerpts from log file

SearcherID	ArticleID	Article element	Grade
cmpinfscnor_searcher002_C	/cs/1998/c2039	/article[1]/bdy[1]/sec[1]	B
cmpinfscnor_searcher002_C	/cs/1998/c2039	/article[1]/bdy[1]/sec[3]/ ss1[2]	I
cmpinfscnor_searcher002_C	/cs/1998/c2039	/article[1]/bdy[1]/sec[3]/ ss1[3]	E

In Table 3 we see that a searcher has assessed three different parts of one article, section 1 (sec[1]), and subsections 2 and 3 in section 3.

In order to investigate our research problem we have investigated the following:

1. the distribution of assessments over article elements, independent of individual searchers, this provides information on what granularity level the searchers generally performed relevance assessments
2. the relationship between an individual searcher's assessments of different elements of the same article
3. the distribution of all assessments for one specific article, which provides information about assessment consistency

4 Findings

4.1 Relationship Between Granularity and Assessments

In total, searchers assessed slightly less than 600 individual documents, of which about 15% were full articles and 85% were sections or subsections of articles (coded with XML codes sec, ss1 or ss2). We do not, unfortunately, know the total distribution of sections and subsections in the 12 000 articles in the database thus we do not know if this reflects the general distribution. Of the 1835 assessments made by the searchers, 24% were article assessments and 76% were assessments of section or subsections. This means that searchers showed a marked tendency towards preferring to assess articles over sections of articles. Of the 1835 assessments, slightly less than 30% were "J", indicating no relevant information, and a small proportion were judged "unspecified". We have chosen to disregard these negative assessments in our further investigation of the material. It is difficult to judge from the logs why searchers have just chosen not to judge some of the documents they find unusable while they give others a negative assessment, so we feel this figure is burdened with too much uncertainty. This leaves us with 1259 individual assessments, distributed as shown in table 4.

Table 4. Distribution of assessments over document elements

	Article	Section	SS1	SS2	
A	33 (13.5%)	164 (67.2%)	42 (17.2%)	5 (2.1%)	244 (100%)
B	32 (28.1%)	56 (49.1%)	24 (21.0%)	2 (1.8%)	114 (100%)
C	9 (31.0%)	15 (51.7%)	5 (17.2%)	-	29 (99.9%)
D	28 (21.0%)	66 (49.6%)	35 (26.3%)	4 (3.0%)	133 (100%)
E	40 (25.0%)	76 (47.5%)	42 (26.3%)	2 (1.2%)	160 (100%)
F	43 (41.7%)	44 (42.7%)	12 (11.7%)	4 (3.9%)	103 (100%)
G	9 (14.3%)	41 (65.1%)	11 (17.5%)	2 (3.2%)	63 (100.1%)
H	23 (18.3%)	78 (61.9%)	21 (16.7%)	4 (3.2%)	126 (100.1%)
I	89 (31.0%)	125 (43.3%)	62 (21.6%)	11 (3.8%)	286 (100%)
Total	306	665	254	34	1259

Table 5. Distribution of various levels of specificity over document elements

	Article	Section	SS1	SS2	
Highly spec.	70	271	88	11	440
A-D-G	22.9%	40.8%	34.6%	32.4%	
Fairly spec.	95	210	87	8	400
B-E-H	31.0%	31.6%	34.3%	23.5%	
Marginally	141	184	79	15	419
spec. C-F-I	46.1%	27.7%	31.1%	44.1%	
Total	306	665	254	34	1259
	100%	100.1%	100%	100.1%	

Table 6. Distribution of various levels of usefulness over document elements

	Article	Section	SS1	SS2	
Highly useful	74	235	71	7	387
A-B-C	24.2%	35.3%	28.0%	20.6%	
Fairly useful	111	186	89	10	396
D-E-F	36.3%	28.0%	35.0%	29.4%	
Marginally	121	244	94	17	476
useful G-H-I	39.5%	36.7%	37.0%	50.0%	
Total	306	665	254	34	1259
	100%	100%	100%	100%	

From table 4, it appears that the distribution of ss1 and ss2 elements deviates little from the average for any of the categories. The most significant deviation from the normal is the relatively low proportion of "A" judgements on the article level and the comparably high proportion of "A"s on the section level. Since "A" includes both maximum specificity and usefulness, and a section of an article might be expected to treat a topic with more specificity than would the entire article, this is no surprise. Tables 5 and 6 show the relative influence of the two relevance dimensions.

As expected, there is a clear inverse relationship between articles and sections in the assessment of specificity; it is apparently (and intuitively) easier to relate the notion of specificity to the section level than to an entire article. It is more difficult to explain the somewhat slighter but still inverse relationship between articles and sections when it comes to judging usefulness. This is, for instance, in opposition to the INEX experiment designers' rules for assessing XML-coded parts of documents, which state that no sub-element can have a lower degree of exhaustivity than the mother element. One would intuitively think that if a section of an article is useful as the answer to a query, the entire article will be useful as well. It is possible that the term "usefulness" is difficult for the searchers to relate to in a setting where the problem which is the basis for judging the material is imposed on them rather than taken from their real-life situation. It might possibly have been easier for them if the searchers were asked to judge "exhaustivity" instead, which is the case for the non-interactive tracks in INEX. It may also be that the combined relevance dimensions makes it difficult to distinguish between "specificity" and "usefulness" – table 4 shows clearly that the three grades which give equal weight to the two measures (A, E and I for high/high, fairly/fairly and marginally/marginally, respectively) are much more heavily used than the others. Again, the use of two separate measures might have provided a more realistic representation of searcher assessments.

4.2 Assessment Overlap

Tables 4-6 show the distribution of assessments without regard to individual searchers or individual search sessions. We find, in general, an increase in both usefulness and in specificity when searchers deal with smaller article element than when they address (and assess) the article as a whole. To investigate whether this is also the case when individual searchers have the chance to see and judge both the full article and its separate sections, we identified the assessment of all overlapping article elements, or *elements*, for each session, i.e. we identified each occurrence in the transaction log where one element and one or more of its sub-elements are assessed in the same session. In total there were 143 such assessments.

In order to identify increase and decrease in assessed usefulness and specificity we treated the two dimensions of the relevance grades separately. Grades A, B, and C were given the score 3 for usefulness; D, E, and F score 2; and G, H, and I scored 1. For specificity grades A, D, and G scored 3; B, E, and H scored 2; whereas C, F, and I were given the score 1. Now we could treat each assessment separately with respect to usefulness and specificity, and thus identify increase and decrease of assessed relevance for overlapping elements. An example is shown in the excerpts in Table 7.

Table 7. Excerpts from log file with overlapping assessments

SearcherID	ArticleID	Article element	Grade
dbdk_searcher012_B	/co/1995/r6057	/article[1]	F
dbdk_searcher012_B	co/1995/r6057	/article[1]/bdy[1]/sec[5]	A

In the Table 7 example we see that the searcher has assessed the article with an "F", meaning it is fairly useful (score: 2) and marginally specific (score: 1). Section 5, however, the searcher thinks is both very useful (score: 3) *and* very specific (score: 3). In this example we see that both the assessed usefulness and specificity increases with the increased document granularity.

The results of a similar treatment of all overlapping assessments in the transaction logs are presented in Table 8. The table should be read from the perspective of the assessment of the super-element, so that increase or decrease is from super-element assessment (e.g. article) to sub-element (e.g. section).

Table 8. Relevance assessment change in overlapping article elements

	Usefulness		Specificity	
Increase	17	(12 %)	36	(25 %)
Unchanged	66	(46 %)	68	(48 %)
Decrease	60	(42 %)	39	(27 %)

From Table 8 we can see that in almost half of all cases there is neither a decrease nor an increase in usefulness or specificity when lower-level elements are assessed. This means that the searcher most often find no difference in relevance between sub-elements and super-element.

The table also shows that searchers are much more likely to assess the sub-elements as less useful than the opposite. This indicates that searchers find the broader article or section more "useful" than the smaller sections and subsections as sources of information. This stands in apparent opposition to the findings in table 6, where we find proportionally more sections than articles judged "highly useful". As mentioned above, what is meant by "useful" is not clearly defined, and this is a source of uncertainty in any attempt to explain the discrepancy. It may seem, however, that even if judged independently a section seems more useful than a full article, the article in its entirety when seen in connection with the sections still offer more towards the searches' problem resolution. A better explanation might be found if we had been able to consider the sequence of the assessments to see if the level of usefulness were influenced by the order in which the searcher viewed the article and the sections.

Table 8 also reveals that there is no clear tendency with respect to increase or decrease in assessed specificity of sub-elements. One might expect that the "deeper" elements, i.e. sections and sub-sections would be assessed as more specific than their super-elements. That is apparently not the case in this experiment.

4.3 Reliability of Searchers' Assessments

The data provides an opportunity to estimate the reliability of the searchers' assessments. In several cases, both whole articles and sections of articles have been assessed by a number of different searchers in relation to the same question. A study of these overlapping judgements shows a remarkable lack of consistency. Of the approximately 50 different articles which were judged by more than one searcher, there was full agreement between assessments in only five cases. Of these only one had more than two different assessments, and in three of these five cases the assessment was "J", i.e. "not relevant". In 10% of the cases both the categories "A" and "J" were included in the assessments of the same article, and more than 30% of the articles were judged to belong to five or more categories. On the section level, the inconsistencies were, if anything, even greater. Here too, the few times where agreement between searchers occurred, it was nearly always agreement on a "J" code.

A closer examination of one particular article the one which was assessed by the largest number of searchers, shows a greater than average agreement on the article level, with 7 assessments divided into 4 "A"s and 3 "B"s. On the section level, however, the four most frequently assessed sections, with 35, 21, 18 and 18 assessments, respectively, have their assessments spread over 6 to 9 of the 10 possible categories, and there is no significant difference in the degree of consistency between the "usefulness" and the "specificity" judgements. In the four sections with the highest number of assessments , assessment of specificity were distributed with 45% "very specific" , 41% "fairly specific" and 14% "marginally" or "not specific", whereas the same figures for usefulness were 54%, 33% and 13%, respectively.

There may be several explanations for this high degree of disagreement. 10 categories may be too many for the searchers to relate to in a consistent manner, or the four-part division of the two dimensions ("very", "fairly", "marginally" or "not") may be a difficult scale to interpret. Obviously a binary but possibly also a 5- or 7-part scale, used separately for the two dimensions, would have been easier to handle. The searcher's familiarity with the topics of the queries or their understanding of the material may of course also influence the reliability of the assessments. This may to an extent be clarified through an investigation of the searcher questionnaires, but since the disparity of assessments is universal over both articles and sections, such an investigation seems to be of dubious value. At any rate, judging of articles and sections seem to be an equally hard task, and the consistency problems calls for caution in the interpretation of the data presented above.

5 Discussion

One of the most alluring features of XML information retrieval has been the ability to perform segment-based indexing and document fragment retrieval (see e.g. [6]). The findings of our investigation support this contention; searchers appear to find more value in section-level than in article-level material, even if they still value the full article more highly in direct comparison. We have not studied the order in which assessments were made, this may throw more light on this apparent discrepancy.

A major limitation of this study is the lack of control with the data collection procedures. Data are collected from searchers around the world, with different backgrounds, pre-knowledge about topics, and information searching competence. Although the simulated work task procedure was used, which aims at providing searchers with a common context, this method has important limitations. The most serious problem, which is also pointed out by [1], is that simulated work tasks should be adjusted somewhat towards the searchers' interest and backgrounds. This has not been the case in the INEX interactive track thus it is difficult, if not impossible, to say how background factors influenced the assessments.

Another weakness in the study is the definition of the XML elements sec, ss1 and ss2. We have not gone into the articles to see whether there are great discrepancies in the amount of text which constitute a section or a subsection, but have assumed them to be comparable with each other. In the main INEX experiments articles have been evaluated to a finer level of granularity, and the problems of evaluation have been even more apparent on the paragraph level; it would be interesting to see whether the same pattern of searcher assessment appears if they were exposed to this level, as a step towards defining the optimal level of text granularity for retrieval. So far, the research reported here only emphasize that this level is difficult to find.

Usefulness is a problematic concept to define; whereas specificity is a clearly defined term, having to do with the focus of topic treatment, usefulness is much vaguer. It may have been confused with or understood as specificity by the searchers. In the other INEX tracks the term "exhaustiveness" has been used to describe this dimension, and this term is easier to define. A better definition is particularly needed in experiments such as the one reported here, where the simulated work tasks were not tuned to fit the searchers performing the tasks, so that the concept of usefulness becomes a very theoretical notion.

A combined measure of relevance with so many alternatives as the one used in this experiment proves difficult for the searchers to relate to. In further experiments it might be fruitful to use another scale and resort to two separate assessments.

As shown in Section 4.3 there is a strong degree Inter-assessor agreement is always a problem, but rarely on the scale observed here.

References

1. Borlund, P.:. Evaluation of interactive information retrieval systems. Åbo: Åbo Akademi University Press (2000)
2. Finesilver, K, Reid, J.: User Behaviour in the Context of Structured Documents. In: Sebastiani, F. (ed.): Advances in Information Retrieval (ECIR 2003). Lecture Notes in Computer Science, Vol. 2633. Springer-Verlag, Berlin Heidelberg New York (2003) 104-119
3. Kekäläinen, J. & Järvelin, K.: Using graded relevance assessments in IR evaluation. Journal of the American Society for Information Science and Technology, 53(13) (2002) 1120-1129.
4. Kazai, G., Lalmas, M., Fuhr, N. Gövert, N.:. A report on the first year of the initiative for the evaluation of XML retrieval (INEX'02). Journal of the American Society for Information Science and Technology, 55(6) (2004) 551-556

5. Kazai, G, Lalmas, M, de Vries, A. P.: The Overlap Problem in Content-Oriented XML Retrieval Evaluation. In: Järvelin, K.,, Allan, J., Bruza, P., Sanderson, M. (eds.) Proceedings of the 27th Annual International ACM SIGIR Conference on Research and Development in Information Retrieval, Sheffield (2004) 72-79
6. Luk, R. W. P. et al.:. A Survey in indexing and searching XML documents. Journal of the American Society for Information Science and Technology, 53(6) (2002) 415-437
7. Malik, S., Tombros, A., Larsen, B.:. HyREX for INEX itrack. (2004) Available: http://inex.is.informatik.uni-duisburg.de:2004/tracks/int/internal/downloads/guide.pdf
8. Saracevic, T., Kantor. P., Chamis, A. Y., Trivison, D.: A Study of Information Seeking and Retrieving. I. Background and Methodology. Journal of the American Society for Information Science, 39 (3) (1988) 161-176
9. Tombros, A., Larsen, B. & Malik, S..: The Interactive track at INEX 2004. To be published in: Fuhr,, N., Lalmas, M., Malik, S., Szlavik, Z. (eds), INEX 2004 workshop pre-proceedings (2005)

Developing a Metadata Lifecycle Model

Jane Barton and R. John Robertson

Centre for Digital Library Research,
Department of Computer & Information Sciences, University of Strathclyde,
Livingstone Tower, 26 Richmond Street, Glasgow G1 1XH, UK
jane.barton@strath.ac.uk
robert.robertson@cis.strath.ac.uk

1 Rationale

Despite substantial investment in the development of digital repositories, and of services based upon their content, there is little real understanding as to how these repositories and services interact beyond a technical level and a marked absence of a conceptual framework for such interactions. As a result, service development takes place with little reference to the context in which repositories are being developed, and repositories derive little benefit from the services that utilise their content. The establishment of such a framework could unlock potential benefits, in terms of metadata quality and metadata workflow efficiency, throughout the community as individual repositories and services understand and exploit their interactions and the context in which they take place [1]. A conceptual framework for the interactions between repositories and services must include not only repository-level interactions - the 'ecology of repositories' [2] - but also the lifecycle of the objects within repositories and the lifecycle of the metadata associated with them.

2 Specific Objectives

The main focus of the workshop is to develop a prototype model of the metadata lifecycle, with reference both to the emerging understanding of the interactions between repositories and services at a conceptual level [3] and to a range of practical examples of metadata lifecycles drawn from existing repositories and services.

More specifically, the workshop will provide a forum in which to:

- present to and debate with a diverse audience the emerging understanding of the interactions between repositories and services at repository, object and metadata level;
- gather a broad range of illustrative examples of metadata lifecycles from various communities of practice;
- facilitate the rapid articulation and refinement of a prototype metadata lifecycle model.

The workshop will build on the 9th DELOS Network of Excellence (Digital Repositories: Interoperability and Common Services) Workshop, held in May 2005 as

F. Crestani and I. Ruthven (Eds.): CoLIS 2005, LNCS 3507, pp. 249–250, 2005.
© Springer-Verlag Berlin Heidelberg 2005

part of the DELOS programme's interoperability strand, reporting on the outcomes of that workshop and seeking to develop them further.

3 Potential Audience

The potential audience includes: digital library managers; institutional, subject or learning object repository managers; virtual learning environment managers; service developers; metadata specialists and librarians; information infrastructure planners and strategists; funding bodies; academics in the field of library and information science (LIS); and researchers and students in these areas.

4 Relationship with Main Conference Theme

The growth of digital libraries and repositories has been one of the key developments in LIS in recent years. They impact nearly every aspect of LIS, from education through cataloguing to management. There is however, no frame of reference or conceptual model which captures the wider context in which funding decisions are made, object and metadata workflows designed and higher level services established. This workshop will make significant progress towards the modelling of this context and assessing its implications for repository management, object creation and metadata quality.

References

1. Robertson, R.J. & Barton, J. (2005). Optimising metadata workflows in a distributed information environment. 9th DELOS Network of Excellence thematic workshop (Digital Repositories: Interoperability & Common Services), Crete.
2. McLean, N. (2004). The ecology of repository services: a cosmic view. European Conference on Digital Libraries, Bath. http://www.ecdl2004.org/presentations/mclean/
3. See, for example, Anderson, S. & Heery, R. (2005). Digital Repositories Review. http://www.jisc.ac.uk/uploaded_documents/rep-review-final-20050220.pdf

Evaluating User Studies in Information Access

Alex Bailey[1], Ian Ruthven[2], and Leif Azzopardi[3]

[1] Canon Technology Europe, UK
alexb@cre.canon.co.uk
[2] Department of Computer and Information Sciences,
University of Strathclyde, UK
ir@cis.strath.ac.uk
[3] Department of Computer Science, University of Glasgow, UK
leif@dcs.gla.ac.uk

1 Introduction

Systems enabling Information Access whether it be; a file browser, a retrieval engine, a mobile device providing content, a personalized agent, etc, need to be evaluated appropriately for the discipline to be considered a science. The problem of how to appropriately evaluate such systems is even more problematic when the evaluation is conducted with human subjects.

The complexity in designing, running and analysing a user study is substantially more time consuming and challenging than a simple comparison of empirical measures such as precision and recall. As a result many researchers avoid the user studies. However, it is only with real user studies that the impact of state of the art research can be truly assessed and the merit of such research validated. How a robust user study should be performed in the context of information access remains a challenge and those researchers wishing to perform such a study are faced with many issues to ensure that the research is carried out in an appropriate and unbiased manner.

The aim of this workshop is to promote a discussion on the methodologies used in user studies in Information Access. The workshop contains sessions to (1) assess current user based studies in Information Access; discussing the advantages and disadvantages of their methodology, (2) to critique proposed evaluations submitted to the workshop and (3) to draw up a list of guidelines for future user studies.

The organizers gratefully acknowledge the support of the workshop program committee: Peter Ingwersen, Royal School of Library and Information Science, Denmark; Kalervo Jarvelin, University of Tampere, Finland; Diane Kelly, University of North Carolina, USA; Iadh Ounis, University of Glasgow, UK; Simon Sweeney, University of Strathclyde, UK; Elaine Toms, Dalhousie University, CA; Ryen White, University of Maryland, US.

F. Crestani and I. Ruthven (Eds.): CoLIS 2005, LNCS 3507, p. 251, 2005.
© Springer-Verlag Berlin Heidelberg 2005

Author Index

Lecture Notes in Computer Science

For information about Vols. 1–3421

please contact your bookseller or Springer

Vol. 3481: O. Gervasi, M.L. Gavrilova, V. Kumar, A. Laganà, H.P. Lee, Y. Mun, D. Taniar, C.J.K. Tan (Eds.), Computational Science and Its Applications – ICCSA 2005, Part II. LXIV, 1316 pages. 2005.

Vol. 3480: O. Gervasi, M.L. Gavrilova, V. Kumar, A. Laganà, H.P. Lee, Y. Mun, D. Taniar, C.J.K. Tan (Eds.), Computational Science and Its Applications – ICCSA 2005, Part I. LXV, 1234 pages. 2005.

Vol. 3479: T. Strang, C. Linnhoff-Popien (Eds.), Location- and Context-Awareness. XII, 378 pages. 2005.

Vol. 3478: C. Jermann, A. Neumaier, D. Sam (Eds.), Global Optimization and Constraint Satisfaction. XIII, 193 pages. 2005.

Vol. 3477: P. Herrmann, V. Issarny, S. Shiu (Eds.), Trust Management. XII, 426 pages. 2005.

Vol. 3475: N. Guelfi (Ed.), Rapid Integration of Software Engineering Techniques. X, 145 pages. 2005.

Vol. 3468: H.W. Gellersen, R. Want, A. Schmidt (Eds.), Pervasive Computing. XIII, 347 pages. 2005.

Vol. 3467: J. Giesl (Ed.), Term Rewriting and Applications. XIII, 517 pages. 2005.

Vol. 3465: M. Bernardo, A. Bogliolo (Eds.), Formal Methods for Mobile Computing. VII, 271 pages. 2005.

Vol. 3464: S.A. Brueckner, G.D.M. Serugendo, A. Karageorgos, R. Nagpal (Eds.), Engineering Self-Organising Systems. XIII, 299 pages. 2005. (Subseries LNAI).

Vol. 3463: M. Dal Cin, M. Kaâniche, A. Pataricza (Eds.), Dependable Computing - EDCC 2005. XVI, 472 pages. 2005.

Vol. 3462: R. Boutaba, K. Almeroth, R. Puigjaner, S. Shen, J.P. Black (Eds.), NETWORKING 2005. XXX, 1483 pages. 2005.

Vol. 3461: P. Urzyczyn (Ed.), Typed Lambda Calculi and Applications. XI, 433 pages. 2005.

Vol. 3460: Ö. Babaoglu, M. Jelasity, A. Montresor, C. Fetzer, S. Leonardi, A. van Moorsel, M. van Steen (Eds.), Self-star Properties in Complex Information Systems. IX, 447 pages. 2005.

Vol. 3459: R. Kimmel, N.A. Sochen, J. Weickert (Eds.), Scale Space and PDE Methods in Computer Vision. XI, 634 pages. 2005.

Vol. 3458: P. Herrero, M.S. Pérez, V. Robles (Eds.), Scientific Applications of Grid Computing. X, 208 pages. 2005.

Vol. 3456: H. Rust, Operational Semantics for Timed Systems. XII, 223 pages. 2005.

Vol. 3455: H. Treharne, S. King, M. Henson, S. Schneider (Eds.), ZB 2005: Formal Specification and Development in Z and B. XV, 493 pages. 2005.

Vol. 3454: J.-M. Jacquet, G.P. Picco (Eds.), Coordination Models and Languages. X, 299 pages. 2005.

Vol. 3453: L. Zhou, B.C. Ooi, X. Meng (Eds.), Database Systems for Advanced Applications. XXVII, 929 pages. 2005.

Vol. 3452: F. Baader, A. Voronkov (Eds.), Logic for Programming, Artificial Intelligence, and Reasoning. XI, 562 pages. 2005. (Subseries LNAI).

Vol. 3450: D. Hutter, M. Ullmann (Eds.), Security in Pervasive Computing. XI, 239 pages. 2005.

Vol. 3449: F. Rothlauf, J. Branke, S. Cagnoni, D.W. Corne, R. Drechsler, Y. Jin, P. Machado, E. Marchiori, J. Romero, G.D. Smith, G. Squillero (Eds.), Applications of Evolutionary Computing. XX, 631 pages. 2005.

Vol. 3448: G.R. Raidl, J. Gottlieb (Eds.), Evolutionary Computation in Combinatorial Optimization. XI, 271 pages. 2005.

Vol. 3447: M. Keijzer, A. Tettamanzi, P. Collet, J.v. Hemert, M. Tomassini (Eds.), Genetic Programming. XIII, 382 pages. 2005.

Vol. 3444: M. Sagiv (Ed.), Programming Languages and Systems. XIII, 439 pages. 2005.

Vol. 3443: R. Bodik (Ed.), Compiler Construction. XI, 305 pages. 2005.

Vol. 3442: M. Cerioli (Ed.), Fundamental Approaches to Software Engineering. XIII, 373 pages. 2005.

Vol. 3441: V. Sassone (Ed.), Foundations of Software Science and Computational Structures. XVIII, 521 pages. 2005.

Vol. 3440: N. Halbwachs, L.D. Zuck (Eds.), Tools and Algorithms for the Construction and Analysis of Systems. XVII, 588 pages. 2005.

Vol. 3439: R.H. Deng, F. Bao, H. Pang, J. Zhou (Eds.), Information Security Practice and Experience. XII, 424 pages. 2005.

Vol. 3438: H. Christiansen, P.R. Skadhauge, J. Villadsen (Eds.), Constraint Solving and Language Processing. VIII, 205 pages. 2005. (Subseries LNAI).

Vol. 3437: T. Gschwind, C. Mascolo (Eds.), Software Engineering and Middleware. X, 245 pages. 2005.

Vol. 3436: B. Bouyssounouse, J. Sifakis (Eds.), Embedded Systems Design. XV, 492 pages. 2005.

Vol. 3434: L. Brun, M. Vento (Eds.), Graph-Based Representations in Pattern Recognition. XII, 384 pages. 2005.

Vol. 3433: S. Bhalla (Ed.), Databases in Networked Information Systems. VII, 319 pages. 2005.

Vol. 3432: M. Beigl, P. Lukowicz (Eds.), Systems Aspects in Organic and Pervasive Computing - ARCS 2005. X, 265 pages. 2005.

Vol. 3431: C. Dovrolis (Ed.), Passive and Active Network Measurement. XII, 374 pages. 2005.

Vol. 3430: S. Tsumoto, T. Yamaguchi, M. Numao, H. Motoda (Eds.), Active Mining. XII, 349 pages. 2005. (Subseries LNAI).

Vol. 3429: E. Andres, G. Damiand, P. Lienhardt (Eds.), Discrete Geometry for Computer Imagery. X, 428 pages. 2005.

Vol. 3428: Y.-J. Kwon, A. Bouju, C. Claramunt (Eds.), Web and Wireless Geographical Information Systems. XII, 255 pages. 2005.

Vol. 3427: G. Kotsis, O. Spaniol (Eds.), Wireless Systems and Mobility in Next Generation Internet. VIII, 249 pages. 2005.

Vol. 3423: J.L. Fiadeiro, P.D. Mosses, F. Orejas (Eds.), Recent Trends in Algebraic Development Techniques. VIII, 271 pages. 2005.

Vol. 3422: R.T. Mittermeir (Ed.), From Computer Literacy to Informatics Fundamentals. X, 203 pages. 2005.